The International Situation and Soviet Foreign Policy

Key reports by Soviet Leaders from the Revolution to the Present

edited by

Myron Rush

Cornell University

Charles E. Merrill Publishing Co.
A Bell & Howell Company
Columbus, Ohio

ISBN: 0-675-09421-6

Library of Congress Catalog Card Number: 74-97723

1 2 3 4 5 – 74 73 72 71 70

Printed in the United States of America

G.H.Bennett.

n

University of Plymouth Library

Subject to status this item may be renewed
via your Voyager account

http://voyager.plymouth.ac.uk

Exeter tel: (01392) 475049
Exmouth tel: (01395) 255331
Plymouth tel: (01752) 232323

Merrill Political Science Series

under the editorship of

John C. Wahlke

Department of Political Science
State University of New York at Stony Brook

Preface

This book is meant for two kinds of readers: for college students who will read it in conjunction with historical and analytical accounts of Soviet foreign policy, and for the general reader who knows something of the political history of the past half-century and wants to know more of the Soviet leaders' perception of major developments and their influence on subsequent events.

My approach to the study of Soviet foreign policy is based on a special practice of the Soviet political system. Top Soviet leaders report periodically to the highest party and state bodies, to the party Congress on behalf of the Central Committee and to the Supreme Soviet on behalf of the Soviet Government. The report usually reviews developments in the interval since the previous report; assesses the current situation; identifies new problems; and states current Soviet policy. The report is in two parts, usually with the international situation discussed first, as though it were primary and must be taken into account before plans can be made for internal development. (Reports to the party Congress contain a third section on party affairs.)

The selections in this book are taken from the key reports by top Soviet leaders since the founding of the USSR. Their order is chronological, not topical, to provide an historical survey of Soviet foreign policy. They are presented relatively intact to preserve their coherence, although some less important passages have been excised. The translations are from Soviet sources.

Reports to the party Congress and the Supreme Soviet are highly authoritative. Their chief authors have been Lenin, Stalin, and Khrushchev; others included in this collection are Molotov, Malenkov, Zhdanov, and Brezhnev. Generally, a report is approved or its main points incorporated in a resolution adopted by the body to which it is addressed. The report is not intended for the masses (although many of its pronouncements subsequently become the basis of mass propaganda), but rather for informing middle-level leaders about the Soviet position in the world and for communicating with foreign statesmen through open channels.

The chief advantages in approaching the study of Soviet foreign policy through these reports are that (1) they are authoritative; (2) they are in the words of the Soviet leaders themselves; (3) they cover the entire period of Soviet history; and (4) they are readily adaptable to comparison, thus facilitating analysis of changes in the Soviet approach to foreign policy as they arise to meet changed circumstances and the passage of time. One must recognize, however, that the reports are not comprehensive; they do not discuss the full range of international problems that the Soviet leadership is actively considering. Also, their contents cannot always be accepted at face value. Soviet pronouncements, at least after the early years of the regime, are much less candid even than official statements in democratic states. They must be read with care; much of what is said must be discounted, or examined carefully for its true meaning. Soviet readers and foreign observers recognize the need to remove the verbal veil which obscures the underlying purpose, and readers of this book are cautioned to do the same.

To assist the reader in probing the text, I have written brief essays introducing each report, which give the background of events and provide analysis and interpretation of the report's significance. My interpretations of Soviet foreign policy are presented with little supporting argument, as my aim is to stimulate and encourage the reader to test my conclusions against the evidence in the reports themselves, and in other books on the subject.

Contents

The International Situation and Soviet Foreign Policy

LENIN

Report to the Congress of Soviets on the Brest-Litovsk Treaty *March 14, 1918*

Introduction After the fall of the Tsarist autocracy in February, 1917, the Bolsheviks came into opposition to the democratic Provisional Government which replaced it. In particular, Lenin and the Bolsheviks opposed Russia's continued participation in the war against Germany. They campaigned for an immediate peace and encouraged desertion from the Army. The Provisional Government's unsuccessful effort to go on fighting lost for it the confidence of the people and contributed importantly to its final collapse and the Bolsheviks' accession to power in the October Revolution. Lenin immediately called for an armistice and began negotiations to end the war. The heavy price demanded by Germany—surrender of the Ukraine, Finland, and the Baltic countries—led a powerful faction in the Soviet leadership to advocate resumption of the war as a revolutionary struggle against Imperial Germany, to be concluded, they hoped, by a proletarian revolution in Germany and in the other warring states of Europe.

1

Lenin, however, opposed this plan, recognizing that the country lacked both the means and the will to resist the German armed forces in Russia. He believed the Bolsheviks could stay in power only if they ended the war, on German terms. After some delay while the matter was disputed, the Germans renewed their advance. This led to the signing of peace, March 3, 1918. Lenin gave his Report on the Brest-Litovsk Treaty several days later, and successfully persuaded the Communist-controlled legislature, the Congress of Soviets, to ratify it.

The speech is important because it expresses some of the principles on which Soviet foreign policy was subsequently based: the need to rely on the cold calculation of reason, rather than on passion and slogans, when deliberating on foreign policy; the need to base calculation on the balance of class forces, in Russia itself and on the world scene; the need to retreat and accept great losses, if necessary, in order to retain the revolutionary base from which advances could later be made. When he delivered this Report, Lenin still believed that the Revolution would be overthrown unless there was an early revolution in Europe. He had already come to realize, however, that the Soviet state would have to accommodate to other states, if only to survive until it could be rescued by the coming proletarian revolution in Europe.

Comrades, today we have to settle a question that marks a turning-point in the development of the Russian revolution, and not only in the Russian but also in the international revolution, and in order to decide correctly on this very harsh peace which representatives of Soviet power have concluded at Brest-Litovsk and which Soviet power asks you to approve, or ratify—in order to settle this question correctly it is more than ever necessary for us to get an understanding of the historical meaning of the turning-point we are witnessing, an understanding of the main feature of the development of the revolution up to now and of the main reason for the severe defeat and the epoch of stern trials we have passed through.

It seems to me that the chief source of disagreement among the Soviet parties on this question is that some people too easily give way to a feeling of just and legitimate indignation at the defeat of the Soviet Republic by imperialism, at times too easily give way to despair instead of considering the historical conditions under which the revolution developed up to the time of the present peace, and as we see them after the peace; instead of doing that they try to answer questions of the tactics of the revolution on the basis of their immediate feelings. The entire history of revolutions, however, teaches us that when we have to do with a mass movement or with the class struggle, especially one like that at present developing, not only throughout a single country, albeit a tremendous country, but also involving all international relations—in such a case we must base our tactics first and mostly on an appraisal of the objective situation, we must make an analytical examination of the course of the revolution up to this moment and the reason it has taken a turn so menacing and so sharp, and so much to our disadvantage.

On examining the development of our revolution from that point of view we see clearly that it has so far passed through a period of relative and largely imaginary independence, being temporarily independent of international relations. The path travelled by our revolution from the end of February 1917 to February 11 of this year when the German offensive began was, by and large, a path of easy and rapid successes. . . .

This period of the victorious, triumphal advance of the dictatorship of the proletariat and Soviet power, when great masses of the working and exploited people of Russia were drawn to the side of Soviet power definitely and irrevocably—this period constituted the last and highest point of development of the Russian revolution which had been progressing all this time, apparently, independently of world imperialism. That was the reason a country that was extremely backward and that was most prepared for the revolution by the experience of 1905 was able to promote one class after another to power rapidly, easily and systematically, getting rid of certain political structures until at last that political structure was reached that was the last word, not only of the Russian revolution, but also of the West-European workers' revolutions, for Soviet power has been consolidated in Russia and has won the absolute sympathy of the working and exploited people; this is because it has destroyed the old state apparatus that was an instrument of oppression and has laid the foundation of a state of a new and higher form of which the Paris Commune was the prototype. . . .

That is what the Russian revolution did in this period and that is why the small vanguard of the Russian revolution is under the impression that this rapid, triumphal advance can be expected to continue in further victory. That is precisely their mistake because the revolution that overthrew the monarchy in a few days, exhausted all possibilities of compromise with the bourgeoisie in a few months and overcame all the resistance of the bourgeoisie in a civil war of a few weeks, this revolution, the revolution of the Socialist Republic, could live side by side with the imperialist powers, among the international predators, the wild beasts of international imperialism, only so long as the bourgeoisie, in a mortal struggle with each other, were paralysed in their offensive against Russia.

And then began the period that we feel so keenly and see before our eyes, the period of disastrous defeats and severe trials for the Russian revolution, the period in which the swift, direct and open offensive against the enemies of the revolution is over and in its place we are experiencing disastrous defeats and have to retreat before forces that are immeasurably greater than ours, before the forces of international imperialism and finance capital, before the military might that the entire bourgeoisie with their modern weapons and their organisation have mustered against us in the interests of plunder, oppression and the strangling of small nations; we had to think of bringing our forces up to their level; we had to face a task of tremendous difficulty, that of direct combat with enemies that differed from Romanov or Kerensky who could not be taken seriously; we had to meet the forces of the international imperialist bourgeoisie, all their military might, we had to stand face to face with the world plunderers. In view of the delay in getting help from the international socialist proletariat we had to take upon ourselves a conflict with these forces and we naturally suffered a disastrous defeat.

And this epoch is one of disastrous defeats, an epoch of retreat, an epoch in which we must save at least a small part of our position by retreating before imperialism, by awaiting the time when there will be changes in the world situation in general, when the forces of the European proletariat arrive, the forces that exist and are maturing but which could not deal with their enemy as easily as we did with ours; it would be a very great illusion, a very great mistake, to forget that it was easy to begin the Russian revolution but difficult to take further steps. This was inevitable because we had to begin with the most backward and most rotten political system. The European revolution will have to deal with the bourgeoisie, with a much more serious enemy and under immeasurably more difficult conditions. It will be much more difficult to begin the European revolution. We see that it is immeasurably more difficult to make the first breach in the system that is holding back the revolution. It will be much easier for the European revolution to advance to the second and third stages. . . . It is an extremely difficult and extremely serious question arising out of the present turning-point in the development of the revolution, the turn from easy victories within the country to exceptionally heavy defeats without; it is also a turning-point in the entire world revolution, a turn from the epoch of propaganda and agitation in the Russian revolution, with imperialism biding its time, to the offensive of imperialism against Soviet power, and this turn raises a particularly difficult and acute question before the international movement in Western Europe. If we are not to forget this historical issue we must try to understand how Russia's basic interests in the question of the present harsh or vile, as it is called, peace took shape.

* * *

When we were about to take power in October it was obvious that events were inevitably leading up to it, that the turn towards Bolshevism in the Soviets indicated a turn throughout the country and that the Bolsheviks must inevitably take power. When we, realising this, took power in October, we said to ourselves and to all the people, very clearly and unequivocally, that it was a transfer of power to the proletariat and the poor peasantry, that the proletariat knew the peasantry would support it—in what you know yourselves—in its active struggle for peace and its readiness to continue the fight against big finance capital. In this we are making no mistake, and nobody who sticks to the concept of class forces and class alignments can get away from the truth that we cannot ask a country of small peasants, a country that has given much for the European and world revolution, to carry on a struggle on the difficult, most difficult conditions when help from the West-European proletariat had undoubtedly been delayed, although there is no doubt that it is coming to us, as the facts, the strikes, etc., show. . . . I realise full well that the Russian bourgeoisie are today urging us on towards a revolutionary war when it is absolutely impossible for us; it is essential to the class interests of the bourgeoisie.

* * *

. . . They know that under no circumstances can Soviet power undertake an imperialist war against mighty imperialism at the present moment. That is why it is only in this international situation, in this general class situation, that we can understand the full depth of the mistake of those who. . . have allowed themselves to be carried away by a theory that is common to the history of all revolutions at moments of difficulty, a theory that is half desperation and half empty phrases; according to this theory, instead of taking a sober view of reality and appraising the tasks of the revolution in respect of the internal and external enemy from the standpoint of class forces, you are asked to settle a serious and very bitter question under the impact of your feelings, from the standpoint of feelings alone. . . .

...Whatever respite we may obtain, no matter how unstable, no matter how brief, harsh and humiliating the peace may be, it is better than war, because it gives the masses a breathing space.

* * *

...The revolution teaches us that when we make diplomatic mistakes, when we assume that the German workers will come to our aid tomorrow, when we hope that Liebknecht will be victorious immediately (and we know that one way or another Liebknecht will win, that is inevitable in the development of the working-class movement), that means that enthusiasm has turned the revolutionary slogans of the difficult socialist movement into empty phrases. There is not a single representative of the working people, there is not a single honest worker who would refuse to make the greatest sacrifice to help the socialist movement of Germany because during all his time at the front he has learned to distinguish between the German imperialists and the soldiers tormented by German discipline, most of whom are in sympathy with us. That is why I say that the Russian revolution has corrected our mistake in practice, has corrected it by giving us the respite. It is very probable that it will be an extremely brief one, but we have the chance of at least a brief respite in which the army, worn out and hungry, will become conscious of the fact that it has been given an opportunity to recuperate. It is clear to us that the period of the old imperialist wars is over and we are threatened with the further horrors of the beginning of fresh wars, but there have been such periods of war in many historical epochs, and they have always become most fierce towards the end. This must be understood, not only at meetings in Petrograd and Moscow; it must be understood by the many tens of millions in the countryside; and the more enlightened part of the rural population, those returning from the front, those who have experienced the horrors of war must help them understand it; the huge masses of peasants and workers must become convinced of the necessity for a revolutionary front—they will then say we have acted correctly.
...They say we are traitors, we have betrayed the Ukraine! I say: Comrades, I've seen enough of the history of revolution not to be embarrassed by the hostile glances and shouts of people who give way to their feelings and are incapable of clear judgement. I will give you a simple example. Suppose that two freinds are out walking at night and they are attacked by ten men. If the scoundrels isolate one of them, what is the other to do? He cannot render assistance and if he runs away is he a traitor? And suppose that it is not a matter of individuals or of areas in which questions of direct feelings are being settled, but of five armies each

a hundred-thousand strong that surround an army of two hundred thousand, and that there is another army that should come to the embattled army's assistance. But if that second army knows that it be certain to fall into a trap, it should withdraw; it must withdraw, even if the retreat had to be covered by the conclusion of an indecent, foul peace—curse as much as you like, but it is necessary to conclude the peace. There is no reason for considering the feelings of a duelist who draws his sword and says that he must die because he is being compelled to conclude a humiliating peace. But we all know, that however we may decide, we have no army, and no gestures will save us from the necessity of withdrawing to gain time and enable our army to recuperate; everybody who looks reality in the face and does not deceive himself with a revolutionary phrase will agree with this.

If we know this, it is our revolutionary duty to conclude even this harsh, super-harsh, and rapacious treaty, for by so doing we shall reach a better position for ourselves and for our allies. Did we actually lose anything by concluding the peace treaty on March 3? Anyone who wants to look at things from the point of view of mass relations, and not from that of the aristocratic duelist, will realise that without an army, or having only the sick remnant of an army, it would be self-deception, it would be the greatest deception of the people, to accept battle and call it a revolutionary war. It is our duty to tell the people the truth; yes, the peace is a harsh one. The Ukraine and Finland will perish but we must accept that peace and all class-conscious working people in Russia will accept it because they know the unvarnished truth, they know the meaning of war, they know that to stake everything on one card on the assumption that the German revolution will begin immediately is self-deception. . . .

Our revolution has been one long triumph since October, and now the lengthy times of hardship have come, we do not know for how long, but we do know that it will be a long and difficult period of defeats and retreats, because the alignment of forces is what it is, because by retreating we shall give the people a chance to recuperate. We shall make it possible for every worker and peasant to realise the truth that will enable him to understand that new wars of the imperialist plunderers against the oppressed peoples are beginning, and every worker and peasant will realise that we must rise in defence of the fatherland, because we have been defencists since October. . . .

I am well aware, comrades, that the banner is in weak hands, I have said that outright several times already, and the workers of the most backward country will not be able to hold that banner unless the workers of all advanced countries come to their aid. The socialist reforms that we have accomplished are far from perfect, they are weak and insufficient; they will serve as a guide to the West-European workers who will say to themselves, "The Russians haven't begun to do properly what has to be done"; the important thing is that our people are not only a weak and backward people as compared with the Germans, but they are the people who have raised the banner of revolution. . . .

Yes, our people have a very heavy burden to bear, the burden they have themselves taken up; but the people who have been able to establish Soviet power cannot perish. Again I repeat—there is not a single politically-conscious socialist, not a single worker of those who think over the history of the revolution, who can dispute the fact that Soviet power—despite all the defects that I know only too well and can fully appreciate—is the highest type of state, the direct successor to the Paris Commune. . . . We have a powerful ally in all West-European countries, the international socialist proletariat, the proletariat that is on our side no matter what our enemies may say. True, it is not easy for that ally to raise his voice, any more than it was easy for us until the end of February 1917. That ally is living in the underground, under conditions of the prison into which all imperialist countries have been turned, but he knows us and understands our cause; it is difficult for him to come to our aid, and Soviet troops, therefore, will need much time and patience and will have to go through many trials before the time comes when he will aid us—we shall use even the slightest chance of procrastination, for time is working on our side. Our cause is gaining strength, the forces of the imperialists are weakening, and no matter what trials and defeats may emerge from the "Tilsit" peace, we shall begin the tactics of withdrawal and, once more I say it, there is no doubt the politically-conscious proletariat and likewise the politically-conscious peasants are on our side, and we are capable not only of making heroic attacks, but also of making a heroic retreat and we shall wait until the international socialist proletariat comes to our aid and shall then begin a second socialist revolution that will be world-wide in its scope.

LENIN

Report to the VIII Party Congress *March 18, 1919*

Introduction Soviet Russia was rescued from the terms of the Brest-Litovsk Treaty not by the revolutionary proletariat of Europe, as Lenin had expected, but by the "imperialist" armies of the Entente, who conquered Germany. Before this occurred, however, the Allied leaders had believed it necessary to intervene in the Russian civil war in order to restore an eastern front against the German armies. But the intervention continued after the defeat of Germany and Lenin saw a need in March, 1919, to end it, even at the cost of new losses of territory like those that had to be accepted at the time of the Brest-Litovsk Treaty. The Soviet Government offered to participate in a Conference on the Prince Islands (Prinkipo), where it was prepared to make far-reaching concessions to the White forces which the Allies were supporting. Instead, the civil war continued and a year later the Bolsheviks were victorious.

Lenin's Report calls attention to the peculiar mix of Marxist doctrine and experimental improvisation which was at the basis of much Soviet policy. Where past experience made it seem possible to avoid improvisation, it was readily seized upon, as in Lenin's argument by analogy to the Brest peace. His assertion that there would "have to be a series of frightful collisions between the Soviet Republic and the bourgeois states" has been prominently quoted by Stalin, at times, as well as by anti-Bolsheviks. Observe, however, that Lenin's assumption of the inevitability of war with capitalist states is here linked with the belief—one he expressed only during the first period of the Revolution—that it was inconceivable for the Soviet Republic to exist alongside the imperialist states for an extended period of time.

At the present time, owing to the difficult food situation and the war which we are still waging against the Entente, a wave of vacillation is again sweeping through the petty-bourgeois democrats. We have been obliged to reckon with these vacillations before; but now we must all learn a tremendously important lesson, namely, that situations never repeat themselves in exactly the same form. The new situation is far more complex. It can be properly assessed, and our policy will be correct, if we draw on the experience of the Brest peace. When we consented to the proposal for a conference on Princes Islands we knew that we were consenting to an extremely harsh peace. On the other hand, however, we now know better how the tide of proletarian revolution is rising in Western Europe, how unrest is changing into conscious discontent, and how the latter is giving rise to a world, Soviet, proletarian movement. At that time we were groping, guessing when the revolution in Europe might break out—we presumed, on the basis of our theoretical conviction, that the revolution must take place—but today we have a number of facts showing how the revolution is maturing in other countries and how the movement began.

That is why, in relation to Western Europe, in relation to the Entente countries, we have, or shall have, to repeat a good deal of what we did at the time of the Brest peace. It will be much easier for us to do this now that we have the experience of Brest. When our Central Committee discussed the question of participating in a conference on Princes Islands together with the Whites—which in fact amounted to the annexation of all the territory the Whites then occupied—this question of an armistice did not evoke a single voice of protest among the proletariat; and that also was the attitude of our Party. At any rate, I did not hear of any dissatisfaction, or indignation, from any quarter. The reason for this was that our lesson in international politics had borne fruit.

Insofar as concerns the petty-bourgeois elements, the problem facing the Party has not yet been fully solved. On a number of questions, in fact on all the questions on the agenda, we have, during the past year, laid the foundation for a correct solution of this problem, particularly in relation to the middle peasants. In theory we agree that the middle peasants are not our enemies, that they need special treatment, and that in their case the situations will vary in accordance with numerous circumstances attending the revolution, in particular, the answer to the question "For or against patriotism?" For us such questions are of second-rate importance, even of third-rate importance; but the petty bourgeoisie is completely blinded by them. Furthermore, all these elements waver in the struggle and become absolutely spineless. They do not know what they want, and are incapable of defending their position. Here we need extremely flexible and extremely cautious tactics, for sometimes it is necessary to give with one hand and take away with the other. . . .

The organisation of a Red Army was an entirely new question which had never been dealt with before, even theoretically. . . . We, however, acted in conformity with the tenets of Marxism. At the same time, the political activities of the Central Committee in each concrete case were determined entirely by what was absolutely indispensable. We were often obliged to feel our way. This will be strongly emphasised by any historian capable of presenting an integrated picture of the activities of the Central Committee of the Party and of the Soviet government during the past year. This fact becomes all the more striking when we try to embrace our past experience in a single glance. But this did not deter us in the least even on October 10, 1917, when the question of seizing power was decided. We did not doubt that we should have to experiment, as Comrade Trotsky expressed it. We undertook a task which nobody in the world has ever attempted on so large a scale.

This is also true of the Red Army. When the war drew to a close the army began to break up, and many people thought at the time that this was a purely Russian phenomenon. But we see that the Russian revolution was in fact the dress rehearsal, or one of the rehearsals, for the world proletarian revolution. When we discussed the Treaty of Brest, when the question of peace arose early in January 1918, we did not yet know when, and in which other countries, armies would begin to disintegrate. We proceeded from experiment to experiment; we endeavoured to create a volunteer army, feeling our way, testing the ground and experimenting to find a solution to the problem in the given situation. And the nature of the problem was clear. Unless we defended the socialist republic by force of arms, we could not exist. A ruling class would never surrender its power to an oppressed class. And the latter would have to prove in practice that it is capable not only of overthrowing the exploiters, but also of organising its self-defence and of staking everything on it. We have always said that there are different kinds of wars. We condemned the *imperialist* war, but we did not reject *war in general*. Those who accused us of being militarists were hopelessly muddled. And when in the report of the Berne Conference of yellow socialists I read that Kautsky had said that the Bolsheviks had introduced not socialism but militarism, I smiled and shrugged my shoulders. As if there was ever a big revolution in history that was not connected with war! Of course not! We are living not merely in a state, but *in a system of states,* and it is inconceivable for the Soviet Republic to exist alongside of the imperialist states for any length of time. One or the other must triumph in the end. And before that end comes there will have to be a series of frightful collisions between the Soviet Republic and the bourgeois states. If the ruling class, the proletariat, wants to hold power, it must, therefore, prove its ability to do so by its military organization. How was a class which had hitherto served as cannon-fodder for the military commanders of the ruling imperialist class to create its own commanders? How was it to solve the problem of combining the enthusiasm, the new revolutionary creative spirit of the oppressed and the employment of the store of the bourgeois science and technology of militarism in their worst forms without which this class would not be able to master modern technology and modern methods of warfare?

Here we were faced with a problem which a year's experience has now summed up for us. When we included the question of bourgeois specialists in the revolutionary programme of our Party, we summed up the Party's practical experience in one of the most important questions. As far as I remember the earlier teachers of socialism, who foresaw a great deal of what would take place in the future socialist revolution and discerned many of its features, never expressed an opinion on this question. It did not exist for them, for it arose only when we proceeded to create a Red Army. . . .

LENIN

Report to the Congress of Soviets *December 5, 1919*

Introduction In this report, written when the Civil War was drawing toward a close, Lenin exults in the Bolshevik victory. He sees in it not only a vindication of the Revolution in Russia but also—despite the absence of Communist revolution in Europe—proof that the Bolsheviks had been right to rely on support from the world proletariat.

Like the world proletariat, world capitalism had also justified the Communist assessment of it. By giving arms and money to the anti-Bolshevik forces in Russia and to the anti-Bolshevik states on its border, world capitalism confirmed Lenin's doctrine that it was committed to the destruction of the Revolution. If capitalism did not bring its full force to bear against the Revolution, Lenin argues, this was only because it could not, since the mass of the people in the great capitalist states "are for us." Though the Bolsheviks had won the civil war, the Revolution would not be secure until the proletariat had won power in several of the "advanced" states. Although it has not done so until today, current Soviet doctrine asserts that the "final" victory of socialism has been achieved.

13

At the time of this Report, it is clear Lenin did not anticipate that almost two decades of peace lay ahead of the Revolution, and that when war finally came the Soviet Union would be allied with powerful capitalist states.

When speaking of the political results and lessons of our activities, the Soviet Republic's international position naturally takes first place. Both prior to October and during the October Revolution, we always said that we regard ourselves and can only regard ourselves as one of the contingents of the international proletarian army, a contingent which came to the fore, not because of its level of development and preparedness, but because of Russia's exceptional conditions; we always said that the victory of the socialist revolution, therefore, can only be regarded as final when it becomes the victory of the proletariat in at least several advanced countries. It was in this respect that we experienced the greatest difficulties.

Our banking on the world revolution, if you can call it that, has on the whole been fully justified. But from the point of view of the speed of its development we have endured an exceptionally difficult period; we have seen for ourselves that the revolution's development in more advanced countries has proved to be considerably slower, considerably more difficult, considerably more complicated. This should not surprise us for it was naturally easier for a country such as Russia to start a socialist revolution than it is for the advanced countries. But, in any case, this slower, more complicated, more zig-zag development of the socialist revolution in Western Europe has burdened us with incredible difficulties.

The question that primarily comes to mind is: how was it possible for such a miracle to have occurred, for Soviet power to have held out for two years in a backward, ruined and war-weary country, in the face of the stubborn struggle waged against it first by German imperialism, which at that time was considered omnipotent, and then by Entente imperialism, which a year ago settled accounts with Germany, had no rivals and lorded it over all the countries on earth? From the point of view of a simple calculation of the forces involved, from the point of view of a military assessment of these forces, it really is a miracle, because the Entente was and continues to be immeasurably stronger than we are. Nevertheless, the year under review is noteworthy most of all for our having won a tremendous victory, so great a victory that I think we may say without exaggeration that our *main difficulties are already behind us.* No matter how great the dangers and difficulties in store for us, the main ones are evidently behind us.

We must understand the reasons for this, and what is most important, must correctly determine our future policy, since the future will almost certainly bring many further attempts by the Entente at intervention, and possibly a rebirth of the previous predatory alliance between international and Russian capitalists to restore the power of the landowners and capitalists, to overthrow Soviet rule in Russia, in short, an alliance pursuing the old aim of extinguishing the centre of the world socialist conflagration—the Russian Socialist Federative Soviet Republic.

Examining the history of the Entente intervention and its political lesson for us from this point of view, I would say that it could be divided into three main stages, each of which has successively given us full and lasting victory.

The first stage, naturally the most convenient and easiest for the Entente countries, involved their attempt to settle matters with Soviet Russia by using their own troops. Of course, after the Entente countries had defeated Germany they had armies of millions of men who had not yet openly declared for peace and who did not immediately recover from the fright given them by the bogey of German imperialism, which had been used to scare them in all the Western countries. At that time, of course, from the military point of view, and from the point of view of foreign policy, it would have been easy for the Entente countries to take a tenth part of their armies and dispatch them to Russia. Note that they completely dominated at sea, that they had complete naval supremacy. Troop transportation and supplies were always completely under their control. Had the Entente countries, who hated us as only the bourgeoisie can hate the socialist revolution, then been able to fling even a tenth part of their armies against us with any success, there cannot be the slightest doubt that Soviet Russia would have been doomed and would have met the same fate as Hungary.

Why did the Entente countries fail to achieve this?... There were no obstacles confronting them. How, then, are we to explain the failure of that attempt? It ended in the Entente countries having to withdraw their troops, because they proved incapable of waging a struggle against revolutionary Soviet Russia. That, comrades, has always been our main and principal argument. From the very outset of the revolution we have said that we constitute a party of the international proletariat, and that, however great the difficulties facing the revolution, there would come a time when, at the most decisive moment, the sympathy, the solidarity of the workers oppressed by international imperialism would make itself felt. For this we are accused of being utopians. But experience has shown that while we cannot always and in all cases rely on action by the proletariat, at any rate we may say that during these two years of the world's history we have been proved correct a thousand times. The attempt by the British and French to crush Soviet Russia with their own troops, an attempt that promised them certain and very easy success in a minimum of time, ended in failure. . . Our response to the unlimited military and technical superiority of the Entente countries was to deprive them of it through the solidarity of the working people against the imperialist governments.

This revealed how superficial and uncertain it is to judge these so-called democratic countries by accepted criteria. Their parliaments have stable bourgeois majorities. This they call "democracy". Capital dominates and weighs down everything and they still resort to military censorship. And they call that "democracy". Among the millions of copies of their newspapers and magazines you would be hard put to find any but an insignificant few that contain even a hint of anything favourable about the Bolsheviks. That is why they say: "We are protected against the Bolsheviks, there is order in our countries", and they call it "democracy". How could it happen that a small section of British soldiers and French sailors were able to compel the withdrawal of the Entente troops from Russia? There is something wrong here. It means that even in Britain, France and America the mass of the people are for us; it means that all these external features, as socialists who refuse to betray socialism have always asserted, are a deception; it means that the bourgeois parliamentary system, bourgeois democracy, bourgeois freedom of the press are merely freedom for the capitalists, freedom to bribe public opinion, to exert pressure on it by all the power of money. That is what socialists always said until the imperialist war scattered them to their national camps and turned each national group of socialists into lackeys of their own bourgeoisie. That was said by socialists before the war, that was always said by the internationalists and Bolsheviks during the war—and it all proved to be absolutely correct. All the external features, all the window-dressings, are a fraud; and this is becoming increasingly obvious to the people. They all shout about democracy, but in no parliament in the world did they dare to say that they were declaring war on Soviet Russia. . . .

That was our first and chief victory, because it was not only a military victory, it was not really a military victory at all—it was actually a victory of that international solidarity of the working people for which we began the whole revolution, and which we pointed to and said that, however numerous the trials we would have to undergo, all these sacrifices would be repaid a hundredfold by the development of the world revolution, which is inevitable. It was apparent from the fact that in the sphere where the grossest material factors play the greatest part, namely, in the military sphere, we defeated the Entente countries by depriving them of the workers and peasants in soldiers' uniforms.

The first victory was followed by the second period of Entente intervention in our affairs. Each nation is headed by a group of politicians who possess wonderful experience, and that is why, after losing this stake, they placed another, taking advantage of their dominant position in the world. There is not a single country, not a single bit of the earth's surface, which is not in fact totally dominated by British, French and American finance capital. That was the basis for the new attempt they made, namely, to compel the small countries surrounding Russia, many of which had been liberated and had been able to declare themselves independent only during the war—Poland, Estonia, Finland, Georgia, the Ukraine, etc.—to compel these small states to go to war against Russia on British, French and American money. . . And what was the result? There was a time when Yudenich's troops were a few versts away from Petrograd, when Denikin stood to the north of Orel, when the slightest assistance to them would have quickly settled the fate of Petrograd, to the advantage of our enemies, in a minimum of time and at negligible cost.

The entire pressure of the Entente countries was brought to bear on Finland, a country that is up to its neck in debt to them. And not only in debt: Finland cannot carry on for one month without the aid of these countries. But how did the "miracle" of our having won the battle against such an enemy happen? And win it we did. Finland did not enter the war, Yudenich was defeated, so was Denikin, and that at a time when joint action by them would most surely, most swiftly have settled the whole struggle to the advantage of international capitalism. We won the battle with international imperialism in this most serious and desperate trial of strength. . . .

The Entente encountered opposition to its pressure on these small countries, on each of these 14 countries. The Finnish bourgeoisie who employed White Terror to crush tens of thousands of Finnish workers know that this will not be forgotten, and that the German bayonets that made it possible no longer exist—these Finnish bourgeois hate the Bolsheviks as intensely as an exploiter would hate the workers who kicked him out. Nevertheless the Finnish bourgeoisie said to themselves, "If we follow the instructions of the Entente, that means we shall undoubtedly lose all hope of independence." And this independence was given to them by the Bolsheviks in November 1917, when Finland was a bourgeois government. The attitude of wide sections of the Finnish bourgeoisie, therefore, proved to be one of vacillation. We won the battle with the Entente countries because they counted on the small nations and at the same time repelled them.

This experience confirms, on an enormous, global scale, what we have always said. There are two forces on earth that can decide the destiny of mankind. One force is international capitalism, and should it be victorious it will display this force in countless atrocities as may be seen from the history of every small nation's development. The other force is the international proletariat that is fighting for the socialist revolution through the dictatorship of the proletariat, which it calls workers' democracy. Neither the vacillating elements here in Russia, nor the bourgeoisie of the small countries believes us; they called us utopians or bandits or even worse, for there is no stupid and monstrous accusation that they will not fling at us. But when they faced up squarely to the issue of either going with the Entente countries and helping them to crush the Bolsheviks, or of helping the Bolsheviks by neutrality, we proved to have won the battle and to have got that neutrality. We had no treaties, whereas Britain, France and America had all sorts of promissory notes, all sorts of treaties; nevertheless the small nations did as we wanted them to; they did so not because the Polish, Finnish, Lithuanian or Latvian bourgeoisie derived satisfaction from conducting their policy in a way that suited the Bolsheviks—that, of course, is nonsense—but because our definition of the historical forces involved was correct, namely, that either brute capital would be victorious, and then, even if it were in the most democratic republic, it would crush all the small nations of the world—or the dictatorship of the proletariat would be victorious, which is the sole hope of all working people and of the small, downtrodden and weak nations. It turned out that we were right not only in theory, but also in practical world politics. When this battle for the troops of Finland and Estonia took place we won it, although they could have crushed us with insignificant forces. We won the battle despite the Entente countries having thrown the enormous weight of their financial pressure, their military might, and their food supplies into the fray in order to compel Finland to take action.

That, comrades, was the second stage of international intervention, our second historic victory. First, we won the workers and peasants away from Britain, France and America. These troops could not fight against us. Secondly, we won away from them these small countries, all of which are against us, and in which not Soviet, but bourgeois rule dominates. They displayed friendly neutrality towards us and acted contrary to the desires of that mighty world force, the Entente, for it was a beast that wanted to crush them. . . .

This victory at the second stage is a far more lasting one than is apparent at the moment. I am not exaggerating at all, and consider exaggerations to be extremely dangerous. I have not the slightest doubt that further attempts will be made by the Entente to set against us now one, now another of the small states that are our neighbors. Such attempts will occur because all this talk about freedom, independence and democracy is sheer hypocrisy, and the Entente may compel them once again to raise their hand against us. But if this attempt was foiled at such a convenient moment when it was so easy to wage a struggle against us, we may, I think, say definitely that in this respect the main difficulty is undoubtedly behind us. We are entitled to say this, and to say it without the slightest exaggeration, fully conscious that the Entente countries possess a tremendous advantage in strength. We have won a lasting victory. Attempts will be made against us, but we shall defeat them with greater ease, because the small states, despite their bourgeois system, have become convinced by experience, not theory—these gentlemen are theory-proof—that the Entente is a more brazen and predatory brute than the one they have in their minds when they think of the Bolsheviks, the bogey used to scare children and cultured philistines all over Europe.

But our victories were not limited to this. In the first place we won over to our side the workers and peasants of the Entente countries; secondly, we gained the neutrality of the small nations under the Entente's domination and, thirdly, we began to win over, within the Entente countries, the petty bourgeoisie and educated townsfolk who had been completely opposed to us.

Comrades, I repeat that it would be a great mistake to jump to hasty conclusions because of all this. There can be no doubt that the imperialists will resume their attempts, but we are absolutely confident that these attempts, no matter by what powerful forces they may be undertaken, will end in failure. We can say that the Civil War which we conducted with such tremendous sacrifices has ended in victory. It has been victorious, not only on a Russian scale, but on a world-historical scale. . . .

LENIN

Report to the IX Party Congress *March 29, 1920*

Introduction The international situation in the aftermath of the civil war was still hazardous. In Russia's weakened condition Lenin had reason to fear attack even from minor powers. But though internally weak, Soviet Russia expected to derive strength from the revolutionary forces of Europe. Thus the situation was seen to be highly fluid. Lenin fears invasion by Poland, yet he expresses confidence that Soviet Russia will soon have a powerful ally in a Soviet Government of Germany. Lenin's fear of a Polish attack proved warranted, but not his belief in the German Revolution.

According to Lenin, the Political Bureau of the Communist Party's Central Committee, a handful of men, made decisions on all questions of foreign policy. It has remained true throughout Soviet history that foreign policy has been made by the Political Bureau or (as in Stalin's time) by its leading figure.

Comrades, we are opening this present Congress of the Party at a highly important moment. The internal development of our revolution has led to very big and rapid victories over the enemy in the Civil War, and, in view of the international situation, these victories, we find, are nothing more nor less than than the victory of the Soviet revolution in the first country to make this revolution—a very weak and backward country—a victory over the combined forces of world capitalism and imperialism. And after these victories we may now proceed with calm and firm assurance to the immediate tasks of peaceful economic development, confident that the present Congress, having reviewed the experience of over two years of Soviet work, will be able to utilise the lesson gained in order to cope with the more difficult and complex task of economic development that now confronts us. From the international standpoint, our position has never been as favourable as it is now; and what fills us with particular joy and vigour is the news we are daily receiving from Germany, which shows that, however difficult and painful the birth of a socialist revolution may be, the proletarian Soviet power in Germany is spreading irresistibly. The part played by the German Kornilov-type putsch was similar to that of Kornilov revolt in Russia. After that a swing towards a workers' government began, not only among the masses of urban workers, but also among the rural proletariat of Germany. And this swing is of historic importance. Not only is it the more absolute confirmation of the correctness of the line, but it gives us the assurance that the time is not far off when we shall be marching hand in hand with a German Soviet government. . . .

[The above paragraph is from Lenin's greeting to the Congress and is not part of his formal Report.]

To present a report on the political work of the Central Committee is a highly difficult task if understood literally. A large part of the work of the Political Bureau has this year consisted in making the current decision on the various questions of co-ordinating the activities of the Soviet and Party institutions and all organizations of the working class, of co-ordinating and doing their utmost to direct the work of the entire Soviet Republic. The Political Bureau adopted decisions on all questions of foreign and domestic policy. Naturally, to attempt to enumerate these questions, even approximately, would be impossible. . . . Now, when I am called upon to make a general report, instead of giving a chronological review and a grouping of subjects, I shall take the liberty of dwelling on the main and most essential points, such, moreover, as link up the experience of yesterday, or, more correctly, of the past year, with the tasks that now confront us.

The time is not yet ripe for a history of Soviet government. And even if it were, I must say for myself—and I think for the Central Committee as well–that we have no present intention of becoming historians. What interests us is the present and the future. We take the past year under review as material, as a lesson, as a stepping-stone, from which we must proceed further. Regarded from this point of view, the work of the Central Committee falls into two big categories–work connected with war problems and those determining the international position of the Republic, and work of internal, peace-time economic development, which only began to come to the fore at the end of the last year perhaps, or the beginning of this year, when it became quite clear that we had won a decisive victory on the decisive fronts of the Civil War. Last spring our military situation was an extremely difficult one; as you remember, we were still to experience quite a number of defeats, of new, huge and unexpected offensives on the part of the counter revolution and the Entente, none of which could have been anticipated by us. It was therefore only natural that the greater part of this period was devoted to the military problem, the problem of the Civil War, which seemed unsolvable to all the faint-hearted, not to speak of the parties of the Mensheviks and Socialist Revolutionaries and other petty-bourgeois democrats, and to all the intermediate elements; this induced them to declare quite sincerely that the problem could not be solved, that Russia was backward and enfeebled and could not vanquish the capitalist system of the entire world, seeing that the revolution in the West had been delayed. And we therefore had to maintain our position and to declare with absolute firmness and conviction that we would win, we had to implement the slogans "Everything for victory!" and "Everything for the war!" . . . Our enemies grew more and more disunited as time went on. They were disunited by capitalist property, by private property under commodity production, whether they were small proprietors who profiteered by selling surplus grain at exorbitant prices and enriched themselves at the expense of the starving workers, or the capitalists of the various countries, even though they possessed military might and were creating a League of Nations a "great united league" of all the foremost nations of the world. Unity of this kind is a sheer fiction, a sheer fraud, a sheer lie. And we have seen–and this was a great example–that this notorious League of Nations, which attempted to hand out mandates for the government of states, to divide up the world–that this notorious alliance proved to be a soap-bubble which at once burst, because it was an alliance founded on capitalist property. We have seen this on a vast historical scale, and it confirms that fundamental truth which told us that our cause was just, that the victory of the October Revolution was absolutely certain, and that the cause we were embarking on was one to which, despite all difficulties and obstacles, millions and millions of working people in all countries would rally. We knew that we had allies, that it was only necessary for the one country to which history had presented this honourable and most difficult task to display a spirit of self-sacrifice, for these incredible sacrifices to be repaid a hundredfold— every month we held out in our country would win us millions and millions of allies in all countries of the world.

If, after all, we give some thought to the reason we were able to win, were bound to win, we shall find that it was only because all our enemies—who were formally tied by all sorts of bonds to the most powerful governments and capitalists in the world—however united they may have been formally, actually turned out to be disunited. . . . In the final analysis this was the fundamental reason, the underlying reason, that made our victory certain and which is still the chief, insuperable and inexhaustible source of our strength; and it permits us to affirm that when we in our country achieve the dictatorship of the proletariat in full measure, and the maximum unity of its forces, through its vanguard, its advanced party, we may expect the world revolution. And this in fact is an expression of the proletarian determination to fight; it is an expression of the proletarian determination to achieve an alliance of millions upon millions of workers of all countries.

The bourgeoisie and the pseudo-socialist gentry of the Second International have declared this to be mere propagandist talk. But it is not, it is historical reality, borne out by the bloody and painful experience of the Civil War in Russia. For this Civil War was a war against world capital; and world capital disintegrated of itself, devoured itself, amidst strife, whereas we, in a country where the proletariat was perishing from hunger and typhus, emerged more hardened and stronger than ever. In this country we won the support of increasing numbers of working people. What the compromisers formerly regarded as propagandist talk and the bourgeoisie were accustomed to sneer at, has been transformed in these years of our revolution, and particularly in the year under review, into an absolute and indisputable historical fact, which enables us to say with the most positive conviction that our having accomplished this is evidence that we possess a world-wide basis, immeasurably wider than was the case in any previous revolution. We have an international alliance, an alliance which has nowhere been registered, which has never been given formal embodiment, which from the point of view of "constitutional law" means nothing, but which, in the disintegrating capitalist world, actually means everything. Every month that we gained positions, or merely held out against an incredibly powerful enemy, proved to the whole world that we were right and brought us millions of new supporters.

This process has been a difficult one; it has been accompanied by tremendous defeats. In this very year under review the monstrous White terror in Finland was followed by the defeat of the Hungarian revolution, which was stifled by the governments of the Entente countries that deceived their parliaments and concluded a secret treaty with Rumania. . . .

And it seems to me that we must first and foremost draw a lesson from this fundamental experience. Here we must make a special point of basing our agitation and propaganda on an analysis, an explanation of why we were victorious, why the sacrifices made in the Civil War have been repaid a hundredfold, and how we must act, on the basis of this experience, in order to succeed in another war, a war on a bloodless front, a war which has only changed its form, but which is being waged against us by those same representatives, lackeys and leaders of the old capitalist world, only still more vigorously, still more furiously, still more zealously. More than any other, our revolution has proved the rule that the strength of a revolution, the vigour of its assault, its energy, determination, its victory and its triumph intensify the resistance of the bourgeoisie. The more victorious we are the more the capitalist exploiters learn to unite and the more determined their onslaught. For, as you all distinctly remember—it was not so long ago when judged by the passage of time, but a long time ago when judged by the march of events—at the beginning of the October Revolution Bolshevism was regarded as a freak; this view, which was a reflection of the feeble development and weakness of the proletarian revolution, very soon had to be abandoned in Russia and has now been abandoned in Europe as well. Bolshevism has become a world-wide phenomenon, the workers' revolution has raised its head. The Soviet system, in creating which in October we followed the traditions of 1905, developing our own experience—this Soviet system has become a phenomen of world-historic importance.

Two camps are now quite consciously facing each other all over the world; this may be said without the slightest exaggeration. It should be noted that only this year have they become locked in a decisive and final struggle. And now, at the time of this very Congress, we are passing through what is perhaps one of the greatest, most acute but not yet completed periods of transition from war to peace.

You all know what happened to the leaders of the imperialist powers of the Entente who loudly announced to the whole world: "We shall never stop fighting those usurpers, those bandits those arrogators of power, those enemies of democracy, those Bolsheviks"—you know that they lifted the blockade, that their attempt to unite the small states failed, because we succeeded in winning over not only the workers of all countries, but also the bourgeoisie of the small countries, for the imperialists oppress not only the workers of their own countries but the bourgeoisie of the small states as well. You know that we won over the vacillating bourgeoisie in the advanced countries. And the present position is that the Entente is breaking its former promises and assurances and is violating the treaties which incidentally, it concluded dozens of times with various Russian whiteguards. And now, as far as these treaties are concerned, the Entente is the loser, for it squandered hundreds of millions on them but failed to complete the job.

It has now lifted the blockade and has virtually begun peace negotiations with the Soviet Republic. But it is not completing these negotiations, and therefore the small states have lost faith in it and in its might. So we see that the position of the Entente, its position in foreign affairs, defies all definition from the standpoint of the customary concepts of law. The states of the Entente are neither at peace with the Bolsheviks nor at war with them, they have recognised us and they have not recognised us. And this utter confusion among our opponents, who were so convinced that they represented something, proves that they represent nothing but a pack of capitalist beasts who have fallen out among themselves and are absolutely incapable of doing us any harm.

The position today is that Latvia has officially made peace proposals to us. Finland has sent a telegram which officially speaks of a demarcation line but actually implies a swing to a policy of peace. Lastly, Poland, the Poland whose representatives have been, and still are, sabre-rattling so vigorously, the Poland that has been, and still is, receiving so many trainloads of artillery and promises of help in everything, if only she would continue the war with Russia—even Poland, the unstable position of whose government compels her to consent to any military gamble, has invited us to begin negotiations for peace. We must be extremely cautious. Our policy demands the most careful thought. Here it is hardest of all to find the proper policy, for nobody as yet knows on what track the train is standing; the enemy himself does not know what he is going to do next. The gentlemen who represent French policy and who are most zealous in egging Poland on, and the leaders of landowner and bourgeois Poland do not know what will happen next; they do not know what thet want. Today they say, "Gentlemen, let us have a few trainloads of guns and a few hundred millions and we are prepared to fight the Bolsheviks." They are hushing up the news of the strikes that are spreading in Poland: they are tightening up the censorship so as to conceal the truth. But the revolutionary movement in Poland is growing. The spread of revolution in Germany, in its new phase, in its new stage, now that the workers, after the German Kornilov-type putsch, are creating Red Armies, plainly shows (as can be seen from the recent dispatches from Germany) that the temper of the workers is rising more and more. The Polish bourgeoisie and landowners are themselves beginning to wonder whether it is not too late, whether there will not be a Soviet Republic in Poland before the government acts either for war or for peace. They do not know what the morrow will bring.

But we know that our forces are growing vastly every month, and will grow even more in future. The result is that our international position is now more stable than ever. But we must watch the international crisis with extreme care and be prepared for any eventuality. We have received a formal offer of peace from Poland. . . . Knowing that our enemy is in desperate straits, that our enemy does not know what he wants to do or what he will do tomorrow, we must tell ourselves quite definitely that in spite of the peace overtures war is possible. It is impossible to foretell what their future conduct will be. . . . Therefore we grasp at the proposal of peace with both hands and are prepared to make the maximum concessions, in the conviction that the conclusion of peace with the small states will further our cause infinitely more than war. For the imperialists used war to deceive the working masses, they used it to conceal the truth about Soviet Russia. Any peace, therefore, will open channels for our influence a hundred times wider, which, as it is, has grown considerably in these past few years. The Third, Communist International has achieved unparalleled successes. But at the same time we know that war may be forced upon us any day. Our enemies do not themselves know as yet what they are capable of doing in this respect.

That war preparations are under way, of that there is not the slightest doubt. Many of the states bordering on Russia—and perhaps many of those not bordering on Russia—are now arming. That is why we must manoeuvre so flexibly in our international policy and adhere so firmly to the course we have taken, that is why we must be prepared for anything. We have waged the war for peace with extreme vigour. This war is yielding splendid results. We have made a very good showing in this sphere of the struggle, at any rate, not inferior to the showing made by the Red Army on the front where blood is being shed. But the conclusion of peace with us does not depend on the will of the small states even if they desire it. They are up to their ears in debt to the countries of the Entente, who are wrangling and competing desperately among themselves. We must therefore remember that peace is of course possible from the point of view of the world situation, the historical situation created by the Civil War and by the war against the Entente.

But the measures we take for peace must be accompanied by intensified preparedness for defence, and in no case must our army be disarmed. Our army offers a real guarantee that the imperialist powers will not make the slightest attempt or encroachment on us; for although they might count on certain ephemeral successes at first, not one of them would escape defeat at the hands of Soviet Russia. . . .

LENIN

Report to the Congress of Soviets
December 23, 1921

Introduction The war against Poland was over by the fall of 1920, and Russia again had peace. Nevertheless drought brought famine and epidemic in the following year. Instead of again intervening with force to bring down the Bolsheviks, the capitalist world, and the United States in particular, sent large quantities of food and medicine, thereby protecting the regime from the worst consequences of the natural disaster and of its own mistaken policies.

Almost incredulously, and despite his philosophy, Lenin at the end of 1921 finds himself compelled to acknowledge a most unexpected outcome of the October Revolution: "only one Socialist Soviet Republic" is in existence, surrounded by hostile imperialist powers. Despite the failure of world revolution, Soviet Russia has survived. What had "seemed inconceivable" was a fact. (Oddly, Lenin concludes from this that "our forecasts and calculations" were correct.) While Lenin acknowledges that an equilibrium has been established on the world scene, he does not feel that this gives Russia any basis for relaxation: intervention is "always a hair's breadth away."

Lenin's discussion of the problems of winning recognition for the Soviet Government, obtaining foreign credits, and settling Soviet debts became the basis for subsequent policy. On the whole, the Soviet Union did win recognition and obtain extensive credits without making large payments on the debts it had inherited from the Tsarist regime and the Provisional Government.

Comrades, I have to make a report on the foreign and domestic position of the Republic. This is the first time I have been able to make such a report when a whole year has passed without one, at any rate, large-scale attack against our Soviet power by Russian or foreign capitalists. This is the first year that we have been able to enjoy a relative respite from intervention, even though to a limited extent, and that we have been able in some measure to apply our energies to our chief and fundamental tasks, namely, the rehabilitation of our war-devastated economy, to healing the wounds inflicted on Russia by the exploiting classes that had been in power, and to laying the foundations for socialist construction.

Firstly, in touching upon the question of the international position of our Republic, I must repeat what I have already said, namely, that a certain equilibrium has been created in international relations, although it is highly unstable. This is now evident. It is very strange for those of us who have lived through the revolution from its inception, who have experienced and observed our incredible difficulties in breaching the imperialist fronts, to see now the way in which things have developed. Probably, at that time none of us expected or could have expected that things would take such a turn.

We imagined (and it is perhaps well worth remembering this now because it will help us in our practical conclusions on the main economic problems) that future development would take a more simple, a more direct form, than the one it took. We told ourselves, we told the working class and the working people both of Russia and of other countries that there was no way out of the terrible and criminal imperialist slaughter except through revolution and that by breaking off the imperialist war by revolution we were opening up the only possible way out of this criminal slaughter for all peoples. It seemed to us then, and it could not seem otherwise, that this was the obvious, direct and easiest path to take. This direct path, which alone had enabled us to break free of imperialist ties, of imperialist crimes and of the imperialist war continuing to threaten the rest of the world, proved to be one which other nations were unable to take at least as quickly as we had thought they would. When, despite this, we now see what has taken place, when we see that there is only one Socialist Soviet Republic and that it is surrounded by a whole array of frenziedly hostile imperialist powers, we ask ourselves—how was it possible for this to happen?

One may reply without any exaggeration: this happened because basically our understanding of events was correct, because basically our appraisal of the imperialist slaughter and the confusion in the relations between the imperialist powers was correct. It is only due to this that such a strange situation has arisen, that we witness such an unstable, inexplicable, and yet to a certain extent, indisputable equilibrium. The fact of the matter is that, although completely surrounded by countries economically and militarily immensely more powerful than ourselves, whose open hostility to us quite often borders on frenzy, we nevertheless see that they were unable to bring about the actual and instant destruction of Soviet Russia on which for three years they had spent so much of their resources and their strength. When we ask ourselves how this could happen, how it could be that one of the most backward and very weak states succeeded in resisting the attacks of the openly hostile, most powerful countries in the world, when we try to examine this question, we see clearly that it was because we proved to be correct on the most fundamental issues. Our forecasts and calculations proved to be correct. It turned out that although the support of the working people of the world was not the swift and direct support that we had counted on, and which we had regarded as the basis of the whole of our policy, we did receive considerable support of another kind, not a direct support, not a swift support. It was precisely this support, precisely this sympathy both of the workers and peasants, the farm workers, throughout the world, even in countries most hostile to us, that were the final and most decisive sources, the decisive reasons for the complete failure of all the attacks directed against us. It was due to this that the alliance of the working people of all countries, which we had proclaimed, strengthened and which had been realised within the borders of our Republic, that had an effect on all countries. No matter how precarious this support may be, as long as capitalism exists in other countries (this we must of course see clearly and frankly acknowledge), we may say that this support can already be relied on. Because of this sympathy and support, the intervention, which we have endured during the past three years, which has caused us so much incredible destruction and suffering, is, I will not say impossible—one has to be very cautious and circumspect here—but, at any rate, it has to a great extent been made far more difficult for our enemies to carry it out. And it is this that, in the final analysis, is responsible for the situation that we see now and which at first glance appears so strange and incomprehensible.

When we quite calmly weigh up the sympathy felt for Bolshevism and the socialist revolution, when we survey the international situation from the point of view of the balance of forces, irrespective of whether these forces favour a just or an unjust cause, whether they favour the exploiting class or the working people—we shall ignore this aspect and attempt an appraisal of how these forces are grouped on an international scale—then we shall see that they are grouped in a manner that basically confirms our predictions and calculations. These were: that capitalism is disintegrating and that after the war, which ended first with the Brest-Litovsk peace and subsequently the Versailles peace—and I don't know which is worse—even in the countries which emerged as victors the hatred and loathing for the war increases as time passes. And the further we get from the war, the clearer it becomes, not only to the working people, but to a very large extent also to the bourgeoisie of the victorious countries, that capitalism is disintegrating, that the world economic crisis has created an intolerable situation from which there is no escape, despite the victories achieved. That is why we, very much weaker than all the other powers, economically, politically and militarily, are at the same time stronger, because we are aware of, and correctly assess, all that emerges and must emerge from this imperialist confusion, from this bloody tangle and from those contradictions (to take only the currency contradictions, I will not mention the others) in which they have become enmeshed and are becoming enmeshed still more deeply, unable to see a way out.

Today we see how the representatives of the most moderate bourgeoisie, who are definitely and without doubt far removed from socialist ideas, to say nothing of "that awful Bolshevism", change their tune; we see how even such people change their tune as the famous writer Keynes, whose book has been translated into all languages, who himself took part in the Versailles negotiations, and who devoted himself heart and soul to helping his governments—even he, subsequently, has had to abandon this path, to give it up, while continuing to curse socialism. I repeat, he does not mention, nor does he wish to think about Bolshevism—but he tells the capitalist world: "What you are doing will lead you into a hopeless situation," and he even proposes something like annulment of all debts.

Excellent, gentlemen! You should have followed our example long ago.

We see, nevertheless, that some kind of equilibrium has been created. This is the objective political situation which is quite independent of our victories, which proves that we fathomed the depth of the contradictions connected with the imperialist war, and that we are gauging them more correctly than ever before, than other powers, who despite all their victories, despite all their strength, have not yet found a way out, nor see any. That is the substance of the international situation which accounts for what we now see. We have before us a highly unstable but, nevertheless, a certain obvious, indisputable equilibrium.

I do not know whether this is for long, and I do not think that anyone can know. That is why we, for our part, must display the utmost caution. And the first precept of our policy, the first lesson that emerges from our governmental activities for the past year, the lesson which must be learned by all workers and peasants, is to be on the alert, to remember that we are surrounded by people, classes, governments which openly express the utmost hatred for us. We must remember that we are always a hair's breadth away from intervention. We shall do all that lies within our power to prevent this misfortune. We experienced such a burden of the imperialist war which is unlikely to have been experienced by any other nation. Then we bore the burden of the Civil War forced on us by the ruling classes, who fought for the Russia of the emigres, the Russia of the landowners, the Russia of the capitalists. We know, we know only too well, the incredible misfortunes that war brings to the workers and peasants. For this reason our attitude to this question must be most cautious and circumspect. We are ready to make the biggest concessions and sacrifices in order to preserve peace for which we have paid a high price. We are ready to make big concessions and sacrifices, but we are not prepared to make any kind of concessions or sacrifices, or do this forever. Let those, fortunately not numerous, representatives of the war parties and aggressive cliques of Finland, Poland, and Rumania who make great play of this, let them mark this well.

Anyone who has any political sense or acumen at all, will say that there has not been—nor can there be—a government in Russia, other than the Soviet Government, prepared to make such concessions and sacrifices in relation to nationalities which had been within our state, and also those which joined the Russian Empire. There is not, and cannot be, another government which would recognise as clearly as we do and declare so distinctly to one and all that the relation of old Russia, tsarist Russia, Russia of the war parties, that her relation to the nationalities populating Russia was criminal, that these relations were impermissible, that they aroused rightful and indignant protest and discontent of the oppressed nationalities. There is not, and cannot be, another government which would so openly admit this position, which would conduct this propaganda, propaganda against chauvinism, propaganda which recognises the guilt of old Russia, tsarist Russia, Kerensky Russia; a government which would conduct propaganda against the forcible incorporation of other nationalities in Russia. This is not mere words—this is a simple political fact, absolutely indisputable and plain for all to see. So long as there are no intrigues against us on the part of any nationality which would bind these nationalities to the imperialists, so long as they do not erect a springboard from which to crush us, we shall not be deterred by formalities. We shall not forget that we are revolutionaries. But . . . we are as firm as ever in our desire at all costs, and at the price of enormous sacrifices and concessions, to maintain peace with all nationalities that belonged to the former Russian Empire, but who do not wish to remain with us. . . .

Comrades, what I have just said is perfectly clear and comprehensible to you, and you could not expect anything else from anyone reporting to you on our policy. You know that such, and no other, is our policy. But, unfortunately, there are now two worlds: the old world of capitalism that is in a state of confusion, but which will never surrender voluntarily, and the rising new world, which is still very weak, but which will grow, for it is invincible. This old world has its old diplomacy, which cannot believe that it is possible to speak frankly and straightforwardly. This old diplomacy thinks to itself—there must be a trap of some sort here. When a representative of this economically and militarily all-powerful old world was sent to us—that was some time ago—I have in mind Bullitt, the representative of the United States Government who was sent to us with the proposal that we should conclude peace with Kolchak and Denikin on terms that were most unfavourable to us—we said that we hold so dear the blood of the workers and peasants, shed for so long in Russia, that although the terms were extremely unfavourable we were prepared to accept them, because we were convinced that the forces of Kolchak and Denikin would collapse from within. We said this quite frankly, with the minimum of diplomatic subtlety, and so they concluded that we must be trying to dupe them. . . . But the upshot was that we, who at that time had proposed a peace that was to our disadvantage, obtained a peace on much more favourable terms. . . .

This, comrades, is what I think it necessary to say about our international situation. A certain unstable equilibrium has been reached. Materially—economically and militarily—we are extremely weak; but morally—by which, of course, I mean not abstract morals, but the alignment of the real forces of all classes in all countries—we are the strongest of all. This has been proved by practice, it has been proved not merely by words but by deeds; it has been proved once and, if history takes a certain turn, it will, perhaps be proved many times again. That is why we say: having started on our work of peaceful construction we shall exert all efforts to continue it without interruption. At the same time, comrades, be vigilant, safeguard the defence potential of our country, look after our Red Army like the apple of your eye, and remember that we have no right to permit an instant's slackening where our workers and peasants and their achievements are concerned.

Comrades, having thus briefly outlined the most essential features of our international position, I shall now deal with the manner in which economic relations are developing in our country and in Western Europe, in the capitalist countries. The great difficulty here has been the absence of definite relations with the capitalist countries, which has made it impossible for us to establish stable economic relations. Events show very clearly that it is also impossible for the capitalist countries to do so. But today we are not in an altruistic mood, and our minds are more taken up with the problem of how to continue in existence in spite of the hostility of other countries.

But is the existence of a socialist republic in a capitalist environment at all conceivable? It seemed inconceivable from the political and military aspects. That it is possible both politically and militarily has now been proved; it is a fact. But what about trade? What about economic relations? Intercourse, assistance, the exchange of services between backward, ruined agricultural Russia and the advanced, industrially developed group of capitalist countries—is that possible? Did they not threaten to surround us with a barbed wire fence so as to prevent any economic relations with us whatever? "War did not scare them, so we will reduce them by means of a blockade."

Comrades, during the past four years we have heard so many threats, and such terrible ones, that none of them can frighten us any more. As for the blockade, experience has shown that it is an open question as to who suffers from it most, the blockaded or the blockaders. Experience has shown undoubtedly that in the first year on which I am able to report as a period of relative, elementary respite from direct brute force, we have not been recognised, we have been rejected, relations with us have been declared non-existent (let them be recognised as non-existent by the bourgeois courts), but they nevertheless exist. I deem it my right to report to you what is, without the slightest exaggeration, one of the main results achieved in 1921, the year under discussion.

I do not know whether the report of the People's Commissariat for Foreign Affairs to the Ninth Congress of Soviets has been, or will be, distributed to you today. In my opinion, the defect in this report is that it is too bulky and is difficult to read to the end. But, perhaps, this is my own failing, and I have no doubt that the overwhelming majority of you, as well as all those who are interested in politics, will read it, even if not immediately. Even if you do not read it in its entirety, but only glance through its pages, you will see that Russia has sprouted, if one may so express it, a number of fairly regular and permanent commercial relations, representations, treaties, etc. True, we are not yet recognised *de jure*. This is still important, because the danger of the unstable equilibrium being upset, the danger of new attempts at invasion has, as I have said, increased; the relations, however are a fact.

In 1921–the first year of trade with foreign countries–we made considerable progress. . . . I must say that for the first time we are beginning to obtain assistance from abroad. We have ordered thousands of locomotives, and we have already received the first thirteen from Sweden and thirty-seven from Germany. It is a very small beginning, but a beginning, nevertheless. After all, we have ordered hundreds of tank cars, about 500 of which arrived here in the course of 1921. We are paying a high, an exorbitant price for these things, but still, it shows that we are receiving the assistance of the large-scale industry of the advanced countries; it shows that the large-scale industry of the capitalist countries is helping us to restore our economy, despite all these countries being governed by capitalists who hate us heart and soul. All of these capitalists are united by governments which continue to make statements in their press about how matters stand with the *de jure* recognition of Soviet Russia, and about whether or not the Bolshevik Government is a legitimate government. Lengthy research revealed that it is a legitimate government, but it cannot be recognised. I have no right to conceal the sad truth that we are not yet recognised, but I must tell you that our commercial relations are nevertheless developing.

All these capitalist countries are in a position to make us pay through the nose, we pay more than the goods are worth, but for all that, they are helping our economy. Why is this? Why are they acting against their own inclinations and in contradiction to what they are constantly asserting in their press–and this press is more than a match for ours in respect of circulation, and the force and venom with which it attacks us. They call us criminals, and all the same they help us. It turns out, therefore, that economically, they are bound up with us. It turns out, as I have already said, that our calculations, made on a grand scale, are more correct than theirs. This is not because they lack people capable of making correct calculations–they have far more than we have; it is because it is impossible to make proper calculations when one is heading for destruction. . . .

You know what that calamity, the famine, cost us, what incredible difficulties it is still causing in agriculture, industry and in our life generally. Nevertheless, in spite of the fact that our country has been devastated by war, has suffered tremendous hardship as a result of all the wars and of the rule of tsars and capitalists, we are now on the road that opens up a prospect of improvement, in spite of the unceasing hostility towards us. This is the main factor. That is why, when we read recently about the Washington Conference, when we heard the news that the countries hostile to us will be obliged to convene a second conference next summer and to invite Germany and Russia to discuss the terms of a genuine peace, we said: Our terms are clear and definite; we have formulated them we have published them. How much hostility shall we encounter? We have no illusions about that; but we know that the economic position of those who blockaded us has proved to be vulnerable. There is a force that is more potent than the wishes, the will and the decisions of any of the governments or classes that are hostile to us. That force is general, economic world relations, which compel them to establish intercourse with us. . . .

. . . You are fully aware, comrades, of the incredible hardships of the 1921 famine. It was inevitable that the misfortunes of old Russia should have been carried over to our times, because the only solution of this problem is the rehabilitation of the productive forces, but not on the old, paltry, petty basis, but on the new basis, the basis of large scale industry and electrification. Only in this way shall we be rid of our poverty and of endless famines. . . . No doubt you have all read how, at the news of the famine, influential statesmen grandiloquently and solmnly declared that to take advantage of the famine in order to raise the question of old debts would be a develish thing to do. I am not so sure that the devil is worse than modern imperialism. What I do know is that in actual fact, despite the famine, they did try to recover their old debts on particularly severe conditions. We do not refuse to pay, and solemnly declare that we are prepared to discuss things in a business-like fashion. But you all understand, and there can be no doubt about this, that we shall never under any circumstances allow ourselves to be tied hand and foot in this matter without considering all its aspects, without taking into account reciprocal claims, without a business-like discussion.

I have to inform you that during recent days we have had considerable success in the struggle against the famine. You have no doubt read in the newspapers that America has allocated 20 million dollars for the relief of the starving in Russia, probably on the same conditions as A.R.A.–the American famine relief organization. Krasin sent us a telegram a few days ago saying that the American Government is formally proposing to guarantee the dispatch to us over a period of three months of foodstuffs and seeds worth those 20 million dollars, provided we, on our part, can agree to the expenditure of 10 million dollars (20 million gold rubles) for the same purpose. We immediately agreed to this and have telegraphed accordingly. And I think we may say that, during the first three months, we shall be able to supply the starving with seeds and food worth 30 million dollars, that is, 60 million gold rubles. This is, of course, very little;

it is by no means sufficient for the terrible misfortune that has struck us. You all understand this perfectly well. But at any rate this is aid which will undoubtedly help to relieve our desperate need and desperate famine. And if in the autumn we were able to achieve certain successes in providing the starving areas with seeds, in extending the sown areas in general, then we now have hopes for far greater success in the spring.

STALIN

Report to the XIV Party
Congress *December 18, 1925*

Introduction The Soviet Union achieved substantial
economic recovery in the next four years (1921-1925) on
the basis of "state capitalism." It also won increased
recognition from the established powers. The situation in
the leadership, however, had grown more complicated.
During 1922 Lenin's personal rule was weakened by an
illness that was to prove fatal, and power was arrogated
by a triumvirate. One of its members, Gregory Zinoviev,
reported for the Central Committee to the next two Party
Congresses. Not he but another triumvir, general secretary
of the Central Committee Joseph Stalin, was to emerge as
the dominant leader. In 1925, Stalin delivered the Report
to the Party Congress (XIV) for the first time. Although
he held no position in the Soviet Government, Stalin soon
established himself as the author of Soviet foreign policy.
He went on to deliver the Report of the Central Committee to the next four Party Congresses (XV - XVIII), thereby establishing the pattern that has been followed since in
its composition. With Stalin, the Reports become more
systematic and comprehensive. He provides a record of

what has happened (which Lenin was unwilling to do), and laboriously, pedantically, and schematically draws instruction from it.

The international equilibrium which Lenin characterized in 1921 as unstable, is thought by Stalin in 1925 to be more durable: he speaks of a "period of 'peaceful coexistence'." (Note that Stalin puts quotation marks around the phrase. Incidentally, although Moscow never tires of invoking "Lenin's principle of peaceful coexistence," the term was never used by Lenin.) The period of peaceful coexistence is linked to the temporary stabilization of capitalism and to the shifting equilibrium of forces between capitalism and socialism. Stalin still looks forward to future victories of the international proletariat, but the survival of the Soviet Union is no longer thought by him to depend upon *world revolution.* As a result, not surprisingly, this phrase nowhere appears in his Report.

The International Situation

The basic and new feature, the decisive feature that has affected all the events in the sphere of foreign relations during this period, is the fact that a certain temporary equilibrium of forces has been established between our country, which is building socialism, and the countries of the capitalist world, an equilibrium which has determined the present period of "peaceful co-existence" between the Land of Soviets and the capitalist countries. What we at one time regarded as a brief respite after the war has become a whole period of respite. Hence a certain equilibrium of forces and a certain period of "peaceful co-existence" between the bourgeois world and the proletarian world.

At the bottom of all this lies an internal weakness, the weakness and infirmity of world capitalism, on the one hand, and the growth of the workers' revolutionary movement in general, and particularly the growth of strength in our country, the Land of Soviets, on the other.

What lies at the bottom of this weakness of the capitalist world?

At the bottom of this weakness lie the contradictions which capitalism cannot overcome, and within the framework of which the entire international situation is taking shape—contradictions which the capitalist countries cannot overcome, and which can be overcome only in the course of development of the proletarian revolution in the West.

What are these contradictions? They can be reduced to five groups.

The first group of contradictions are those between the proletariat and the bourgeoisie in the capitalist countries.

The second group of contradictions are those between imperialism and the liberation movement in the colonies and dependent countries.

The third group of contradictions are those that are developing, and cannot but develop, between the countries that were victorious in the imperialist war and those that were defeated.

The fourth group of contradictions are those that are developing, and cannot but develop, among the victor countries themselves.

And the fifth group of contradictions are those that are developing between the Land of Soviets and the countries of capitalism as a whole.

Such are the five principal groups of contradictions, within the framework of which the development of our international position is proceeding.

Comrades, unless we briefly examine the nature and the growth of these contradictions, we shall not be able to understand the present international position of our country. Therefore, a brief review of these contradictions must necessarily form part of my report.

The Stabilisation of Capitalism

And so, let us begin with the first series of contradictions, those between the proletariat and the bourgoisie in the capitalist countries. In this sphere, the basic facts may be reduced to the following.

Firstly. Capitalism is emerging, or has already emerged, from the chaos in production, trade and in the sphere of finance which set in, and in which it found itself, after the war. The Party called this the partial, or temporary, stabilisation of capitalism. What does that mean? It means that the production and trade of the capitalist countries, which had become terribly low at one time in the period of the post-war crisis (I have in mind the years 1919-20), have begun to make progress, and the political power of the bourgeoisie has begun to become more or less consolidated. It means that capitalism has temporarily extricated itself from the chaos in which it found itself after the war. . . .

Secondly. Instead of the period of flow of the revolutionary tide that we observed in Europe in the years of the post-war crisis, we now see a period of ebb. This means that the question of taking power, of the proletariat capturing power any day, is not now on the order of the day in Europe. The period of rising revolutionary tide, when the movement pushes forward and upward and the Party's slogans cannot keep pace with the movement, as was the case in our country, for example, in 1905 or in 1917—that period of rising tide still lies ahead. At present, however, it does not exist;

instead, there is a period of temporary ebb, a period in which the proletariat is accumulating forces, a period which is giving big results as regards indicating new forms of the movement, as regards the existence and growth of a mass movement under the banner of the struggle for trade-union unity, as regards establishing and strengthening ties between the working-class movement in the West and the working-class movement in the Soviet Union, as regards a swing to the Left—the British working-class movement for example—as regards the disintegration of Amsterdam, the deep fissure in it, etc., etc. I repeat, we are in a period of accumulation of forces, which is of great importance for future revolutionary actions. It is the period in which the conquest of the mass organisations of the proletariat (the trade unions, etc.) and the "removal from their posts" of the Social-Democratic leaders becomes the slogan of the communist movement, as was the case in our country in 1911-12.

Thirdly. The centre of financial power in the capitalist world, the centre of the financial exploitation of the whole world, has shifted from Europe to America. Formerly, France, Germany and Britain usually formed the centre of the financial exploitation of the world. That cannot be said now without special reservations. Now, the centre of the financial exploitation of the world is mainly the United States of America. . . . As regards export of capital, America, at the present time, is almost the only country that is exporting capital in ever-growing proportions. The amount exported by France and Germany is terribly small; Britain has also considerably reduced her export of capital.

Fourthly. The temporary stabilisation of European capitalism to which I referred above has been achieved mainly with the aid of American capital, and at the price of the financial subordination of Western Europe to America. . . .

Fifthly. In view of this, in order to be able to pay interest and principal, Europe is forced to increase the burden of taxation on the population, to worsen the conditions of the workers. . . .

Such are the principal facts which show that the temporary stabilisation of capitalism which Europe has achieved is a putrid stabilisation that has grown up on putrid soil.

It is very likely—I do not exclude the possibility—that production and trade in Europe will reach the pre war level. But that does not mean that capitalism will thereby reach the degree of stability it possessed before the war. That degree of stability it will never reach again. . . .

Imperialism, the Colonies and Semi-Colonies

Let us pass to the second series of contradictions, those between the imperialist countries and the colonial countries.

The basic facts in this sphere are: the development and growth of industry and of the proletariat in the colonies, especially during and after the war; the growth of culture in general, and of the national intelligentsia in particular, in these countries; the growth of the national-revolutionary movement in the colonies and the crisis in the world domination of imperialism in general; the struggle for liberation waged by India and Egypt against British imperialism; the war for liberation waged by Syria and Morocco against French imperialism; China's struggle for liberation against Anglo-Japanese-American imperialism, etc.; the growth of the working-class movement in India and China and the increasingly important role of the working class in these countries in the national-revolutionary movement.

From this it follows that the Great Powers are faced with the danger of losing their chief rear, i.e., the colonies. Here, the stabilisation of capitalism is in a bad way; for the revolutionary movement in the oppressed countries, growing step by step, is beginning in some places to assume the form of open war against imperialism (Morocco, Syria, China), while imperialism is obviously unable to cope with the task of curbing "its" colonies.

It is said—especially by bourgeois writers—that the Bolsheviks are to blame for the growing crisis in the colonies. I must say that they do us too much honour by blaming us for that. Unfortunately, we are not yet strong enough to render all the colonial countries direct assistance in securing their liberation. It is necessary to delve deeper to find the cause. The cause is, apart from everything else, that the European states, being obliged to pay interest on debts to America, are compelled to intensify oppression and exploitation in the colonies and dependent countries, and this cannot but lead to an intensification of the crisis and of the revolutionary movement in these countries.

All this goes to show that, in this sphere, the affairs of world imperialism are more than in a bad way. Whereas, in the sphere of the first series of contradictions, European capitalism has become partly stabilised and the question of the proletariat seizing power any day does not arise for the time being, in the colonies the crisis has reached a climax and the question of expelling the imperialists from a number of colonies is on the order of the day.

Victors and Vanquished

I pass to the third series of contradictions, those between the victor countries and the defeated countries.

The basic facts in this sphere are the following. Firstly, after the Versailles Peace, Europe found herself split up into two camps—the camp of the vanquished (Germany, Austria and other countries) and the camp of the victors (the Entente plus America). Secondly, the circumstance must be noted that the victors, who had previously tried to strangle the defeated countries by means of occupation (I remind you of the Ruhr), have abandoned this line and have adopted a different method, the method of financial exploitation—of Germany in the first place, and of Austria in the second place. This new method finds expression in the Dawes Plan, the unfavourable results of which are only now making themselves felt. Thirdly, the Locarno Conference, which was supposed to have eliminated all the contradictions between the victors and the vanquished, but which, actually, in spite of all the hullabaloo around this question, did not eliminate any of the contradictions but only aggravated them.

* * *

If the Dawes Plan is fraught with a revolution in Germany, Locarno is fraught with a new war in Europe.

The British Conservatives think that they can both maintain the "status quo" against Germany and use Germany against the Soviet Union. Are they not wanting too much?

There is talk about pacifism, there is talk about peace among the states of Europe. Briand and Chamberlain embrace, Stresemann lavishes compliments on Britain. That is all nonsense. We know from the history of Europe that every time treaties were concluded about the disposition of forces for a new war, those treaties were called peace treaties. Treaties were concluded that determined the elements of the subsequent war, and the conclusion of such treaties was always accompanied by a hullabaloo and clamour about peace. False bards of peace were always found on those occasions. . . .

Have we any grounds, after this, for believing the songs about the League of Nations and Locarno? Of course not. That is why we can believe neither Chamberlain and Briand when they embrace, nor Stresemann when he is lavish with his compliments. That is why we think that Locarno is a plan for the disposition of forces for a new war and not for peace.

. . . What does the present position of the Second International in relation to Locarno show? That the Second International is not only an organisation for the bourgeois corruption of the working class, but also an organisation for the moral justification of all the injustices of the Versailles Peace; that the Second International is a subsidiary of the Entente, an organisation whose function is, by its activities and its clamour in support of Locarno and the League of Nations, to give moral justification to all the injustices and all the oppression that have been created by the Versailles—locarno regime.

The Contradictions between the Victor Countries

I pass to the fourth series of contradictions, to those between the victor countries. The basic facts here are that, in spite of the existence of a sort of bloc between America and Britain, a bloc founded on an agreement between America and Britain against the annulment of Allied debts, in spite of this bloc, I say, the conflict of interests between Britain and America is not being allayed, on the contrary, it is becoming more intense. One of the principal problems now facing the world powers is the problem of oil. If, for example, we take America, we find that she produces about 70 per cent of the world output of oil and accounts for over 60 per cent of total world consumption. Well, it is just in this sphere, which is the principal nerve of the entire economic and military activities of the world powers, that America everywhere and always encounters opposition from Britain. If we take the two world oil companies—Standard Oil and Royal Dutch-Shell, the former representing America and the latter Britain—we find that the struggle between those companies is going on in all parts of the world, wherever oil is obtainable. It is a struggle between America and Britain. For the problem of oil is a vital one; because who will command in the next war depends on who will have most oil. Who will command world industry and trade depends on who will have most oil. Now that the fleets of the advanced countries are passing over to oil propulsion, oil is the vital nerve of the struggle among the world states for supremacy both in peace and in war. . . . That is apart from such a fact of no little importance as the conflict of interests between Britain and America in China. You no doubt know that the struggle there is a concealed one, and that very often America, operating in a more flexible manner and refraining from the crude colonial methods which the British lords have not yet abandoned, succeeds in putting a spoke in Britain's wheel in China in order to oust Britain and pave the way for herself in China. Obviously, Britain cannot look upon this with indifference.

I shall not dwell at length on the opposition of interests between France and Britain arising from the struggle for supremacy on the European continent. That is a generally known fact. It is also clear that the conflict of interests between Britain and France takes place not only over the question of hegemony on the continent, but also in the colonies. Information has got into the press that the war in Syria and Morocco against French imperialism was organised not without Britain's participation. I have no documents, but I think that this information is not altogether groundless.

Lastly, I must mention a fact which must surprise everybody, namely, the colossal growth of armaments in the victor countries. I am speaking about the victors, about the contradictions among the victor states. These victors are called allies. True, America does not belong to the Entente, but she fought in alliance with it against Germany. Well, those allies are now arming themselves to the utmost. Against whom are they arming? In the past, when the Entente countries piled up armaments, they usually referred to Germany, saying that she was armed to the teeth and constituted a danger to world peace, owing to which it was necessary to arm for defence. But what about now? Germany as an armed force no longer exists; she has been disarmed. Nevertheless, the growth of armaments in the victor countries is proceeding as never before.... What have the League of Nations and the Second International done to put a stop to this furious growth of armaments? Don't they know that with the growth of armaments "the guns begin to go off of their own accord"? Don't expect a reply from the League of Nations and the Second International. The point here is that the conflict of interests among the victor countries is growing and becoming more intense, that a collision among them is becoming inevitable, and, in anticipation of a new war, they are arming with might and main. I shall not be exaggerating if I say that in this case we have not a friendly peace among the victor countries, but an armed peace, a state of armed peace that is fraught with war. What is now going on in the victor countries reminds us very much of the situation that prevailed before the war of 1914—a state of armed peace.

The rulers of Europe are now trying to cover up this fact with clamour about pacifism. But I have already said what this pacifism is worth and what value should be attached to it. The Bolsheviks have been demanding disarmament ever since the time of Genoa. Why do not the Second International and all the others who are chattering about pacifism support our proposal?

This circumstance shows once again that the stabilisation, the temporary, partial stabilisation, that Europe has achieved at the price of its own enslavement, is not lasting, for the contradictions between the victor countries are growing and becoming more intense, not to speak of the contradictions between the victor countries and the defeated countries.

The Capitalist World
and the Soviet Union

I pass to the fifth series of contradictions, those between the Soviet Union and the capitalist world.

The basic fact in this sphere is that an all-embracing world capitalism no longer exists. After the Land of Soviets came into being, after the old

Russia was transformed into the Soviet Union, an all-embracing world capitalism ceased to exist. The world split up into two camps: the camp of imperialism and the camp of the struggle against imperialism. That is the first point that must be noted.

The second point that must be noted in this sphere is that two major countries—Britain and America, as an Anglo-American alliance—are coming to stand at the head of the capitalist countries. Our country—the Soviet Union—is coming to stand at the head of those discontented with imperialism and who are engaged in mortal struggle against it.

The third point is that two major, but opposite, centres of attraction are being created and, in conformity with this, two lines of attraction towards those centres all over the world: Britain and America—for the bourgeois governments, and the Soviet Union—for the workers of the West and for the revolutionaries of the East. The power of attraction of Britain and America lies in their wealth; credits can be obtained there. The power of attraction of the Soviet Union lies in its revolutionary experience, its experience in the struggle for the emancipation of the workers from capitalism and of the oppressed peoples from imperialism. I am speaking of the attraction of the workers of Europe and of the revolutionaries of the East towards our country. You know what a visit to our country means to a European worker or to a revolutionary from an oppressed country, how they make pilgrimages to our country, and what an attraction our country has for all that is honest and revolutionary all over the world.

Two camps, two centres of attraction.

The fourth point is that in the other camp, the camp of capitalism, there is no unity of interests and no solidarity; that what reigns there is a conflict of interests, disintegration, a struggle between victors and vanquished, a struggle among the victors themselves, a struggle among all the imperialist countries for colonies, for profits; and that, because of all this, stabilisation in that camp cannot be lasting. On the other hand, in our country there is a healthy process of stabilisation, which is gaining strength, our economy is growing, our socialist construction is growing, and in the whole of our camp all the discontented elements and strata of both the West and the East are gradually and steadily rallying around the proletariat of our country, rallying around the Soviet Union.

Over there, in the camp of capitalism, there is discord and disintegration. Over here, in the camp of socialism, there is solidarity and an ever-increasing unity of interests against the common enemy—against imperialism.

Such are the basic facts which I wanted to point out in the sphere of the fifth series of contradictions—the contradictions between the capitalist world and the Soviet world.

* * *

. . . If we are regarded as part, as the child, of the working class of Europe, if on those grounds the working class of Europe assumes moral responsibility, undertakes the task of defending our state in case, say, of intervention by capitalism, the task of defending our interests against imperialism, what does that show? It shows that our forces are growing and will continue to grow very rapidly. It shows that the weakness of capitalism will increase very rapidly. For without the workers it is impossible to wage war nowadays. If the workers refuse to fight against our Republic, if they regard our Republic as their child in whose fate they are closely concerned, then war against our country becomes impossible. That is the secret, that is the root, that is the significance of the pilgrimages to our country that we have had, which we shall have more of, and which it is our duty to encourage to the utmost as a pledge of solidarity and a pledge that the ties of friendship between the workers of our country and the workers of the Western countries will be strengthened.

* * *

Such are the characteristic features of the basic contradictions that are corroding capitalism.

What follows from all these contradictions? What do they show? They show that the capitalist world is being corroded by a whole series of internal contradictions which are enfeebling capitalism; that, on the other hand, our world, the world socialism, is becoming more and more closely welded, more united; that because of this, on precisely this basis, there arose that temporary equilibrium of forces that put an end to war against us, that ushered in the period of "peaceful co-existence" between the Soviet state and the capitalist states.

I must mention two other facts which also helped to bring it about that instead of a period of war we have a period of "peaceful co-existence."

The first fact is that at the present moment America does not want war in Europe. It is as though she were saying to Europe: I have loaned you thousands of millions; sit still and behave yourself if you want to get more money in future, if you don't want your currency to get into a mess; get down to work, earn money and pay the interest on your debts. It scarcely needs proof that this advice of America's, even if it is not decisive for Europe, is bound to have some effect.

The second fact is that since the victory of the proletarian revolution in our country, a whole vast country with tremendous markets and tremendous sources of raw materials has dropped out of the world capitalist system, and this, of course, was bound to affect the economic situation in Europe. The loss of one-sixth of the globe, the loss of the markets and sources of raw materials of our country, means for capitalist Europe that its production is reduced and experiences a severe shaking. And so, in order to put a stop to this alienation of European capital from our country, from our markets and sources of raw materials, it was found necessary to agree to a certain period of "peaceful co-existence" with us, in order to be able to find a way to our markets and sources of raw materials—without this, it appears, it is impossible to achieve any economic stability in Europe.

The External Position
of the U.S.S.R.

Such are all those factors that have led to a certain equilibrium of forces between the camp of socialism and the camp of capitalism all over the world; that have caused the period of war to be replaced by a period of respite; that have converted the brief respite into a whole period of respite, and have enabled us to carry out a sort of "collaboration," as Ilyich called it, with the capitalist world.

Hence the series of "recognitions" of the Soviet Union which has commenced, and which is bound to continue.

I shall not enumerate the countries that have "recognised" us. I think that America is the only one of the big countries that has not done so. Nor shall I dilate on the fact that after these "recognitions" we concluded trade agreements, with Germany and Italy, for example. I shall not deal at length with the fact that our foreign trade has grown considerably, that America, a country which exports cotton to us, and Britain and Germany, countries which import our grain and agricultural produce, are particularly interested in this trade. There is one thing I must say, namely, that this year is the first year since the advent of the period of "co-existence" with the capitalist states in which we are entering into rich and wide commercial relations with the capitalist world on a more or less large scale.

That, of course, does not mean that we have already done away with all those, so to speak, reservations, and all those claims and counter-claims, as they might be called, that have existed and still exist between our state and the states of the West. We know that payment of debts is being demanded of us. Europe has not yet forgotten this, and probably will not forget it, at any rate, not so soon. We are told that our pre-war debts to Europe amount to 6,000 millions, that the war debts are estimated at over 7,000 million rubles, hence, a total of 13,000 millions. Allowing for depreciation of currency, and subtracting from this sum the share of the border countries, it works out that we owe the West-European states not less than 7,000 millions. It is known that our counter-claims in connection with the intervention of Britain, France and America during the civil war amount, I think, to the figure (if we take Larin's calculations) of 50,000 million rubles. Consequently, they owe us five times more than we owe them. (*Larin from his seat*: "We shall get it.") Comrade Larin says that in good time we shall get all of it. If, however, we make a more conservative calculation, as the People's Commissariat of Finance does, it will amount to no less than 20,000 million. Even then we stand to gain. But the capitalist countries refuse to reconcile themselves to this, and we still figure in their lists as debtors.

Of the questions concerning our foreign policy, of the questions that arose in the period under review, questions that are exceptionally delicate and urgent, that concern the relations between our government and the governments of the West-European countries, I should like to mention two: firstly, the question that the British Conservatives have raised more than once and will raise again—that of propaganda; and, secondly, the question of the Communist International.

We are accused of conducting special propaganda against imperialism both in Europe and in the colonies and dependent countries. The British Conservatives assert that the Russian Communists are people whose mission it is to destroy the might of the British Empire. I should like to state here that all this is utter nonsense. We do not need any special propaganda, either in the West or in the East, now that workers' delegations visit our country, see for themselves the state of things here and carry their information about the state of things here to all the Western countries. We do not need any other propaganda. That is the best, the most potent and most effective propaganda for the Soviet system and against the capitalist system.

We are told that we are conducting propaganda in the East. I assert that this, too, is utter nonsense. We do not need any special propaganda in the East, now that, as we know, the whole of our state system rests on the basis of the co-existence and fraternal co-operation of the extremely diverse nationalities in our country. Any Chinese, any Egyptian, and Indian, who comes to our country and stays here six months, has an opportunity of convincing himself that our country is the only country that understands the spirit of the oppressed peoples and is able to arrange co-operation between the proletarians of the formerly dominant nationality and the proletarians of the formerly oppressed nationalities. We need no other propaganda, no other agitation, in the East except that the delegations that come here from China, India and Egypt, after working here and looking about them, should carry their information about our state of things all over the world. That is the best propaganda, and it is the most effective of all forms and types of propaganda.

* * *

A few words about the Comintern. Hirelings of the imperialists and authors of forged letters are spreading rumors in the West to the effect that the Comintern is an organisation of conspirators and terrorists, that Communists are touring the Western countries for the purpose of hatching plots against the European rulers. Among other things, the Sofia explosion in Bulgaria is being linked with Communists. I must declare what every cultured person must know, if he is not an utter ignoramus, and if he has not been bribed—I must declare that Communists never had, do not have, and cannot have, anything in common with the theory and practice of individual terrorism; that Communists never had, do not have, and cannot have, anything in common with the theory of conspiracies against individual persons. The theory and practice of the Comintern consists in organising the mass revolutionary movement against capitalism. That is true. That is the task of the Communists. Only ignoramuses and idiots can confuse plots and individual terrorism with the Comintern's policy in the mass revolutionary movement.

Two words about Japan. Some of our enemies in the West are rubbing their hands with glee, as much as to say: See, a revolutionary movement has begun in China. It is, of course, the Bolsheviks who have bribed the Chinese people—who else could bribe a people numbering 400 millions?—and this will lead to the "Russians" fighting the Japanese. All that is nonsense, comrades. The forces of the revolutionary movement in China are unbelievably vast. They have not yet made themselves felt as they should. They will make themselves felt in the future. The rulers in the East and West who do not see those forces and do not reckon with them to the degree that they deserve will suffer for this. We, as a state, cannot but reckon with this force. We consider that China is faced with the same problem that faced North America when she was uniting in a single state, that faced Germany when she was uniting and freeing herself from external enemies. Here, truth and justice are wholly on the side of the Chinese revolution. That is why we sympathise and will continue to sympathise with the Chinese revolution in its struggle to liberate the Chinese people from the yoke of the imperialists and to unite China in a single state. Whoever does not and will not reckon with this force will certainly lose. I think that Japan will understand that she, too, must reckon with this growing force of the national movement in China, a force that is pushing forward and sweeping everything from its path. . . .

Every general, every ruler of Manchuria, who bases his policy on conflicts between us and Japan, on a deterioration of our relations with Japan, is certain to go under. Only the one who bases his policy on an improvement of our relations with Japan, on a rapprochement between us and Japan, will remain on his feet; only such a general, and such a ruler, can sit firmly in Manchuria, because we have no interests that lead to our relations with Japan becoming strained. Our interests lie in the direction of rapprochement between our country and Japan.

The Party's Tasks

I pass to the question of our Party's tasks in connection with the external situation.

I think that here our Party's tasks, in the sense of its work, should be outlined in two spheres: the of the *international* revolutionary movement, and then in the sphere of the Soviet Union's *foreign policy.*

What are the tasks in the sphere of the *international* revolutionary movement?

The tasks are, firstly, to work in the direction of strengthening the Communist Parties in the West, of their winning a majority among the masses of the workers. Secondly, to work in the direction of intensifying the struggle of the workers in the West for trade-union unity, for strengthening the friendship between the proletariat in our Union and the proletariat in the capitalist countries. This includes the pilgrimages of which I have spoken and the significance of which I described above. Thirdly, to work in the direction of strengthening the link between the proletariat in our country and the movement for liberation in the oppressed countries, for they are our allies in the struggle against imperialism. And fourthly, to work in the direction of strengthening the socialist elements in our country, in the direction of the victory of these elements over the capitalist elements, a victory that will be of decisive significance for revolutionising the workers of all countries. Usually, when speaking about our Party's tasks in the sphere of the international revolutionary movement, our comrades confine themselves to the first three tasks and forget about the fourth task, namely, that our struggle in our country, the struggle for the victory of the socialist elements in our country over the capitalist elements, our struggle in the work of construction, is also of international significance, for our country is the base of the international revolution, for our country is the principal lever for expanding the international revolutionary movement; and if our work of construction here, in our country, proceeds at the proper tempo, it means that we are performing our work in all the other channels of the international revolutionary movement precisely in the way the Party demands that we should perform it.

Such are the Party's tasks in the sphere of the international revolutionary movement.

Now about the Party's tasks in the sphere of our Union's *foreign* policy.

Firstly, to work in the direction of fighting against new wars, in the direction of maintaining peace and ensuring so-called normal relations with the capitalist countries. The basis of our government's policy, of its foreign policy, is the idea of peace. The struggle for peace, the struggle against new wars, the exposure of all the steps that are being taken to prepare a new war, the exposure of those steps that cover up actual preparation of war with the flag of pacifism—such is the task. It is precisely for this reason that we refuse to join the League of Nations, for the League of Nations is an organisation for covering up the preparations for war; for, to join the League of Nations, we must choose, as Comrade Litvinov has rightly expressed it, between the hammer and the anvil. Well, we do not wish to be either a hammer for the weak nations or an anvil for the strong ones. We want neither the one nor the other; we stand for peace, we stand for the exposure of all those steps that lead to war, no matter by what pacifist bunting they may be concealed. Whether the League of Nations or Locarno, it makes no difference—they can't fool us with a flag, nor frighten us with noise.

Secondly, to work in the direction of expanding our trade with the outside world on the basis of the monopoly of foreign trade.

Thirdly, to work in the direction of rapprochement with the countries that were defeated in the imperialist war, with those capitalist countries which were most humiliated and came off worst, and which, owing to this, are in opposition to the ruling alliance of Great Powers.

Fourthly, to work in the direction of strengthening our link with the dependent and colonial countries.

Such are the tasks that face the Party at the present time in the sphere of international relations and the international working-class movement.

STALIN

Report to the XV Party Congress
December 3, 1927

Introduction The contradictions which Stalin perceived in the capitalist world of 1925 seemed to him two years later to have worsened. In accordance with Lenin's theory of imperialism, these contradictions are giving rise to an acute crisis of capitalism and widespread preparations for a new war to re-divide the world. His theme is no longer temporary stability, but the inevitability of war; not peaceful coexistence, but capitalist encirclement. Stalin even accepts war between the USSR and the capitalist world as inevitable. His stated objective is not to avert such a war but to postpone it until circumstances are more favorable. Never again, to my knowledge, did Stalin say that war with capitalist states was inevitable.

The marked shift in Stalin's appraisal of the international situation between 1925 and 1927 cannot be understood solely by reference to changes in objective reality. It may be accounted for, at least in part, by projected changes in Soviet domestic policy: at the XV Congress Stalin moves sharply to the left, and the danger of war helps to establish a need for his ambitious Five Year Plan, aimed at rapid industrialization. By this time, the USSR so dominates the policy of the Communist International (Comintern) that a move to the left in Soviet domestic policy compels the Comintern to move left in its turn. As a result, "revolutionary situations" are searched for and, not surprisingly, are discovered. The revolutionary ebb of 1925 becomes the revolutionary upsurge of 1927.

The Growing Crisis of World Capitalism and The External Situation of the U.S.S.R.

Our country, comrades, is living and developing in the conditions of capitalist encirclement. Its external position depends not only on its internal forces, but also on the state of that capitalist encirclement, on the situation in the capitalist countries which surround our country, on their strength and weakness, on the strength and weakness of the oppressed classes throughout the world, on the strength and weakness of the revolutionary movement of those classes. That is apart from the fact that our revolution is a part of the international revolutionary movement of the oppressed classes.

That is why I think that the Central Committee's report must start with a sketch of our country's international position, with a sketch of the situation in the capitalist countries and of the state of the revolutionary movement in all countries.

The Economics of World Capitalism and the Intensification of the Struggle for Foreign Markets

a) The first question is that of the state of production and trade in the major capitalist countries.

The basic fact in this sphere, comrades, is that during the past two years, during the period under review, *production* in the capitalist countries has transcended the pre-war level, has gone beyond the pre-war level.

* * *

Does all this mean that, thereby, the stabilisation of capitalism has become firm and lasting? Of course not! It was already stated in the report to the Fourteenth Congress that capitalism might reach the prewar level, might exceed that pre-war level, might rationalise its production, but that this did not mean—did not by a long way mean—that the stabilisation of capitalism could as a result become firm, that capitalism could recover its former, pre-war stability. On the contrary, this very stabilisation, the fact that production is growing, that trade is growing, that technical progress and production potentialities are increasing, whereas the world market, the limits of that market, and the spheres of influence of the individual imperialist groups, remain more or less stable—precisely this is giving rise to a most profound and acute crisis of world capitalism, a crisis which is fraught with new wars and which threatens the existence of any stabilisation at all.

Partial stabilisation is giving rise to an intensification of the crisis of capitalism, and the growing crisis is upsetting stabilisation—such are the dialectics of the development of capitalism in the present period of history.

b) The most characteristic feature of this growth of production and trade of world capitalism is that the development proceeds *unevenly*. Development is not taking place in such a way that the capitalist countries are moving forward one behind the other, smoothly and evenly, without hindering one another and without upsetting each other, but, on the contrary, in such a way that some countries are being ousted and are declining, while others are pushing forward and moving upward; it is proceeding in the form of a mortal struggle of continents and countries for supremacy in the market.

The economic centre is shifting from Europe to America, from the Atlantic to the Pacific. The share of world trade of America and Asia is thereby growing at the expense of Europe.

* * *

. . .Parallel with countries in which capitalism is tearing ahead (the U.S.A. and partly Japan), we have other countries which are in a state of economic decline (Britain). Parallel with growing capitalist Germany and rising countries which have been coming to the front in recent years (Canada, Australia, Argentina, China, India), we have countries in which capitalism is becoming stabilised (France, Italy). The number of claimants to markets is growing, production potentialities are growing, and supply is growing, but the dimensions of markets and the borders of spheres of influence remain more or less stable.

Such is the basis of the growing irreconcilable contradictions of present-day capitalism.

c) This contradiction between the growth of the production potentialities and the relative stability of markets lies at the root of the fact that the problem of markets is today the fundamental problem of capitalism. . . .The peaceful road to the solution of the problem of markets remains closed to capitalism. The *only* "way out" left open for capitalism is a *new* redivision of colonies and of spheres of influence by force, by means of armed collisions, by means of new imperialist wars.

Stabilisation is intensifying the crisis of capitalism.

*The International Policy of
Capitalism and the Preparation of
New Imperialist Wars*

a) In this connection, the question of redividing the world and spheres of influence, which constitute the basis of foreign markets, is today the principal question in the policy of world capitalism. I have already said that the existing distribution of colonies and spheres of influence brought about as a result of the last imperialist war has already become obsolete. It now fails to satisfy either the United States, which, not being content with South America, is trying to penetrate Asia (primarily China); or Britain, whose dominions and a number of whose most important Eastern markets are slipping from her hands; or Japan, which every now and again is "obstructed" in China by Britain and America; or Italy and France, which have an incalculable number of "points of dispute" in the Danubian countries and in the Mediterranean; and least of all does it satisfy Germany, which is still bereft of colonies.

Hence the "general" striving for a new redivision of markets and sources of raw materials. That the Asiatic markets and the routes to them are the chief arena of the struggle needs no proof. Hence a series of key problems, which are veritable hotbeds of new conflicts. Hence the so-called Pacific problem (the America-Japan-Britain antagonism) as the origin of the struggle for supremacy in Asia and on the routes to it. Hence the Mediterranean problem (the Britain-France-Italy antagonism) as the origin of the struggle for supremacy on the shores of the Mediterranean, as the origin of the struggle for the shortest routes to the East. Hence the aggravation of the oil problem (antagonism between Britain and America), for without oil it is impossible to wage war, and whoever has the advantage as regards oil has a chance of victory in the coming war.

This leaves no room for doubt: things are moving towards the organisation of new coalitions of powers in order to prepare new wars for foreign markets, for sources of raw materials, and for the routes to them.

b) Have attempts been made during the period under review to bring about a "peaceful settlement" of the maturing military conflicts? Yes, there have been more of them than might have been expected; but they have led to nothing, absolutely nothing. Not only that; those attempts have turned out to be merely a screen for the preparations that the "powers" are making for new wars, a screen intended to deceive the people, to deceive "public opinion."

Take the League of Nations, which, according to the mendacious bourgeois press, and the no less mendacious Social-Democratic press, is an instrument of peace. What has all the League of Nations' talk about peace, disarmament, reduction of armaments led to? To nothing, except the deception of the masses, except new spurts in armaments, except a further aggravation of the maturing conflicts. Can it be regarded as accidental that although the League of Nations has been talking about peace and disarmament for three years, and although the so-called Second International has been giving its support to this mendacious talk for three years, the "nations" are continuing to arm more and more, expanding the old conflicts among the "powers," piling up new conflicts, and thus undermining the cause of peace?

What does the failure of the tripartite conference for the reduction of naval armaments (Britain, America and Japan) indicate, if not that the Pacific problem is the source of new imperialist wars, that the "powers" do not want either to disarm or to reduce armaments? What has the League of Nations done to avert this danger?

Or take, for example, the recent declarations of the Soviet delegation in Geneva on the question of genuine disarmament (and not window-dressing). What is the explanation of the fact that Comrade Litvinov's straightforward and honest declaration in favour of complete disarmament struck the League of Nations with paralysis and came as a "complete surprise" to it? Does not this fact show that the League of Nations is not an instrument of peace and disarmament, but an instrument for covering up new armaments and the preparation of new wars?

The venal bourgeois press of all countries, from Japan to Britain, from France to America, is shouting at the top of its voice that the Soviet disarmament proposals are "insincere." In that case, why not test the sincerity of the Soviet proposals and proceed at once, in practice, to disarm, or at least considerably to reduce armaments? What prevents this?

Or, for example, the present system of "friendship pacts" between capitalist states: the pact between France and Yugoslavia, the pact between Italy and Albania, the "pact of friendship" between Poland and Lithuania that Pilsudski is preparing, the "Locarno system," the "spirit of Locarno," etc.–what is this if not a system of preparation of new wars and of alignment of forces for future military collisions?

Or take, for example, the following facts: from 1913 to 1927 *the numerical strength of the armies* of France, Britain, Italy, the United States and Japan increased from 1,888,000 to 2,262,000 men. . . .What do these facts show if not that the preparation of a new war is in full swing?

Such are the results of the "peace policy" and of the "disarmament" policy of the bourgeois states in general, of the League of Nations especially, and of Social-Democratic servility to capital in particular.

Formerly, the justification put forward for the growth of armaments was that Germany was armed from head to foot. Today this "justification" falls to the ground because Germany has been disarmed.

Is it not obvious that the growth of armaments is dictated by the inevitability of new imperialist wars between the "powers," that the "spirit of war" is the principal content of the "spirit of Locarno"?

I think that the present "peaceful relations" could be likened to an old, worn-out shirt consisting of patches held together by a thin thread. It is enough to pull this thread fairly hard, to break it in some place or other, for the whole shirt to fall to pieces, leaving nothing but patches. It is enough to shake the present "peaceful relations" somewhere in Albania or Lithuania, in China or North Africa, for the whole "edifice of peaceful relations" to collapse.

That is how things were before the last imperialist war, when the assassination in Sarajevo led to war.

That is how things are now.

Stabilisation is inevitably giving rise to new imperialist wars.

*The State of the World Revolutionary
Movement and the Harbingers of a
New Revolutionary Upsurge*

a) For waging war, increased armaments are not enough, the organisation of new coalitions is not enough. For this it is necessary in addition to strengthen the rear in the capitalist countries. Not a single capitalist country can wage an important war unless it first strengthens its own rear, unless it curbs "its" workers, unless it curbs "its" colonies. Hence the gradual fascisation of the policy of the bourgeois governments.

b) It is not difficult to understand that this brutal pressure of the fascisised governments was bound to meet with a counter-movement on the part of the oppressed peoples in the colonies and of the working class in the metropolises. Facts like the growth of the revolutionary movement in China, Indonesia, India, etc., cannot fail to have a decisive significance for the fate of world imperialism.

Judge for yourselves. Of the 1,905 million inhabitants *of the entire globe,* 1,134 million live in the colonies and dependent countries, 143,000,000 live in the U.S.S.R., 264,000,000 live in the intermediate countries, and only 363,000,000 live in the big imperialist countries, which oppress the colonies and dependent countries.

Clearly, the revolutionary awakening of the colonial and dependent countries presages the end of world imperialism. The fact that the Chinese revolution has not yet led to direct victory over imperialism cannot be of decisive significance for the prospects of the revolution. Great popular revolutions never achieve final victory in the first round of their battles. They grow and gain strength in the course of flows and ebbs. That has been so everywhere, including Russia. So it will be in China.

The most important result of the Chinese revolution is the fact that it has awakened from age-long slumber and has set in motion hundreds of millions of exploited and oppressed people, has utterly exposed the counter-revolutionary character of the cliques of generals, has torn the mask from the faces of the Kuomintang servitors of counter-revolution, has raised the prestige of the Communist Party among the masses of the common people, has raised the movement as a whole to a higher stage and has roused new hope in the hearts of the millions of the oppressed classes in India, Indonesia, etc. Only the blind and the faint-hearted can doubt that the Chinese workers and peasants are moving towards a new revolutionary upsurge.

As regards the revolutionary working-class movement in Europe, here in this sphere, too, we have obvious signs of a swing to the Left on the part of the rank-and-file workers and of a revolutionary revival. Facts like the British general strike and coal strike, the revolutionary action of the workers in Vienna, the revolutionary demonstrations in France and Germany in connection with the murder of Sacco and Vanzetti, the election successes achieved by the German and Polish Communist Parties, the obvious differentiation that is taking place in the British working-class movement, whereby the workers are moving to the Left while the leaders are moving to the Right, into the camp of avowed social-imperialism, the degeneration of the Second International into a direct appendage of the imperialist League of Nations, the decline of the prestige of the Social-Democratic parties among the broad masses of the working class, the universal growth of the influence and prestige of the Comintern and its sections among the proletarians in all countries, the growth of the prestige of the U.S.S.R. among the oppressed classes all over the world, the "Congress of the Friends of the U.S.S.R.," etc.–all these facts undoubtedly indicate that Europe is entering a new period of revolutionary upsurge.

If a fact like the murder of Sacco and Vanzetti could give rise to working-class demonstrations, it undoubtedly indicates that revolutionary energy has accumulated in the depths of the working class and is seeking, and will continue to seek, a cause, an occasion, sometimes seemingly most insignificant, to break to the surface and hurl itself upon the capitalist regime.

We are living on the eve of a new revolutionary upsurge both in the colonies and in the metropolises.

Stabilisation is giving rise to a new revolutionary upsurge.

The Capitalist World and the U.S.S.R.

a) Thus, we have all the symptoms of a most profound crisis of the growing instability of world capitalism.

Whereas the *temporary* post-war economic crisis of 1920-21, with the chaos within the capitalist countries, and the breakdown of their external ties, may be regarded as having been overcome, as a result of which a period of partial stabilisation has begun, the *general* and *fundamental* crisis of capitalism ushered in as a result of the victory of the October Revolution and the dropping out of the U.S.S.R. from the world capitalist system, far from being overcome is, on the contrary, becoming deeper and deeper, and is shaking the very foundations of the existence of world capitalism.

Far from hindering the development of this general and fundamental crisis, stabilisation, on the contrary, has provided the basis and source for its further development. The growing struggle for markets, the necessity of a new redivision of the world and of spheres of influence, the bankruptcy of bourgeois pacifism and of the League of Nations, the feverish efforts to form new coalitions and to align forces in view of the possibility of a new war, the furious growth of armaments, the savage pressure upon the working class and the colonial countries, the growth of the revolutionary movement in the colonies and in Europe, the growth of the prestige of the Comintern throughout the world, and lastly, the consolidation of the might of the Soviet Union and its enhanced prestige among the workers of Europe and the labouring masses in the colonies—all these are facts which cannot but shake the very foundations of world capitalism.

The stabilisation of capitalism is becoming more and more putrid and unstable.

Whereas a couple of years ago it was possible and necessary to speak of the ebb of the revolutionary tide in Europe, today we have every ground for asserting that *Europe is obviously entering a period of new revolutionary upsurge;* to say nothing of the colonies and dependent countries, where the position of the imperialists is becoming more and more catastrophic.

b) The capitalists' hopes of taming the U.S.S.R., of its capitalistic degeneration, of the decline of its prestige among the workers of Europe and the labouring masses of the colonies, have collapsed. The U.S.S.R. is growing and developing precisely as a country which is building socialism. Its influence among the workers and peasants all over the world is growing and gaining strength. The very existence of the U.S.S.R. as a country which is building socialism is one of the greatest factors in the disintegration of world imperialism and in the undermining of its stability both in Europe and in the colonies. The U.S.S.R. is obviously becoming the banner of the working class of Europe and of the oppressed peoples of the colonies.

Therefore, to clear the ground for future imperialist wars, to secure a tighter grip on "their" working class and to curb "their" colonies with the object of strengthening the capitalist rear, it is necessary, the bourgeois bosses think, first of all to curb the U.S.S.R., that seat and hotbed of revolution, which, moreover, could be one of the biggest markets for the capitalist countries. Hence the revival of interventionist tendencies among the imperialists, the policy of isolating the U.S.S.R., the policy of encircling the U.S.S.R., the policy of preparing the conditions for war against the U.S.S.R.

The strengthening of interventionist tendencies in the camp of the imperialists and the threat of war (against the U.S.S.R.) is one of the basic factors in the present situation.

It is considered that the most "threatened" and "injured" party under the conditions of the developing crisis of capitalism is the British bourgeoisie. And it is the British bourgeoisie that has taken the initiative in strengthening interventionist tendencies. Obviously, the assistance that the Soviet workers rendered the British coal miners, and the sympathy of the working class of the U.S.S.R. for the revolutionary movement in China, could not but add fuel to the flames. All these circumstances determined Britain's rupture with the U.S.S.R. and the worsening of relations with a number of other states.

c) The struggle between two tendencies in the relations between the capitalist world and the U.S.S.R., the tendency towards military aggression (primarily Britain) and the tendency to continue peaceful relations (a number of other capitalist countries), is, in view of this, the basic fact in our foreign relations at the present time.

Whereas a year or two ago it was possible and necessary to speak of a period of a certain equilibrium and "peaceful co-existence" between the U.S.S.R. and the capitalist countries, today we have every ground for asserting that *the period of "peaceful co-existence" is receding into the past,* giving place to a period of imperialist assaults and preparation for intervention against the U.S.S.R.

True, Britain's attempts to form a united front against the U.S.S.R. have failed so far. The reasons for this failure are: the contradiction of interests in the camp of the imperialists; the fact that some countries are interested in economic relations with the U.S.S.R.; the peace policy of the U.S.S.R.; the counter-action of the working class of Europe; the imperialists' fear of unleashing revolution in their own countries in the event of war against the U.S.S.R. But this does not mean that Britain will abandon her efforts to organise a united front against the U.S.S.R., that she will fail to organise such a front. The threat of war remains in force, despite Britain's temporary setbacks.

Hence, the task is to take into account the contradictions in the camp of the imperialists, to postpone war by "buying off" the capitalists and to take all measures to maintain peaceful relations.

We must not forget Lenin's statement that as regards our work of construction very much depends upon whether we succeed in postponing war with the capitalist world, which is inevitable, but which can be postponed either until the moment when the proletarian revolution in Europe matures, or until the moment when the colonial revolutions have fully matured, or, lastly, until the moment when the capitalists come to blows over the division of the colonies.

Therefore, the maintenance of peaceful relations with the capitalist countries is an obligatory task for us.

Our relations with the capitalist countries are based on the assumption that the co-existence of two opposite systems is possible. Practice has fully confirmed this. Sometimes the question of debts and credits is a stumbling-block. In this our policy is clear. It is based on the formula: "give and take." If you give us credits with which to fertilise our industry, you will get some part of the pre-war debts, which we regard as extra interest on the credits. If you give nothing, you will get nothing. Facts show that we have some achievements to record as regards receiving industrial credits. I have in mind just now not only Germany, but also America and Britain. Wherein lies the secret? In the fact that our country could be a vast market for imports of equipment, while the capitalist countries need markets for precisely that kind of goods.

Conclusions

To sum up, we have:

Firstly, the growth of the contradictions within the capitalist encirclement; the necessity for capitalism of a new redivision of the world by means of war; the interventionist tendencies of one part of the capitalist world headed by Britain; the reluctance of the other part of the capitalist world to become involved in war against the U.S.S.R., preferring to establish economic relations with it; a conflict between these two tendencies and a certain possibility for the U.S.S.R. to turn these contradictions to account for the purpose of maintaining peace.

Secondly, we have the collapsing stabilisation; the growth of the colonial-revolutionary movement; the signs of a new revolutionary upsurge in Europe; the growth of the prestige of the Comintern and its sections throughout the world; the obvious growth of the sympathy of the working class of Europe for the U.S.S.R.; the growing might of the U.S.S.R. and the growing prestige of the working class of our country among the oppressed classes throughout the world.

Hence the Party's tasks:

1) In the sphere of the international revolutionary movement:

a) *to strive to develop the Communist Parties throughout the world;*

b) *to strive to strengthen the revolutionary trade unions and the workers' united front against the capitalist offensive;*

c) *to strive to strengthen the friendship between the working class of the U.S.S.R. and the working class in the capitalist countries;*

d) *to strive to strengthen the link between the working class of the U.S.S.R. and the liberation movement in the colonies and dependent countries.*

2) In the sphere of the U.S.S.R.'s foreign policy:

a) *to combat the preparations for new imperialist wars;*

b) *to combat Britain's interventionist tendencies and to strive to strengthen the U.S.S.R.'s defensive capacity;*

c) *to pursue a policy of peace and to maintain peaceful relations with the capitalist countries;*

d) *to expand our trade with the outside world on the basis of strengthening the monopoly of foreign trade;*

e) *rapprochement with the so-called "weak" and "unequal" states, which are suffering from oppression and exploitation by the ruling imperialist powers.*

STALIN

Report to the XVI Party Congress
June 27, 1930

Introduction When Stalin next addressed the Congress, the Great Depression had begun. He took this event as confirmation of his 1927 assessment of the capitalist world. In accordance with Lenin's theory, the economic crisis was expected to lead to political conflict, and finally to war. The chief focus of imperialist conflict, it should be noted, both in Lenin's theory and in Stalin's Report, is not the sensitive strategic areas of the metropolitan countries themselves, but the underdeveloped areas of the world. Not until the XVII Congress (1934) did Stalin direct his primary attention to political disputes in Europe. Depression in the capitalist world, according to Stalin, has contradictory implications for the USSR: it improves the chances for proletarian revolutions, but it increases the danger of a new capitalist intervention against the USSR.

Stalin tells foreign Communist Parties to prepare for their coming class battles in the new period of revolution by waging uncompromising struggle against the Social Democrats, or, as he calls them, "social fascists." This policy, duly implemented in Germany, contributed to the triumph of the Nazi Party in 1933 and the immediate destruction of the Communist Party. As to the alleged increase in the danger of war, it is difficult to believe that the USSR would have undertaken its breakneck drive toward industrialization and collective agriculture had Stalin believed war to be imminent. It cannot be ruled out, however, that Stalin believed the world depression to have increased the danger of an attack on the USSR in the long run.

The Growing Crisis of World Capitalism and The External Situation of the U.S.S.R.

Comrades, since the Fifteenth Congress two and a half years have passed. Not a very long period one would think. Nevertheless, during this period most important changes have taken place in the life of peoples and states. If one were to characterise the past period in two words, it could be called a *turning point* period. It marked a turning point not only for us, for the U.S.S.R., but also for the capitalist countries all over the world. Between these two turning points, however, there is a fundamental difference. Whereas for the U.S.S.R. this turning point meant a turn in the direction of a new and bigger economic *upswing,* for the capitalist countries it meant a turn towards economic *decline.* Here, in the U.S.S.R., there is a *growing upswing* of socialist development both in industry and in agriculture. There, among the capitalists, there is *growing* economic *crisis* both in industry and in agriculture.

Such is the picture of the present situation in a few words.

Recall the state of affairs in the capitalist countries two and a half years ago. Growth of industrial production and trade in nearly all the capitalist countries. Growth of production of raw materials and food in nearly all the agrarian countries. A halo around the United States as the land of the most full-blooded capitalism. Triumphant hymns of "prosperity." Grovelling to the dollar. Panegyrics in honour of the new technology, in honour of capitalist rationalisation. Proclamation of an era of the "recovery" of capitalism and of the unshakable firmness of capitalist stabilisation. "Universal" noise and clamour about the "inevitable doom" of the Land of Soviets, about the "inevitable collapse" of the U.S.S.R.

That was the state of affairs yesterday.

And what is the picture today?

Today there is an economic crisis in nearly all the industrial countries of capitalism. Today there is an agricultural crisis in all the agrarian countries. Instead of "prosperity" there is mass poverty and a colossal growth of unemployment. Instead of an upswing in agriculture there is the ruin of the vast masses of the peasants. The illusions about the omnipotence of capitalism in general, and about the omnipotence of North American capitalism in particular, are collapsing. The triumphant hymns in honour of the dollar and of capitalist rationalisation are becoming fainter and fainter. Pessimistic wailing about the "mistakes" of capitalism is growing louder and louder. And the "universal" clamour about the "inevitable doom" of the U.S.S.R. is giving way to "universal" venomous hissing about the necessity of punishing "that country" that dares to develop its economy when crisis is reigning all around.

Such is the picture today.

Things have turned out exactly as the Bolsheviks said they would two or three years ago.

The Bolsheviks said that in view of the restricted limits of the standard of living of the vast masses of the workers and peasants, the further development of technology in the capitalist countries, the growth of productive forces and of capitalist rationalisation, must inevitably lead to a severe economic crisis. The bourgeois press jeered at the "queer prophesies" of the Bolsheviks. The Right deviators dissociated themselves from this Bolshevik forecast and for the Marxist analysis substituted liberal chatter about "organised capitalism." But how did things actually turn out? They turned out exactly as the Bolsheviks said they would.

Such are the facts.

* * *

The Intensification of the
Contradictions of Capitalism

A most important result of the world economic crisis is that it is laying bare and intensifying the contradictions inherent in world capitalism.

a) It is laying bare and intensifying the *contradictions between the major imperialist countries,* the struggle for markets, the struggle for raw materials, the struggle for the export of capital. None of the capitalist states is now satisfied with the old distribution of spheres of influence and colonies. They see that the relation of forces has changed and that it is necessary in accordance with it to redivide markets, sources of raw materials, spheres of influence, and so forth. The chief contradiction here is that between the United States and Britain. Both in the sphere of the export of manufactured goods and in the sphere of the export of capital, the struggle is raging chiefly between the United States and Britain. It is enough to read any journal dealing with economics, any document concerning exports of goods and capital, to be convinced of this. The principal arena of the struggle is South America, China, the colonies and dominions of the old imperialist states. Superiority of forces in this struggle—and a definite superiority—is on the side of the United States.

After the chief contradiction come contradictions which, while not the chief ones, are, however, fairly important: between America and Japan, between Germany and France, between France and Italy, between Britain and France, and so forth.

There can be no doubt whatever that owing to the developing crisis, the struggle for markets, for raw materials and for the export of capital will grow more intense month by month and day by day.

Means of struggle: tariff policy, cheap goods, cheap credits, regrouping of forces and new military-political alliances, growth of armaments and preparation for new imperialist wars, and finally—war.

I have spoken about the crisis embracing all branches of production. There is one branch, however, that has not been affected by the crisis. That branch is the armament industry. It is growing continuously, notwithstanding the crisis. The bourgeois states are furiously arming and rearming. What for? Not for friendly chats, of course, but for war. And the imperialists need war, for it is the only means by which to redivide the world, to redivide markets, sources of raw materials and spheres for the investment of capital.

It is quite understandable that in this situation so-called pacifism is living its last days, that the League of Nations is rotting alive, that "disarmament schemes" come to nothing, while conferences for the reduction of naval armaments become transformed into conferences for renewing and enlarging navies.

This means that the danger of war will grow at an accelerated pace.

* * *

b) [The world economic crisis] is laying bare and will intensify the *contradictions between the victor countries and the vanquished countries.* Among the latter I have in mind chiefly Germany. Undoubtedly, in view of the crisis and the aggravation of the problem of markets, increased pressure will be brought to bear upon Germany, which is not only a debtor, but also a very big exporting country... To think that such a situation will have no effect upon world capitalism means not to understand anything in life. To think that the German bourgeoisie will be able to pay 20,000 million marks within the next ten years and that the German proletariat, which is living under the double yoke of "its own" and the "foreign" bourgeoisie, will allow the German bourgeoisie to squeeze these 20,000 million marks out of it without serious battles and convulsions, means to go out of one's mind. Let the German and French politicians pretend that they believe in this miracle. We Bolsheviks do not believe in miracles.

c) It is laying bare and intensifying *the contradictions between the imperialist states and the colonial and dependent countries.* The growing economic crisis cannot but increase the pressure of the imperialists upon the colonies and dependent countries, which are the chief markets for goods and sources of raw materials. Indeed, this pressure is increasing to the utmost degree. It is a fact that the European bourgeoisie is now in a state of war with "its" colonies in India, Indo-China, Indonesia and North Africa. It is a fact that "independent" China is already virtually partitioned into spheres of influence, while the cliques of counter-revolutionary Kuomintang generals, warring among themselves and ruining the Chinese people, are obeying the will of their masters in the imperialist camp.

* * *

It would be ridiculous to think that these outrages will be without consequences for the imperialists. The Chinese workers and peasants have already retaliated to them by forming Soviets and a Red Army. It is said that a Soviet government has already been set up there. I think that if this is true, there is nothing surprising about it. There can be no doubt that only Soviets can save China from utter collapse and pauperisation.

As regards India, Indo-China, Indonesia, Africa, etc., the growth of the revolutionary movement in those countries, which at times assumes the form of a national war for liberation, leaves no room for doubt. Messieurs the bourgeois count on flooding those countries with blood and on relying on police bayonets, calling people like Gandhi to their assistance. There can be no doubt that police bayonets make a poor prop. Tsarism, in its day, also tried to rely on police bayonets, but everybody knows what kind of a prop they turned out to be. As regards assistants of the Gandhi type, tsarism had a whole herd of them in the shape of liberal compromisers of every kind, but nothing came of this except discomfiture.

d) [The world economic crisis] is laying bare and intensifying *the contradictions between the bourgeoisie and the proletariat* in the capitalist countries. The crisis has already increased the pressure exerted by the capitalists on the working class. The crisis has already given rise to another wave of capitalist rationalisation, to a further deterioration of the conditions of the working class, to increased unemployment, to an enlargement of the permanent army of unemployed, to a reduction of wages. It is not surprising that these circumstances are revolutionising the situation, intensifying the class struggle and pushing the workers towards new class battles.

As a result of this, Social-Democratic illusions among the masses of workers are being shattered and dispelled. After the experience of Social-Democrats being in power, when they broke strikes, organised lockouts and shot down workers, the false promises of "industrial democracy," "peace in industry," and "peaceful methods" of struggle sound like cruel mockery to the workers. Will many workers be found today capable of believing the false doctrines of the social-fascists? The well-known workers' demonstrations of August 1, 1929 (against the war danger) and of March 6, 1930 (against unemployment) show that the best members of the working class have already turned away from the social-facists. . . .

. . . All that is necessary is that the Communists should be capable of appraising the situation and making proper use of it. By developing an uncompromising struggle against Social-Democracy, which is capital's agency in the working class, and by reducing to dust all and sundry deviations from Leninism, which bring grist to the mill of Social-Democracy, the Communist Parties have shown that they are on the right road. They must definitely fortify themselves on this road; for only if they do that can they count on winning over the majority of the working class and successfully prepare the proletariat for the coming class battles. Only if they do that can we count on a further increase in the influence and prestige of the Communist International.

Such is the state of the principal contradictions of world capitalism, which have become intensified to the utmost by the world economic crisis.

What do all these facts show?

That the stabilisation of capitalism is coming to an end.

That the upsurge of the mass revolutionary movement will increase with fresh vigour.

That in a number of countries the world economic crisis will grow into a political crisis.

This means, firstly, that the bourgeoisie will seek a way out of the situation through further fascisation in the sphere of domestic policy, and will utilise all the reactionary forces, including Social-Democracy, for this purpose.

It means, secondly, that in the sphere of foreign policy the bourgeoisie will seek a way out through a new imperialist war.

It means, lastly, that the proletariat, in fighting capitalist exploitation and the war danger, will seek a way out through revolution.

The Relations Between the U.S.S.R. and the Capitalist States

a) I have spoken above about the contradictions of world capitalism. In addition to these, however, there is one other contradiction. I am referring to the contradiction between the capitalist world and the U.S.S.R. True, this contradiction must not be regarded as being of the same order as the contradiction *within capitalism*. It is a contradiction between capitalism as a whole and the country that is building socialism. This, however, does not prevent it from corroding and shaking the very foundations of capitalism. More than that, it lays bare all the contradictions of capitalism to the roots and gathers them into a single knot, transforming them into an issue of the life and death of the capitalist order itself. That is why, every time the contradictions of capitalism become acute, the bourgeoisie turns its gaze towards the U.S.S.R., wondering whether it would not be possible to solve this or that contradiction of capitalism, or all the contradictions together, at the expense of the U.S.S.R., of that Land of Soviets, that citadel of revolution which, by its very existence, is revolutionising the working class and the colonies, which is hindering the organisation of a new war, hindering a new redivision of the world, hindering the capitalists from lording it in its extensive home market which they need so much, especially now, in view of the economic crisis.

Hence the tendency towards adventurist attacks on the U.S.S.R. and towards intervention, a tendency which will certainly grow owing to the development of the economic crisis.

The most striking expression of this tendency at the present time is present-day bourgeois France, the birthplace of the philanthropic "Pan-Europe" scheme, the "cradle" of the Kellogg Pact, the most aggressive and militarist of all the aggressive and militarist countries in the world.

But intervention is a two-edged sword. The bourgeoisie knows this perfectly well. It will be all right, it thinks, if intervention goes off smoothly and ends in the defeat of the U.S.S.R. But what if it ends in the defeat of the capitalists? There was intervention once and it ended in failure. If the first intervention, when the Bolsheviks were weak, ended in failure, what guarantee is there that the second will not end in failure too? Everybody sees that the Bolsheviks are far stronger now, both economically and politically, and as regards preparedness for the country's defence. And what about the workers in the capitalist countries, who will not permit intervention in the U.S.S.R., who will fight intervention and, if anything happens, may attack the capitalists in the rear? Would it not be better to proceed along the line of increasing trade connections with the U.S.S.R., to which the Bolsheviks do not object?

Hence the tendency towards continuing peaceful relations with the U.S.S.R.

* * *

b) It is said that the stumbling block to the improvement of economic relations between the U.S.S.R., and the bourgeois states is the question of the debts. I think that this is not an argument in favour of paying the debts, but a pretext advanced by the aggressive elements for interventionist propaganda. . . . If Messieurs the capitalists could somehow "fence themselves off" from the economic crisis, from mass poverty, from unemployment, from low wages and from the exploitation of labour, it would be another matter; then there would be no Bolshevik movement in their countries. But the whole point is that every rascal tries to justify his weakness or impotence by pleading Russian Bolshevik propaganda.

It is said, further, that another stumbling block is our Soviet system, collectivisation, the fight against the kulaks, anti-religious propaganda, the fight against wreckers and counter-revolutionaries among "men of science". . . . Since, however, we have agreed not to intervene in the internal affairs of other countries, is it not obvious that it is not worth while reverting to this question? Collectivisation, the fight against the kulaks, the fight against wreckers, anti-religious propaganda, and so forth, are the inalienable right of the workers and peasants of the U.S.S.R., sealed by our Constitution. . . .

That is how the matter stands with the "obstacles" that hinder the establishment of "normal" relations between the U.S.S.R. and other countries.

It turns out that these "obstacles" are fictitious "obstacles" raised as a pretext for anti-Soviet propaganda.

Our policy is a policy of peace and of increasing trade connections with all countries. A result of this policy is an improvement in our relations with a number of countries and the conclusion of a number of agreements for trade, technical assistance, and so forth. Another result is the U.S.S.R.'s adherence to the Kellogg Pact, the signing of the well-known protocol along the lines of the Kellogg Pact with Poland, Rumania, Lithuania, and other countries, the signing of the protocol on the prolongation of the treaty of friendship and neutrality with Turkey. And lastly, a result of this policy is the fact that we have succeeded in maintaining peace, in not allowing our enemies to draw us into conflicts, in spite of a number of provocative acts and adventurist attacks on the part of the warmongers. We shall continue to pursue this policy of peace with all our might and with all the means at our disposal. We do not want a single foot of foreign territory; but of our territory we shall not surrender a single inch to anyone.

Such is our foreign policy.

The task is to continue this policy with all the perserverance characteristic of Bolsheviks.

STALIN

Report to the XVII
Party Congress
January 26, 1934

Introduction When Stalin next spoke, Japan had taken
the course of aggression in China (1931) and Germany
had come under the rule of Hitler (January 1933). For a
year, Stalin's response to the unexpected and potentially
dangerous developments in Germany was a cautious
silence. Now he spoke out, though still cautiously, in
what was till then his most important pronouncement on
foreign policy.

The coming to power of fascism in Germany and its
increased strength elsewhere meant to Stalin that the
bourgeoisie could find no other way out of its difficulties
except through a policy of internal repression and war.
While the war of which Stalin spoke in 1930 was a new
war of intervention against the Soviet Union, in 1934 he
considers at length the four kinds of war he believes
possible:

1. War between the great capitalist powers;
2. Colonial war against a country like China;
3. Racist war by the Germans to conquer the Slavs (by
   implication, Russians are among the potential victims); and

4. War against the USSR, which military circles in Japan and political leaders in "certain states" of Europe have begun to plan.

Stalin does not speak explicitly of a war by Germany against the Soviet Union—almost as though it is too fearful to mention.

Stalin tries to deter war against the Soviet Union by threatening the USSR's enemies with revolution. With respect to Germany, this was an empty threat, since the German Communist Party had already been destroyed by Hitler. Later, after Hitler attacked the USSR in 1941, Stalin again threatened Germany with revolution, but there was none.

In a striking passage, Stalin says that Soviet diplomacy (which at that moment happened to favor France and Poland) is not ideologically committed against fascist states. For the USSR, the decisive question is not Germany's *fascism*, but the friendship or hostility of Germany's policy towards Russia—a question that is prior to, and independent of, ideology. Political leaders among the Western allies (and also many liberals) failed to take Stalin at his word, and lived to regret it: in August 1939 Stalin acted on this principle when he made his crucial pact with Hitler.

Of the five great powers in the world aside from itself, the USSR is developing favorable relations with the *United States* and *France;* on the other hand, it is having some difficulties with *Japan,* which could be amicably settled, and has been subjected to pressure by the Conservative government in *Britain,* with whom improved relations evidently are not expected; finally, the USSR has had to cope with hostile changes in the foreign policy of *Germany* after Hitler's advent to power. Unless Hitler's government were to maintain a policy hostile to the USSR, however, Stalin at this time shows no inclination to oppose fascist Germany.

As in previous Reports to the party congress, Stalin does not hesitate to state the Comintern's policy, which is to be followed by the various Communist Parties. It remains a leftist policy of preparation for the revolutionary seizure of power. Significantly, however, Stalin mentions that "some comrades" oppose this policy.

This is probably an esoteric reference to top Soviet leaders who believed that foreign Communist Parties should abandon the tactics that helped bring the Nazis to power in Germany and should initiate instead a policy of cooperating with right wing Socialists against the common fascist enemy. Conceivably, these "comrades" also opposed Stalin's policy of ideological neutrality between the fascist and the democratic states.

The Continuing Crisis of World Capitalism and the External Situation of the Soviet Union

Comrades, more than three years have passed since the Sixteenth Congress. That is not a very long period. But it has been fuller in content than any other period. I do not think that any period in the last decade has been so rich in events as this one.

In the *economic* sphere these years have been years of continuing world economic crisis. The crisis has affected not only industry, but also agriculture as a whole. The crisis has raged not only in the sphere of production and trade; it has also extended to the sphere of credit and money circulation, and has completely upset the established credit and currency relations among countries. While formerly people here and there still disputed whether there was a world economic crisis or not, now they no longer do so, for the existence of the crisis and its devastating effects are only too obvious. Now the controversy centres around another question: Is there a way out of the crisis or not; and if there is, then what is to be done?

In the *political* sphere these years have been years of further tension both in the relations between the capitalist countries and in the relations within them. Japan's war against China and the occupation of Manchuria, which have strained relations in the Far East; the victory of fascism in Germany and the triumph of the idea of revenge, which have strained relations in Europe; the withdrawal of Japan and Germany from the League of Nations, which has given a new impetus to the growth of armaments and to the preparations for an imperialist war; the defeat of fascism in Spain, which is one more indication that a revolutionary crisis is maturing and that fascism is far from being long-lived—such are the most important events of the period under review. It is not surprising that bourgeois pacifism is breathing its last and that the trend towards disarmament is openly and definitely giving way to a trend towards armament and rearmament.

Amid the surging waves of economic perturbations and military-political catastrophes, the U.S.S.R. stands out like a rock, continuing its work of socialist construction and its fight to preserve peace. Whereas in the capitalist countries the economic crisis is still raging, in the U.S.S.R. the advance continues both in industry and in agriculture. Whereas in the capitalist countries feverish preparations are in progress for a new war for a new redivision of the world and of spheres of influence, the U.S.S.R. is continuing its systematic and persistent struggle against the menace of war and for peace; and it cannot be said that the efforts of the U.S.S.R. in this direction have had no success.

Such is the general picture of the international situation at the present moment.

Let us pass to an examination of the principal data on the economic and political situation in the capitalist countries.

The Course of the Economic Crisis in the Capitalist Countries

The present economic crisis in the capitalist countries differs from all analogous crises, among other things, in that it is the longest and most protracted crisis. Formerly crises would come to an end in a year or two; the present crisis, however, is now in its fifth year, devastating the economy of the capitalist countries year after year and draining it of the fat accumulated in previous years. It is not surprising that this is the most severe of all the crises that have taken place.

How is this unprecedentedly protracted character of the present industrial crisis to be explained?

...It is to be explained [chiefly] by the fact that industrial crisis broke out in the conditions of the *general* crisis of capitalism, when capitalism no longer has, nor can have, either in the major countries or in the colonial and dependent countries, the strength and stability it had before the war and the October Revolution; when industry in the capitalist countries has acquired, as a heritage from the imperialist war, chronic under-capacity operation of plants, and armies of millions of unemployed of which it is no longer able to rid itself.

* * *

Evidently, what we are witnessing is a transition from the lowest point of decline of industry, from the lowest point of the industrial crisis, to a depression—not an ordinary depression, but a depression of a special kind, which does not lead to a new upswing and flourishing of industry, but which, on the other hand, does not force industry back to the lowest point of decline.

The Growing Tension in the Political Situation in the Capitalist Countries

A result of the protracted economic crisis has been an unprecedented increase in the tension of the political situation in the capitalist countries, both within those countries and in their mutual relations.

The intensified struggle for foreign markets, the abolition of the last vestiges of free trade, the prohibitive tariffs, the trade war, the foreign currency war, dumping, and many other analogous measures which demonstrate extreme *nationalism* in economic policy have strained to the utmost the relations among the various countries, have created the basis for military conflicts, and have put war on the order of the day as a means for a new redivision of the world and of spheres of influence in favour of the stronger states.

Japan's war against China, the occupation of Manchuria, Japan's withdrawal from the League of Nations, and her advance in North China, have made the situation still more tense. The intensified struggle for the Pacific and the growth of naval armaments in Japan, the United States, Britain and France are results of this increased tension.

Germany's withdrawal from the League of Nations and the spectre of revanchism have further added to the tension and have given a fresh impetus to the growth of armaments in Europe.

It is not surprising that bourgeois pacifism is now dragging out a miserable existence, and that idle talk of disarmament is giving way to "business-like" talk about armament and rearmament.

Once again, as in 1914, the parties of bellicose imperialism, the parties of war and revanchism are coming into the foreground.

Quite clear things are heading for a new war.

The internal situation of the capitalist countries, in view of the operation of these same factors, is becoming still more tense. Four years of industrial crisis have exhausted the working class and reduced it to despair. Four years of agricultural crisis have utterly ruined the poorer strata of the peasantry, not only in the principal capitalist countries, but also—and particularly—in the dependent and colonial countries. It is a fact that, notwithstanding all kinds of statistical trickery designed to minimise unemployment, the number of unemployed, according to the official figures of bourgeois institutions, reaches 3,000,000 in Britain, 5,000,000 in

Germany and 10,000,000 in the United States, not to mention the other European countries. Add to this the more than ten million partially unemployed; add the vast masses of ruined peasants—and you will get an approximate picture of the poverty and despair of the labouring masses. The masses of the people have not yet reached the stage when they are ready to storm capitalism; but the idea of storming it is maturing in the minds of the masses—of that there can hardly be any doubt. This is eloquently testified to by such facts as, say, the Spanish revolution which overthrew the fascist regime, and the expansion of the Soviet districts in China, which the united counter-revolution of the Chinese and foreign bourgeoisie is unable to stop.

This, indeed, explains why the ruling classes in the capitalist countries are so zealously destroying or nullifying the last vestiges of parliamentarism and bourgeois democracy which might be used by the working class in its struggle against the oppressors, why they are driving the Communist Parties underground and resorting to openly terrorist methods of maintaining their dictatorship.

Chauvinism and preparation of war as the main elements of foreign policy; repression of the working class and terrorism in the sphere of home policy as a necessary means for strengthening the rear of future war fronts—that is what is now particularly engaging the minds of contemporary imperialist politicians.

It is not surprising that fascism has now become the most fashionable commodity among war-mongering bourgeois politicians. I am referring not only to fascism in general, but, primarily, to fascism of the German type, which is wrongly called national-socialism—wrongly because the most searching examination will fail to reveal even an atom of socialism in it.

In this connection the victory of fascism in Germany must be regarded not only as a symptom of the weakness of the working class and a result of the betrayals of the working class by Social-Democracy, which paved the way for fascism; it must also be regarded as a sign of the weakness of the bourgeoisie, a sign that the bourgeoisie is no longer able to rule by the old methods of parliamentarism and bourgeois democracy, and, as a consequence, is compelled in its home policy to resort to terrorist methods of rule—as a sign that it is no longer able to find a way out of the present situation on the basis of a peaceful foreign policy, and, as a consequence, is compelled to resort to a policy of war.

Such is the situation.

As you see, things are heading towards a new imperialist war as a way out of the present situation.

Of course, there are no grounds for assuming that war can provide a real way out. On the contrary, it is bound to confuse the situation still more.

More than that, it is sure to unleash revolution and jeopardise the very existence of capitalism in a number of countries, as happened in the course of the first imperialist war. And if, in spite of the experience of the first imperialist war, the bourgeois politicians clutch at war as a drowning man clutches at a straw, that shows that they have got into a hopeless muddle, have landed in an impasse, and are ready to rush headlong into the abyss.

It is worth while, therefore, briefly to examine the plans for the organisation of war which are now being hatched in the circles of bourgeois politicians.

Some think that war should be organised against one of the great powers. They think of inflicting a crushing defeat upon that power and of improving their affairs at its expense. Let us assume that they organise such a war. What may be the result of that?

As is well known during the first imperialist war it was also intended to destroy one of the great powers, viz., Germany, and to profit at her expense. But what was the upshot of this? They did not destroy Germany; but they sowed in Germany such a hatred of the victors, and created such a rich soil for revenge, that even to this day they have not been able to clear up the revolting mess they made, and will not, perhaps, be able to do so for some time. On the other hand, the result they obtained was the smashing of capitalism in Russia, the victory of the proletarian revolution in Russia, and—of course—the Soviet Union. What guarantee is there that a second imperialist war will produce "better" results for them than the first? Would it not be more correct to assume that the opposite will be the case?

Others think that war should be organised against a country that is weak in the military sense, but represents an extensive market—for example, against China, which, it is claimed, cannot even be described as a state in the strict sense of the word, but is merely "unorganised territory" which needs to be seized by strong states. They evidently want to divide her up completely and improve their affairs at her expense. Let us assume that they organise such a war. What may be the result of that?

It is well known that at the beginning of the nineteenth century Italy and Germany were regarded in the same light as China is today, i.e., they were considered "unorganised territories" and not states, and they were subjugated. But what was the result of that? As is well known, it resulted in wars for independence waged by Germany and Italy, and the union of these countries into independent states. It resulted in increased hatred for the oppressors in the hearts of the peoples of these countries, the effects of which have not been removed to this day and will not, perhaps, be removed for some time. The question arises: What guarantee is there that the same thing will not result from a war of the imperialists against China?

Still others think that war should be organised by a "superior race," say, the German "race," against an "inferior race," primarily against the Slavs; that only such a war can provide a way out of the situation, for it is the mission of the "superior race" to render the "inferior race" fruitful and to rule over it. Let us assume that this queer theory, which is as far removed from science as the sky from the earth, let us assume that this queer theory is put into practice. What may be the result of that?

It is well known that ancient Rome looked upon the ancestors of the present-day Germans and French in the same way as the representatives of the "superior race" now look upon the Slav races. It is well known that ancient Rome treated them as an "inferior race," as "barbarians," destined to live in eternal subordination to the "superior race," to "great Rome"; and, between ourselves be it said, ancient Rome had some grounds for this, which cannot be said of the representatives of the "superior race" of today. But what was the upshot of this? The upshot was that the non-Romans, i.e., all the "barbarians," united against the common enemy and brought Rome down with a crash. The question arises: What guarantee is there that claims of the representatives of the "superior race" of today will not lead to the same lamentable results? What guarantee is there that the fascist literary politicians in Berlin will be more fortunate than the old and experienced conquerors in Rome? Would it not be more correct to assume that the opposite will be the case?

Finally, there are others who think that war should be organised against the U.S.S.R. Their plan is to defeat the U.S.S.R., divide up its territory, and profit at its expense. It would be a mistake to believe that it is only certain military circles in Japan who think in this way. We know that similar plans are being hatched in the circles of the political leaders of certain states in Europe. Let us assume that these gentlemen pass from words to deeds. What may be the result of that?

There can hardly be any doubt that such a war would be the most dangerous war for the bourgeoisie. It would be the most dangerous war, not only because the peoples of the U.S.S.R. would fight to the death to preserve the gains of the revolution; it would be the most dangerous war for the bourgeoisie for the added reason that it would be waged not only at the fronts, but also in the enemy's rear. The bourgeoisie need have no doubt that the numerous friends of the working class of the U.S.S.R. in Europe and Asia will endeavour to strike a blow in the rear at their oppressors who have launched a criminal war against the fatherland of the working class of all countries. And let not Messieurs the bourgeoisie blame us if some of the governments near and dear to them, which today rule happily "by the grace of God," are missing on the morrow after such a war.

There has been one such war against the U.S.S.R., if you remember, fifteen years ago. As is well known, the universally esteemed Churchill clothed that war in poetic formula—"the campaign of fourteen states." You remember, of course, that that war rallied all the working people of our country into one united camp of self-sacrificing warriors, who with their lives defended their workers' and peasants' motherland against the foreign foe. You know how it ended. It ended in the ejection of the invaders from our country and the formation of revolutionary Councils of Action in Europe. It can hardly be doubted that a second war against the U.S.S.R. will lead to the complete defeat of the aggressors, to revolution in a number of countries in Europe and in Asia, and to the destruction of the bourgeois-landlord governments in those countries.

Such are the war plans of the perplexed bourgeois politicians.

As you see, they are not distinguished either for their brains or for their valour.

But while the bourgeoisie chooses the path of war, the working class in the capitalist countries, brought to despair by four years of crisis and unemployment, is beginning to take the path of revolution. This means that a revolutionary crisis is maturing and will continue to mature. And the more the bourgeoisie becomes entangled in its war schemes, the more frequently it resorts to terrorist methods of fighting against the working class and the labouring peasantry, the more rapidly will the revolutionary crisis develop.

Some comrades think that, once there is a revolutionary crisis, the bourgeoisie is bound to get into a hopeless position, that its end is therefore a foregone conclusion, that the victory of the revolution is thus assured, and that all they have to do is to wait for the fall of the bourgeoisie and to draw up victorious resolutions. That is a profound mistake. The victory of the revolution never comes of itself. It must be prepared for and won. And only a strong proletariat revolutionary party can prepare for and win victory. Moments occur when the situation is revolutionary, when the rule of the bourgeoisie is shaken to its very foundations, and yet the victory of the revolution does not come, because there is no revolutionary party of the proletariat with sufficient strength and prestige to lead the masses and to take power. It would be unwise to believe that such "cases" cannot occur. . . .

The Relations Between the U.S.S.R.
And the Capitalist States

It is easy to understand how difficult it has been for the U.S.S.R. to pursue its peace policy in this atmosphere poisoned with the miasma of war schemes.

In the midst of this eve-of-war frenzy which has affected a number of countries, the U.S.S.R. during these years has stood firmly and unshakably by its position of peace: fighting against the menace of war; fighting to preserve peace; meeting halfway those countries which in one way or another stand for the preservation of peace; exposing and tearing the masks from those who are preparing for and provoking war.

What did the U.S.S.R. rely on in this difficult and complicated struggle for peace;

a) On its growing economic and political might.

b) On the moral support of the vast masses of the working class of all countries, who are vitally interested in the preservation of peace.

c) On the prudence of those countries which for one motive or another are not interested in disturbing the peace, and which want to develop trade relations with such a punctual client as the U.S.S.R.

d) Finally—on our glorious army, which stands ready to defend our country against assaults from without.

It was on this basis that we began our campaign for the conclusion with neighbouring states of pacts of non-aggression and of pacts defining aggression. You know that this campaign has been successful. As you know, pacts of non-aggression have been concluded not only with the majority of our neighbours in the West and in the South, including Finland and Poland, but also with such countries as France and Italy; and pacts defining aggression have been concluded with those same neighbouring states, including the Little Entente.

On the same basis the friendship between the U.S.S.R. and Turkey has been consolidated; relations between the U.S.S.R. and Italy have improved and have indisputably become satisfactory; relations with France, Poland and other Baltic states have improved; relations have been restored with the U.S.A., China, etc.

Of the many facts reflecting the successes of the peace policy of the U.S.S.R. two facts of indisputably material significance should be noted and singled out.

1) I have in mind, firstly, the change for the better that has taken place recently in the relations between the U.S.S.R. and France. In the past, as you know, our relations with Poland were not at all good. Representatives of our state were assassinated in Poland. Poland regarded herself as the barrier of the Western states against the U.S.S.R. All the various imperialists counted on Poland as their advanced detachment in the event of a military attack on the U.S.S.R. The relations between the U.S.S.R. and France were no better. We need only recall the facts relating to the trial of the Ramzin group of wreckers in Moscow to bring to mind a picture of the relations between the U.S.S.R. and France. But now those undesirable relations are

gradually beginning to disappear. They are giving way to other relations, which can only be called relations of rapprochment.

The point is not merely that we have concluded pacts of non-aggression with these countries, although the pacts in themselves are of very great importance. The point is, primarily, that the atmosphere of mutual distrust is beginning to be dissipated. This does not mean, of course, that the incipient process of rapprochement can be regarded as sufficiently stable and as guaranteeing ultimate success. Surprises and zigzags in policy, for example in Poland, where anti-Soviet sentiments are still strong, can as yet by no means be regarded as out of the question. But the change for the better in our relations, irrespective of its results in the future, is a fact worthy of being noted and emphasised as a factor in the advancement of the cause of peace.

What is the cause of this change? What stimulates it?

Primarily the growth of the strength and might of the U.S.S.R.

In our times it is not the custom to take any account of the weak—only the strong are taken into account. Furthermore, there have been some changes in the policy of Germany which reflect the growth of revanchist and imperialist sentiments in Germany.

In this connection some German politicians say that the U.S.S.R. has now taken an orientation towards France and Poland; that from an opponent of the Versailles Treaty it has become a supporter of it, and that this change is to be explained by the establishment of the fascist regime in Germany. That is not true. Of course, we are far from being enthusiastic about the fascist regime in Germany. But it is not a question of fascism here, if only for the reason that fascism in Italy, for example, has not prevented the U.S.S.R. from establishing the best relations with that country. Nor is it a question of any alleged change in our attitude towards the Versailles Treaty. It is not for us, who have experienced the shame of the Brest Peace, to sing the praises of the Versailles Treaty. We merely do not agree to the world being flung into the abyss of a new war on account of that treaty. The same must be said of the alleged new orientation taken by the U.S.S.R. We never had any orientation towards Germany, nor have we any orientation towards Poland and France. Our orientation in the past and our orientation at the present time is towards the U.S.S.R. alone. (*Stormy applause*) And if the interests of the U.S.S.R. demand rapprochement with one country or another which is not interested in disturbing peace, we adopt this course without hesitation.

No, that is not the point. The point is that Germany's policy has changed. The point is that even before the present German politicians came to power, and particularly after they came to power, a contest began in Germany between two political lines: between the old policy, which was reflected in the treaties between the U.S.S.R. and Germany, and the "new" policy, which, in the main, recalls the policy of the former German Kaiser, who at one time occupied the Ukraine and marched against Leningrad, after converting the Baltic countries into a place d'armes for this march; and this "new" policy is obviously gaining the upper hand over the old policy. The fact that the advocates of the "new" policy are gaining supremacy in all things, while the supporters of the old policy are in disfavour, cannot be regarded as an accident. Nor can the well-known statement made by Hugenberg in London, and the equally well-known declarations of Rosenberg, who directs the foreign policy of the ruling party in Germany, be regarded as accidents. That is the point, comrades.

2) I have in mind, secondly, the restoration of normal relations between the U.S.S.R. and the United States of America. There cannot be any doubt that this act is of very great significance for the whole system of international relations. The point is not only that it improves the chances of preserving peace, improves the relations between the two countries, strengthens trade connections between them and creates a basis for mutual collaboration. The point is that it forms a landmark between the old position, when in various countries the U.S.A. was regarded as the bulwark for all sorts of anti-Soviet trends, and the new position, when that bulwark has been voluntarily removed, to the mutual advantage of both countries.

Such are the two main facts which reflect the successes of the Soviet policy of peace.

It would be wrong, however, to think that everything went smoothly in the period under review. No, not everything went smoothly, by a long way.

Recall, say, the pressure that was brought to bear upon us by Britain; the embargo on our exports, the attempt to interfere in our internal affairs and to use this as a probe—to test our power of resistance. True, nothing came of this attempt, and later the embargo was lifted; but the unpleasant after-effect of these sallies still makes itself felt in everything connected with the relations between Britain and the U.S.S.R., including the negotiations for a commercial treaty. And these sallies against the U.S.S.R. must not be regarded as accidental. It is well known that a certain section of the British Conservatives cannot live without such sallies. And precisely because they are not accidental we must reckon that in the future, too, sallies will be made against the U.S.S.R., all sorts of menaces will be created, attempts will be undertaken to damage the U.S.S.R., etc.

Nor must we lose sight of the relations between the U.S.S.R. and Japan, which stand in need of considerable improvement. Japan's refusal to conclude a pact of non-aggression, of which Japan stands in no less need than the U.S.S.R., once again emphasises the fact that all is not well in the sphere of our relations. The same must be said of the rupture of negotiations concerning the Chinese-Eastern Railway, due to no fault of the U.S.S.R.; and also of the outrageous actions of the Japanese agents on the Chinese-Eastern Railway, the illegal arrests of Soviet employees on the Chinese-Eastern Railway, etc. That is apart from the fact that one section of the military in Japan, with the obvious approval of another section of the military, is openly advocating in the press the necessity for a war against the U.S.S.R. and the seizure of the Maritime Province; while the Japanese Government, instead of calling these instigators of war to order, pretends that the matter is no concern of its. It is not difficult to understand that such circumstances cannot but create an atmosphere of uneasiness and uncertainty. Of course, we shall persistently continue to pursue a policy of peace and strive for an improvement in our relations with Japan, because we want to improve these relations. But it does not depend entirely upon us. That is why we must at the same time take all measures to guard our country against surprises, and be prepared to defend it against attack.

As you see, alongside the successes in our peace policy there are also a number of unfavourable features.

Such is the external situation of the U.S.S.R.

Our foreign policy is clear. It is a policy of preserving peace and strengthening trade relations with all countries. The U.S.S.R. does not think of threatening anybody—let alone of attacking anybody. We stand for peace and uphold the cause of peace. But we are not afraid of threats and are prepared to answer the instigators of war blow for blow. Those who want peace and seek business relations with us will always have our support. But those who try to attack our country will receive a crushing repulse to teach them in future not to poke their pig snouts into our Soviet garden.

Such is our foreign policy.

The task is to continue to implement this policy with unflagging perseverance and consistency.

STALIN

Report to the XVIII Party
Congress *March 10, 1939*

Introduction When Stalin next addressed the Party
Congress, the international situation had changed
radically. In 1935, the USSR had become allied with
France and had adopted a policy of "collective security"
against aggression by Germany. Nevertheless, German
power had continued to grow. The USSR's value as an
ally had been brought in question in the West by Stalin's
blood purge of Soviet institutions, in particular of the
Red Army. Fearing that war might result from strong
opposition to Hitler's demands, France and Great Britain
tried to appease him, a policy which culminated in the
late Summer of 1938 in the Munich Conference, from
which the USSR was excluded.

The USSR was now in grave danger. Instead of the
relatively disarmed Germany with which the USSR had
been able to maintain friendly relations from 1918 to
1933, there was now a Germany possessed of a vast and
powerful war machine proclaiming its hostility to
Bolshevik Russia. The USSR would have to meet this
danger from Germany alone and unaided unless it could

restore and extend its ties with France and her allies. There were two possible solutions to this problem: one was to participate in a reliable military coalition that was more powerful than Germany, which thus could deter war or win it; the other was to reach an agreement with Germany that would avert the danger of an attack on the USSR. Each solution had its advantages and disadvantages. Stalin's preferred solution during this period probably changed according to circumstances.

Stalin characterizes the international scene as one in which economic crisis in the capitalist countries has given rise to a "second imperialist war" to redistribute markets and territories. While Stalin distinguishes between "aggressive" and "non-aggressive states," the importance of this distinction for Soviet foreign policy is somewhat reduced by the fact that the aims of both sides are alleged to be imperialistic. The aggressive states (Germany, Italy, and Japan) infringe upon the interests of the non-aggressive states (England, France and the USA) which make concessions and fail to resist. Why this policy of "non-intervention?" It is not because of weakness, since the "non-aggressive, democratic states" unquestionably are stronger militarily. (Here Stalin miscalculated seriously, as became apparent a year later when German arms rapidly conquered France.) Is it because they fear the outbreak of revolution if they become involved in war? Stalin does not deny the existence of such fears, or that they are well-founded. But fear of revolution is not the chief reason for the non-intervention policy. The concessions of the non-aggressive states result from their intention to avoid war themselves while encouraging the aggressor states to become involved in war, either colonial war or war against the USSR. In a weakened condition, the aggressive states could then be readily dealt with by their imperialist rivals. The non-aggressors egg on Germany, in particular, to war with the USSR, at the same time trying to incense the Soviet Union against Germany, "to provoke a conflict with Germany without any valid grounds." Stalin warns that this strategy, which he has attributed to the Western democracies, may end in a fiasco.

Stalin's speech is largely an analysis of the foreign policy of the Western democracies. While he treats Germany as an aggressor state which is hostile to the interests of England and France, he leaves open the question of whether it is also hostile to Soviet interests. He asserts that there are no grounds for conflict between the two states—but he does not say that this is Germany's understanding of the situation. There is a message here for Hitler. Just as Stalin, in 1934, informed Hitler that Germany's internal regime, its fascism, did not preclude close relations with the USSR, he now tells him that Germany's aggressive foreign policy (which had been clearly revealed in the intervening years) is also no obstacle so long as German aggression is not directed against the USSR. There is a message in the Report for the West's leaders as well. If they read carefully, they will perceive Stalin's invitation to Hitler to improve relations. But Stalin does not leave it at that; he warns that the USSR will not "pull the chestnuts out of the fire" for them, that is, the USSR will not be drawn into a war against Germany from which France and Britain may stand aside, or in which they may fail to make a proper contribution.

A few days after Stalin's Report, Europe received a new shock from Hitler, who destroyed the remnants of the Czechoslovak state. Even so, Stalin's message to Hitler had results. Negotiations were begun which led to the Nazi-Soviet Pact of August, 1939, enabling Germany to go to war without fear of a Soviet attack on its eastern front. The price paid to Stalin was a Soviet share in the division of Poland.

The Soviet Union and International Affairs

Comrades, five years have elapsed since the Seventeenth Party Congress. No small period, as you see. During this period the world has undergone considerable changes. States and countries, and their mutual relations, are now in many respects totally altered.

What changes exactly have taken place in the international situation in this period? In what way exactly have the foreign and internal affairs of our country changed?

For the capitalist countries this period was one of very profound perturbations in both the economic and political spheres. In the economic sphere these were years of depression, followed, from the beginning of the latter half of 1937, by a period of new economic crisis, of a new decline of industry in the United States, Great Britain and France; consequently, these were years of new economic complications. In the political sphere they were years of serious political conflicts and perturbations. A new imperialist war is already in its second year, a war waged over a huge territory stretching from Shanghai to Gibralter and involving over five hundred million people. The map of Europe, Africa and Asia is being forcibly re-drawn. The entire post-war system, the so-called regime of peace, has been shaken to its foundations.

For the Soviet Union, on the contrary, these were years of growth and prosperity, of further economic and cultural progress, of further development of political and military might, of struggle for the preservation of peace throughout the world.

Such is the general picture.

Let us now examine the concrete data illustrating the changes in the international situation.

New Economic Crisis in the Capitalist Countries.
Intensification of the Struggle for Markets and Sources of
Raw Material, and for a New Redivision of the World

The economic crisis which broke out in the capitalist countries in the latter half of 1929 lasted until the end of 1933. After that the crisis passed into a depression, and was then followed by a certain revival, a certain upward trend of industry. But this upward trend of industry did not develop into a boom, as is usually the case in a period of revival. On the contrary, in the latter half of 1937 a new economic crisis began which seized the United States first of all and then England, France and a number of other countries.

The capitalist countries thus found themselves faced with a new economic crisis before they had even recovered from the ravages of the recent one.

This circumstance naturally led to an increase of unemployment. The number of unemployed in capitalist countries, which had fallen from thirty million in 1933 to fourteen million in 1937, has now again risen to eighteen million as a result of the new economic crisis.

A distinguishing feature of the new crisis is that it differs in many respects from the preceding one, and, moreover, differs for the worse and not for the better.

Firstly, the new crisis did not begin after an industrial boom, as was the case in 1929, but after a depression and a certain revival, which, however, did not develop into a boom. This means that the present crisis will be more severe and more difficult to cope with than the previous crisis.

Further, the present crisis has broken out not in time of peace, but at a time when a second imperialist war has already begun; at a time when Japan, already in the second year of her war with China, is disorganizing the immense Chinese market and rendering it almost inaccessible to the goods of other countries; when Italy and Germany have already placed their national economy on a war footing, squandering their reserves of raw material and foreign currency for this purpose; and when all the other big capitalist powers are beginning to reorganize themselves on a war footing. This means that capitalism will have far less resources at its disposal for a normal way out of the present crisis than during the preceding crisis.

Lastly, as distinct from the preceding crisis, the present crisis is not a general one, but as yet involves chiefly the economically powerful countries which have not yet placed themselves on a war economy basis. As regards the aggressive countries, such as Japan, Germany and Italy, who have already reorganized their economy on a war footing, they, because of the intense development of their war industry, are not yet experiencing a crisis of overproduction, although they are approaching it. This means that by the time the economically powerful, non-aggressive countries begin to emerge from the phase of crisis the aggressive countries, having exhausted their reserves of gold and raw material in the course of the war fever, are bound to enter a phase of a very severe crisis. . . .

Naturally, such an unfavourable turn of economic affairs could not but aggravate relations between the powers. The preceding crisis had already mixed the cards and intensified the struggle for markets and sources of raw materials. The seizure of Manchuria and North China by Japan, the seizure of Abyssinia by Italy—all this reflected the acuteness of the struggle among the powers. The new economic crisis must lead, and is actually leading, to a further sharpening of the imperialist struggle. It is no longer a question of competition in the markets, of a commercial war, of dumping. These methods of struggle have long been recognized as inadequate. It is now a question of a new redivision of the world, of spheres of influence and colonies, by military action.

Japan tried to justify her aggressive actions by the argument that she had been cheated when the Nine-Power Pact was concluded and had not been allowed to extend her territory at the expense of China, whereas Britain and France possess enormous colonies. Italy recalled that she had been cheated during the division of the spoils after the first imperialist war and that she must recompense herself at the expense of the spheres of influence of Britain and France. Germany, who had suffered severely as a result of the first imperialist war and the Peace of Versailles, joined forces with Japan and Italy, and demanded an extension of her territory in Europe and the return of the colonies of which the victors in the first imperialist war had deprived her.

Thus the bloc of three aggressor states came to be formed.

A new redivision of the world by means of war became imminent.

Aggravation of the International Political Situation.
Collapse of the Post-War System of Peace Treaties.
Beginning of a New Imperialist War

Here is a list of the most important events during the period under review which mark the beginning of the new imperialist war. In 1935 Italy attacked and seized Abyssinia. In the summer of 1936 Germany and Italy organized military intervention in Spain, Germany entrenching herself in the north of Spain and in Spanish Morocco, and Italy in the south of Spain and in the Balearic Islands. Having seized Manchuria, Japan in 1937 invaded North and Central China, occupied Peking, Tientsin and Shanghai and began to oust her foreign competitors from the occupied zone. In the beginning of 1938 Germany seized Austria, and in the autumn of 1938 the Sudeten region of Czechoslovakia. At the end of 1938 Japan seized Canton, and at the beginning of 1939 the Island of Hainan.

Thus the war, which has stolen so imperceptibly upon the nations, has drawn over five hundred million people into its orbit and has extended its sphere of action over a vast territory, stretching from Tientsin, Shanghai and Canton, through Abyssinia, to Gibraltar.

After the first imperialist war the victor states, primarily Britain, France and the United States, had set up a new regime in the relations between countries, the post-war regime of peace. The main props of this regime were the Nine-Power Pact in the Far East, and the Versailles Treaty and a number of other treaties in Europe. The League of Nations was set up to regulate relations between countries within the framework of this regime, on the basis of a united front of states, of collective defence of the security of states. However, three aggressive states, and the new imperialist war launched by them, have upset the entire system of this post-war peace regime. Japan tore up the Nine-Power Pact, and Germany and Italy the Versailles Treaty. In order to have their hands free, these three states withdrew from the League of Nations.

The new imperialist war became a fact.

It is not so easy in our day to suddenly break loose and plunge straight into war without regard for treaties of any kind or for public opinion. Bourgeois politicians know this very well. So do the fascist rulers. That is why the fascist rulers decided, before plunging into war, to frame public opinion to suit their ends, that is, to mislead it, to deceive it.

A military bloc of Germany and Italy against the interests of England and France in Europe? Bless us, do you call that a bloc! "We" have no military bloc. All "we" have is an innocuous "Berlin-Rome axis"; that is, just a geometrical equation for an axis.

A military bloc of Germany, Italy and Japan against the interests of the United States, Great Britain and France in the Far East? Nothing of the kind! "We" have no military bloc. All "we" have is an innocuous "Berlin-Rome-Tokyo triangle"; that is, a slight penchant for geometry.

A war against the interests of England, France, the United States? Nonsense! "We" are waging war on the Comintern, not on these states. If you don't believe it, read the "anti-Comintern pact" concluded between Italy, Germany and Japan.

That is how Messieurs the aggressors thought of framing public opinion, although it was not hard to see how preposterous this whole clumsy game of camouflage was; for it is ridiculous to look for Comintern "hotbeds" in the deserts of Mongolia, in the mountains of Abyssinia, or in the wilds of Spanish Morocco.

But war is inexorable. It cannot be hidden under any guise. For no "axes," "triangles" or "anti-Comintern pacts" can hide the fact that in this period Japan has seized a vast stretch of territory in China, that Italy has seized Abyssinia, that Germany has seized Austria and the Sudeten region, that Germany and Italy together have seized Spain—and all this in defiance of the interests of the non-aggressive states. The war remains a war; the military bloc of aggressors remains a military bloc; and the aggressors remain aggressors.

It is a distinguishing feature of the new imperialist war that it has not yet become universal, a world war. The war is being waged by aggressor states, who in every way infringe upon the interests of the non-aggressive states, primarily England, France and the U.S.A., while the latter draw back and retreat, making concession after concession to the aggressors.

Thus we are witnessing an open redivision of the world and spheres of influence at the expense of the non-aggressive states, without the least attempt at resistance, and even with a certain amount of connivance, on the part of the latter.

Incredible, but true.

To what are we to attribute this one-sided and strange character of the new imperialist war?

How is it that the non-aggressive countries, which possess such vast opportunities, have so easily, and without any resistance, abandoned their positions and their obligations to please the aggressors?

Is it to be attributed to the weakness of the non-aggressive states? Of course not! Combined, the non-aggressive, democratic states are unquestionably stronger than the fascist states, both economically and militarily.

To what then are we to attribute the systematic concessions made by these states to the aggressors?

It might be attributed, for example, to the fear that a revolution might break out if the non-aggressive states were to go to war and the war were to assume world-wide proportions. The bourgeois politicians know, of course, that the first imperialist world war led to the victory of the revolution in one of the largest countries. They are afraid that the second imperialist world war may also lead to the victory of the revolution in one or several countries.

But at present this is not the sole or even the chief reason. The chief reason is that the majority of the non-aggressive countries, particularly England and France, have rejected the policy of collective security, the policy of collective resistance to the aggressors, and have taken up a position of non-intervention, a position of "neutrality."

Formally speaking, the policy of non-intervention might be defined as follows: "Let each country defend itself from the aggressors as it likes and as best it can. That is not our affair. We shall trade both with the aggressors and with their victims." But actually speaking, the policy of non-intervention means conniving at aggression, giving free rein to war, and, consequently, transforming the war into a world war. The policy of non-intervention reveals an eagerness, a desire, not to hinder the aggressors in their nefarious work: not to hinder Japan, say, from embroiling herself in a war with China, or, better still, with the Soviet Union; not to hinder Germany, say, from enmeshing herself in European affairs, from embroiling herself in a war with the Soviet Union; to allow all the belligerents to sink deeply into the mire of war, to encourage them surreptitiously in this; to allow them to weaken and exhaust one another; and then, when they have become weak enough, to appear on the scene with fresh strength, to appear, of course, "in the interests of peace," and to dictate conditions to the enfeebled belligerents.

Cheap and easy!

Take Japan, for instance. It is characteristic that before Japan invaded North China all the influential French and British newspapers shouted about China's weakness and her inability to offer resistance, and declared that Japan with her army could subjugate China in two or three months.

Then the European and American politicians began to watch and wait. And then, when Japan started military operations, they let her have Shanghai, the vital centre of foreign capital in China; they let her have Canton, a centre of Britain's monopoly influence in South China; they let her have Hainan, and they allowed her to surround Hongkong. Does not this look very much like encouraging the aggressor? It is as though they were saying: "Embroil yourself deeper in war; then we shall see."

Or take Germany, for instance. They let her have Austria, despite the undertaking to defend her independence; they let her have the Sudeten region; they abandoned Czechoslovakia to her fate, thereby violating all their obligations; and then they began to lie vociferously in the press about "the weakness of the Russian army," "the demoralization of the Russian air force," and "riots" in the Soviet Union, egging the Germans on to march farther east, promising them easy pickings, and prompting them: "Just start war on the Bolsheviks, and everything will be all right." It must be admitted that this too looks very much like egging on and encouraging the aggressor.

The hullabaloo raised by the British, French and American press over the Soviet Ukraine is characteristic. The gentlemen of the press there shouted until they were hoarse that the Germans were marching on Soviet Ukraine, that they now had what is called the Carpathian Ukraine, with a population of some seven hundred thousand, and that not later than this spring the Germans would annex the Soviet Ukraine, which has a population of over thirty million, to this so-called Carpathian Ukraine. It looks as if the object of this suspicious hullabaloo was to incense the Soviet Union against Germany, to poison the atmosphere and to provoke a conflict with Germany without any visible grounds.

It is quite possible, of course, that there are madmen in Germany who dream of annexing the elephant, that is, the Soviet Ukraine, to the gnat, namely, the so-called Carpathian Ukraine. If there really are such lunatics in Germany, rest assured that we shall find enough strait-jackets for them in our country. But if we ignore the madmen and turn to normal people, is it not clearly absurd and foolish to seriously talk of annexing the Soviet Ukraine to this so-called Carpathian Ukraine? Imagine: The gnat comes to the elephant and says perkily: "Ah, brother, how sorry I am for you. . . . Here you are without any landlords, without any capitalists, with no national oppression, without any fascist bosses. Is that a way to live? . . . As I look at you I can't help thinking that there is no hope for you unless you annex yourself to me. . . . Well, so be it: I allow you to annex your tiny domain to my vast territories. . . ."

Even more characteristic is that fact that certain European and American politicians and pressmen, having lost patience waiting for "the march on the Soviet Ukraine," are themselves beginning to disclose what is really behind the policy of non-intervention. They are saying quite openly, putting it down in black on white, that the Germans have cruelly "disappointed" them, for instead of marching farther east, against the Soviet Union, they have turned, you see, to the west and are demanding colonies. One might think that the districts of Czechoslovakia were yielded to Germany as the price of an undertaking to launch war on the Soviet Union, but that now the Germans are refusing to meet their bills and are sending them to Hades.

Far be it from me to moralize on the policy of non-intervention, to talk of treason, treachery and so on. It would be naive to preach morals to people who recognize no human morality. Politics is politics, as the old, case-hardened bourgeois diplomats say. It must be remarked, however, that the big and dangerous political game started by the supporters of the policy of non-intervention may end in a serious fiasco for them.

Such is the true face of the prevailing policy of non-intervention.

Such is the political situation in the capitalist countries.

The Soviet Union and the Capitalist Countries

The war has created a new situation with regard to the relations between countries. It has enveloped them in an atmosphere of alarm and uncertainty. By undermining the post-war peace regime and overriding the elementary principles of international law, it cast doubt on the value of international treaties and obligations. Pacifism and disarmament schemes are dead and buried. Feverish arming has taken their place. Everybody is arming, small states and big states, including primarily those which practise the policy of non-intervention. Nobody believes any longer in the unctuous speeches which claim that the Munich concessions to the aggressors and the Munich agreement opened a new era of "appeasement." They are disbelieved even by the signatories to the Munich agreement, Britain and France, who are increasing their armaments no less than other countries.

Naturally, the U.S.S.R. could not ignore these ominous events. There is no doubt that any war, however small, started by the aggressors in any remote corner of the world constitutes a danger to the peaceable countries. All the more serious then is the danger arising from the new imperialist war, which has already drawn into its orbit over five hundred million people in Asia, Africa and Europe. In view of this, while our country is unswervingly pursuing a policy of preserving peace, it is at the same time doing a great deal to increase the preparedness of our Red Army and our Red Navy.

At the same time, in order to strengthen its international position, the

Soviet Union decided to take certain other steps. At the end of 1934 our country joined the League of Nations, considering that despite its weakness the League might nevertheless serve as a place where aggressors can be exposed, and as a certain instrument of peace, however feeble, that might hinder the outbreak of war. The Soviet Union considers that in alarming times like these even so weak an international organization as the League of Nations should not be ignored. In May 1935 a treaty of mutual assistance against possible attack by aggressors was signed between France and the Soviet Union. A similar treaty was simultaneously concluded with Czechoslovakia. In March 1936 the Soviet Union concluded a treaty of mutual assistance with the Mongolian People's Republic. In August 1937 the Soviet Union concluded a pact of non-aggression with the Chinese Republic.

It was in such difficult international conditions that the Soviet Union pursued its foreign policy of upholding the cause of peace.

The foreign policy of the Soviet Union is clear and explicit.

1. We stand for peace and the strengthening of business relations with all countries. That is our position; and we shall adhere to this position as long as these countries maintain like relations with the Soviet Union, and as long as they make no attempt to trespass on the interests of our country.

2. We stand for peaceful, close and friendly relations with all the neighbouring countries which have common frontiers with the U.S.S.R. That is our position; and we shall adhere to this position as long as these countries maintain like relations with the Soviet Union, and as long as they make no attempt to trespass, directly or indirectly, on the integrity and inviolability of the frontiers of the Soviet state.

3. We stand for the support of nations which are the victims of aggression and are fighting for the independence of their country.

4. We are not afraid of the threats of aggressors, and are ready to deal two blows for every blow delivered by instigators of war who attempt to violate the Soviet borders.

Such is the foreign policy of the Soviet Union.

In its foreign policy the Soviet Union relies upon:

1. Its growing economic, political and cultural might;

2. The moral and political unity of our Soviet society;

3. The mutual friendship of the nations of our country;

4. Its Red Army and Red Navy;

5. Its policy of peace;

6. The moral support of the working people of all countries, who are vitally concerned in the preservation of peace;

7. The good sense of the countries which for one reason or another have no interest in the violation of peace.

* * *

The tasks of the Party in the sphere of foreign policy are:

1. To continue the policy of peace and of strengthening business relations with all countries;

2. To be cautious and not allow our country to be drawn into conflicts by warmongers who are accustomed to have others pull the chestnuts out of the fire for them;

3. To strengthen the might of our Red Army and Red Navy to the utmost;

4. To strengthen the international bonds of friendship with the working people of all countries, who are interested in peace and friendship among nations.

MOLOTOV

Report to the Supreme Soviet
August 31, 1939

Introduction In this speech Molotov justifies the Nazi-Soviet Pact and presents it to the Supreme Soviet for ratification. He argues that the negotiations between the USSR on the one hand and France and Britain on the other, which began soon after Hitler swallowed up Czechoslovakia, were doomed to fail because the Western powers were fundamentally unwilling to contribute to Soviet security. Therefore, since no effective alliance against Germany could be created, there was but one solution to the problem of Soviet security—to reach agreement, if possible, with Germany. Using Stalin's March 1939 Report as his text, Molotov says that Stalin's message was correctly understood by the German Government which acted on Stalin's invitation to seek a German-Soviet understanding. The menace of war with Germany was thus eliminated.

From the moment of the Pact's signing the distinction that had previously been made between aggressor and non-aggressor states collapsed. Britain and France, along with Germany, were now equally "enemies of peace" and remained so until June 1941, when Hitler attacked the USSR. Molotov refutes the charge that the Pact enabled Germany to go to war, arguing instead that it served the cause of peace by narrowing the zone of possible hostilities in Europe. In any case, according to Molotov, Soviet policy is "based on the interests of the peoples of the USSR and only their interests." At a moment of great danger to the USSR, the head of the Soviet Government disavowed by his silence the cause of the world proletariat.

Comrades: Since the third session of the Supreme Soviet the international situation has shown no change for the better. On the contrary, it has become even more tense. The steps taken by various governments to put an end to this state of tension have obviously proved inadequate. They met with no success. This is true of Europe.

Nor has there been any change for the better in East Asia. Japanese troops continue to occupy the principal cities and a considerable part of the territory of China. Nor is Japan refraining from hostile acts against the U.S.S.R. Here, too, the situation has changed in the direction of further aggravation.

In view of this state of affairs, the conclusion of a pact of non-aggression between the U.S.S.R. and Germany is of tremendous positive value, eliminating the danger of war between Germany and the Soviet Union. In order more fully to define the significance of this pact, I must first dwell on the negotiations which have taken place in recent months in Moscow with representatives of Great Britain and France. As you know, Anglo-French-Soviet negotiations for conclusion of a pact of mutual assistance against aggression in Europe began as far back as April.

True, the initial proposals of the British Government were, as you know, entirely unacceptable. They ignored the prime requisites for such negotiations—they ignored the principle of reciprocity and equality of obligations. In spite of this, the Soviet Government did not reject the negotiations and in turn put forward its own proposals. We were mindful of the fact that it was difficult for the Governments of Great Britain and France to make an abrupt change in their policy from an unfriendly attitude towards the Soviet Union which had existed quite recently to serious negotiations with the U.S.S.R. based on the condition of equality of obligation.

However, the subsequent negotiations were not justified by their results. The Anglo-French-Soviet negotiations lasted four months. They helped to elucidate a number of questions. At the same time they made it clear to the representatives of Great Britain and France that the Soviet Union has to be seriously reckoned with in international affairs. But these negotiations encountered insuperable obstacles. The trouble, of course, did not lie in individual "formulations" or in particular clauses in the draft of the pact. No, the trouble was much more serious.

The conclusion of a pact of mutual assistance against aggression would have been of value only if Great Britain, France and the Soviet Union had arrived at agreement as to definite military measures against the attack of an aggressor. Accordingly, for a certain period not only political but also military negotiations were conducted in Moscow with representatives of the British and French armies. However, nothing came of the military negotiations. . . .

What is the root of [the] contradictions in the position of Great Britain and France? In a few words, it can be put as follows: On the one hand, the British and French governments fear aggression, and for that reason they would like to have a pact of mutual assistance with the Soviet Union provided it helped strengthen them, Great Britain and France.

But, on the other hand, the British and French governments are afraid that the conclusion of a real pact of mutual assistance with the U.S.S.R. may strengthen our country, the Soviet Union, which, it appears, does not answer their purpose. It must be admitted that these fears of theirs outweighed other considerations. Only in this way can we understand the position of Poland, who acts on the instructions of Great Britain and France.

I shall now pass to the Soviet-German Non-Aggression Pact.

The decision to conclude a non-aggression pact between the U.S.S.R. and Germany was adopted after military negotiations with France and Great Britain had reached an impasse owing to the insuperable differences I have mentioned. As the negotiations had shown that the conclusion of a pact of mutual assistance could not be expected, we could not but explore other possibilities of ensuring peace and eliminating the danger of war between Germany and the U.S.S.R. If the British and French governments refused to reckon with this, that is their affair. It is our duty to think of the interests of the Soviet people, the interests of the Union of Soviet Socialist Republics. All the more since we are firmly convinced that the interests of the U.S.S.R. coincides with the fundamental interests of the peoples of other countries. But that is only one side of the matter.

Another circumstance was required before the Soviet-German Non-Aggression Pact could come into existence. It was necessary that in her foreign policy Germany should make a turn towards good-neighborly relations with the Soviet Union.

Only when this second condition was fulfilled, only when it became clear to us that the German Government desired to change its foreign policy so as to secure an improvement of relations with the U.S.S.R. was the basis found for the conclusion of a Soviet-German Non-Aggression Pact. Everybody knows that during the last six years, ever since the National-Socialists [Nazis] came into power, political relations between Germany and the U.S.S.R. have been strained. Everybody also knows that despite the differences of outlook and political systems, the Soviet Government endeavored to maintain normal business and political relations with Germany. There is no need now to revert to individual incidents of these relations during recent years, which are well known to you.

I must, however, recall the explanation of our foreign policy given several months ago at the Eighteenth Party Congress. Speaking of our tasks in the realm of foreign policy, Stalin defined our attitude to other countires as follows:

1. To continue the policy of peace and of strengthening business relations with all countries:

2. To be cautious and not to allow our country to be drawn into conflicts by war-mongers who are accustomed to have others pull the chestnuts out of the fire for them.

As you see, Stalin declared in conclusion that the Soviet Union stands for strengthening business relations with all countries. But at the same time Stalin warned us against warmongers who are anxious in their own interests to involve our country in conflicts with other countries.

Exposing the hullabaloo raised in the British, French, and American press about Germany's "plans" for the seizure of the Ukraine, Stalin said:

It looks as if the object of this suspicious hullabaloo was to incense the Soviet Union against Germany, to poison the atmosphere and to provoke a conflict with Germany without any visible grounds.

As you see, Stalin hit the nail on the head when he exposed the machinations of the Western European politicians who were trying to set Germany and the Soviet Union at loggerheads.

It must be confessed that there were some short-sighted people even in our own country who, carried away by oversimplified anti-fascist propaganda, forgot about this provocative work of our enemies. Mindful of this, Stalin even then suggested the possibility of other, unhostile, good-neighborly relations between Germany and the U.S.S.R. It can now be seen that on the whole Germany correctly understood these statements of Stalin and drew practical conclusions from them. The conclusion of the Soviet-German Non-Aggression Pact shows that Stalin's historic pre-vision has been brilliantly confirmed.

In the spring of this year the German Government made a proposal to resume commercial and credit negotiations. Soon after, the negotiations were resumed. By making mutual concessions, we succeeded in reaching an agreement. As you know, this agreement was signed on August 19. This is not the first commercial and credit agreement concluded with Germany under her present government.

But this agreement differs favorably not only from the 1935 agreement but from all previous agreements, not to mention the fact that we had no economic agreement equally advantageous with Great Britain, France or any other country. The agreement is advantageous to us because its credit conditions (a seven-year credit) enables us to order a considerable additional quantity of such equipment as we need. By this agreement, the U.S.S.R. undertakes to sell to Germany a definite quantity of our surplus raw materials for her industry, which fully answers the interests of the U.S.S.R.

Why should we reject such an advantageous economic agreement? Surely not to please those who are generally averse to the Soviet Union having advantageous economic agreements with other countries? And it is clear that the commercial and credit agreement with Germany is fully in accord with the economic interests and defense needs of the Soviet Union. This agreement is fully in accord with the decision of the Eighteenth Congress of our Party, which approved Stalin's statement as to the need for "strengthening business relations with all countries."

When, however, the German government expressed the desire to improve political relations as well, the Soviet government had no grounds for refusing. This gave rise to the question of concluding a non-aggression pact.

Voices are now being heard testifying to the lack of understanding of the most simple reasons for the improvement of political relations between the Soviet Union and Germany which has begun. For example, people ask with an air of innocence how the Soviet Union could consent to improve political relations with a state of a fascist type. "Is that possible?" they ask. But they forget that this is not a question of our attitude towards the internal regime of another country but of the foreign relations between the two states. They forget that we hold the position of not interfering in the internal affairs of other countries and, correspondingly, of not tolerating interference in our own internal affairs. Furthermore, they forget the important principle of our foreign policy which was formulated by Stalin at the Eighteenth Party Congress as follows:

We stand for peace and the strengthening of business relations with all countries. That is our position; and we adhere to this position as long as these countries maintain like relations with the Soviet Union, and as long as they make no attempt to trespass on the interests of our country.

The meaning of these words is quite clear: the Soviet Union strives to maintain friendly relations with all non-Soviet countries, provided that these countries maintain a like attitude towards the Soviet Union. In our foreign policy towards non-Soviet countries, we have always been guided by Lenin's well-known principle of the peaceful coexistence of the Soviet state and of capitalist countries. . . .

Since 1926, the political basis of our relations with Germany has been the treaty of neutrality which was already extended by the present German Government in 1933. This treaty of neutrality remains in force to this day. The Soviet Government considered it desirable even before this to take a further step towards improving political relations with Germany, but the circumstances have been such that this has become possible only now.

It is true that it is not a pact of mutual assistance that is in question, as in the case of the Anglo-French-Soviet negotiations, but only of a non-aggression pact. Nevertheless, conditions being what they are, it is difficult to overestimate the international importance of the Soviet-German pact. That is why we favored the visit of Von Ribbentrop, the German Minister for Foreign Affairs, to Moscow.

August 23, 1939, the day the Soviet-German Non-Aggression Pact was signed, is to be regarded as a date of great historical importance. The Non-Aggression Pact between the U.S.S.R. and Germany marks a turning point in the history of Europe, and not only of Europe. Only yesterday the German fascists were pursuring a foreign policy hostile to us. Yes, only yesterday we were enemies in the sphere of foreign relations. Today, however, the situation has changed and we are enemies no longer.

The art of politics in the sphere of foreign relations does not consist in increasing the number of enemies for one's country. On the contrary, the art of politics in this sphere is to reduce the number of such enemies and to make the enemies of yesterday good neighbors, maintaining peaceable relations with one another.

History has shown that enmity and wars between our country and Germany have been to the detriment of our countries, not to their benefit. Russia and Germany suffered most of all countries in the war of 1914-1918. Therefore the interests of the peoples of the Soviet-Union and Germany stand in need of peaceable relations. The Soviet-German Non-Aggression Pact puts an end to enmity between Germany and the U.S.S.R. and this is in the interests of both countries. The fact that our outlooks and political systems differ must not and cannot be obstacles to the establishment of good political relations between both states, just as like differences are not impediments to good political relations which the U.S.S.R. maintains with other non-Soviet capitalist countries. Only enemies of Germany and the U.S.S.R. can strive to create and foment enmity between the peoples of these countries. We have always stood for amity between the peoples of the U.S.S.R. and Germany, for the growth and development of friendship between the peoples of the Soviet Union and the German People.

The importance of the Soviet-German Non-Aggression Pact lies in the fact that the two largest states of Europe have agreed to put an end to the enmity between them, to eliminate the menace of war and live at peace one with the other, narrowing thereby the zone of possible military conflicts in Europe. Even if military conflicts in Europe should prove unavoidable, the scope of hostilities will now be restricted. Only the instigators of a general European war can be displeased by this state of affairs, those who under the mask of pacifism would like to ignite a general conflagration in Europe.

The Soviet-German Pact has been the object of numerous attacks in the English, French and American press. Conspicuous in these efforts are certain "Socialist" newspapers, diligent servitors of "their" national capitalism, servitors of gentlemen who pay them decently. It is clear that the real truth cannot be expected from gentry of this caliber. Attempts are being made to spread the fiction that the signing of the Soviet-German Pact disrupted the negotiations with England and France on a mutual assistance pact. This lie has already been nailed in the interview given by Voroshilov.

In reality, as you know, the very reverse is true. The Soviet Union signed the Non-Aggression Pact with Germany, for one thing, in view of the fact that the negotiations with France and England had run into insuperable differences and ended in failure through the fault of the ruling classes of England and France.

Finally, there are wiseacres who construe from the pact more than is written in it. For this purpose, all kinds of conjectures and hints are mooted in order to cast doubt on the pact in one or another country. But all this merely speaks for the hopeless impotence of the enemies of the pact who are exposing themselves more and more as enemies of both the Soviet Union and Germany, striving to provoke war between these countries.

In all this, we find fresh corroboration of Stalin's warning that we must be particularly cautious with warmongers who are accustomed to have others pull the chestnuts out of the fire for them. We must be on guard against those who see an advantage to themselves in bad relations between the U.S.S.R. and Germany, in enmity between them, and who do not want peace and good neighborly relations between Germany and the Soviet Union.

We can understand why this policy is being pursued by out-and-out imperialists. But we cannot ignore such facts as the especial zeal with which some leaders of the Socialist Parties of Great Britain and France have recently distinguished themselves in this matter. And these gentlemen have really gone the whole hog, and no mistake. These people positively demand that the U.S.S.R. get itself involved in war against Germany on the side of Great Britain. Have not these rabid warmongers taken leave of their senses? It is really difficult for these gentlemen to understand the purpose of the Soviet-German Non-Aggression Pact, on the strength of which the U.S.S.R. is not obligated to involve itself in war either on the side of Great Britain against Germany or on the side of Germany against Great Britain? Is it really difficult to understand that the U.S.S.R. is pursuing and will continue to pursue its own independent policy, based on the interests of the peoples of the U.S.S.R. and only their interests?

If these gentlemen have such an uncontrollable desire to fight, let them do their own fighting without the Soviet Union. We would see what fighting stuff they are made of.

In our eyes, in the eyes of the entire Soviet people, these are just as much enemies of peace as all other instigators of war in Europe. Only those who desire a grand new slaughter, a new holocaust of nations, only they want to set the Soviet Union and Germany at loggerheads, they are the only people who want to destroy the incipient restoration of good-neighborly relations between the peoples of the U.S.S.R. and Germany.

The Soviet Union signed a pact with Germany, fully assured that peace between the peoples of the U.S.S.R. and Germany is in the interests of all peoples, in the interests of universal peace. Every sincere supporter of peace will realize the truth of this. This pact corresponds to the fundamental interests of the working people of the Soviet Union and cannot weaken our vigilance in defense of these interests. This pact is backed by firm confidence in our real forces, in their complete preparedness to meet any aggression against the U.S.S.R.

This pact, like the unsuccessful Ango-French-Soviet negotiations, proves that no important questions of international relations, and questions of Eastern Europe even less, can be settled without the active participation of the Soviet Union, that any attempts to shut out the Soviet Union and decide such questions behind its back are doomed to failure.

The Soviet-German Non-Aggression Pact spells a new turn in the development of Europe, a turn towards improvement of relations between the two largest states of Europe. This pact not only eliminates the menace of war with Germany, narrows down the zone of possible hostilities in Europe, and serves thereby the cause of universal peace: it must open to us new possibilities of increasing our strength, of further consolidation of our position, of further growth of the influence of the Soviet Union on international developments.

There is no need to dwell here on the separate clauses of the pact. The Council of People's Commissars has reason to hope that the pact will meet with your approval as a document of cardinal importance to the U.S.S.R.

The Council of People's Commissars submits the Soviet-German Non-Aggression pact to the Supreme Soviet and proposes that it be ratified.

STALIN

Report Delivered on the 24th Anniversary of the October Revolution November 6, 1941

Introduction Hitler's surprise attack on the USSR in
June 1941 exposed the fundamental failure of Stalin's
diplomacy in dealing with Hitlerite Germany since 1933.
The USSR now faced a tremendously powerful German
army which had conquered Europe, and was saved from
isolation only by the fact that Britain and the United
States immediately allied themselves with the USSR
against Hitler. Their action—which Stalin says confounded
Hitler, and on which Stalin himself could not have
calculated—saved the USSR from the worst consequences
of his policies. Stalin's speech combines an effort to
establish the grounds of confidence in ultimate victory
with a realistic assessment of the dangers arising from the
German invasion—for which Soviet propaganda had failed
to prepare the people. He says that the German army has
been favored in its Russian campaign because it is fighting
on only a single front in Europe and has superiority in
materiel (specifically tanks), which it obtained through
German control of the industry of most of Europe. He
fails to mention that this is the result of his own policies

106

in signing the Pact with Hitler in 1939 and subsequently providing economic assistance to German's war effort.

Because Soviet propaganda against fascist Germany had ceased with the signing of the Pact of 1939, Stalin now had to explain to the Soviet people that National Socialist Germany was not socialist in the Soviet sense, and was actually an inferior regime to the "democracies" allied with the USSR. He thus restored the distinction between the two kinds of capitalist state which between 1939 and 1941 had been obscured.

What are the grounds of Stalin's confidence in final victory? There is the struggle of the conquered peoples of Europe against their German masters and the opposition of the German people to the war. Actually, both proved less significant than Stalin had supposed. (He also says, incorrectly, that German reserves of man-power are giving out.) Ultimately, however, Stalin bases his confidence of victory on a simple material factor which is decisive: the great industrial superiority of the allies over Germany. (What a far cry this is from Mao's professed belief in the superiority of man over arms!)

In his brief statement of war aims, Stalin gives assurance that the USSR will allow the liberated nations of East Europe to organize their lives freely as they think fit, a policy which, if carried out, would have avoided the cold war.

. . . I have already said in one of my public speeches at the beginning of the war that the war has created a grave menace for our country, that serious danger threatens our country, that we must understand and realize this danger and place all our work on a war footing. Today, after four months of war, I must emphatically state that far from having abated, this danger is greater than ever. The enemy has seized a large part of the Ukraine, Byelorussia, Moldavia, Lithuania, Latvia, Esthonia and a number of other regions, has forced his way into the Donets Basin, hangs like a black cloud over Leningrad and is threatening our glorious capital, Moscow. The German-fascist invaders are plundering our country, destroying the towns and villages created by the efforts of the workers, farmers and intellectuals. Hitler's hordes are slaughtering and outraging the civilian population of our country showing no mercy to women, children or the aged. Our brothers in the regions of our country seized by the Germans are groaning beneath the yoke of the German oppressors.

Rivers of enemy blood have been shed by the men of our Army and Navy, who are defending the honour and liberty of their native land, manfully repulsing the attacks of a bestial enemy and displaying examples of valour and heroism. But the enemy stops at no sacrifice, he does not care one iota for the blood of his soldiers, he keeps flinging ever fresh detachments into the field to replace those that have been shattered, and is straining every effort to capture Leningrad and Moscow before the advent of winter, for he knows that winter bodes him no good.

In four months of war we have lost 350,000 killed and 378,000 missing and our wounded number 1,020,000. In this same period the enemy has lost over four and a half million men, killed, wounded and taken prisoner.

There can be no doubt that as a result of four months of war Germany, whose reserves of man-power are already giving out, has been far more weakened than the Soviet Union, whose reserves are only just beginning to come into full play.

Failure of the "Blitzkrieg"

In launching their attack on our country the German-fascist invaders calculated that they would be able to "finish off" the Soviet Union for certain in one and a half or two months, and in this short period would succeed in reaching the Urals. It must be said that the Germans made no concealment of this plan for a "lightning" victory. On the contrary, they gave it the utmost publicity. The facts, however, have revealed the utter frivolity and goundlessness of this "lightning" plan. Today this crazy plan must be regarded as having definitely failed.

How is it to be explained that the "lightning war," which succeeded in Western Europe, failed and collapsed in the East?

What did the German-fascist strategists count on when they asserted that they would finish off the Soviet Union in two months and reach the Urals in this short period?

They seriously counted in the first place on creating a universal coalition against the U.S.S.R., on enlisting Great Britain and the U.S.A. in this coalition, after having frightened the ruling circles of these countries with the bogey of revolution, and thus completely isolating our country from other powers. The Germans knew that their policy of playing on the contradictions among the classes of the individual states, and between these states and the Soviet country, had already yielded fruit in France, the rulers of which, having allowed themselves to be frightened by the bogey of revolution, in their fright laid their country at the feet of Hitler and renounced all resistance. The German-fascist strategists thought that the same thing would happen in the case of Great Britain and the United States. The notorious Hess was in fact sent to England by the German-fascists precisely in order to persuade the English statesmen to join a universal campaign against the U.S.S.R. But the Germans sadly miscalculated. Notwithstanding all Hess's efforts, Great Britain and the United States, far from joining the campaign of the German-fascist robbers against the U.S.S.R., proved to be in one camp with the U.S.S.R. against Hitlerite Germany. Far from being isolated, the U.S.S.R. acquired new allies in the shape of Great Britain, the United States and countries occupied by the Germans. It turned out that the German policy of playing on contradictions and using the bogey of revolution has lost its effect and is unsuitable in the new situation. And not only is it unsuitable, but it is even fraught with grave danger for the German robbers, for under the new conditions of the war it leads to diametrically opposite results.

Secondly, the Germans counted on the Soviet system being unstable, on the Soviet hinterland being unstable, and believed that after the first serious blow and the first reverses suffered by the Red Army conflicts would break out between the workers and farmers, squabbling would begin among the peoples of the U.S.S.R., uprisings would occur, and the country would fall to pieces—which it was expected would facilitate the advance of the German invaders to the Urals. But here, too, the Germans sadly miscalculated. Far from weakening, the reverses of the Red Army only served still further to strengthen both the alliance of the workers and farmers and the friendship of the peoples of the U.S.S.R. More, they converted the family of peoples of the U.S.S.R. into a single and unshakable camp, selflessly supporting their Red Army and their Red Navy. Never has the Soviet hinterland been as solid as it is today. It is quite likely that if any other country had lost as much territory as we have lost now it would not have stood the test and would have fallen into decline. If the Soviet system has stood the test so well and has even strengthened its hinterland, it must mean that the Soviet system is now a most stable one.

Lastly, the German robbers counted on the weakness of the Red Army and Red Navy, believing that the German army and German navy would succeed at the very first blow in overwhelming and scattering our army and navy and opening the way for an unhindered advance into the depths of our country. But here, too, the Germans sadly miscalculated, overrating their own strength and underrating our army and navy.

Of course, our army and navy are still young, they have been fighting for only four months, they have not yet succeeded in becoming a thoroughly seasoned army and navy, whereas they are confronted by the seasoned navy and seasoned army of the Germans, who have already been at war for two years. But, in the first place, the morale of our army is higher than that of the German, for it is defending its native land from alien invaders and believes in the justice of its cause, whereas the German army is waging a war of annexation, is plundering a foreign country, and is unable to believe even for a moment in the justice of its vile cause. There can be no doubt that the idea of defending their native land, which is what our people are fighting for, is bound to breed, and actually is breeding in our army heroes who are cementing the Red Army, whereas the idea of seizing and plundering a foreign country, which is what the Germans are in fact waging the war for, is bound to breed, and actually is breeding in the German army professional looters, devoid of all moral principles and corrupting the German army. Secondly, as it advances into the interior of our country, the German army is moving farther and farther away from its own German hinterland, is forced to operate in hostile surroundings, is forced to create a new hinterland in an alien country, a hinterland, moreover, that is being disrupted by our guerillas—all of which is radically disorganizing the supply of the German army, causes it to fear its own hinterland, and destroys its faith in the stability of its position, whereas our army is operating in its own native surroundings, enjoys the constant support of its hinterland, is assured supplies of men, munitions and food, and has a profound faith in its hinterland. That is why our army has proved to be stronger than the Germans anticipated and the German army weaker than might have been expected judging by the boastful self-advertisement of the German invaders. The defence of Leningrad and Moscow, where our divisions lately wiped out about a score and a half of seasoned German divisions, shows that in the fire of our patriotic war there are being forged, and already have been forged, new Soviet men and commanders, airmen, artillerymen, trench mortar men, tankmen, infantrymen and seamen, who tomorrow will become the terror of the German army.

There can be no doubt that all these factors, taken together, predetermine the inevitable collapse of the "blitzkrieg" in the East.

All that, of course, is true. But it is likewise true that alongside these favourable factors, there are a number of factors unfavourable to the Red Army, as a result of which our army is suffering temporary reverses, is obliged to retreat and to surrender a number of regions of our country to the enemy.

What are these unfavourable factors? What are the reasons for the temporary military reverses of the Red Army?

One of the reasons for the reverses of the Red Army is the absence of a ·second front in Europe against the German-fascist troops. The fact of the matter is that at the present time there are no armies of Great Britain or the United States of America on the European continent to wage war against the German-fascist troops, with the result that the Germans are not compelled to divide their forces and to wage war on two fronts, in the West and in the East. Well, the effect of this is that the Germans, considering their rear in the West secure, are able to send all their troops and the troops of their allies in Europe against our country. The situation at present is such that our country is waging the war of liberation singlehanded, without military help from anyone, against the combined forces of Germans, Finns, Rumanians, Italians and Hungarians. The Germans plume themselves on their temporary successes and are lavish in the praises of their army, claiming that it can always defeat the Red Army in single combat. But the Germans' claims are nothing but an empty boast, for it is incomprehensible why in that case the Germans have resorted to the aid of the Finns, Rumanians, Italians and Hungarians against the Red Army, which is fighting absolutely singlehanded without any military help from outside. There can be no doubt that the absence of a second front in Europe against the Germans makes the position of the German army considerably easier. But neither can there be any doubt that the appearance of a second front on the European continent—and it must unquestionably appear in the near future—will materially ease the situation of our army to the detriment of the German army.

Another reason for the temporary reverses of our army is our lack of an adequate number of tanks and partly of aircraft. In modern warfare it is very hard for infantry to fight without tanks and without adequate aircraft protection. Our aircraft are superior in quality to the German, and our splendid airmen have covered themselves with glory as dauntless fighters. But we still have less airplanes than the Germans. Our tanks are superior in quality to the German, and our glorious tankmen and artillerymen have on more than one occasion put the vaunted troops of the Germans, with their numerous tanks, to flight. But we still have several times less tanks than the Germans. Therein lies the secret of the temporary successes of the German army. It cannot be said that our tank-building industry is working badly and is supplying our front with few tanks. No, it is working very well and is producing quite a number of splended tanks. But the Germans are producing far more tanks, for they now have at their disposal not only their own tank-building industry, but also the industry of Czechoslovakia, Belgium, Holland and France. Were it not for this the Red Army would long ago have smashed the German army, which never ventures into action without tanks and cannot withstand the onslaught of our troops if it has not a superiority in tanks.

There is only one way of nullifying the German's superiority in tanks and thus radically improving the position of our army, and that is, not only to increase the output of tanks in our country several times over, but also sharply to increase the production of anti-tank aircraft, anti-tank rifles and guns, and anti-tank grenades and trench mortars, and to build as large a number as possible of anti-tank traps and every other kind of tank obstacle.

That is the task now.

We can accomplish this task, and we must accomplish it at all costs!

In our country the German robbers, i.e., the Hitlerites, are usually called fascists. The Hitlerites, it seems, consider this wrong and insist on calling themselves "National-Socialists." Hence, the Germans are trying to assure us that the Hitlerite party, the party of German robbers, which is plundering Europe and has engineered the dastardly attack on our socialist country, is a socialist party. Is this possible? What can there be in common between socialism and the bestial Hitlerite robbers who are plundering and oppressing the nations of Europe?

Can the Hitlerites be regarded as nationalists? No, they cannot. Actually the Hitlerites now are not nationalists but imperialists. As long as the Hitlerites were engaged in assembling the German lands and reuniting the Rhine district, Austria, etc., there may have been some ground for calling them nationalists. But after they seized foreign territories and enslaved European nations—the Czechs, Slovaks, Poles, Norwegians, Danes, Hollanders, Belgians, Frenchmen, Serbs, Greeks, Ukrainians, Byelorussians, the inhabitants of the Baltic countries, etc.—and began to reach out for world domination, the Hitlerite party ceased to be a nationalist party, for from that moment on it became an imperialist, predatory, oppressor party.

The Hitlerite party is a party of imperialists, and of the most rapacious and predatory imperialists in the world at that.

Can the Hitlerites be regarded as socialists? No, they cannot. Actually the Hitlerites are the sworn enemies of socialism, arrant reactionaries and Black-Hundreds who have robbed the working class and the peoples of Europe of the most elementary democratic liberties. In order to cover up their reactionary, Black-Hundred essence the Hitlerites denounce the internal regime of England and America as a plutocratic regime. But in England and the United States there are elementary democratic liberties, there exist trade unions of workers and salaried employees, there exist workers' parties, there exist parliaments; whereas in Germany, under the Hitler regime, all these institutions have been destroyed. One need but compare these two sets of facts to perceive the reactionary essence of the Hitler regime and the utter hypocrisy of the German-fascist buncombe about a plutocratic regime in England and in America. In point of fact the Hitler regime is a copy of the reactionary regime which existed in Russia under tsardom. As we know, the Hitlerites suppress the rights of the workers, the rights of the intellectuals and the rights of nations as readily as the tsarist regime suppressed them, they organize the medieval Jewish pogroms as readily as the tsarist regime did.

The Hitlerite party is a party of enemies of democratic liberties, a party of medieval reaction and Black-Hundred pogroms.

And if these brazen imperialists and arrant reactionaries still continue to don the toga of "nationalists" and "socialists," they do so for the purpose of deceiving the people, of hoodwinking the credulous and of using the flag of "nationalism" and "socialism" to cover up their predatory imperialist essence.

The German robbers want a war of extermination with the peoples of the U.S.S.R. Well, if the Germans want a war of extermination, they will get it.

From now on our task, the task of the peoples of the U.S.S.R., the task of the men, commanders and the political staff of our Army and our Navy is to exterminate to a man all the Germans who have intruded into the territory of our country as its invaders.

No mercy should be shown the German invaders!

Death to the German invaders!

The very fact that in their moral degradation the German robbers, who have lost every semblance of human beings, have long ago sunk to the level of wild beasts tells us that they have doomed themselves to inevitable destruction.

But the inevitable destruction of the Hitlerite robbers and their armies is not determined by moral factors alone.

There exist three other basic factors, which are operating more powerfully with each day that passes, and which are bound to lead in the not distant future to the inevitable defeat of Hitler's robber imperialism.

Firstly, there is the instability of the *European* hinterland of imperialist Germany, the instability of the "New Order" in Europe. The German robbers have enslaved the peoples of the European continent—from France to the Soviet Baltic countries, from Norway, Denmark, Belgium, Holland and Soviet Byelorussia to the Balkans and the Soviet Ukraine; they have robbed them of their elementary democratic liberties; they have deprived them of the right to order their own destiny; they have taken away their grain, meat and raw materials; they have turned them into their slaves; they have crucified the Poles, Czechs, Serbs, and decided that, having achieved supremacy in Europe, they can now use it as a basis for building up Germany's world supremacy. That is what they call the "New Order in Europe." But what is this "basis," what is this "New Order"? Only the self-admiring Hitlerite fools fail to see that the "New Order" in Europe and the infamous "basis" of this order represent a volcano which is ready to erupt at any moment and overwhelm the German imperialist house of cards. They talk about Napoleon and say that Hitler is acting like him, that he resembles Napoleon in every way. But, firstly, they should not forget Napoleon's fate. And, secondly, Hitler no more resembles Napoleon than a kitten resembles a lion. For Napoleon fought against the forces of reaction and relied on progressive forces, whereas Hitler, on the contrary, relies on the forces of reaction and fights the forces of progress. Only the Hitlerite fools in Berlin fail to realize that the enslaved peoples of Europe will fight and revolt against Hitler's tyranny. Who can doubt that the U.S.S.R., Great Britain and the U.S.A. will give every support to the peoples of Europe in their struggle for liberation against Hitler's tyranny?

Secondly, there is the instability of the *German* hinterland of the Hitlerite robbers. So long as the Hitlerites were engaged in the assembling of Germany, which had been carved up by the Versailles Treaty, they could enjoy the support of the German people, who were inspired by the ideal of the restoration of Germany. But after this aim had been achieved and the Hitlerites entered the road of imperialism, of the seizure of foreign lands and the subjugation of foreign nations, thereby converting the peoples of Europe and the peoples of the U.S.S.R. into sworn enemies of present day Germany, a profound change of heart took place among the German people—against the continuation of the war, in favour of ending the war. Over two years of sanguinary war, the end of which is not in sight; the millions of human lives sacrificed; starvation; impoverishment; epidemics; the atmosphere of hostility to the Germans all around them; Hitler's stupid policy, which has turned the peoples of the U.S.S.R. into sworn enemies of present-day Germany—all this could not but set the German people against the unnecessary and ruinous war. Only the Hitlerite fools fail to see that not only the European hinterland but also the German hinterland of the German troops represents a volcano which is ready to erupt and overwhelm the Hitlerite adentures.

Lastly, there is the coalition of the U.S.S.R., Great Britain and the United States of America against the German fascist imperialists. It is a fact that Great Britain, the United States of America and the Soviet Union have united into a single camp, which has set itself the aim of defeating the Hitlerite imperialists and their robber armies. Modern war is a war of engines. The war will be won by the side that has an overwhelming preponderance in the output of engines. The combined engine output of the U.S.A., Great Britain and the U.S.S.R. is at least three times as large as that of Germany. That is one of the grounds for the inevitable doom of Hitler's robber imperialism.

The recent three-power conference in Moscow, attended by Lord Beaverbrook as representative of Great Britain and by Mr. Harriman as representative of the United States, has decided to give our country systematic aid in the way of tanks and aircraft. As you know, we have already begun to receive tanks and airplanes in accordance with that decision. Even prior to that England undertook to supply us with materials of which there is a scarcity in our country, such as aluminium, lead, tin, nickel and rubber. If we add the fact that a few days ago the United States of America decided to grant the Soviet Union a loan of 1,000,000,000 dollars, we can confidently state that the coalition of the United States of America, Great Britain and the U.S.S.R. is something real, and that it is growing and will continue to grow to the benefit of our common cause of liberation.

Such are the factors which determine the irrevocable doom of German fascist imperialism.

Lenin distinguished between two kinds of war—predatory, and, consequently, unjust wars, and wars of liberation, just wars.

The Germans are now waging a predatory war, an unjust war, for the purpose of seizing foreign territory and subjugating foreign peoples. That is why all honest people must rise against the German robbers, as enemies.

Unlike Hitlerite Germany, the Soviet Union and its allies are waging a war of liberation, a just war, for the purpose of liberating the enslaved peoples of Europe and the U.S.S.R. from Hitler's tyranny. That is why all honest people must support the armies of the U.S.S.R., Great Britain and the other allies, as armies of liberation.

We have not, and cannot have, any such war aims as the seizure of foreign territories and the subjugation of foreign peoples—whether it be peoples and territories of Europe or peoples and territories of Asia, including Iran. Our first aim is to liberate our territories and our peoples from the German-fascist yoke.

We have not, and cannot have, any such war aims as that of imposing our will and our regime upon the Slavonic or other enslaved nations of Europe, who are expecting our help. Our aim is to help these nations in the struggle of liberation they are waging against Hitler's tyranny and then to leave it to them quite freely to organize their life on their lands as they think fit. There must be no interference whatever in the internal affairs of other nations!

But if these aims are to be achieved, we must crush the military might of the German invaders, we must destroy, to the last man, the German forces of occupation who have intruded into our country for the purpose of enslaving it.

STALIN

Election Speech
February 9, 1946

Introduction This is one of the very few extended speeches Stalin gave after World War II, and one of the key documents for analysis of Soviet foreign policy. Though Stalin does not here engage in the vituperative discourse which later became characteristic of the cold war, he makes it clear that Soviet policy is premised on the development of hostile relations among the victorious powers.

Against the opinion of Winston Churchill and others that the war could have been averted, Stalin contends that it was inevitable. This of course exculpates him from a possible charge that his mistakes helped to precipitate the war. The implications, however, are more far-reaching. Since the war was an inevitable consequence of the existence of capitalism, and capitalism continues to exist, war must also be expected in the future.

From this reaffirmation of the Leninist theory that capitalism in the imperialist stage of development inevitably gives rise to war, Stalin evidently drew an important practical conclusion: it is necessary to raise the

Soviet economy to a level where "our homeland will be guaranteed against all possible accidents." Achievement of this level requires the tripling of pre-war industrial production by 1960. Now, in view of the devastated condition of the Soviet economy in the aftermath of war, this program entailed a rate of industrial growth comparable to that achieved by the USSR during the decade of the 'thirties. The Soviet people would again have to make sacrifices like those of the decade before the War.

After what the Soviet people had just suffered in war, new sacrifices could be justified only by the argument that there was a serious risk of war between the victorious powers in the years ahead. Stalin did not argue this explicitly, but his reaffirmation of Lenin's doctrine that war was inevitable under capitalism may have been intended to serve the same purpose. While this speech is not a declaration of cold war, it seems intelligible only if one supposes that Stalin anticipated the cold war.

Comrades!

Eight years have elapsed since the last election to the Supreme Soviet. This was a period abounding in events of decisive moment. The first four years passed in intensive effort on the part of Soviet men and women to fulfill the Third Five-Year Plan. The second four years embrace the events of the war against the German and Japanese aggressors, the events of the Second World War. Undoubtedly, the war was the principal event in the past period.

It would be wrong to think that the Second World War was a casual occurrence or the result of mistakes of any particular statesmen, though mistakes undoubtedly were made. Actually, the war was the inevitable result of the development of world economic and political forces on the basis of modern monopoly capitalism. Marxists have declared more than once that the capitalist system of world economy harbors elements of general crises and armed conflicts and that, hence, the development of world capitalism in our time proceeds not in the form of smooth and even progress but through crises and military catastrophes.

The fact is, that the unevenness of development of the capitalist countries usually leads in time to violent disturbance of equilibrium in the world system of capitalism, that group of capitalist countries which considers itself worse provided than others with raw materials and markets usually making attempts to alter the situation and repartition the "spheres of influence" in its favor by armed force. The result is a splitting of the capitalist world into two hostile camps and war between them.

Perhaps military catastrophes might be avoided if it were possible for raw materials and markets to be periodically redistributed among the various countries in accordance with their economic importance, by agreement and peaceable settlement. But that is impossible to do under present capitalist conditions of the development of world economy.

Thus the First World War was the result of the first crisis of the capitalist system of world economy, and the Second World War was the result of a second crisis.

That does not mean of course that the Second World War is a copy of the first. On the contrary, the Second World War differs materially from the first in nature. It must be borne in mind that before attacking the Allied countries the principal fascist states—Germany, Japan and Italy—destroyed the last vestiges of bourgeois democratic liberties at home, established a brutal terrorist regime in their own countries, rode roughshod over the principles of sovereignty and free development of small countries, proclaimed a policy of seizure of alien territories as their own policy and declared for all to hear that they were out for world domination and the establishment of a fascist regime throughout the world.

Moreover, by the seizure of Czechoslovakia and of the central areas of China, the Axis states showed that they were prepared to carry out their threat of enslaving all freedom-loving nations. In view of this, unlike the First World War, the Second World War against the Axis states from the very outset assumed the character of an anti-fascist war, a war of liberation, one the aim of which was also the restoration of democratic liberties. The entry of the Soviet Union into the war against the Axis states could only enhance, and indeed did enhance, the anti-fascist and liberation character of the Second World War.

It was on this basis that the anti-fascist coalition of the Soviet Union, the United States of America, Great Britain and other freedom-loving states came into being—a coalition which subsequently played a decisive part in defeating the armed forces of the Axis states.

That is how matters stand as regards the origin and character of the Second World War.

By now I should think everyone admits that the war really was not and could not have been an accident in the life of nations, that actually this war became the war of nations for their existence, and that for this reason it could not be a quick lightning affair.

As regards our country, for it this war was the most bitter and arduous of all wars in the history of our Motherland.

But the war was not only a curse. It was at the same time a great school in which all the forces of the people were tried and tested. The war laid bare all facts and events in the rear and at the front, it tore off relentlessly all veils and coverings which had concealed the true faces of the states, governments and parties and exposed them to view without a mask or embellishment, with all their shortcomings and merits.

And so, how is our victory over our enemies to be understood? What is the significance of this victory as regards the State and the development of the internal forces of our country?

Our victory means, first of all, that our Soviet social order has triumphed, that the Soviet social order has successfully passed the ordeal in the fire of war and has proved its unquestionable vitality.

* * *

More than that, there is no longer any question today whether the Soviet social order is or is not capable of enduring, for after the object lessons of war none of the skeptics ventures any longer to voice doubts as to the vitality of the Soviet social order. The point now is that the Soviet social order has shown itself more stable and capable of enduring than a non-Soviet social order, that the Soviet social order is a form of organization, a society superior to any non-Soviet social order.

Second, our victory means that our Soviet state system has triumphed, that our multinational Soviet State has stood all the trials of war and has proved its vitality.

* * *

Today it is no longer a question of the vitality of the Soviet state system, for that vitality can no longer be doubted; the point now is that the Soviet state system has proved itself a model for a multinational state, has proved that the Soviet state system is a system of state organization in which the national question and the problem of collaboration among nations has been settled better than in any other multinational state.

Third, our victory means that the Soviet armed forces have triumphed, that our Red Army has triumphed, that the Red Army bore up heroically under all the trials of war, utterly routed the armies of our enemies and came out of the war as a victor.

* * *

Today we can say that the war has refuted all such statements as unfounded and absurd. The war showed that the Red Army is not a "colossus with feet of clay," but a first-class contemporary army with fully modern armaments, highly experienced commanding personnel and high moral and fighting qualities. It must not be forgotten that the Red Army is the army that utterly routed the Germany army which but yesterday was striking terror into the armies of the European states.

* * *

It would be a mistake to think that such a historic victory could have been won if the whole country had not prepared beforehand for active defense. It would be no less mistaken to imagine that such preparations could be carried through in a short time—in the space of some three or four years. It would be a still greater mistake to say that we won only owing to the gallantry of our troops.

Of course, victory cannot be achieved without gallantry. But gallantry alone is not enough to vanquish an enemy who has a large army, first-class armaments, well-trained officer cadres, and a fairly good organization of supplies. To meet the blow of such an enemy, to repulse him and then to inflict utter defeat upon him required, in addition to the matchless gallantry of our troops, fully up-to-date armaments and adequate quantities of them as well as well-organized supplies in sufficient quantities.

But that, in turn, necessitated having—and in adequate amounts—such elementary things as metal for the manufacture of armaments, equipment and machinery for factories, fuel to keep the factories and transport going, cotton for the manufacture of uniforms, and grain for supplying the Army.

Can it be claimed that before entering the Second World War our country already commanded the necessary minimum material potentialities for satisfying all these requirements in the main? I think it can. In order to prepare for this tremendous job we had to carry out three Five-Year Plans of national economic development. It was precisely these three Five-Year Plans that helped us to create these material potentialities. At any rate, our country's position in this respect before the Second World War, in 1940, was several times better than it was before the First World War, in 1913.

* * *

This historic transformation was accomplished in the course of three Five-Year Plan periods, beginning with 1928, the first year of the First Five-Year Plan. Up to that time we had to concern ourselves with rehabilitating our ravaged industry and healing the wounds received in the First World War and the Civil War. Moreover, if we bear in mind that the

First Five-Year Plan was fulfilled in four years, and that the fulfillment of the Third Five-Year Plan was interrupted by war in its fourth year, we find that it took only about 13 years to transform our country from an agrarian into an industrial one.

* * *

By what policy did the Communist Party succeed in providing these material potentialities in the country in such a short time?

First of all, by the Soviet policy of industrializing the country.

The Soviet method of industrializing the country differs radically from the capitalist method of industrialization. In capitalist countries industrialization usually begins with light industry. Since in light industry smaller investments are required and there is more rapid turnover of capital and since, furthermore, it is easier to make a profit there than in heavy industry, light industry serves as the first object of industrialization in these countries.

Only after a lapse of much time, in the course of which light industry accumulates profits and concentrates them in banks, does the turn of heavy industry arrive and accumulated capital begin to be transferred gradually to heavy industry in order to create conditions for its development.

But that is a lengthy process requiring an extensive period of several decades, in the course of which these countries have to wait until light industry has developed and must make shift without heavy industry. Naturally, the Communist Party could not take this course. The Party knew that a war was looming, that the country could not be defended without heavy industry, that the development of heavy industry must be undertaken as soon as possible, that to be behind with this would mean to lose out. The Party remembered Lenin's words to the effect that without heavy industry it would be impossible to uphold the country's independence, that without it the Soviet order might perish.

Accordingly, the Communist Party of our country rejected the "usual" course of industrialization and began the work of industrializing the country by developing heavy industry. It was very difficult, but not impossible. A valuable aid in this work was the nationalization of industry, and banking, which made possible the rapid accumulation and transfer of funds to heavy industry.

There can be no doubt that without this it would have been impossible to secure our country's transformation into an industrial country in such a short time.

Second, by a policy of collectivization of agriculture.

The method of collectivization proved a highly progressive method not only because it did not involve the ruination of the peasants but especially because it permitted, within a few years, the covering of the entire country with large collective farms which are able to use new machinery, take advantage of all the achievements of agronomic science and give the country greater quantities of marketable produce.

There is no doubt that without a collectivization policy we could not in such a short time have done away with the age-old backwardness of our agriculture.

It cannot be said that the Party's policy encountered no resistance. Not only backward people, such as always decry everything new, but many prominent members of the Party as well, systematically dragged the Party backward and tried by hook or by crook to divert it to the "usual" capitalist path of development. All the anti-Party machinations of the Trotskyites and the Rightists, all their "activities" in sabotaging the measures of our Government, pursued the single aim of frustrating the Party's policy and obstructing the work of industrialization and collectivization. But the Party did not yield either to the threats from one side or the wails from the other and advanced confidently regardless of everything.

Was the Communist Party able to make proper use of the material potentialities thus created in order to develop war production and provide the Red Army with the weapons it needed?

I think that it was able to do so and with maximum success.

* * *

If we leave out of account the first year of war, when the evacuation of industry to the East held up the development of war production, we see that in the remaining three years of the war the Party scored such successes as allowed it not only to furnish the front with sufficient quantities of artillery, machine guns, rifles, aircraft, tanks and ammunition, but to accumulate reserves. Moreover, it is known that in quality our weapons were not only nothing inferior to the German, but, taken on the whole, were actually superior to them.

As regards the supply of the Red Army with provisions and uniforms, it is known to all that far from experiencing any shortage in this respect, the front actually had the reserves it required.

That is how matters stand with regard to the work of the Communist Party of our country in the period up to the outbreak of war and during the war itself.

Now a few words about the Communist Party's plans of work for the immediate future. As is known these plans are set forth in the new Five-Year Plan which is shortly to be endorsed. The principal aims of the new Five-Year Plan are to rehabilitate the ravaged areas of the country, to restore the prewar level in industry and agriculture, and then to surpass this level in more or less substantial measure. To say nothing of the fact that the rationing system will shortly be abolished, special attention will be devoted to extending the production of consumer goods, to raising the living standard of the working people by steadily lowering the prices of all goods, and to the widespread construction of all manner of scientific research institutions that can give science the opportunity to develop its potentialities.

I have no doubt that if we give our scientists proper assistance they will be able in the near future not only to overtake but to surpass the achievements of science beyond the boundaries of our country.

As regards the plans for a longer period ahead, the Party means to organize a new mighty upsurge in the national economy, which would allow us to increase our industrial production, for example, three times over as compared with the prewar period. We must achieve a situation where our industry can produce annually up to 50 million tons of pig iron, up to 60 million tons of steel, up to 500 million tons of coal, and up to 60 million tons of oil. Only under such conditions can we consider that our homeland will be guaranteed against all possible accidents. That will take three more Five-Year Plans, I should think, if not more. But it can be done and we must do it.

Such is my brief report on the Communist Party's work in the recent past and its plans of work for the future.

It is for you to judge how correctly the Party has been working and whether it could not have worked better.

In conclusion, allow me to thank you for the confidence you have shown me in nominating me to the Supreme Soviet. You need not doubt that I shall do my best to justify your trust.

ZHDANOV

Report on the International Situation to the Cominform
September 22, 1947

Introduction In the eighteen months between Stalin's election speech and the founding of the Cominform, the cold war took shape. The United States and the USSR consolidated their alliances and hardened their positions towards each other. The speech of Andrei Zhdanov, then Stalin's heir presumptive, is the classic Soviet statement on the origin and significance of the cold war, and its themes and vituperative rhetoric established the basis of Soviet propaganda for the years following.

The world was perceived as two camps, just as in the early years of the Soviet regime. (The distinction between fascist and democratic capitalist states, which was held significant in the mid-thirties and again during the war years, was abandoned.) The capitalist camp was the incarnation of evil, the democratic camp, the incarnation of good.

Zhdanov called upon the newly established Cominform to help consolidate the Soviet sphere in East Europe. Within a few months, Tito's Yugoslavia was expelled from the Cominform for its unwillingness to knuckle under to Soviet control, and Czechoslovakia's ambivalent status was ended as it was compelled by the threat of civil war and armed Soviet intervention to become a new "people's democracy." At the same time, the Cominform—which included the Communist Parties of France and Italy—was called upon to prevent the consolidation of "bourgeois democracy" in West Europe. Communists and Communist-dominated labor unions responded by launching numerous political strikes, but they failed in their efforts to disrupt national life and to influence the governments' foreign policies.

The bellicosity of the Zhdanov line, particularly the charge that the imperialist camp was trying to instigate a new war, posed a problem. The Soviet people and the people of other Communist countries had just fought a terrible war, and were still working to repair its destruction. Their morale could be endangered if they believed a new war to be imminent. Zhdanov is reassuring. Although the imperialists seek a solution to their difficulties in a new war, they lack the means to bring it about. The imperialists dwell on the danger of war "to frighten the weak-nerved and unstable and to extort concessions." Since there is no immediate danger of war, there is no need to make concessions in order to avert war. The Zhdanov line implied a tough, aggressive foreign policy toward the West, based on confidence that this involved slight risk of war.

The Post-War World Situation

The end of the Second World War brought with it big changes in the world situation. The military defeat of the bloc of fascist states, the character of the war as a war of liberation from fascism, and the decisive role played by the Soviet Union in the vanquishing of the fascist aggressors sharply altered the alignment of forces between the two systems—the socialist and the capitalist—in favour of socialism.

What is the essential nature of these changes?

The principal outcome of World War II was the military defeat of Germany and Japan—the two most militaristic and aggressive of the capitalist countries. The reactionary imperialist elements all over the world, notably in Britain, America and France, had reposed great hopes in

Germany and Japan, and chiefly in Hitler Germany: firstly as in a force most capable of inflicting a blow on the Soviet Union in order to, if not having it destroyed altogether, weaken it at least and undermine its influence; secondly, as in a force capable of smashing the revolutionary labour and democratic movement in Germany herself and in all countries singled out for Nazi aggression, and thereby strengthening capitalism generally. This was the chief reason for the pre-war policy of "appeasement" and encouragement of fascist aggression, the so-called Munich policy consistently pursued by the imperialist ruling circles of Britain, France, and the United States.

But the hopes reposed by the British, French, and American imperialists in the Hitlerites were not realized. The Hitlerites proved to be weaker, and the Soviet Union and the freedom-loving nations stronger than the Munichists had anticipated. As the result of World War II the major forces of bellicose international fascist reaction had been smashed and put out of commission for a long time to come.

This was accompanied by another serious loss to the world capitalist system generally. Whereas the principal result of World War I had been that the united imperialist front was breached and that Russia dropped out of the world capitalist system, and whereas, as a consequence of the triumph of the socialist system in the U.S.S.R., capitalism ceased to be an integral, world wide economic system, World War II and the defeat of fascism, the weakening of the world position of capitalism and the enhanced strength of the anti-fascist movement resulted in a number of countries in Central and Southeastern Europe dropping out of the imperialist system. . . .

The new democratic power in Yugoslavia, Bulgaria, Rumania, Poland, Czechoslovakia, Hungary and Albania, backed by the mass of the people, was able within a minimum period to carry through such progressive democratic reforms as bourgeois democracy is no longer capable of effecting. Agrarian reform turned over the land to the peasants and led to the elimination of the landlord class. Nationalization of large-scale industry and banks, and the confiscation of the property of traitors who had collaborated with the Germans radically undermined the position of monopoly capital in these countries and redeemed the masses from imperialist bondage. Together with this, the foundation was laid of state, national ownership, and a new type of state was created—the people's republic, where the power belongs to the people, where large-scale industry, transport and banks are owned by the state, and where a bloc of the labouring classes of the population, headed by the working class, constitute a leading force. As a result, the peoples of these countries have not only torn themselves from the clutches of imperialism, but are paving the way for entry onto the path of socialist development.

The war immensely enhanced the international significance and prestige of the U.S.S.R. The U.S.S.R. was the leading force and the guiding spirit in the military defeat of Germany and Japan. The progressive democratic forces of the whole world rallied around the Soviet Union. The socialist state successfully stood the strenuous test of the war and emerged victorious from the mortal struggle with a most powerful enemy. Instead of being enfeebled, the U.S.S.R. became stronger.

The capitalist world has also undergone a substantial change. Of the six so-called great imperialist powers (Germany, Japan, Great Britain, the U.S.A., France and Italy), three have been eliminated by military defeat (Germany, Italy and Japan). France has also been weakened and has lost its significance as a great power. As a result, only two great imperialist world powers remain—the United States and Great Britain. But the position of one of them, Great Britain, has been undermined.

World War II aggravated the crisis of the colonial system, as expressed in the rise of a powerful movement for national liberation in the colonies and dependencies. This has placed the rear of the capitalist system in jeopardy. The peoples of the colonies no longer wish to live in the old way. The ruling classes of the metropolitan countries can no longer govern the colonies on the old lines. Attempts to crush the national liberation movement by military force now increasingly encounter armed resistance on the part of the colonial peoples and lead to protracted colonial wars (Holland—Indonesia, France—Viet Nam).

The war—itself a product of the unevenness of capitalist development in the different countries—still further intensified this unevenness. Of all the capitalist powers, only one—the United States—emerged from the war not only unweakened, but even considerably stronger economically and militarily. The war greatly enriched the American capitalists. The American people on the other hand, did not experience the privations that accompany war, the hardship of occupation, or aerial bombardment; and since America entered the war practically in its concluding stage, when the issue was already decided, her human casualties were relatively small. For the U.S.A., the war was primarily and chiefly a spur to extensive industrial development and to substantial increase of exports (principally to Europe).

But the end of the war confronted the United States with a number of new problems. The capitalist monopolies were anxious to maintain their profits at the former high level, and accordingly pressed hard to prevent a reduction of the wartime volume of deliveries. But this meant that the United States must retain the foreign markets which had absorbed American products during the war, and moreover, acquire new markets, inasmuch as the war had substantially lowered the purchasing power of most of the countries. The financial and economic dependence of these countries on the U.S.A. had likewise increased. The sharp decline of the economic power of the other capitalist states makes it possible to speculate on their post-war economic difficulties, and, in particular, on the post-war economic difficulties of Great Britain, which makes it easier to bring these countries under American control. The United States proclaimed a new frankly predatory and expansionist course.

The purpose of this new, frankly expansionist course is to establish the world supremacy of American imperialism. With a view to consolidating America's monopoly position in the markets gained as a result of the disappearance of her two biggest competitors, Germany and Japan, and the weakening of her capitalist partners, Great Britain and France, the new course of United States policy envisages a broad program of military, economic and political measures, designed to establish United States political and economic domination in all countries marked out for American expansion, to reduce these countries to the status of satellites of the United States, and to set up regimes within them which would eliminate all obstacles on the part of the labour and democratic movement to the exploitation of these countries by American capital. The United States is now endeavouring to extend this new line of policy not only to its enemies in the war and to neutral countries, but in an increasing degree to its wartime allies.

* * *

Thus the new policy of the United States is designed to consolidate its monopoly position and to reduce its capitalist partners to a state of subordination and dependence on America.

But America's aspirations to world supremacy encountered an obstacle in the U.S.S.R., the stronghold of anti-imperialist and anti-fascist policy, and its growing international influence, in the new democracies, which have escaped from the control of Britain and American imperialism, and in the workers of all countries, including America itself, who do not want a new war for the supremacy of their oppressors. Accordingly, the new expansionist and reactionary policy of the United States envisages a struggle against the U.S.S.R., against the labour movement in all countries, including the United States, and against the emancipationist, anti-imperialist forces in all countries.

Alarmed by the achievements of socialism in the U.S.S.R., by the achievements of the new democracies, and by the post-war growth of the labour and democratic movement in all countries, the American reactionaries are disposed to take upon themselves the mission of "saviours" of the capitalist system from Communism.

The frank expansionist program of the United States is therefore highly reminiscent of the reckless program, which failed so ignominiously, of the fascist aggressors, who, as we know, also made a bid for world supremacy.

*   *   *

The American imperialists regard themselves as the principal force opposed to the U.S.S.R., the new democracies and the labour and democratic movement in all countries of the world, as the bulwark of the reactionary, anti-democratic forces in all parts of the globe. Accordingly, literally on the day following the conclusion of World War II, they set to work to build up a front hostile to the U.S.S.R. and world democracy, and to encourage the anti-popular reactionary forces—collaborationists and former capitalist stooges—in the European countries which had been liberated from the Nazi yoke and which were beginning to arrange their affairs according to their own choice.

The more malignant and unbalanced imperialist politicians followed the lead of Churchill in hatching plans for the speedy launching of a preventive war against the U.S.S.R. and openly called for the employment of America's temporary monopoly of the atomic weapon against the Soviet people. The new warmongers are trying to intimidate and browbeat not only the U.S.S.R., but other countries as well, notably China and India, by libellously depicting the U.S.S.R. as a potential aggressor, while they themselves pose as "friends" of China and India, as "saviours" from the Communist peril, their mission being to "help" the weak. By these means they are seeking to keep India and China under the sway of imperialism and in continued political and economic bondage.

The New Post-War Alignment of Political Forces and the Formation of Two Camps: The Imperialist and Anti-Democratic Camp, and The Anti-Imperialist and Democratic One

The fundamental changes caused by the war on the international scene and in the position of individual countries has entirely changed the political landscape of the world. A new alignment of political forces has arisen. The more the war recedes into the past, the more distinct become two major trends in post-war international policy, corresponding to the division of the political forces operating on the international arena into two major camps: the imperialist and anti-democratic camp, on the one hand, and the anti-imperialist and democratic camp, on the other. The principal driving force of the imperialist camp is the U.S.A. Allied with it are Great Britain and France. The existence of the Atlee-Bevin Labour Government in Britain and the Ramadier Socialist Government in France does not hinder these countries from playing the part of satellites of the United States and following the lead of its imperialist policy on all major questions. The imperialist camp is also supported by colony-owning countries, such as Belgium and Holland, by countries with reactionary anti-democratic regimes, such as Turkey and Greece, and by countries politically and economically dependent upon the United States, such as the Near-Eastern and South-American countries and China.

The cardinal purpose of the imperialist camp is to strengthen imperialism, to hatch a new imperialist war, to combat socialism and democracy, and to support reactionary and anti-democratic profascist regimes and movements everywhere.

In the pursuit of these ends the imperialist camp is prepared to rely on reactionary and anti-democratic forces in all countries, and to support its former adversaries in the war against its wartime allies.

The anti-fascist forces comprise the second camp. This camp is based on the U.S.S.R. and the new democracies. It also includes countries that have broken with imperialism and have firmly set foot on the path of democratic development, such as Rumania, Hungary and Finland. Indonesia and Viet Nam are associated with it; it has the sympathy of India, Egypt and Syria. The anti-imperialist camp is backed by the labour and democratic movement and by the fraternal Communist parties in all countries, by the fighters for national liberation in the colonies and dependencies, by all progressive and democratic forces in every country. The purpose of this camp is to resist the threat of new wars and imperialist expansion, to strengthen democracy and to extirpate the vestiges of fascism.

The end of the Second World War confronted all the freedom-loving nations with the cardinal task of securing a lasting democratic peace sealing victory over fascism. In the accomplishment of this fundamental task of the post-war period the Soviet Union and its foreign policy are playing a leading role. This follows from the very nature of the Soviet socialist state, to which motives of aggression and exploitation are utterly alien, and which is interested in creating the most favourable conditions for the building of a Communist society. One of these conditions is external peace. As embodiment of a new and superior social system, the Soviet Union reflects in its foreign policy the aspirations of progressive mankind, which desires lasting peace and has nothing to gain from a new war hatched by capitalism. The Soviet Union is a staunch champion of the liberty and independence of all nations, and a foe of national and racial oppression and colonial exploitation in any shape or form. The change in the general alignment of forces between the capitalist world and the socialist world brought about by the war has still further enhanced the significance of the foreign policy of the Soviet state and enlarged the scope of its activity on the international arena.

* * *

The successes and the growing international prestige of the democratic camp were not to the liking of the imperialists. Even while World War II was still on, reactionary forces in Great Britain and the United States became increasingly active, striving to prevent concerted action by the Allied powers, to protract the war, to bleed the U.S.S.R., and to save the fascist aggressors from utter defeat. The sabotage of the Second Front by the Anglo-Saxon imperialists, headed by Churchill, was a clear reflection of this tendency, which was in point of fact a continuation of the Munich policy in the new and changed conditions. But while the war was still in progress British and American reactionary circles did not venture to come out openly against the Soviet Union and the democratic countries, realizing that they had the undivided sympathy of the masses all over the world. But in the concluding months of the war the situation began to change. The British and American imperialists already manifested their unwillingness to respect the legitimate interests of the Soviet Union and the democratic countries at the Potsdam tripartite conference, in July 1945.

The foreign policy of the Soviet Union and the democratic countries in these two past years has been a policy of consistently working for the observance of the democratic principles in the post-war settlement. The countries of the anti-imperialist camp have loyally and consistently striven for the implementation of these principles, without deviating from them one iota. Consequently, the major objective of the post-war foreign policy of the democratic states has been a democratic peace, the eradication of the vestiges of fascism and the prevention of a resurgence of fascist imperialist aggression, the recognition of the principle of the equality of nations and respect for their sovereignty, and general reduction of all armaments and the outlawing of the most destructive weapons, those designed for the mass slaughter of the civilian population. . . .

Of immense importance are the joint efforts of the diplomacy of the U.S.S.R. and that of the other democratic countries to secure a reduction of armaments and the outlawing of the most destructive of them—the atomic bomb.

* * *

Soviet foreign policy proceeds from the fact of the co-existence for a long period of the two systems—capitalism and socialism. From this it follows that co-operation between the U.S.S.R. and countries with other systems is possible, provided that the principle of reciprocity is observed and that obligations once assumed are honoured. Everyone knows that the U.S.S.R. has always honoured the obligations it has assumed. The Soviet Union has demonstrated its will and desire for co-operation.

Soviet foreign policy, defending the cause of peace, discountenances a policy of vengeance towards the vanquished countries.

It is known that the U.S.S.R. is in favour of a united, peace-loving, demilitarized and democratic Germany. Comrade Stalin formulated the Soviet policy towards Germany when he said: "In short, the policy of the Soviet Union on the German question reduces itself to the demilitarization and democratization of Germany. The demilitarization and democratization of Germany is one of the most important guarantees for the establishment of a solid and lasting peace". However, this policy of the Soviet Union towards Germany is being encountered by frantic opposition from the imperialist circles in the United States and Great Britain.

The meeting of the Council of Foreign Ministers in Moscow in March and April 1947 demonstrated that the United States, Great Britain and France are prepared not only to prevent the democratic reconstruction and demilitarization of Germany, but even to liquidate her as an integral state, to dismember her, and to settle the question of peace separately.

Today this policy is being conducted under new conditions, now that America has abandoned the old course of Roosevelt and is passing to a new policy, a policy of preparing for new military adventures.

The American Plan for the Enthrallment of Europe

The aggressive and frankly expansionist course to which American imperialism has committed itself since the end of World War II finds expression in both the foreign and home policy of the United States. The active support rendered to the reactionary, anti-democratic forces all over the world, the sabotage of the Potsdam decisions which call for the democratic reconstruction and demilitarization of Germany, the protection given to Japanese reactionaries, the extensive war preparations and the accumulation of atomic bombs—all this goes hand in hand with an offensive against the elementary democratic rights of the working people in the United States itself.

* * *

American imperialism is persistently pursuing a policy of militarizing the country. Expenditure on the U. S. army and navy exceeds 11,000 million dollars per annum. In 1947–48, 35 per cent of America's budget was appropriated for the armed forces, or eleven times more than in 1937–1938.

On the outbreak of World War II the American army was the seventeenth largest in the capitalist world; today it is the largest one. The United States is not only accumulating stocks of atomic bombs; American strategists say quite openly that it is preparing bacteriological weapons.

The strategical plans of the United States envisages the creation in peacetime of numerous bases and vantage grounds situated at great distances from the American continent and designed to be used for aggressive purposes against the U.S.S.R. and the countries of the new democracy.

Although the war has long since ended, the military alliance between Britain and the United States and even a combined Anglo-American military staff continue to exist. Under the guise of agreement for the standardization of weapons the United States has established its control over the armed forces and military plans of other countries, notably of Great Britain and Canada. . . .

The military circles are becoming an active political force in the United States, supplying large numbers of government officials and diplomats who are directing the whole policy of the country into an aggressive military course.

Economic expansion is an important supplement to the realization of America's strategical plan. American imperialism is endeavouring like a usurer, to take advantage of the post-war difficulties of the European countries, in particular of the shortage of raw materials, fuel and food in the Allied countries that suffered most from the war, to dictate to them extortionate terms for any assistance rendered. . . .American economic "assistance" pursues the broad aim of bringing Europe into bondage to American capital. . . .

But economic control logically leads to political subjugation to American imperialism. . . .In "saving" a country from starvation and collapse, the American monopolies at the same time seek to rob it of all vestige of independence. American "assistance" automatically involves a change in the policy of the country to which it is rendered: parties and individuals come to power that are prepared, on directions from Washington, to carry out a program of home and foreign policy suitable to the United States (France, Italy, and so on).

Lastly, the aspiration to world supremacy and the anti-democratic policy of the United States involve an ideological struggle. . . .The warmongers fully realize that long ideological preparation is necessary before they can get their soldiers to fight the Soviet Union.

In their ideological struggle against the USSR, the American imperialists, who have no great insight into political questions, demonstrate their ignorance by laying primary stress on the allegation that the Soviet Union is undemocratic and totalitarian, while the United States and Great Britain and the whole capitalist world are democratic. On this platform of ideological struggle—on this defence of bourgeois pseudo-democracy and condemnation of Communism as totalitarian—are united all the enemies of the working class without exception, from the capitalist magnates to the right socialist leaders, who seize with the greatest eagerness on any slanderous imputations against the USSR suggested to them by their imperialist masters. The pith and substance of this fraudulent propaganda is the claim that the earmark of true democracy is the existence of a plurality of parties and of an organized opposition minority. On these grounds the British Labourites, who spare no effort in their fight against Communism, would like to discover antagonistic classes and a corresponding struggle of parties in the USSR. Political ignoramuses that they are, they cannot understand that capitalists and landlords, antagonistic classes, and hence a plurality of parties have long ceased to exist in the USSR. . . .

One of the lines taken by the ideological campaign that goes hand in hand with the plans for the enslavement of Europe is an attack on the principle of national sovereignty, an appeal for the renouncement of the sovereign rights of nations, to which is opposed the idea of a world government. The purpose of this campaign is to mask the unbridled expansion of American imperialism which is ruthlessly violating the sovereign rights of nations, to represent the United States as a champion of universal laws, and those who resist American penetration as believers in obsolete and selfish nationalism. . .

At this present juncture the expansionist ambitions of the United States find concrete expression in the Truman doctrine and the Marshall Plan. Although they differ in form of presentation, both are an expression of a single policy, they are both an embodiment of the American design to enslave Europe.

* * *

Acting on instructions from Washington, the British and French governments invited the Soviet Union to take part in a discussion of the

Marshall proposals. This step was taken in order to mask the hostile nature of the proposals with respect to the USSR. The calculation was that, since it was well known beforehand that the USSR would refuse American assistance on the terms proposed by Marshall, it might be possible to shift the responsibility on the Soviet Union for "declining to assist the economic restoration of Europe," and thus incite against the USSR the European countries that are in need of real assistance. If, on the other hand, the Soviet Union should consent to take part in the talks, it would be easier to lure the countries of east and south-east Europe into the trap of the economic restoration of Europe with American assistance. Whereas the Truman plan was designed to terrorize and intimidate these countries, the "Marshall Plan" was designed to test their economic staunchness, to lure them into a trap and then shackle them in the fetters of dollar "assistance."

In that case, the "Marshall Plan" would facilitate one of the most important objectives of the general American program, namely, to restore the power of imperialism in the countries of the new democracy and to compel them to renounce close economic and political co-operation with the Soviet Union.

The representatives of the USSR, having agreed to discuss the Marshall proposals in Paris with the governments of Great Britain and France, exposed at the Paris talks the unsoundness of attempting to work out an economic program for the whole of Europe, and showed that the attempt to create a new European organization under the aegis of France and Britain was a threat to interfere in the internal affairs of the European countries and to violate their sovereignty. They showed that the "Marshall Plan" was in contradiction to the normal principles of international co-operation, that it harboured the danger of splitting Europe and the threat of subjugating a number of European countries to American capitalist interests, that it was designed to give priority of assistance to the monopolistic concerns of Germany over the Allies, and that the restoration of these concerns was obviously designated in the "Marshall Plan" to play a special role in Europe.

It should be noted that the American variant of the Western bloc is bound to encounter serious resistance even in countries already so dependent on the United States as Britain and France. The prospect of the restoration of German imperialism, as an effective force capable of opposing democracy and Communism in Europe, cannot be very alluring either to Britain or to France. Here we have one of the major contradictions within the Anglo-French-American bloc. Evidently, the American monopolies, and the international reactionaries generally, do not regard Franco and the Greek fascists as a very reliable bulwark of the

United States against the USSR and the new democracies in Europe. They are, therefore, staking their main hopes on the restoration of capitalist Germany, which they consider would be a major guarantee of the success of the fight against the democratic forces of Europe. They trust neither the British Labourites nor the French Socialists, whom, in spite of their manifest desire to please, they regard as "semi-Communists", insufficiently worthy of confidence. . . .

The Soviet government has never objected to using foreign, and in particular American, credits as a means capable of expediting the process of economic rehabilitation. However, the Soviet Union has always taken the stand that the terms of credits must not be extortionate, and must not result in the economic and political subjugation of the debtor country to the creditor country. From this political stand, the Soviet Union has always held that foreign credits must not be the principal means of restoring a country's economy. The chief and paramount condition of a country's economic rehabilitation must be the utilization of its own internal forces and resources and the creation of its own industry. Only in this way can its independence be guaranteed against encroachments on the part of foreign capital, which constantly displays a tendency to utilize credits as an instrument of political and economic enthrailment. Such precisely is the "Marshall Plan", which would strike at the industrialization of the European countries and is consequently designed to undermine their independence.

The exposure of the American plan for the economic enslavement of the European countries is an indisputable service rendered by the foreign policy of the USSR and the new democracies.

It should be borne in mind that America herself is threatened with an economic crisis. There are weighty reasons for Marshall's official generosity. If the European countries do not receive American credits, their demand for American goods will diminish, and this will tend to accellerate and intensify the approaching economic crisis in the United States. Accordingly, if the European countries display the necessary stamina and readiness to resist the enthralling terms of the American credit, America may find herself compelled to beat a retreat.

The Tasks of the Communist Parties in Uniting the Democratic, Anti-Fascist, Peace-Loving Elements to Resist the New Plans of War and Aggression

The dissolution of the Comintern, which conformed to the demands of the development of the labour movement in the new historical situation, played a positive role. The dissolution of the Comintern once and for all disposed of the slanderous allegation of the enemies of Communism and the labour movement that Moscow was interfering in the internal affairs of other states, and that the Communist Parties in the various countries were acting not in the interests of their nations, but on orders from outside.

The Comintern was founded after the first world war, when the Communist Parties were still weak, when practically no ties existed between the working classes of the different countries, and when the Communist Parties had not yet produced generally recognized leaders of the labour movement. The service performed by the Comintern was that it restored and strengthened the ties between the working people of the different countries, that it elaborated theoretical questions of the labour movement in the new, post-war conditions of development, that it established general standards of propaganda of the ideas of Communism, and that it facilitated the preparation of leaders of the labour movement. This created the conditions for the conversion of the young Communist Parties into mass labour parties. But once the young Communist Parties had become mass labour parties, the direction of these parties from one centre became impossible and inexpedient. As a result, the Comintern, from a factor promoting the development of the Communist Parties began to turn into a factor hindering their development. The new stage in the development of the Communist Parties demanded new forms of contact among the parties. It was these considerations that made it necessary to dissolve the Comintern and to devise new forms of connection between the parties.

In the course of the four years that have elapsed since the dissolution of the Comintern, the Communist Parties have grown considerably in strength and influence in nearly all the countries of Europe and Asia. The influence of the Communist Parties has increased not only in Eastern Europe, but in practically all European countries where fascism held sway, as well as in those which were occupied by the German fascists—France, Belgium, Holland, Norway, Denmark, Finland, etc. The influence of the Communists has increased especially in the new democracies, where the Communist Parties are among the most influential parties in the state.

But the present position of the Communist Parties has its shortcomings. Some comrades understood the dissolution of the Comintern to imply the elimination of all ties, of all contact, between the fraternal Communist Parties. But experience has shown that such mutual isolation of the Communist Parties is wrong, harmful and, in point of fact, unnatural. The Communist movement develops within national frameworks, but there are tasks and interests common to the parties of various countries. . . .The need for mutual consultation and voluntary coordination of action between individual parties has become particularly urgent at the present juncture when continued isolation may lead to a slackening of mutual understanding, and at times, even to serious blunders.

In view of the fact that the majority of the leaders of the Socialist parties (especially the British Labourites and the French Socialists) are acting as agents of United States imperialist circles, there has devolved upon the Communists the special historical task of leading the resistance to the American plan for the enthrallment of Europe, and of boldly denouncing all coadjutors of American imperialism in their own countries. At the same time, Communists must support all the really patriotic elements who do not want their countries to be imposed upon, who want to resist enthrallment of their countries to foreign capital, and to uphold their national sovereignty. The Communists must be the leaders in enlisting all anti-fascist and freedom-loving elements in the struggle against the new American expansionist plans for the enslavement of Europe.

It must be borne in mind that a great gulf lies between the desire of the imperialists to unleash a new war and the possibility of engineering such a war. The peoples of the world do not want war. The forces that stand for peace are so big and influential that if they are staunch and determined in defence of peace, if they display fortitude and firmness, the plans of the aggressors will come to grief. It should not be forgotten that all the hullabaloo of the imperialist agents about the danger of war is designed to frighten the weak-nerved and unstable and to extort concessions to the aggressor by means of intimidation.

The chief danger to the working class at this present juncture lies in underrating its own strength and overrating the strength of the enemy. Just as in the past the Munich policy untied the hands of the Nazi aggressors, so today concessions to the new course of the United States and the imperialist camp may encourage its inspirers to be even more insolent and aggressive. The Communist Parties must therefore head the resistance to the plans of imperialist expansion and aggression along every line—state, economic and ideological; they must rally their ranks and unite their efforts on the basis of a common anti-imperialist and democratic platform, and gather around them all the democratic and patriotic forces of the people.

A special task devolves on the fraternal Communist Parties of France, Italy, Great Britain and other countries. They must take up the standard in defence of the national independence and sovereignty of their countries. If the Communist Parties firmly stick to their position, if they do not allow themselves to be intimidated and blackmailed, if they act as courageous sentinels of enduring peace and popular democracy, of the national sovereignty, liberty and independence of their countries, if, in their struggle against the attempts to economically and politically enthrall their countries, they are able to take the lead of all the forces prepared to uphold the national honour and independence, no plans for the enthrallment of Europe can possibly succeed.

MALENKOV

Report to the XIX Party
Congress *October 5, 1952*

Introduction The most important event in the interval
between Zhdanov's speech and Malenkov's was the
outbreak of the Korean War in June, 1950. It would be
difficult to exaggerate its consequences. It caused the
West to revise its estimate of the Communists' willingness
to risk war and led to a four-fold increase in United
States military spending. The USSR also revised its
estimate of the risk of war, although Stalin apparently
still believed he could control it, presumably by making
concessions to the West if necessary. Nevertheless, the
military forces and defense spending of the Soviet Union
and of the whole Communist bloc increased sharply. This
produced severe strains that led to economic and political
difficulties, particularly in the satellite regimes of Eastern
Europe.

The contrast drawn by Zhdanov between the two camps
is retraced by Malenkov–Stalin's new heir presumptive–
who argues that the United States leaders are committed
to the imposition of fascism at home and abroad. U.S.
domination of the imperialist camp may be drawing to an
end, however, as its allies grow more restive. Malenkov

invites dissident allies of the United States to seek an accommodation with the USSR. He even asserts that the divisions in the imperialist camp are so great that its members may find themselves at war with each other. In this he follows—as he must—Stalin's argument in a work just published, *The Economic Problems of Socialism.*

Stalin's discussion of the problem of war is so important for an understanding of Soviet foreign policy during his last years that it warrants quotation at length, and some comment:

> Some comrades* maintain that as a result of the development of the new international conditions after the second world war, wars between capitalist countries have ceased to be inevitable. They think that the contradictions between the camp of socialism and the camp of capitalism are greater than the contradictions between the capitalist countries, that the USA has sufficiently subjected the other capitalist countries to itself not to allow them to wage war among themselves and weaken one another, that the more advanced people of capitalism have learned enough from the experience of two world wars, which inflicted serious damage on the whole capitalist world, not to allow themselves again to involve capitalist countries in war against each other, that in view of all this, wars between capitalist countries have ceased to be inevitable.
>
> These comrades are mistaken. They see the external phenomena twinkling on the surface but they do not see those profound forces which, though acting imperceptibly at present, will nevertheless determine the course of events.
>
> Outwardly it would seem "all is well"... However, would it not be more correct to say that capitalist Britain and in her footsteps capitalist France will finally be forced to tear themselves from the embraces of the USA and enter into conflict with it in order to assure themselves an independent position and, of course, high profits? ...

---

* Oddly, this may be an allusion to Malenkov himself. (See below.) The translation of this passage is my own.

It is said that the contradictions between capitalism and socialism are stronger than the contradictions between the capitalist countries. Theoretically, of course, this is true. Not only is it true now, at the present time, but it was also true before the second world war. And the leaders of the capitalist countries more or less understood this. All the same, the second world war began not with war against the USSR but with war between capitalist countries. . . . Thus the struggle of the capitalist countries for markets and the desire to sink their competitors turned out in practice to be stronger than the contradictions between the camp of capitalism and the camp of socialism.

The question is, what guarantee is there that Germany and Japan will not again rise to their feet, that they will not try to break loose from American bondage. . . ? I think there are no such guarantees.

But it follows from this that the inevitability of wars between capitalist countries remains valid. Some say of Lenin's thesis that imperialism inevitably begets wars, that it is necessary to consider it obsolete, since at the present time powerful popular forces have appeared that are taking a stand in defence of peace, against a new world war. This is not correct. . . In order to eliminate the inevitability of wars it is necessary to destroy imperialism.

For Stalin, war was inevitable, and the aim of Soviet foreign policy (as in 1939) was to assure that the war was waged between capitalist states, not against the USSR. To achieve this objective, the USSR had to be very strong, economically and militarily. For this reason, Stalin set extremely high targets for industry in 1946, and military spending for both nuclear and conventional forces was at a remarkably high level throughout the post-war period, especially after the onset of the Korean War (1950). Granted such strength, however, it was not necessary to conciliate the capitalist world. Since the "contradictions" in the imperialist camp were so great that they might readily lead to war among its members, there was small reason for the USSR to seek to negotiate a settlement of outstanding differences between the two sides: it had only to stay strong and wait for the imperialist camp to weaken itself by internecine struggle.

In his discussion of war, Stalin says nothing of nuclear weapons and their bearing on the problem. Malenkov, in his Report, refers several times to nuclear weapons but, in accordance with the current Soviet propaganda line, displays little appreciation of their unprecedented destructiveness. Malenkov even asserts that a new world war—presumably one fought with nuclear weapons—would result in the "collapse of the world capitalist system," and says nothing of the consequences for the "democratic camp." In a later speech, however, after Stalin was dead and both sides had exploded thermonuclear devices, Malenkov was to change his publicly-expressed views. In March, 1954, he said that a new world war would mean the destruction of world civilization. Thus, while Stalin continued in the nuclear age to rely on war to further Soviet security and the progress of Communism (just as he had in the period of Soviet "neutrality," from 1939 to 1941), at least some among his heirs apparently had already begun to question privately the utility of war.

International Position of the Soviet Union

Further Weakening of the World Capitalist System and Economic Position of the Capitalist Countries

Far from eliminating the economic and political contradictions of capitalism, the second world war aggravated these contradictions still more, undermined the economies of the capitalist countries and deepened the general crisis of the world capitalist system. The second world war failed to justify the hopes of the big bourgeoisie of the imperialist countries. Each of the two belligerent capitalist groups calculated on redividing the world by armed force, on seizing new raw material sources and expanding the markets for its goods, that is, on strengthening its own economic position at the expense of its adversaries and establishing world domination.

But these calculations miscarried. Although Germany and Japan were knocked out as the chief rivals of the three main capitalist countries—the United States, Britain and France—the hopes of these countries, especially of the United States, of being thus able to increase industrial output four or five-fold, were shattered. In addition, China and the European People's Democracies dropped out of the capitalist system, and, together with the Soviet Union, formed a united and powerful camp of peace and democracy which stands opposed to the camp of imperialism.

The economic result of the rise of two opposing camps, as Comrade Stalin has pointed out, was the disintegration of the single, all-embracing world market and the emergence of two parallel world markets: that of the countries of the camp of peace and democracy, and that of the aggressive, Imperialist camp. The disintegration of the single world market is the most important economic outcome of the Second World War and its economic consequences.

*   *   *

This economic policy of American imperialism could not but sharpen the antagonisms between the United States and the other capitalist countries. The chief of these remains the antagonism between the United States and Britain, taking form of open struggle between the American and British monopolies for sources of oil, rubber, non-ferrous and rare metals, sulphur and wool, and for markets.

To this should be added the very serious antagonisms between the United States and Japan, the United States and Italy, and the United States and Western Germany—the countries subjected to the occupation yoke of the United States dictators. It would be naive to think that these vanquished countries will agree to remain indefinitely under the heel of the American occupationists. It would be folly to think that they will not attempt, in one way or another, to throw off the American yoke and live free and independent lives.

The antagonisms between the United States and Britain, and between the United States and France, are becoming increasingly acute and will become still more acute as American capitalism, to the accompaniment of noise about "aid," and by granting credits, insinuates itself into the economics of Britain, France and Italy, seizing raw material sources and markets in the British and French colonies. Britain and, following her, France and the other capitalist countries are endeavoring to break away from subordination to the United States in order to secure for themselves an independent position and high profits. Even now British capitalists are putting up a stubborn fight against American dictation in world trade.

* * *

The United States as well as Britain and France, thought that their economic "blockade" of the U.S.S.R., China and the European People's Democracies would strangle these countries. Actually the effect has been not the strangling but the strengthening of the new democratic world market. The imperialists have thereby delivered a telling blow to their own export trade and have aggravated still more the contradiction between the production potential of their industry and the possibilities for the sale of its products.

All this signifies that even deeper contradictions have arisen in the capitalist economy, and that the world system of capitalist economy as a whole has become considerably narrower and weaker and even less stable than before the war.

Conscious of these economic difficulties the United States capitalists are endeavoring to overcome them by means of the war in Korea, the armaments drive and the militarization of industry.

Having launched a reactionary war against the Korean people, and whipping up war hysteria against the democratic camp, the United States, British and French imperialists have converted their economies to a war footing and have carried militarization of the economy and the arms drive to colossal dimensions in their countries. . .

The switch to a war economy has enabled the United States and other capitalist countries to raise industrial output for the time being. . . At the same time the militarization of the economy results in the population being robbed of their money through higher taxes. All this turns the budgets of the capitalist countries into a means by which the billionaires rob the people; it substantially lowers the purchasing power of the population, reduces the demand for manufactured goods and agricultural produce, drastically curtails civilian production and creates the conditions for the onset of a severe economic crisis.

Militarization of the national economy does not do away with but, on the contrary, increases the disproportion between production capacity and the diminishing purchasing power of the population, which the ruling clique in the capitalist countries is reducing to the very minimum, and this in turn leads to a steady contraction of the capitalist market. Thus, the expansion of war production is inevitably leading to the maturing of a new deep economic crises.

The armaments drive is a particularly heavy burden on the economy of the satellites of the United States of America. . . The armaments drive conducted by the rulers of Britain, France, Italy, Western Germany, Belgium, Norway and other capitalist countries, on orders from the

American monopolies, is ruining the economy of these countries and pushing them towards diaster.

* * *

At the same time militarization has led to a sharp decline in the conditions of the masses. Increased taxes, rising prices for goods of mass consumption and inflation have increased the relative and absolute impoverishment of the working people. . . Class contradictions between the imperialist bourgeoisie, on the one hand, and the working class and all the toiling people, on the other, are rapidly becoming more acute. A strike wave is spreading wider and wider throughout the capitalist world.

The situation in which the world capitalist system finds itself is complicated by the fact that, as a result of the war and the new upsurge of the national-liberation struggle in the colonial and dependent countries, the disintegration of the colonial system of imperialism is actually taking place.

As a direct result of the defeat of fascist Germany and imperialist Japan, the imperialist front was breached in China, Korea and Viet Nam, where People's Republics have arisen in place of the former semi-colonies and colonies. The victory of the Chinese people revolutionized the East still more and helped to stimulate the liberation struggle waged by the peoples oppressed by imperialism. . . .

*Aggravation of the International Situation.   Threat of a
New War Emanating from the U.S.-British Aggressive
Bloc. Struggle of the Peoples for Peace*

The postwar activity of the U. S. British and French ruling circles in the sphere of international relations, too, has been marked by preparations for a new war.

Almost immediately after the second world war, the United States of America renounced the line of policy agreed upon and pursued by the wartime allies and laid down in the decisions of the Teheran, Yalta and Potsdam conferences of the powers. By a series of aggressive actions the U.S.A. aggravated the international situation and brought the world face to face with the danger of a new war.

* * *

The U.S. attack on the Korean People's Democratic Republic marked the transition of the U.S.-British bloc from preparation for aggressive war to direct acts of aggression. The Korean people, who in close co-operation with the valiant Chinese volunteers are heroically defending the freedom and independence of their homeland and giving a rebuff to the violators of peace, enjoy the warmest sympathy of all democratic and peace-loving man-kind.

* * *

Once free capitalist states, Britain, France, the Netherlands, Belgium and Norway are now in fact abandoning their own national policy and carrying out a policy dictated by the U.S. imperialists, yielding their territories for American bases and military springboards, thereby endangering their own countries in the event of hostilities breaking out. On American bidding they conclude alliances and blocs directed against their own national interests. . .

As for such "free" countries as Greece, Turkey and Yugoslavia, they have already been turned into American colonies, while the rulers of Yugoslavia—all these Titos, Kardeljs, Rankovics, Djilases, Pijades and others—who long ago became American agents, engage in espionage and subversion against the U.S.S.R. and the People's Democracies on assignments from their American "bosses."

The ruling circles of France, Italy, Britain, Western Germany and Japan have harnessed themselves to the chariot of U.S. imperialism and have renounced a national, independent foreign policy of their own. . . .

The Right-wing Social Democrats, and the top leaders of the British Labor Party, of the French Socialist Party and of the Social Democratic Party of Western Germany in the first place, also bear direct responsibility for this anti-national policy of the ruling circles . . . Present-day right-wing Social Democracy, in addition to its old role of lackey of the national bourgeoisie, has become an agency of foreign, U.S. imperialism, carrying out its foulest assignments in preparing for war and in fighting against its own people.

A distinctive feature of the strategy of U.S. imperialism is that its bosses base their war plans on the utilization of the territory of others and the armies of others—primarily the West German and Japanese armies, as well as the British, French and Italian—on utilization of other peoples who are to serve, according to the schemes of the U.S. strategists, as blind instruments and cannon fodder in the conquest of world dominion by the U.S. monopolists.

But even now the more sober and progressive politicians in the European and other capitalist countries, men who have not been blinded by hatred of the Soviet Union, see clearly the abyss into which the American adventurists, who have run amuck, are plunging them; they are beginning to take a stand against war. It should be assumed that genuine peace-loving democratic forces will be found in the countries that are doomed to the role of pawns in the hands of the U.S. dictators, forces which will follow their own independent, peaceful policy and will find a way out of the impasse into which they have been driven by the U.S. dictators. The European and other countries taking this new path will meet with complete understanding in all the peace-loving countries.

In their endeavors to mask their policy of conquest, the ruling circles of the United States seek to pass off the so-called "cold war" against the democratic camp as a peaceful defensive policy and frighten their own people with the non-existent danger of attack from the U.S.S.R. Masking the aggressive plans and the military operations now in progress with demagogic phrasemongering about peace is a characteristic feature of the policy of the bosses of the Atlantic bloc. The crux of the matter is that today it is not so easy to drive peoples who only recently bore the full brunt of a bloody shambles, into a new war, a war against the peace-loving peoples. Hence all the efforts of the aggressive Atlantic wolf to appear in sheep's clothing.

In these circumstances it would be dangerous to underestimate the harm of the pharisaical peace camouflage resorted to by the present-day aggressors.

War preparations are accompanied by an unprecedented wave of unbridled militarism which affects every aspect of the life of the people in the countries of the imperialist camp, by a frenzied offensive of reaction against the working people, and by fascization of the entire regime in these countries.

*   *   *

U.S. imperialism is at present not only the aggressor, it is the world gendarme seeking to strangle freedom wherever possible and to implant fascism.

*   *   *

In connection with the growing danger of war a popular peace movement is developing, an anti-war coalition is being created of different classes and social strata interested in ending the international tension and preventing a new world war. . . . This peace movement does not pursue the aim of abolishing capitalism, for it is not a socialist, but a democratic movement of hundreds of millions of people. The peace partisans are advancing demands and suggestions which are bound to contribute to preserving peace and preventing another war. The achievement of this goal would, in the present historical conditions, be a tremendous victory for the cause of democracy and peace.

The present correlation of forces between the camp of imperialism and war and the camp of democracy and peace makes this prospect a completely real one. For the first time in history there exists a mighty and united camp of peace-loving states. In the capitalist countries the working class is better organized than before, powerful democratic international organizations of workers, peasants, women and the youth have been established. The Communist Parties, fighting heroically for the cause of peace have grown in numbers and strength.

The peoples of all countries, including the broad masses in the United States of America, for in the event of war they would suffer no less than the population of other countries, are interested in combating the danger of a new war. The war in Korea despite the vast preponderance of American technique, has already taken from the American people a toll of hundreds of thousands in killed and wounded. It is not difficult to visualize how enormous the sacrifices of the American people would be should the bloated financial tycoons of the U.S.A. hurl them into war against the peace-loving peoples.

The task now is to activate the popular masses still more, to strengthen the organization of the partisans of peace, to expose the warmakers tirelessly and not allow them to enmesh the peoples in a web of lies. To bridle and isolate the gamblers of the camp of the imperialist aggressors who seek to embroil the peoples in a sanguinary slaughter for the sake of their profits—such is the principal task of all progressive and peace-loving mankind.

The Soviet Union in the Struggle for the Preservation and Consolidation of Peace

. . . The peacefulness of the Soviet Union is illustrated not only by its proposals but also by its deeds. After the war the Soviet Union considerably reduced its armed forces, which are now numerically not superior to the forces it had before the war. In the briefest space of time after the war the Soviet Government withdrew its troops from the territory of China, Korea, Norway, Czechoslovakia, Yugoslavia and Bulgaria, whither those troops had been moved in the course of military operations against the fascist aggressors. . . .

During the most serious complications in the international arena in recent years, it was the Soviet Union that advanced proposals providing a basis for a peaceful settlement of outstanding questions. It suffices to recall that it was the Soviet side which advanced the proposals that served as the basis for the truce talks in Korea.

The Government of the U.S.S.R. attaches much importance to the United Nations Organization, holding that it could be an important instrument for maintaining peace. But at present the United States is turning the United Nations from the organ of international co-operation which it should be according to the Charter, into an organ of its dictatorial policy in the struggle against peace and is using it as a screen for its aggressive actions. However, notwithstanding the tremendous obstacles put in its way by the voting machine which the United States has set up in the United Nations, the Soviet Union upholds peace there and works for the adoption of realistic proposals arising from the present-day international situation; proposals aimed at curbing the aggressive forces, at preventing another war, and at stopping hostilities where they are already in progress.

It would be incorrect to consider that war could be directed only against the Soviet state. The First World War, as we know, was unleashed by the imperialists long before the U.S.S.R. came into being. The Second World War began as a war among capitalist states, and the capitalist countries themselves suffered heavily from it. The contradictions which today rend the imperialist camp may lead to war between one capitalist state and another. Taking all these circumstances into consideration, the Soviet Union is working to prevent any war among states and is acting for a peaceful settlement of international conflicts and disagreements.

However, in pursuing its policy of ensuring lasting peace, the Soviet Union finds itself up against the aggressive policy pursued by the ruling circles of the United States of America.

Moreover, bellicose American circles are endeavoring to put the blame where it does not belong. They are inflating in every possible way their propaganda of lies about a supposed threat on the part of the Soviet Union. As for these lies and inventions about the Soviet Union, it would be ridiculous to go into them, for they completely lack foundation. Indisputable facts show who really is the aggressor.

Everybody knows that the United States of America is intensifying its armaments drive, refuses to ban the atomic and germ weapons and to reduce conventional armaments, while the Soviet Union proposes a ban on the atomic and germ weapons and a reduction of other armaments and armed forces.

Everybody knows that the United States refuses to conclude a Peace Pact, while the Soviet Union proposes the conclusion of such a Pact.

Everybody knows that the United States is forming aggressive blocs against the peace-loving peoples, while the exclusive object of the treaties concluded between the Soviet Union and foreign states is to combat revival of Japanese or German aggression.

Everybody knows that the United States attacked Korea and is trying to enslave it, while the Soviet Union has not conducted any hostilities anywhere since the end of the Second World War.

The United States is carrying out aggression also against China. It has seized ancient Chinese territory—the island of Taiwan. Its air force is bombing Chinese territory in violation of all accepted standards of international law. Everybody knows that the air force of the U.S.S.R. is not bombing anybody and that the U.S.S.R. has not seized any foreign territory.

Such are the indisputable facts.

Passing over to our relations with Britain and France, it must be said that these relations ought to be in keeping with the spirit of the treaties we concluded with those countries during the second world war and which stipulate co-operation with them in the postwar period. However, the British and French Governments are grossly violating these treaties. Contrary to the solemn pledges of postwar co-operation which they gave to the Soviet Union at the time it was waging a sanguinary war to liberate the peoples of Europe from German-fascist enslavement, the rulers of Britain and France have joined completely in carrying out the American imperialists' aggressive plans against the peace-loving states. It is clear that in view of such a stand taken by the Governments of Britain and France, our relations with these countries leave much to be desired.

The position of the U.S.S.R. as regards the United States, Britain, France, and the other bourgeois states is clear, and our side has stated that position on many occasions. Now, as well, the U.S.S.R. is ready for co-operation with these states, having in mind the observance of peaceful international standards and the guaranteeing of a stable and lasting peace.

With regard to the defeated countries—Germany, Italy and Japan—the Soviet Government pursues a policy entirely different in principle from the policy of the imperialist powers. The fact that the Soviet socialist state was among the victors has created an absolutely new, unprecedented situation and possibilities for the peoples of the defeated countries. For every country which signed an unconditional surrender the policy of the Soviet state opens up the possibility of peaceful, democratic development of progress for civilian industries and agriculture, of selling foods on foreign markets, and of creating national armed forces essential for the country's defense. In conformity with the Potsdam Agreement, the Soviet Union unswervingly pursues a policy aimed at the speediest conclusion of a peace treaty with Germany, the withdrawal of all occupation forces from

Germany, and the establishment of a united, independent, peace-loving, democratic Germany, having in mind that the existence of such a Germany, together with the existence of the peace-loving Soviet Union, excludes the possibility of new wars in Europe and makes the enslavement of European countries by the world imperialists impossible.

It is to be hoped that the German people, who are faced with the dilemma of either taking that path or of being turned into mercenary soldiers of the American and British imperialists, will choose the correct path—the path of peace.

The same must be said with regard to Italy, to whose fraternal people the Soviet Union wishes complete restoration of their national independence.

The Soviet Government considers that Japan should also become an independent democratic peace-loving state, as envisaged by joint decisions of the Allies. The Soviet Government refused to sign the one-sided treaty which the American dictators forced upon the San Francisco Conference, since that treaty tramples upon the principles of the Cairo and Potsdam declarations and the Yalta Agreement, and is aimed at turning Japan into an American Far Eastern military base. The peoples of the Soviet Union have deep respect for the Japanese people, who have to endure the yoke of foreign bondage, and they believe that the Japanese people will achieve national independence for their homeland and take the path of peace.

The Soviet policy of peace and security of the peoples proceeds from the fact that the peaceful co-existence and co-operation of capitalism and Communism are quite possible provided there is a mutual desire to cooperate, readiness to adhere to commitments entered into, and observance of the principle of equality and non-interference in the internal affairs of other states.

*   *   *

While American and British bellicose circles keep reiterating that only the armaments drive keeps industry in the capitalist countries going at full capacity, there is in actual fact another prospect—the prospect of developing and extending trade relations between all countries, irrespective of differences in their social systems which could keep the factories and mills in the industrially developed countries working to capacity for years, that could ensure markets in other countries for the goods in which some countries are rich, promote economic advance in the under-developed countries and thereby establish lasting economic co-operation.

In pursuing its policy of peace the Soviet Union is in complete unanimity with the other democratic peace-loving states: the Chinese People's

Republic, Poland, Romania, Czechoslovakia, Hungary, Bulgaria, Albania, the German Democratic Republic, the Korean People's Democratic Republic, the Mongolian People's Republic. The relations between the U.S.S.R. and these countries are an example of completely new relations among states, relations such as have never been witnessed in history. They are based on the principles of equality, economic co-operation and respect for national independence. True to its treaties of mutual aid, the U.S.S.R. has rendered and will render aid and support in the further strengthening and development of these countries.

We are confident that in peaceful competition with capitalism, the socialist system of economy will prove its superiority over the capitalist system more and more vividly year by year. We have no intention, however, of forcing our ideology or our economic system on anybody. "Export of revolution is nonsense," says Comrade Stalin. "Every country will make its own revolution if it wants to, and if it does not want to there will be no revolution."

While it steadfastly pursues its policy of peaceful co-operation with all countries, the Soviet Union takes into account the existence of the threat of new aggression on the part of the warmongers who have lost all restraint. Hence, it is strengthening its defense capacity and will continue to strengthen it.

* * *

The facts of history cannot be ignored. And the facts show that as a result of the first world war Russia dropped out of the system of capitalism, while as a result of the second world war a whole series of countries in Europe and Asia dropped out of the system of capitalism. There is every reason to assume that a third world war would bring about the collapse of the world capitalist system.

That, so to speak, is the prospect of a war and its consequences if war is forced on the peoples by the warmongers, by the aggressors.

But there is another prospect, the prospect of preserving peace, the prospect of peace among nations. That prospect calls for prohibition of war propaganda in accordance with the resolution adopted by the United Nations, a ban on atomic and germ weapons, consistent reduction of the armed forces of the Great Powers, conclusion of a Peace Pact among the powers, extension of trade among countries, restoration of the single international market, and other analogous measures in the spirit of strengthening peace.

Implementation of these measures would strengthen peace, rid the peoples of fear of the war danger, put an end to the unparalleled expenditure of material resources on armaments and preparation for a war of annihilation, and provide the possibility of diverting them for the welfare of the peoples.

The Soviet Union stands for implementation of these measures, for the prospect of peace among nations.

* * *

The tasks of the Party in the sphere of foreign policy:

1. To continue the struggle against the plotting and unleashing of another war, to rally the powerful anti-war, democratic front for the strengthening of peace, to strengthen the bonds of friendship and solidarity with peace supporters all over the world, persistently to expose all the preparations for another war, all the machinations and intrigues of the warmongers;

2. To continue to pursue a policy of international co-operation and promotion of business relations with all countries;

3. To strengthen and develop inviolable relations of friendship with the Chinese People's Republic, with the European People's Democracies— Poland, Czechoslovakia, Romania, Hungary, Bulgaria, Albania, with the German Democratic Republic, with the Korean People's Democratic Republic and with the Mongolian People's Republic;

4. Tirelessly to strengthen the defense might of the Soviet state and to increase our preparedness to give any aggressor a crushing blow.

MALENKOV

Report to the Supreme Soviet   *August 8, 1953*

Introduction Midway between Malenkov's two speeches, in March 1953, Stalin died. His death led to important changes in Soviet policy. Malenkov's programmatic speech in August was unusual in several respects. The order of topics, international and domestic, is reversed, suggesting the primacy of domestic reform. One of the first things the post-Stalin leadership did was to end the Korean War, which liberated the necessary funds for measures to improve agriculture and raise living standards generally. Malenkov personally, though not all his colleagues in the leadership, wanted to cut back Soviet commitments abroad where he thought this could be done safely. Malenkov's speech is also unusual in that he tried to assert the primacy of the Government (the Council of Ministers) over party bodies in the making of policy, both domestic and foreign. After a struggle lasting more than a year, he was defeated and forced to step down from his post as head of the Government.

While Malenkov tried to set in motion important changes in foreign policy, he proceeded cautiously. Stalin's heirs faced a difficult problem in relaxing the state's tight grip over society, both in the USSR and in the European satellites. (A curiosity may be mentioned. When Malenkov reminds the People's Democracies of the need to consolidate the "firm alliance of the working class and the peasantry," (Section III) he is signaling Moscow's approval of a policy of shifting resources from heavy and defense industry to agriculture.) The perils of relaxation were made strikingly evident in East Germany three months after Stalin died, when a Moscow-instigated program of reform led to a revolt against the puppet Communist regime. The revolt quickly collapsed when Soviet occupation troops attacked the rebels, but the need to move cautiously in enacting reforms had been made clear.

Unlike the Malenkov of October 1952—who still had to satisfy his master, Stalin—the Malenkov of August 1953 is not content to rely on contradictions in the opposing camp to weaken it. He advocates an *active* policy of improving the international atmosphere and attempting to lessen international tension, to be achieved, in part, presumably by an easing of Soviet pressure on the West. If détente is achieved, he suggests, the North Atlantic bloc may lose its cohesion and come apart. But Malenkov is sensitive to the charge that the USSR wants to reduce tension because of internal weakness. He announces that "the United States has no monopoly of the hydrogen bomb." (Several days later the Soviet Union exploded a thermonuclear device.) Speaking from nuclear strength, Malenkov proceeds to call for great-power negotiations.

Malenkov's insistence that a sober policy must be based on actual realities, on facts, while formally directed to the West, may be an implicit criticism of Stalin's unrealistic policies in his last years. It seems to point toward a settlement with the West that would preserve the 1953 *status quo.*

The International Situation and the Foreign Policy of the Soviet Union

Comrade Deputies, when examining our internal problems, we cannot, of course, abstract our attention from the international situation.

The distinguishing feature of the international situation today is the big successes achieved by the Soviet Union, the Chinese People's Republic and the entire camp of peace and democracy in their struggle to lessen international tensions, in their struggle for peace and the prevention of another world war.

In the East, the bloodshed which has carried off so many human lives and which harboured a threat of the most serious international complications has been stopped.

The peoples of the whole world hailed the signing of the Korean armistice with the greatest joy. They rightly regard it as a victory for the peace-loving forces. For over three years the camp of peace and democracy had been striving to stop the war in Korea. Its efforts have been crowned by the signing of the armistice. The will to peace of the millions has become so powerful and effective a force that the aggressors are compelled to reckon with it.

The aggressive elements started the war in Korea in the hope that they could bring the Korean people to their knees. But, in embarking on war against the Korean People's Democratic Republic, the interventionists miscalculated. They were unable to crush the heroic Korean people. The interventionists launched their armed venture in the belief that they could achieve their object by a lightning stroke and without particular strain. But it turned out otherwise. They became involved in a protracted and sanguinary war and after sustaining heavy losses in men and materiel and thoroughly damaging their military prestige were forced to abandon their plans of aggrandizement. This is truly a case of going out for wool and coming home shorn.

The Korean people's struggle against the interventionists and their hirelings, the Syngman Rhee clique, has shown that devotion to the cause of liberty and independence of one's country engenders supreme fortitude, courage and mass heroism. Against the Korean people was hurled the most powerful military machine commanded by modern imperialism; yet they were invincible, because they were fighting in a righteous cause. Nor will the noble deed of the glorious Chinese People's Volunteers in coming to the aid of the Korean people ever be obliterated from the memory of man. It is a deed of which not only the great Chinese people, but all progressive men and women are proud.

The peoples of the Soviet Union heartily congratulate the Korean and Chinese peoples on the achievement of an armistice.

The task now is to ensure the rebuilding of the peaceful life of the Korean people, who have suffered so severely and at the cost of such heavy sacrifice have upheld the right to be the arbiters of their own destiny, the destiny of their country.

We, Soviet people, ardently wish that the glorious Korean people may live and prosper in peace. The Soviet Union will help the Korean people to heal the severe wounds inflicted by the war. The Government has decided to assign at once 1,000 million rubles for the rehabilitation of Korea's devastated economy. We are confident that the Supreme Soviet will unanimously approve this decision.

In the West, the Soviet Union's consistency and perseverance in pursuing a policy of peace has foiled the provocative venture in Berlin.

The organizers of the Berlin venture had far-reaching aims. Their idea was to suppress Germany's democratic forces, to destroy the German Democratic Republic, which is the bulwark of the peace-loving forces of the German people, to convert Germany into a militarist state, and to re-create a hotbed of war in the heart of Europe. There can be no doubt that if the Soviet Union had not displayed firmness and steadfastness in upholding the interests of peace, the Berlin venture might have had very grave international consequences.

That is why the liquidation of the Berlin venture must also be regarded as an important victory for the cause of peace.

Among the Soviet Union's successes in its effort to lessen international tensions is the improvement of its relations with the neighbouring countries.

Desirous of promoting peaceful co-operation with all countries, the Soviet Government attaches particular importance to strengthening the Soviet Union's relations with its neighbours. To elevate these relations to the level of genuine good-neighbourliness is the aim for which we are striving and will continue to strive.

The Soviet Union has no territorial claims on any country, neighbouring countries included. Respect for the national liberty and sovereignty of all countries, big and small, is an inviolable principle of our foreign policy. . .

Our neighbour in the south is Iran. The experience of three and a half decades has shown that mutual friendship and co-operation is to the interest of the Soviet Union and Iran. Hence, there is a firm basis for Soviet-Iranian relations, which makes it possible to settle issues arising between the two parties to their mutual satisfaction.

Improvement of relations between Turkey and the Soviet Union would certainly redound to the benefit of both parties and would be a valuable contribution to greater security in the Black Sea area.

* * *

Desirous of lessening general tension, the Soviet Government consented to the re-establishment of diplomatic relations with Israel. In doing so, it took into consideration the fact that the Israeli Government had given an undertaking that "Israel would not be a party to any alliance or pact aiming at aggression against the Soviet Union." We believe that resumption of diplomatic relations will facilitate co-operation between the two states.

The assertion made by certain foreign newspapers that resumption of diplomatic relations with Israel will tend to weaken the Soviet Union's relations with the Arab states is devoid of foundation. The activities of the Soviet Government will be directed in the future, too, to furthering friendly co-operation with the Arab states.

Our Government took the initiative in exchanging Ambassadors with Yugoslavia and Greece, after a long interruption. We expect this to lead to normalization of relations with both countries and to produce good results.

There are no objective causes which might prevent an improvement of relations between the Soviet Union and Italy. It goes without saying that relations between states can be strengthened if the mutual obligations they have assumed are observed. With favourable development of Soviet-Italian relations, Italian industry, which is now experiencing great difficulties, might receive substantial support from improved economic intercourse between our countries. A mutually advantageous agreement would ensure Italy coal and grain, and also orders for her industries. This would undoubtedly help to improve the living conditions of Italy's splendid people.

The peoples of all countries hope that the conclusion of the Korean armistice will be an important contribution to the furtherance of peace and security, first and foremost, in the Far East.

In this connection, normalization of relations between all the Far Eastern states, and with Japan in particular, is a matter of urgent moment. There are serious obstacles to this, inasmuch as the United States of America has violated the agreements concluded by the Allies during and after the war, and is pursuing a policy of suppressing Japan's national independence and converting her into a strategic bridgehead. The healthy forces of the Japanese nation are coming more and more to realize that the existing obstacles must be overcome and the national independence of their country upheld. They understand that this is the only way to ensure the peaceful development of their country and the necessary political and quite feasible economic relations with neighbouring countries. Any steps that Japan takes along these lines will meet with the sympathy and support of the Soviet Union and of all peace-loving nations.

Of great importance for the promotion of peace in the East is the attitude of so big a country as India. India has made a substantial contribution to the efforts of the peace-loving countries to stop the Korean war. Our relations with India are growing firmer, and cultural and economic intercourse with her is becoming wider. We hope that relations between India and the Soviet Union will become stronger and develop in a spirit of friendly cooperation.

The desire of business circles in a number of countries to remove discriminatory measures of every description which hamper world trade is understandable and timely. Restoration of normal trade relations between countries with whom mutual trade is an established tradition has long become a necessity. All who believe, and rightly, that broader economic relations will help to promote peace cannot but work for sounder international trade.

The Government of the Soviet Union considers it of prime importance to continue to strengthen relations with the countries of the democratic camp. These relations are marked by close co-operation and real brotherly friendship.

Strong and unbreakable ties of friendship bind the Soviet Union and the Chinese People's Republic; economic and cultural intercourse between the two countries is on a vast scale and growing apace.

On an ever broader and firmer basis, the Soviet Union is co-operating in all spheres with Poland, Czechoslovakia, Rumania, Hungary, Bulgaria, Albania, the Mongolian People's Republic, and the People's Democratic Republic of Korea.

Our friendly relations with the German Democratic Republic are carried on an ever firmer footing; the Soviet Union renders, and will continue to render, assistance and support to the German Democratic Republic, which is the bulwark of the struggle for a united, peaceable and democratic Germany.

One of the decisive advantages of the democratic camp, and a point in which it differs fundamentally from the imperialist camp, is that it is not torn by internal contradictions and conflicts, that a major source of its strength and progress is the mutual concern displayed by all the countries of the democratic camp for one another's interests, and their close economic co-operation. The friendly ties and brotherly co-operation between the countries of the democratic camp will therefore grow ever firmer and stronger.

The active struggle for peace conducted with fixity of purpose by the Soviet Union and the entire democratic camp has yielded definite results. A change in the international atmosphere is to be observed. After a long period of mounting tension, one feels for the first time since the war a certain easing of the international situation. Hundreds of millions of people are becoming increasingly hopeful that a way can be found of settling disputes and outstanding issues. This is a reflection of the deep desire of the people for stable and lasting peace.

We cannot, however, close our eyes to the fact that there are also forces which are working against the policy of relaxing international tension and trying to frustrate it at any cost. That is why the Korean armistice negotiations were so protracted, why strategic bridgeheads are being built in West Germany and Japan, why provocations are instigated against the countries of the democratic camp, and why a policy of atomic blackmail is carried on.

The aggressive elements are stubbornly working against relaxation of international tension because they fear that if developments take this course they will have to curtail armaments programmes, which are a source of huge profit to the munitions manufacturers and which create artificial employment for industry. They fear for their fabulous profits. These elements are also afraid that if international tension is lessened, more millions upon millions of people will realize that the North-Atlantic bloc, which was ostensibly established for defence, actually is the chief danger to peace. The aggressive circles are equally aware that if now, at this time of international tension, the North-Atlantic bloc is torn by internal conflicts and contradictions, it may fall to pieces altogether if that tension is relaxed.

It is quite obvious that, alongside the peace-loving forces, there are forces in the world which have too definitely committed themselves to a policy of aggravating international tension. These forces bank on war; peace does not suit them. They consider that any lessening of tension would be a misfortune. They are committed to a course of adventurism and a policy of aggression.

This policy is served by the so-called "cold war strategy" and international provocations of every description.

Absorbed in the policy of aggravating international tension, certain conspicuous but—let it be said—not very perspicacious transatlantic leaders consider the Soviet Union's efforts to safeguard peace between nations, its concern to lessen international tensions, as a manifestation of weakness. It is precisely this preposterous assumption that explains the flagrantly unreasonable approach of certain U.S. circles to the settlement of international issues, and their policy of pressure and indiscriminate adventurism.

There is nothing new, of course, in this "philosophy." The world has not yet forgotten that none other than Hitler acted on the unwise assumption that the Soviet Union was a "colossus with feet of clay" and embarked on his criminal venture against our country. Everyone knows that this ended in the downfall of German fascism.

One may be allowed to ask: on what grounds do certain American politicians reiterate today the talk about the weakness of the Soviet Union?. . .

True, there are politicians abroad, it appears, who profess to see a sign of our country's weakness in the fact that enemy of the people Beria has been exposed and rendered harmless. But these are short-sighted politicians. It is clear to everyone that the timely exposure of a double-dyed agent of imperialism and rendering him harmless cannot in any way be taken as evidence of weakness of the Soviet state.

We know that the war advocates abroad for a long time cherished the illusion that the United States had a monopoly of the atomic bomb. But developments showed that they were greatly mistaken. The United States had long ceased to have a monopoly of the atomic bomb. The transatlantic enemies of peace have lately found a new consolation. The United States, you see, possess a more powerful weapon than the atomic bomb; it has a monopoly of the hydrogen bomb. That might presumably be some consolation to them if it tallied with the facts. But it does not. The Government considers it necessary to inform the Supreme Soviet that the United States has no monopoly of the hydrogen bomb either.

* * *

Comrades, the present stage of international development is an exceptionally important and responsible one. It would be a crime against humanity if a certain easing of the international situation which is now to be observed were to give way to a new increase of tension.

Soviet foreign policy is clear.

The Soviet Union will consistently and firmly pursue a policy of preserving and consolidating peace, will promote cooperation and business relations with all states which have a like desire, and strengthen the ties of brotherly friendship and solidarity with the great Chinese people, with all the People's Democracies.

We firmly stand by the belief that there are no disputed or outstanding issues today which cannot be settled peacefully by mutual agreement between the parties concerned.

This also relates to disputed issues between the United States of America and the Soviet Union. We stand, as we have stood in the past, for the peaceful co-existence of the two systems. We hold that there are no objective reasons for clashes between the United States of America and the Soviet Union. The security of the two states and of the world, and the development of trade between the United States and the Soviet Union can be ensured on the basis of normal relations between the two countries.

Today, the government of any country, if it is seriously concerned for the future of its people, is in duty bound practically to assist the settlement of international disputes. No small part could, of course, be played by Great-Power negotiations. Naturally, the appropriate prerequisites must be created for this.

A broad public demand has lately arisen in Britain and other countries for effective measures to lessen international tensions. The recognition is growing in political quarters in these countries that disputed issues can be settled. However, mere verbal recognition of this possibility is today insufficient.

The President of the U.S.A. declared in his speech to the American Society of Newspaper Editors on April 16 that no dispute, "great or small, is insoluable—given only the will to respect the rights of all nations." This is an important statement, which might only be welcomed. But, unfortunately, the actual policy of the ruling circles in the U.S.A. stands in irreconcilable contradiction to this statement of President Eisenhower.

If respect for the rights of all nations is seriously meant, then an aggressive policy must be abandoned and the course adopted of settling international issues by mutual agreement between the parties concerned.

If respect for the rights of all nations is seriously meant, then the policy of ignoring China must be ended and the violated rights of the Chinese People's Republic in the United Nations must be restored. The great Chinese Power must occupy its legitimate place both in the United Nations and in the whole system of international relations.

The entire present day situation stresses the especial responsibility which lies upon the Great Powers to bring about a further relaxation of international tension by means of negotiation and settlement of disputed issues. It is upon them that the U.N. Charter puts the chief responsibility for the maintenance of world peace and security. . . .

It is also necessary to solve such urgent problems as the German question, which is of cardinal importance. . . .

They want us to agree to the rebuilding of an aggressive militarist Germany, and take the liberty of talking in this connection of safeguarding peace in Europe. But our people did not shed the blood of millions of their sons and daughters in war with militarist Germany in order to permit the rebuilding of this most dangerous hotbed of war in Europe.

The Great Powers bound themselves to preserve German's national unity, not to destroy it, to ensure the transformation of Germany into a peaceable democratic state, not to assist the rebuilding of German militarism. The Soviet Union, for its part, will do everything in its power to assist the carrying out of these obligations. . . .

A militarist Germany, irrespective of whether it appears in its former guise or under the screen of a "European Defence Community," would be a mortal enemy of France and other neighbouring states. Therefore, any attempt to bind France to a "European Defence Community" would be a betrayal of France to the German revanchists. . .

We heartily wish the French people—with whom our people are bound by ties of long-standing friendship and by the blood they shed in common struggle against their common enemy, the German militarists—success in this course. We do not forget that the Soviet Union and France have a treaty of alliance and mutual assistance,which can serve as a basis for developing and strengthening the relations between our countries, and help to safeguard European security.

It is likewise necessary to settle the Austrian question. This presupposes, first of all, the removal of artificial obstacles, such as the "abbreviated treaty," which contradicts existing Four-Power agreements. No one can deny that a proper settlement of the German question would assist the settlement of the Austrian question too.

An important condition for the furtherance of peace is the enhancement of the prestige and weight of the United Nations. Today, this international organization is actually in a state of deep crisis, because it has been reduced to the role of an instrument of the North-Atlantic bloc.

The United Nations must return to the path mapped out by its Charter. It is its direct duty to assist the settlement of international problems and to rule out the possibility of aggression on the part of any of its members against other states. The Soviet Government will energetically support this.

The Soviet Union unswervingly pursues and will pursue a policy of peace. The Soviet Union has no intention of attacking anyone. Aggressive designs are alien to it. Of this the peoples of all countries may be assured.

However, while persistently working for peace, we must firmly remember our sacred duty constantly to strengthen and perfect the defence of the great Soviet Union. This we must do against the event of anyone taking it into his head to commit an act of insanity and attempt to violate the security of our Motherland. The Soviet people must be prepared at any moment to cool the hot heads of adventurers and war instigators of every description and compel them to respect the socialist gains and the might of the Soviet Union.

For the Soviet Government and for all of us Soviet people, promoting peace and safeguarding the security of nations is not a matter of tactics or diplomatic manoeuvering. It is our general line in the sphere of foreign policy.

Hundreds of millions of people believe and hope that the near future will witness a further relaxation of international tension. We must see to it that the expectations and hopes of the peoples are not disappointed.

Our Cause is Invincible

... It is rightly considered in the People's Democracies that an indispensable condition for and guarantee of, their successful progress is consolidation of the firm alliance of the working class and the peasantry. It is clear that all the tasks confronting the People's Democracies can be accomplished only if this tried and tested Leninist policy is unswervingly adhered to.

In the sphere of foreign relations, the People's Democracies, shoulder to shoulder with the Soviet Union, are resolutely defending the peace and security of nations.

* * *

Whoever does not understand that the 800 million human beings who constitute the great family of nations of the democratic camp cannot be compelled to relinquish the historic gains they have won with their sweat and blood, to relinquish their own rule, the rule of the people, and to restore the rule of the exploiters—whoever does not understand that is simply foolish. It is clear to the whole world that the aggressive forces will not succeed in reversing the course of history. Anyone who desires to pursue a sober policy in international affairs must take his stand on actual realities, on facts, whether they are pleasant or not.

It must be realized that, with the present alignment of forces, and with the firm determination of the Soviet Union and the countries of the democratic camp to uphold their vital interests in the international arena, it is the duty not only of the countries of the democratic camp, but of all countries to conduct a policy based upon the peaceful co-existence of the two systems. For any other course is a course of hopeless ventures and inevitable failures.

* * *

Our cause is invincible!

We shall continue to march forward confidently to the building of a Communist society in our country.

KHRUSHCHEV

Report to the XX Party Congress *February 14, 1956*

Introduction During 1954, Khrushchev emerged as the dominant figure in the "collective leadership." At the Geneva Summit Conference of July, 1955, he was a representative of the Soviet Union. While the Conference made little progress toward settling outstanding issues, Khrushchev gained from his talks with President Eisenhower a large measure of assurance that the United States, despite its great quantitative superiority in strategic nuclear forces, would not attack the USSR except under the most extreme provocation, i.e., unless the USSR acted in ways that it did not intend. President Eisenhower's stress on the destructiveness to both sides of a nuclear war led Khrushchev to say in his Report that prominent bourgeois leaders frankly admit that they cannot win a war in which atomic weapons are used. (The reassurance that Khrushchev derived from this seems not altogether consistent with his denial that an arms race can have the effect of reducing the danger of war.) From Geneva on, Khrushchev hoped to develop a new relationship with the U.S., one that would make Soviet political gains possible, in Europe and elsewhere, without increasing the risk of war.

The post-Stalin leadership looked more favorably on the countries of the third world than had Stalin and adopted friendlier policies toward them. Khrushchev voices approval of non-Communist states that refuse to participate in blocs, and includes them, along with the Soviet bloc itself, in his zone of peace. In the following years the USSR increasingly cultivated these states through offers of economic and military assistance.

After surveying the international situation and outlining Soviet foreign policy, Khrushchev devotes a section of his Report to updating doctrine. He rejects the view that capitalism is in a state of complete stagnation, but he still retains faith in the coming economic crisis of capitalism, which will benefit the Communist world. (This faith is somewhat analogous to the West's faith in the liberalization of the USSR.) The crisis, when it occurs, will provide an opportunity for revolution in particular countries and for the Communist seizure of power. Until then, however, the world Communist movement must follow a "rightist" policy of cooperation with any group that is willing to oppose the imperialists. Moscow subsequently tried to establish contact with European leaders of democratic socialism, but the Soviet suppression of the Hungarian revolt in October, 1956, put a quick end to these efforts.

The theme of peaceful coexistence, of course, is not new. However, Khrushchev asserts that peaceful coexistence is "the general line of our country's foreign policy," and this *is* unusual. It implies an unwillingness to accept a substantial risk of war in the pursuit of Soviet foreign policy objectives. Communist China took exception to this implication, and it became an important point of contention between the two countries.

Khrushchev's boldest ideological innovation is his denial of the key Leninist teaching that wars are inevitable as long as imperialism exists. Observe that he does not justify his revision of Lenin's doctrine by the advent of thermonuclear weapons—which, he might have argued, made it inexpedient for capitalism to defend itself by war. Instead, it is the world socialist camp which had come into being while Stalin was still alive that makes possible the prevention of war. Khrushchev says little explicitly about nuclear weapons, but they were unquestionably in his mind at many points in the Report.

Khrushchev's increased confidence in the international situation is reflected in the changed order of topics in his Report. The section on the international situation does not begin with an analysis of the *capitalist* world as heretofore, but with a discussion of "economic advance in the USSR and the People's Democracies." The implication (later made explicit) is that the capitalist world is no longer the dominant factor in the international situation around which the USSR must orient its foreign policy; the socialist camp is here presented as the full equal of the capitalist camp.

The International Position
of the Soviet Union

The emergence of socialism from within the bounds of a single country and its transformation into a world system is the main feature of our era. Capitalism has proved powerless to prevent this process of world-historic significance. The simultaneous existence of two opposite world economic systems, the capitalist and the socialist, developing according to different laws and in opposite directions, has become an indisputable fact.

* * *

The Steady Economic Advance in the U.S.S.R.
and the People's Democracies

... The industrial base of socialism is growing stronger. The share of the socialist countries in world industrial output is steadily increasing. This fact is a material expression of a progressive historical process: contraction of the sphere of capitalist exploitation, of the world positions of capitalism and expansion of the world positions of socialism.

High rates of development of industrial production are a guarantee of new successes for socialism in its economic competition with capitalism. The U.S.S.R. now holds second place in total volume of industrial output ...

A feature of the Soviet economy and of that of all the socialist countries is their all-round development and general peaceful trend. The countries of socialism are giving unremitting attention above all to the development of heavy industry, which is the foundation for the continuous expansion of social production as a whole. At the same time they are giving great attention to the growth of agriculture and the light industries. Living standards are steadily rising: culture is flowering.

* * *

We note China's achievements in socialist industrialization with great satisfaction. Never before has a highly industrialized country voluntarily helped other countries to become industrialized. On the contrary, the small group of highly developed countries which emerged in the capitalist world have always hindered the industrialization of other countries, particularly colonies and semi-colonies. That is why the bulk of the countries in Asia, South America, and Africa have no large-scale industry of their own. The Soviet Union, to which such purposes are alien, is doing everything to help the fraternal people of China establish a powerful industry of their own. Our country is helping the People's Republic of China to build, within one five-year period alone, 156 enterprises and 21 separate workshops, supplying industrial plant to a total value of about 5,600 million rubles.

In exchange for these deliveries the Soviet Union is receiving products from China and other People's Democracies in which it is interested, the materials and consumer goods usually exported by these countries.

* * *

The Economic Situation in the Capitalist Countries and the Further Aggravation of The Contradictions of Capitalism

. . . In 1955 industrial output in the capitalist world as a whole was 93 per cent greater than in 1929.

Does this mean that capitalism has succeeded in overcoming its internal contradictions and acquiring stability? No, it does not. The capitalist world economy is developing extremely unevenly and has become still more unstable. . . .

The general crisis of capitalism continues to deepen. Capitalism's insoluble contradiction—the contradiction between the modern productive forces and capitalist relations of production—has become still more acute. The rapid development of present-day technology does not remove this contradiction but only emphasizes it.

It should be said that the idea that the general crisis of capitalism means complete stagnation, a halt in production and technical progresss, has always been alien to Marxism-Leninism. Lenin pointed out that capitalism's general tendency to decay did not preclude technical progress or an upswing in production in one period or another.... Therefore we must study the capitalist economy attentively and not over-simplify Lenin's thesis on the decay of imperialism but study the best that capitalist science and technology have to offer, in order to use the achievements of world technological progress in the interests of socialism.

* * *

Based on the present business activity, talk about "prosperity" has again begun in some Western circles. They are attempting to prove that the Marxist theory of crises has "become antiquated." Bourgeois economists are silent about the fact that only a temporary coincidence of circumstances favourable to capitalism prevented the crisis phenomena from developing into a deep economic crisis...

The capitalists and the learned defenders of their interests are circulating the "theory" that uninterrupted expansion of arms manufacture brings salvation from economic crisis. The representatives of Marxist-Leninist science have more than once pointed out that this is a hollow illusion. The arms race does not cure the disease, it drives it deeper. And the more extensive the militarization of the economy, the graver will be its consequences for capitalism.

The representatives of the capitalist groups repose special hopes in government regulation of the economy. Monopoly capital is establishing direct control over government agencies, sending its representatives to work in them and making the government "regulate" the country's economy in the interests of the monopolies....However, the state's intervention in economic activity does not eliminate the fundamental defects of the capitalist system. The state is powerless to do away with the objective laws of capitalist economy, which lead to anarchy of production and economic crises. Crises are inherent in the very nature of capitalism, they are inevitable.

* * *

The United States of America is losing the monopoly position it held during the first post-war years... In 1947-48 the United States accounted for nearly three-fifths of the industrial output of the capitalist world, but today it accounts for only half. The United States has already made the most of its post-war economic opportunities; no new markets are in sight. There is therefore no prospect of a further substantial increase in production.

The situation in the capitalist world market has become especially aggravated since the re-appearance in it of Western Germany and Japan.

They, like Britain and France, have practically regained their pre-war positions in the world market. Today a further increase in each country's exports is possible only as a result of fierce struggle against competitors. . . .The economic struggle between the capitalist countries is gaining momentum. As before, the main conflict is that between the United States and Great Britain. . . .

The revival of Western Germany's economic power is especially aggravating the situation in the world market. . . .

The problem of markets is becoming all the more acute, because the capitalist world market is steadily shrinking as a result of the formation of the new and growing socialist world market. Besides, the underdeveloped countries, on casting off the colonial yoke, begin to develop their own industry, which inevitably leads to a further narrowing of markets for industrial products. All this means that the struggle for markets and spheres of influence will become still sharper within the imperialist camp.

* * *

Thus, capitalism is steadily moving towards new economic and social upheavals.

The Imperialist Policy of Lining Up
Aggressive Blocs and Fanning the "Cold War."
The Struggle of the Peoples for Relaxation
of International Tension

. . . The organizers of military blocs allege that they have united for defence, for protection against the "communist threat." But that is sheer hypocrisy. We know from history that when planning a redivision of the world, the imperialist powers have always lined up military blocs. Today the "anti-communism" slogan is again being used as a smokescreen to cover up the claims of one power for world domination. The new thing here is that the United States wants, by means of all kinds of blocs and pacts, to secure a dominant position in the capitalist world for itself, and to reduce all its partners in the blocs to the status of obedient executors of its will.

The inspirers of the "positions of strength" policy assert that this policy makes another war impossible, because it ensures a "balance of power" in the world arena. This view is widespread among Western statesmen and it is therefore all the more important to thoroughly expose its real meaning.

Can peace be promoted by an arms race? It would seem that it is simply absurd to pose such a question. Yet the adherents of the "positions of strength" policy offer the arms race as their main recipe for the preservation of peace! It is perfectly obvious that when nations compete to increase their military might, the danger of war becomes greater, not lesser.

The arms race, the "positions of strength" policy, the lining up of aggressive blocs and the "cold war"—all this could not but aggravate the international situation, and it did. This has been one trend of world events during the period under review.

But other processes have also taken place in the international arena during these years, processes showing that in the world today monopolist circles are by no means controlling everything.

The steady consolidation of the forces of socialism, democracy and peace, and of the forces of the national-liberation movement is of decisive significance. The international position of the Soviet Union, the People's Republic of China, and the other socialist countries has been further strengthened during this period, and their prestige and international ties have grown immeasurably. The international camp of socialism is exerting ever-growing influence on the course of international events.

The forces of peace have been considerably augmented by the emergence in the world arena of a group of peace-loving European and Asian states which have proclaimed non-participation in blocs as a principle of their foreign policy. The leading political circles of these states rightly hold that to participate in restricted military imperialist alignments would merely increase the danger of their countries being involved in military gambles by the aggressive forces and draw them into the maelstrom of the arms drive.

As a result, a vast Zone of Peace including peace-loving states, both socialist and non-socialist, of Europe and Asia, has emerged in the world. This zone includes vast areas inhabited by nearly 1,500 million people, that is, the majority of the population of our planet.

The vigorous efforts for peace of the broadest masses have greatly influenced international events. For the scale and organization of the struggle against the war danger waged by the masses the present period is without precedent.

The Communist Parties have proved to be the most active and consistent fighters against the war danger and reaction. Throughout these years, as before, they have been in the very thick of the struggle to preserve peace, to uphold the vital interests of the working people, and the national independence of their countries. . . .

Not a few of the misfortunes harassing the world today are due to the fact that in many countries the working class has been split for many years and its different groups do not present a united front, which only plays into the hands of the reactionary forces. Yet, today, in our opinion, the prospect of changing this situation is opening up. Life has put on the agenda many questions which not only demand rapprochement and co-operation between all workers' parties but also create real possibilities for this co-operation. The most important of these questions is that of preventing a new war. If the working class comes out as a united organized force and acts with firm resolution, there will be no war.

All this places an historic responsibility upon all leaders of the labour movement. The interests of the struggle for peace make it imperative to find points of contact and on these grounds to lay the foundations for co-operation, sweeping aside mutual recriminations. Here co-operation with those circles of the socialist movement whose views on the forms of transition to socialism differ from ours is also possible and essential. Among them are not a few people who are honestly mistaken on this question, but this is no obstacle to co-operation. Today many Social-Democrats stand for active struggle against the war danger and militarism, for rapprochement with the socialist countries, for unity of the labour movement. We sincerely greet these Social-Democrats and are willing to do everything necessary to join our efforts in the struggle for the noble cause of upholding peace and the interests of the working people.

All international developments in recent years show that big popular forces have risen to fight for the preservation of peace. The ruling imperialist circles cannot but reckon with this factor. Their more far-sighted representatives are beginning to admit that the "positions of strength" policy could not put pressure on the countries against which it was directed and that it has failed. At the same time this policy weighs heavily on the masses in the capitalist world and has increased their dissatisfaction. The overwhelming majority of mankind rejects the "positions of strength" policy as a policy of gambles directed against the people and enhancing the war danger.

Under the impact of these incontestable facts, symptoms of a certain sobering up are appearing among influential Western circles. More and more people among these circles are realizing what a dangerous gamble war against the socialist countries may prove for the destinies of capitalism. Undoubtedly, the working class and the labouring masses of the capitalist countries, should their rulers dare to precipitate such a war, would draw decisive conclusions regarding the system which periodically plunges the nations into the blood bath of war. Nor is it fortuitous that prominent leaders of bourgeois countries frankly admit with increasing frequency that "there will be no victor" in a war in which atomic weapons are used. These leaders still do not venture to state that capitalism will find its grave in another world war, should it unleash it, but they are already compelled openly to admit that the socialist camp is invincible.

Disintegration of the Imperialist Colonial System

. . . The disintegration of the imperialist colonial system now taking place is a post-war development of history-making significance. Peoples who for centuries were kept away by the colonialists from the high road of progress followed by human society are now going through a great process of regeneration. People's China and the independent Indian Republic have joined the ranks of the Great Powers. We are witnessing a political and economic upsurge of the peoples of South-East Asia and the Arab East. The awakening of the peoples of Africa has begun. The national-liberation movement has gained in strength in Brazil, Chile and other Latin-American countries. The outcome of the wars in Korea, Indo-China and Indonesia has demonstrated that the imperialists are unable, even with the help of armed intervention, to crush the peoples who are resolutely fighting for a life of freedom and independence. The complete abolition of the infamous system of colonialism has now been put on the agenda as one of the most acute and pressing problems.

The new period in world history which Lenin predicted has arrived, and the peoples of the East are playing an active part in deciding the destinies of the whole world, are becoming a new mighty factor in international relations. In contrast to the pre-war period, most Asian countries now act in the world arena as sovereign states or states which are resolutely upholding their right to an independent foreign policy. International realtions have spread beyond the bounds of relations between the countries inhabited chiefly by peoples of the white race and are beginning to acquire the character of genuinely world-wide relations.

The winning of political freedom by the peoples of the former colonies and semi-colonies is the first and most important prerequisite of their full independence, that is, of the achievement of economic independence. The liberated Asian countries are pursuing a policy of building up their own industry, training their own technicians, raising the living standards of the people, and regenerating and developing their age-old national culture. History-making prospects for a better future are opening up before the countries which have embarked upon the path of independent development.

These countries, although they do not belong to the socialist world system, can draw on its achievements to build up an independent national economy and to raise the living standards of their peoples. Today they need not go begging for up-to-date equipment to their former oppressors. They can get it is the socialist countries, without assuming any political or military commitments.

The very fact that the Soviet Union and the other countries of the socialist camp exist, their readiness to help the underdeveloped countries in advancing their industries on terms of equality and mutual benefit are a major stumbling-block to colonial policy. The imperialists can no longer regard the underdeveloped countries solely as potential sources for making maximum profits. They are compelled to make concessions to them.

* * *

The contradictions and rivalry between the colonial powers for spheres of influence, sources of raw materials, and markets are growing. The United States is out to grab the colonial possessions of the European powers. South Viet-Nam is passing from France to the United States. The American monopolies are waging an offensive against the French, Belgian and Portuguese possessions in Africa. Once Iran's oil riches were fully controlled by the British, but now the British have been compelled to share them with the Americans; moreover, the American monopolists are fighting to oust the British entirely. American influence in Pakistan and Iraq is increasing under the guise of "free enterprise."

* * *

The monopolists are interested in continuing the "positions of strength" policy; the ending of the "cold war" is to their disadvantage. Why? Because the fanning of war hysteria is used to justify imperialist expansion, to intimidate the masses and dope their minds in order to justify the higher taxes which then go to pay for war orders and flow into the safes of the millionaires. Thus, the "cold war" is a means for maintaining the war industry at a high level and for extracting colossal profits.

Naturally, "aid" to underdeveloped countries is granted on definite political terms, terms providing for their integration into aggressive military blocs, the conclusion of joint military pacts, and support for American foreign policy aimed at world domination, or "world leadership," as the American imperialists themselves call it.

The struggle of the peoples of the Eastern countries against participation in blocs is a struggle for national independence. It is not fortuitous that the overwhelming majority of countries in South-East Asia and the Middle East have rejected the importunate attempts of the Western Powers to inveigle them into closed military alignments.

Despite all the efforts to set the peoples of the under-developed countries at loggerheads with each other and with the peoples of the socialist camp, their friendship and co-operation is growing ever stronger. The Bandung Conference of 29 Asian and African countries has strikingly demonstrated the growing solidarity of the Eastern peoples. Its decisions reflected the will of hundreds of millions of people in the East. It struck a powerful blow at the plans of the colonialists and aggressors.

The friendship and co-operation between the Eastern peoples who have thrown off the colonial yoke and the peoples of the socialist countries is growing and strengthening. This was graphically revealed by the visits of the leaders of India and Burma to the Soviet Union and by the visit of the Soviet leaders to India, Burma and Afghanistan. Those visits confirmed the identity of views existing between the Soviet Union and the Republic of India, one of the Great Powers of the world, and between the Soviet Union, Burma, and Afghanistan, on the fundamental international issue of today: the preservation and consolidation of universal peace and the national independence of all states.

* * *

The Soviet Union in the Struggle for the Consolidation of Peace and International Security

Loyal to the Leninist principles of peaceful foreign policy, the Soviet Union has vigorously worked to ease international tension and strengthen peace, and has scored big successes. I should like to call your attention to the most important directions in which the Soviet Union's initiative for peace developed.

First, improving relations between the Great Powers.

Second, elimination of the breeding grounds of war that existed in the East and the prevention of the development of new breeding grounds of war and conflict in Europe and Asia.

Third, adjusting relations with a number of countries in order to ease tension in Europe (normalization of relations with fraternal Yugoslavia, conclusion of the State Treaty with Austria, establishment of diplomatic relations between the U.S.S.R. and the German Federal Republic, etc.)

Fourth, exploration of new ways to settle such questions as the establishment of a collective security system in Europe, disarmament, prohibition of atomic weapons, the German problem, etc.

Fifth, rapprochement with all countries desiring to preserve peace.

Sixth, expanding in every way international contacts: personal contacts between Soviet statesmen and those of other countries; contacts between representatives of our Party and workers' parties of other countries and between trade unions; greater exchange of parliamentary, social, and other delegations: the development of trade and other economic ties; and the expansion of tourist travel and student exchange.

The peace initiative of the Soviet Union has become one of the most important factors exerting a tremendous influence on international events.

The success of the Soviet Union's peace initiative has been greatly facilitated by the support and joint action of all the peace-loving countries. A particularly important part in this respect has been, and is being, played by the great People's Republic of China which did so much to end the bloodshed in Korea and Indo-China and has made the well-known proposal for a Collective Peace Pact in Asia. The great Indian Republic has made a big contribution to strengthening peace in Asia and the whole world. Millions of ordinary people in all countries have ardently supported the Soviet steps to put international relations on a healthy basis.

The efforts of the peace-loving states and peoples have not been in vain. For the first time since the war a certain relaxation of international tension has set in. In this atmosphere the Geneva Conference of the Heads of Government of the Four Powers became possible. The Conference demonstrated the vitality and correctness of the method of negotiation between countries. It confirmed the Soviet view that the most intricate international issues can be settled through negotiation, given a mutual desire for cooperation and agreement.

Some people are now trying to bury the Geneva spirit. The facts show that certain circles in the West have still not given up hope of putting pressure on the Soviet Union and wresting unilateral concessions from it. But it is high time to understand that such calculations are unrealistic. The Soviet Union has done much to bring the positions of the Great Powers closer together. Now it is up to the United States, Britain, and France. This of course does not mean that the Soviet Union will refuse to make further efforts to ease international tension and strengthen peace. On the contrary, since it has become possible to bring the positions of the powers closer together on a number of major international issues, the Soviet Union will strive with still greater persistence to establish confidence and co-operation between all countries, above all between the Great Powers. Equal effort and reciprocal concessions are absolutely indispensable in the relations between the Great Powers. The method of negotiation must become the sole method of solving international problems.

Assuring collective security in Europe, assuring collective security in Asia, disarmament—these are the three cardinal problems whose solution can lay the foundation for lasting and durable peace.

Establishment of a collective security system in Europe would meet the vital interests of all European countries, large and small, and would simultaneously serve as a solid guarantee of peace throughout the world. It would at the same time make it possible to settle the German issue as well. The present situation as regards this problem cannot but arouse alarm. Germany still remains divided and the arming of Western Germany is being accelerated. It is no secret that in reviving German militarism each of the three Western Powers pursues its own ends. But who stands to gain from this short-sighted policy? Above all the imperialist forces of Western Germany. Among the losers, however, first place should go to France, which this policy seeks to reduce to the status of a third-rate power. A new Washington-Bonn axis is more and more clearly emerging and aggravating the war danger.

Compelled to pool their forces and resources, our states have concluded the Warsaw Treaty, which is an important stabilizing factor in Europe. They are fully resolved to do their utmost to protect the peaceful life of their peoples and to prevent the outbreak of another conflagration in Europe.

As for disarmament, we will spare no effort to solve this most important problem.

We will continue to work to end the arms drive and ban atomic and hydrogen weapons. Prior to agreement on important aspects of disarmament we are willing to take certain partial steps, for example, to discontinue thermonuclear weapon tests, to see that the troops stationed in Germany should have no atomic weapons, and to cut military budgets. Implementation of such measures by the nations could pave the way to understanding on other, more intricate aspects of disarmament.

The Soviet Union is firmly resolved to do everything necessary to safeguard international peace and security.

The establishment of firm friendly relations between the two biggest powers of the world, the Soviet Union and the United States of America, would be of great significance for the strengthening of world peace. We think that if the well-known Five Principles of peaceful co-existence were to underlie the relations between the U.S.S.R. and the United States, that would be of truly great importance for all mankind and would, of course benefit the people of the United States no less than the Soviet peoples and all other peoples. These principles—mutual respect for territorial integrity and sovereignty, non-aggression, non-interference in each other's domestic affairs, equality and mutual advantage, peaceful co-existence and economic co-operation—are now subscribed to and supported by a score of states.

We have recently taken new important steps with a view to achieving a fundamental improvement in Soviet-American relations. I mean the proposal for the conclusion of a Treaty of Friendship and Co-operation between the U.S.S.R. and the United States, contained in the letter of Comrade N.A. Bulganin to President Dwight D. Eisenhower.

We want to be friends with the United States and to co-operate with it for peace and international security and also in the economic and cultural spheres. We propose this with good intentions, without holding a knife behind our back. We have put forward our proposal not because the Soviet

Union cannot live without such a treaty with the United States. The Soviet state existed and developed successfully even when it had no normal diplomatic relations with the United States. We have proposed a treaty to the United States because the conclusion of such a treaty would meet the profoundest aspirations of the peoples of both countries to live in peace and friendship.

If good relations between the Soviet Union and the United States are not established and mutual distrust continues, it will lead to an arms race on a still bigger scale and to a still more dangerous build-up of strength on both sides. Is this what the peoples of the Soviet Union and the United States want? Of course not.

So far our initiative has not met with due understanding and support in the United States, which shows that the advocates of settling outstanding issues by means of war still hold strong positions there, and that they continue to exert big pressures on the President and the Administration. But we hope that our peaceful aspirations will be more correctly appraised in the United States and that matters will take a turn for the better.

As before, we intend to work for the further improvement of our relations with Great Britain and France. . . .

The Soviet Union will continue to strive unswervingly for the extension and strengthening of friendship and co-operation with the Eastern countries. We can note with satisfaction that good, friendly relations have developed between our country and the Republic of India and we are confident that these relations have a great future. We acclaim the desire of the peoples of the Arab countries to uphold their national independence. We also believe that Iran, Turkey, and Pakistan will realize that normal relations with the U.S.S.R. are in their vital interest. . .

Some Fundamental Questions of
Present-Day International Developments

Comrades, I should like to dwell on some fundamental questions concerning present-day international development, which determine not only the present course of events, but also the prospects for the future.

These questions are the peaceful co-existence of the two systems, the possibility of preventing wars in the present era, and the forms of transition to socialism in different countries.

Let us examine these questions in brief.

The peaceful co-existence of the two systems. The Leninist principle of peaceful co-existence of states with different social systems has always been and remains the general line of our country's foreign policy.

It has been alleged that the Soviet Union advances the principle of peaceful co-existence merely out of tactical considerations, considerations of expediency. Yet it is common knowledge that we have always, from the very first years of Soviet power, stood with equal firmness for peaceful co-existence. Hence, it is not a tactical move, but a fundamental principle of Soviet foreign policy.

This means that if there is indeed a threat to the peaceful co-existence of countries with differing social and political systems, it by no means comes from the Soviet Union or the rest of the socialist camp. Is there a single reason why a socialist state should want to unleash aggresssive war? Do we have classes and groups that are interested in war as a means of enrichment? We do not. We abolished them long ago. Or, perhaps, we do not have enough territory or natural wealth, perhaps we lack sources of raw materials or markets for our goods? No, we have sufficient of all those and to spare. Why then should we want war? We do not want it, as a matter of principle we renounce any policy that might lead to millions of people being plunged into war for the sake of the selfish interests of a handful of multi-millionaires. Do those who shout about the "aggressive intentions" of the U.S.S.R. know all this? Of course they do. Why then do they keep up the old monotonous refrain about some imaginary "communist aggression"? Only to stir up mud, to conceal their plans for world domination, a "crusade" against peace, democracy, and socialism.

To this day the enemies of peace allege that the Soviet Union is out to overthrow capitalism in other countries by "exporting" revolution. It goes without saying that among us Communists there are no supporters of capitalism. But this does not mean that we have interfered or plan to interfere in the internal affairs of countries where capitalism still exists. Romain Rolland was right when he said that "freedom is not brought in from abroad in baggage trains like Bourbons." It is ridiculous to think that revolutions are made to order. We often hear representatives of bourgeois countries reasoning thus: "The Soviet leaders claim that they are for peaceful co-existence between the two systems. At the same time they declare that they are fighting for communism, and say that communism is bound to win in all countries. Now if the Soviet Union is fighting for communism, how can there be any peaceful co-existence with it?" This view is the result of bourgeois propaganda. The ideologists of the bourgeoisie distort the facts and deliberately confuse questions of ideological struggle with questions of relations between states in order to make the Communists of the Soviet Union look like advocates of aggression.

When we say that the socialist system will win in the competition between the two systems—the capitalist and the socialist—this by no means signifies that its victory will be achieved through armed interference by the socialist countries in the internal affairs of the capitalist countries. Our certainty of the victory of communism is based on the fact that the socialist mode of production possesses decisive advantages over the capitalist mode of production. Precisely because of this, the ideas of Marxism-Leninism are more and more capturing the minds of the broad masses of the working people in the capitalist countries, just as they have captured the minds of millions of men and women in our country and the People's Democracies. We believe that all working men in the world, once they have become convinced of the advantages communism brings, will sooner or later take the road of struggle for the construction of socialist society. Building communism in our country, we are resolutely against war. We have always held and continue to hold that the establishment of a new social system in one or another country is the internal affair of the peoples of the countries concerned. This is our attitude, based on the great Marxist-Leninist teaching.

The principle of peaceful co-existence is gaining ever wider international recognition. This principle is one of the cornerstones of the foreign policy of the Chinese People's Republic and the other People's Democracies. It is being actively implemented by the Republic of India, the Union of Burma, and a number of other countries. And this is natural, for there is no other way in present-day conditons. Indeed, there are only two ways: either peaceful co-existence or the most destructive war in history. There is no third way.

* * *

The possibility of preventing war in the present era. Millions of people all over the world are asking whether another war is really inevitable, whether mankind which has already experienced two devastating world wars must still go through a third one? Marxists must answer this question taking into consideration the epoch-making changes of the last decades.

There is, of course, a Marxist-Leninist precept that wars are inevitable as long as imperialism exists. This precept was evolved at a time when 1) imperialism was an all-embracing world system, and 2) the social and political forces which did not want war were weak, poorly organized, and hence unable to compel the imperialists to renounce war.

People usually take only one aspect of the question and examine only the economic basis of wars under imperialism. This is not enough. War is not only an economic phenomenon. Whether there is to be a war or not depends in large measure on the correlation of class, political forces, the degree of organization and the awareness and resolve of the people.

Moreover, in certain conditons the struggle waged by progressive social and political forces may play a decisive role. Hitherto the state of affairs was such that the forces that did not want war and opposed it were poorly organized and lacked the means to check the schemes of the war-makers. Thus it was before the First World War, when the main force opposed to the threat of war—the world proletariat—was disorganized by the treachery of the leaders of the Second International. Thus it was on the eve of the Second World War, when the Soviet Union was the only country that pursued an active peace policy, when the other Great Powers to all intents and purposes encouraged the aggressors, and the Right-wing Social-Democratic leaders had split the labour movement in the capitalist countries.

In that period this precept was absolutely correct. At the present time, however, the situation has changed radically. Now there is a world camp of socialism, which has become a mighty force. In this camp the peace forces find not only the moral, but also the material means to prevent aggression. Moreover, there is a large group of other countries with a population running into many hundreds of millions which are actively working to avert war. The labour movement in the capitalist countries has today become a tremendous force. The movement of peace supporters has sprung up and developed into a powerful factor.

In these circumstances certainly the Leninist precept that so long as imperialism exists, the economic basis giving rise to wars will also be preserved remains in force. That is why we must display the greatest vigilance. As long as capitalism survives in the world, the reactionary forces representing the interests of the capitalist monopolies will continue their drive towards military gambles and aggression, and may try to unleash war. But war is not fatalistically inevitable. Today there are mighty social and political forces possessing formidable means to prevent the imperialists from unleasing war, and if they actually try to start it, to give a smashing rebuff to the aggressors and frustrate their adventurist plans. To be able to do this all anti-war forces must be vigilant and prepared, they must act as a united front and never relax their efforts in the battle for peace. The more actively the peoples defend peace, the greater the guarantees that there will be no new war.

Forms of transition to socialism in different countries. In connection with the radical changes in the world arena new prospects are also opening up in respect to the transistion of countries and nations to socialism.

Much that is unique in socialist construction is being contributed by the Chinese People's Republic, whose economy prior to the victory of the revolution was exceedingly backward, semi-feudal and semi-colonial in character. Having taken over the decisive commanding positions, the people's democratic state is using them in the social revolution to implement a policy of peaceful reorganization of private industry and trade and their gradual transformation into a component of socialist economy

* * *

It is probable that more forms of transition to socialism will appear. Moreover, the implementation of these forms need not be associated with civil war under all circumstances. Our enemies like to depict us Leninists as advocates of violence always and everywhere. True, we recognize the need for the revolutionary transformation of capitalist society into socialist society. It is this that distinguishes the revolutionary Marxists from the reformists, the opportunists. There is no doubt that in a number of capitalist countries the violent overthrow of the dictatorship of the bourgeoisie and the sharp aggravation of class struggle connected with this are inevitable. But the forms of social revolution vary. It is not true that we regard violence and civil war as the only way to remake society.

It will be recalled that in the conditions that arose in April 1917 Lenin granted the possibility that the Russian Revolution might develop peacefully, and that in the spring of 1918, after the victory of the October Revolution, Lenin drew up his famous plan for peaceful socialist construction. It is not our fault that the Russian and international bourgeoisie organized counter-revolution, intervention, and civil war against the young Soviet state and forced the workers and peasants to take up arms. It did not come to civil war in the European People's Democracies, where the historical situation was different.

Leninism teaches us that the ruling classes will not surrender their power voluntarily. And the greater or lesser degree of intensity which the struggle may assume, the use or the non-use of violence in the transition to socialism depends on the resistance of the exploiters, on whether the exploiting class itself resorts to violence, rather than on the proletariat.

In this connection the question arises of whether it is possible to go over to socialism by using parliamentary means. No such course was open to the Russian Bolsheviks, who were the first to effect this transition. Lenin showed us another road, that of the establishment of a republic of Soviets, the only correct road in those historical conditions. Following that course we achieved a victory of history-making significance. Since then, however, the historical situation has undergone radical changes which make possible a new approach to the question. . . .

The winning of a stable parliamentary majority backed by a mass revolutionary movement of the proletariat and of all the working people could create for the working class of a number of capitalist and former colonial countries the conditions needed to secure fundamental social changes.

In the countries where capitalism is still strong and has a huge military and police apparatus at its disposal, the reactionary forces will of course inevitably offer serious resistance. There the transition to socialism will be attended by a sharp class, revolutionary struggle.

Whatever the form of transition to socialism, the decisive and indispensable factor is the political leadership of the working class headed by its vanguard. Without this there can be no transition to socialism.

It must be strongly emphasized that the more favourable conditions for the victory of socialism created in other countries are due to the fact that socialism has won in the Soviet Union and is winning in the Peoople's Democracies. Its victory in our country would have been impossible had Lenin and the Bolshevik Party not upheld revolutionary Marxism in battle against the reformists, who broke with Marxism and took the path of opportunism.

Such are the considerations which the Central Committee of the Party finds necessary to set out in regard to the forms of transition to socialism in present-day conditions.

* * *

What are the tasks confronting the Party in the sphere of foreign policy? They are:

1. To pursue steadfastly the Leninist policy of peaceful co-existence between different states irrespective of their social systems. To work vigorously for the cause of peace and the security of the peoples, for the establishment of confidence between states, with a view to transforming the relaxation of international tension achieved to date into a stable peace.

2. To strengthen in every way our fraternal relations with the People's Republic of China, Poland, Czecholovakia, Bulgaria, Hungary, Rumania, Albania, the German Democratic Republic, the Korean People's Democratic Republic, the Democratic Republic of Viet-Nam, and the Mongolian People's Republic, bearing in mind that the greater the unity and might of the socialist countries the more secure is the cause of peace.

To strengthen in every way friendship and co-operation with the fraternal peoples of the Federative People's Republic of Yugoslavia.

3. To consolidate untiringly the bonds of friendship and co-operation with the Republic of India, Burma, Indonesia, Afghanistan, Egypt, Syria, and other countries which stand for peace; to support countries which refuse to be involved in military blocs; to co-operate with all forces seeking to preserve peace.

To develop and strengthen friendly relations with Finland, Austria, and other neutral countries.

4. To pursue a vigorous policy of further improving relations with the United States of America, Britain, France, Western Germany, Japan, Italy, Turkey, Iran, Pakistan, and other countries with a view to strengthening mutual confidence, extending trade, and expanding contacts and co-operation in the sphere of culture and science.

5. To follow vigilantly the intrigues of circles that do not want a relaxation of international tension; to expose in good time the subversive activities of the enemies of peace and the peoples' security; to take all measures necessary to further strengthen the defence potential of our socialist state; to maintain our defences at the level required by present-day military science, and to ensure the security of our socialist country.

KHRUSHCHEV

Report to XXI (Extraordinary) Party Congress January 27, 1959

Introduction Khrushchev's attack on Stalin in his 1956 "secret speech," delivered with little or no forewarning to foreign Communist leaders, caused deep fissures in the world Communist movement. In particular, it led to a weakening of Soviet authority in East Europe. The divided leadership in Moscow could not agree on a consistent policy to deal with emergent problems there. The result was the Hungarian revolution and its bloody suppression, which brought Soviet fortunes and prestige to a new low. By the end of 1957, however, recovery had begun. Khrushchev purged his rivals and established a personal rule that provided relatively unified direction for Soviet policy. Sputnik was launched in October, 1957, giving a great boost to the Soviet economic and political system in the world's eyes and raising serious question about the United States' strategic nuclear superiority. The Soviet economy, particularly agriculture, performed well in 1958. Reflecting on these things, Khrushchev apparently was carried away by dreams of the world's peaceful conquest by Communism.

The Report to the XXI Congress is buoyant and optimistic. Extrapolating recent trends, Khrushchev concludes that the USSR will surpass the United States in *per capita* production in little more than a decade. The material superiority of the USSR over the United States and of the socialist camp over the imperialist camp is expected, somehow, to bring new successes to Soviet foreign policy. We will never know whether Khrushchev's belief in "economics over politics" (i.e., economic success brings political success), was warranted, since the Seven Year Plan, which embodied his high hopes, proved far too ambitious and was abandoned.

The success of Sputnik, and Khrushchev's heightened confidence that the United States feared taking actions that might lead to war, encouraged him to attempt a more venturesome foreign policy. In November, 1958 he issued a virtual ultimatum to the Western powers to agree to end their occupation of West Berlin by May, 1959. When he delivered his Report (January, 1959), the West was in disarray and uncertain how to respond. Khrushchev was unwilling to take provocation action in the center of Europe, however, and the deadline passed (as later deadlines were to pass) without any change in West Berlin's status. One consequence of the Berlin Crisis of 1959 was Khrushchev's long-sought visit that fall to the United States.

The USSR had supported a number of Arab states (particularly the United Arab Republic) after 1955. With the passage of time difficulties arose, especially from the oppressive measures of Premier Nasser against native Communists. The problem this posed—whether to support leaders of "the national liberation movement" or local Communists, when the two clashed—has confronted Moscow on numerous occasions in its history. In his Report, Khrushchev offers a relatively strong defense of the local Communists, but in his "concluding remarks" he seems more conciliatory. In the years following, Khrushchev was somewhat reconciled to the abuse of Egyptian Communists. In this connection, it is interesting to observe that De Gaulle's accession to power in 1958 was not immediately welcomed by Khrushchev, who saw a danger that De Gaulle might try to suppress French

Communism and possibly spur a renewal of fascism in Europe. Subsequently, however, he tried to exploit De Gaulle's hostility to the United States.

In his "concluding remarks" (made towards the end of the Congress) Khrushchev encourages speculation in the United States about the progress of the Soviet ICBM program, which was widely believed to be in advance of our own. He asserts that the USSR has organized "serial production" of the ICBM, which implies a substantial rate of production. In retrospect, this claim appears exaggerated; it was part of a systematic effort by Khrushchev to deceive the West about the pace and scope of the Soviet ICBM program.

There is a curious passage near the end of his Report in which Khrushchev denies—or seems to deny—that in a recent private talk with Senator Hubert Humphrey he discussed Moscow's disagreements with Peking. In retrospect, it seems likely that Khrushchev did speak confidentially to Humphrey of Moscow's increasing difficulties with Peking, but later felt obliged to disavow his remarks.

Decisive Stage in the Economic Competition Between Socialism and Capitalism and the Present International Situation

Comrades, the Seven-Year Plan will have a powerful impact on the international situation and will be a new triumph for Marxism-Leninism. Our successes in fulfilling the plan will attract millions of new adherents to socialism, consolidate the forces of peace and weaken the forces of war and cause tremendous changes not only in our country, but all over the world. There will be in the world a decisive shift in favour of socialism in the economic field.

Economy is the main field in which the peaceful competition between socialism and capitalism is unfolding, and it is in our interests to win this competition in a historically short period.

* * *

The Seven-Year Plan and the
Basic Economic Task of the U.S.S.R.

What are the immediate prospects in the economic development of the two world systems?

The time in which the U.S.S.R. will accomplish its basic economic task depends above all on the initial ratio of the production level of the U.S.S.R. to that of the U.S.A. What can be said on that score?

The volume of Soviet industrial production is roughly half that of America's, and that of Soviet agricultural production is 20 to 25 percent lower than America's.

U.S. industrial output per head of population is more than double that of the U.S.S.R., and agricultural output about 40 per cent higher.

How soon can we close this gap, draw level, and then surpass the U.S.A. in these indices?

Rates of production growth are decisive. And the advantage in rates rests with the socialist economic system.

Today our country is ahead of the U.S.A. both in rates and in annual absolute growth of production. We go forward four times as fast, and we add more to our output each year. Consequently, it is now much easier to overtake the Americans.

Soviet and U.S. rates of industrial growth being what they are, the Soviet Union will, by fulfilling the plan, surpass the United States for absolute output in some key items and draw near to America's present level of output in others. By that time the output of key agricultural products, both in absolute figures and in output per head of population, will exceed the present U.S. level. The population both in the U.S.S.R. and in the U.S.A. will grow, and it is to be expected that in our country it will grow more. The population in the U.S.S.R. will probably be about l5 to 20 per cent greater than in the U.S.A. Hence, if we reckon per head of population, it will probably take us another five years or so after fulfilling the Seven-Year Plan to catch up and surpass the United States in industrial production. *Consequently, by that time [1970] – or possibly earlier – the Soviet Union will rank first in the world for both absolute volume of production and per capita output. That will be a historic victory for socialism in the peaceful competition with capitalism in the international arena.*

It is not the Soviet Union alone which is faced with the problem of making the most of the time factor in its economic competition with capitalism. It may be recalled, for example, that the Communist Party of China in 1957 set the task of surpassing Britain in volume of output in the key industries within the next fifteen years. The great popular movement for the "big leap," which has begun in that country, shows that the Chinese people will achieve that goal much sooner. The Czechoslovak Republic intends by 1965 to raise industrial output by 90 to 95 per cent over 1957, and the Polish People's Republic by 80 per cent over 1958. . . .

In the world socialist system, all countries join and co-ordinate their production efforts, while the relations between capitalist countries are dominated by irreconcilable contradictions. The co-ordination of national economic plans is the form in which the production efforts of the socialist countries are being pooled at this stage. International division of labour—particularly its higher forms, specialization and co-operation—has to play a big part in the economic development of the socialist camp. It offers new, additional opportunities of increasing production in the socialist camp as a whole and in each particular socialist country. Acting on its own, no country could develop as rapidly as it is developing within the system of socialist countries.

* * *

The Peace Policy of the U.S.S.R. and
International Relations

The Seven-Year Plan is a fresh manifestation of the Leninist peace policy of the Soviet Union. Its fulfilment will play a very big part in solving the cardinal problem of our time—the preservation of world peace.

The importance of the plan lies, first of all, in the spirit of peace which imbues it. A state which undertakes the building of new factories, plants, power stations, mines and other institutions on a giant scale, which allocates nearly 400,000 million rubles for housing and communal-service development and aims at substantially raising the living standard of its people, is a state that is looking forward to peace and not war.

Secondly, the plan, when fulfilled, will so greatly increase the economic potential of the U.S.S.R. that it will, together with the growth of the economic potential of all the socialist countries, give peace a decisive advantage in the international balance of forces. Thereby new, still more favourable conditions will be provided for averting a world war and preserving peace on earth.

The conclusion drawn by the 20th Congress of the Party that war is not [fatalistically] inevitable has been fully justified. Today we have all the more reason to insist that the conclusion was correct. There are now tremendous forces capable of rebuffing the imperialist aggressors and defeating them if they should start a world war.

What new elements will arise in the international situation with the implementation of the economic plans of the Soviet Union and the other socialist countries of Europe and Asia? Their fulfilment will *create a real possibility of eliminating war as a means of settling international issues.*

Indeed, when the U.S.S.R. becomes the foremost industrial power in the world, when the Chinese People's Republic becomes a mighty industrial power and the industrial output of all the socialist countries combined is more than half the world industrial output, the international situation will change radically. The successes of the socialist countries will unquestionably go a long way towards strengthening the forces of peace throughout the world. By that time the countries championing a durable peace will no doubt be joined by new countries that will have thrown off colonial oppression. The idea that war is impermissible will take still firmer root in the minds of men. The new balance of forces will be so obvious that even the most die-hard imperialists will clearly see the futility of any attempt to start a war against the socialist camp. Backed by the might of the socialist camp, the peaceful nations will then be able to make bellicose imperialist groups abandon their plans for a new world war.

In this way, it will become really possible to exclude world war from the life of society even before the complete triumph of socialism on earth, with capitalism still existing in part of the world.

It may be argued that capitalism will still exist and so there will still be adventurers who might start a war. That is true, and we must not forget it. As long as capitalism exists it may always be possible to find people who, contrary to the dictates of common sense, will want to rush headlong into a hopeless venture. But in that way they will merely hasten the death of the capitalist system. Any attempt at aggression will be curbed and the adventurers put where they belong.

Such are the prospects, comrades, that stand out as we discuss our plans.

Allow me to turn to specific problems of the international situation. I shall not deal with all international problems—I will only touch on the more pressing ones.

The right solution to the German problem is of great importance to peace and international security. Twice in the first half of the twentieth century, German imperialism started world wars. Today, with the assistance of the monopolists of the U.S.A., Britain and the other partners of the aggressive North-Atlantic Treaty, West Germany is being turned into the main atomic and rocket base of NATO. Even now West Germany is coming to play a leading role in that aggressive bloc. Some Western politicians are evidently thinking of again spearheading the German threat eastwards, forgetting that German militarism also knows the way to the West.

A situation is arising in which German militarism may for the third time drag mankind into a world war. When we point to the grave danger involved in the arming of West Germany, we are told that as a member of NATO West Germany is kept under control and is not dangerous. But anyone can now see that militarism and revanchism has reared its ugly head in West Germany and threatens peaceful nations.

*   *   *

In view of the growing military threat from the Federal Republic of Germany, the Soviet Union has recently made a number of new proposals on the German problem. We have proposed a gradual reduction of foreign troops in Germany, or better still, their complete withdrawal. We stand for a "zone of disengagement" of armed forces. The farther apart they will be, the [less] the danger of clashes and conflicts. The Soviet Union is prepared to withdraw its forces not only from Germany, but also from Poland and Hungary, where they are stationed under the Warsaw Treaty, if all the NATO countries withdraw their troops to within their national boundaries and abolish their military bases in other countries.

The Soviet Union supports the Polish plan for an "atomic-free zone" in Europe and a reduction of conventional armaments in that zone.

Last November the Soviet Government approached the United States, Britain and France with a proposal to do away with the remnants of the occupation regime in Berlin and make West Berlin a demilitarized free city. Such a settlement of the Berlin question would make for a durable peace in Europe and serve to ease international tension.

The German problem would be radically solved through the conclusion of a German peace treaty. There is nothing to justify the fact that, fourteen years after the end of the war, no peace treaty has yet been signed between Germany and the countries which fought against her. Such a situation virtually benefits those who want the "cold war" to continue. The Western Powers are taking advantage of it to keep their troops in the heart of Europe, to maintain an atomic bridgehead there and to prepare a new war, unceremoniously playing with Germany and her people as though they were small change.

The Soviet Union, for its part, will spare no effort to have a peace treaty concluded. It will work for it consistently and indefatigably. The peace treaty would also serve to solve the Berlin problem on peaceful and democratic lines. It would lead to West Berlin being made a free city and provide the necessary guarantee of non-interference in its affairs. The United Nations should be called on to enforce this guarantee. We want negotiations on all these problems so as to find a reasonable solution to them. Our proposals are in line with this purpose. They help to eliminate many of the causes of tension in the relations between states in the heart of Europe, and will strengthen peace.

The peace treaty will mean a big step forward towards German reunification, now hindered by the existing international tension, particularly in the relations between the two German states.

It must be clearly understood that the reunification of Germany is wholly and entirely the business of the German people. Since there are two sovereign states today and neither can be eliminated without touching off a world war, Germany's reunification can only be achieved through negotiations between the German Democratic Republic and the Federal Republic of Germany. There is no other way.

* * *

Western propaganda makes a great deal of noise, alleging that the Soviet Union is opposed to German reunification by free elections. We have never objected to free elections, nor do we object now. But again, the issue must be settled by the Germans themselves. . .

In this connection, we must again mention the role being played by Chancellor Adenauer, who fears German reunification on peaceful and democratic lines. . . . He ought to consider that it is not only his allies that have nuclear weapons, but also the Soviet Union. One should not forget that those are weapons whose use may lead to the loss of many human lives. Since West Germany is being turned into an atomic base, her population will be the first to suffer in the event of an armed conflict.

In another part of the world—the Far East—the aggressive policy of the United States toward the Chinese People's Republic and other peace-loving countries is the main source of tension. Some time ago the world saw with anxiety how America's aggressive moves threatened to develop into a huge military conflagration. It was the resolute action of the Chinese People's Republic and other peace-loving forces that averted the threat.

The Pacific area has become the main testing ground for U.S. atomic weapons. . . *A zone of peace, above all an atom-free zone, can and should be created in the Far East and the rest of the Pacific area.*

* * *

After the colonialists have been expelled and the country's national problems essentially solved, the people seek a solution to vital social problems. This applies above all to the land and peasant problem and the problem of labour's struggle against capital. Social processes arise within the national-liberation movement such as inevitably engender different opinions on the further course of development of the state.

Our country, like the other socialist countries, has always supported, and will continue to support, the national-liberation movement. The Soviet Union has never interfered, and has no intention of interfering, in the domestic affairs of other countries. But we feel we must state our attitude to the fact that a campaign is being conducted in some countries against progressive forces under the spurious slogans of anti-communism. Since in the United Arab Republic statements have recently been made against the ideas of communism and accusations levelled at Communists, I who am a Communist think it necessary to declare at this congress of our Communist Party that it is wrong to accuse Communists of helping to weaken or divide the national effort in the struggle against imperialsim. On the contrary, no one is more staunch and more devoted to the struggle against colonialists than the Communists. There are no forces more steadfast in the struggle against imperialism than the forces of communism. And that is why the imperialists are spearheading their struggle against the communist movement.

The struggle against the Communist and other progressive parties is a reactionary cause. Anti-communist policy does not unite the national forces but disunites them. Thereby it weakens the effort of a nation in defending its interests against imperialism. It is wrong to accuse Communists of acting against the national interests of the Arab peoples. It is also naive to equate communism with Zionism. Everyone knows that Communists, those of Israel included, are fighting against Zionism.

It is unreasonable to see "communist intrigue" in everything. Problems of social development should be viewed more deeply. There are objective laws of social development and these tell us that within nations there exist classes with different interests. After imperialist oppression has been abolished in a colonial country, its workers want to have shorter working hours and higher wages; its peasants want to have more land and an opportunity to enjoy the fruits of their labour; both workers and peasants want to have political rights. But the capitalists want to make more profit, and landed proprietors want to keep their land. The progressive elements want their country to make social progress. They strive to strengthen its national independence and to protect it from imperialist plots. Internal reaction, which is often instigated by the imperialists from without, resist that.

These processes, which take place in the countries that have shaken off imperialist tyranny; do not arise by the will or whim of any party. They arise because there are classes and different class interests. We who are Communists, and all progressive people in general, naturally sympathize with those who fight for social justice.

We do not deny that we and some of the leaders of the United Arab Republic have divergent views in the ideological sphere. But in the matter of fighting against imperialism, of consolidating the political and economic independence of the countries which have freed themselves from colonialism, of combating the war danger, our attitude coincides with theirs. Differences in ideological views should not impede the development of friendly realtions between our countries or our joint struggle against imperialism.

Imperialist agents travelling in the Middle East seek to put the fear of communism into certain people, hoping thereby to assure imperialist influence and to support the reactionaries. For this reason, the people there must be on guard against imperialist intrigue.

The countries which have achieved their national liberation need, and will continue to need, the support of the socialist countries and all progressive people. The Soviet Union and the other socialist countries are promoting friendly relations with the countries which have won freedom from colonial tyranny; they are helping them and will continue to do so.

The imperialists use their economic relations with the underdeveloped countries as instruments of blackmail and extortion. They impose military and political conditions on those countries. Our country bases its relations with all states on complete equality and co-operation, with no military or political strings attached. We do not engage in charity. The Soviet Union renders aid on a fair commercial basis. The socialist countries help the underdeveloped countries to set up industries of their own, whereas the United States tries to sell them consumer goods which have no market at home. The Seven-Year Plan offers new opportunities for Soviet economic co-operation with the industrially underdeveloped countries.

* * *

Measures to ease the situation in the various regions should be combined with efforts to improve the over-all international climate.

The task of tasks today is to break the deadlock over the *disarmament issue*. The armament race continues, swallowing up ever more financial and material resources. . . .

The need to ban tests of atomic and hydrogen weapons is particularly compelling. Now that it is generally recognized that atomic explosions can be detected at any point of the globe, there is no reason to delay the settlement of the issue of banning nuclear weapons tests. The peoples of all countries demand that a stop be put to these tests which contaminate the world atmosphere with harmful fall-out. And this demand must be met.

We hold the view that relations between states with different social systems should be based on peaceful co-existence. We and the ruling circles of the capitalist countries have different views and different world outlooks. We shall never renounce our views and have no illusions about our class opponents changing their ideology. But this does not imply that we must go to war over our divergence in views. In every country, it is the people themselves who shape their own destiny and choose their course of development. The Soviet Union has no intention of forcing on anyone the path it has chosen. We are wholly guided by Lenin's principle that revolution is not an export item.

Would it not be better for the leaders of states with different social systems to come—as soon as possible—to the conclusion that since we share one planet, and not too big a planet by present technological standards, it would be advisable to live on it without elbowing each other, or shaking fists at each other all the time in the shape of atom or hydrogen bombs. We must learn to settle our disputes by peaceful negotiation.

It is high time to see that threats are no good as far as the Soviet Union, the socialist camp are concerned, and to realize the radical changes which have come about in the world strategic situation.

Today all admit the successes achieved by Soviet science and technology, which have blazed man's trail into outer space. These achievements indicate the potentialities of the Soviet Union, of the world socialist system. It should be perfectly obvious that since the Soviet Union can launch a rocket hundreds of thousands of kilometres into outer space, it can launch powerful rockets with pinpoint accuracy to any place on the globe. . . . And now that we lead in rocket engineering, we again say to the United States, Britain and France: let us ban for all time the testing, production and use of atomic, hydrogen and rocket weapons; let us destroy all stockpiles of these deadly weapons; let us use the great discovery of human genius exclusively for peaceful purposes, for the welfare of man. Our Government is prepared to sign an appropriate treaty, tomorrow, if you like.

The only reasonable policy for the Great Powers is to proceed to a peaceful settlement of international problems and to start on general disarmament.

More than a year ago the Soviet Government proposed an East-West meeting of heads of government. Through the fault of the Western Powers, no progress has been made in the matter since then. But we consider it our duty to the peoples of all countries to work for this meeting, on which all who are concerned with peace and international security are pinning so much hope.

We have had more than one occasion to point out the great responsibility for the preservation of peace which rests with the two Great Powers—the Soviet Union and the United States. As far as the Soviet Union is concerned, it has more than once expressed its sincere desire to normalize relations with the United States, and has backed its words with deeds. The

Soviet Union proposed a fifty-year non-aggression pact. It proposed that the two countries should engage in extensive trade on mutually advantageous terms, encourage cultural relations, etc. But every time we came up against an outright refusal or veiled resistance.

Our two countries have never had any territorial claims on each other, nor have they any today. There are no grounds for clashes between our two peoples. Yet the relations between the U.S.S.R. and the U.S.A. have long been abnormal.

We know that many politicians and financiers, Senators and newspaper publishers in the U.S.A. have an interest in maintaining such relations. But the number of people who favour friendly, good-neighbour relations with the Soviet Union is growing in the United States. The reception accorded to A. I. Mikoyan in America was forceful proof of this. His visit evoked among the American people a demonstration of friendly sentiment for the peoples of the Soviet Union. Most of the Americans whom he met expressed their sincere and outspoken sympathy for the Soviet people, and a desire for friendship and peaceful co-operation with the Soviet Union. Among them were people of different political and religious views and of different social standing—scientists, cultural workers, businessmen and people from other walks of life. Evidently, most Americans no longer believe the anti-Soviet propaganda of the reactionary bourgeois newspapers in the U.S.A. The attempts made by certain elements to organize provocative action during Comrade Mikoyan's visit failed completely, because those elements did not represent the sentiments and views of the American people.

We welcome the efforts of all Americans who advocate an end to the "cold war" and support peaceful coexistence and co-operation between all countries. Sympathy for the American people, whose industrial genius and efficiency are known all over the world, is strong in our country.

There are, of course, quite a few difficulties along the path of peaceful coexistence. In following this path, both sides will have to show a great deal of willingness for mutual understanding, great restraint and, if you will, great patience.

Communist Construction in the U.S.S.R. and the
International Working-Class Movement

There was a time when, in their struggle against feudalism, bourgeois revolutions proclaimed the alluring slogan of liberty, equality and fraternity, but it was proclaimed by the bourgeoisie primarily to push aside the aristocracy and pave the way for capital. As it consolidated its rule, the bourgeoisie ignored that slogan more and more.

Today, though they still gamble on the slogan of liberty, equality and fraternity, the imperialists turn more and more frequently to outright dictatorship. There are sinister symptoms in the capitalist countries today of an onset of reaction and fascism. It is this reactionary path that has been chosen by West Germany, where the Communist Party has been banned, democrats are persecuted, and fascist and revanchist organizations are given free rein. The trend towards an open dictatorship has taken shape in France, where the democratic freedoms and the gains of the masses are being trampled underfoot. The onslaught of reaction in France, a country once famed for its democratic traditions, causes concern to all champions of democracy and progress. The military coups in Pakistan and Thailand have shown that an offensive is under way against the democratic gains of peoples that have won national independence. The forces of reaction are becoming more active also in a number of other capitalist countries.

What we have is thus not isolated facts, but a clear-cut general tendency typical of many capitalist countries.

The reactionaries are taking recourse to the old anti-popular method of doing away with the democratic system and setting up "strong-arm" governments. But now, just as when fascist dictatorships were being established in Italy and Germany, the tendency towards an open dictatorship of the monopoly bourgeoisie is a sign of the weakness and not strength of the bourgeoisie. It should be borne in mind, however, that under an unlimited dictatorship reaction has a better chance of using terror and repression, of suppressing all opposition, of indoctrinating the masses to suit its ends, of infecting them with the poison of chauvinism, and of getting its hands free for military ventures. For this reason, the people must be vigilant. They must be ever ready to repel the offensive of reaction and the menace of a revival of fascism.

Millions of people usually associate fascism with Hitler and Mussolini. But we must not dismiss the possibility of fascism reviving in forms other than those which have already discredited themselves in the eyes of peoples.

Now that there exists a powerful socialist camp, now that the working-class movement has much experience in combating reaction, and that the working class is better organized, the peoples have greater opportunities of blocking the advance of fascism. The broadest sections of the people, all democratic, genuinely national forces, can and must be rallied against fascism. In this connection, it is important completely to eliminate sectarian narrow-mindedness which may hamper the mobilization of the masses against reaction and fascism. Unity of the democratic forces, above all of the working class, is the most reliable barrier to the fascist danger.

Who obstructs working-class unity? Imperialist reaction and its henchmen in the working-class movement, such as Guy Mollet or Spaak, the anti-Communist-minded Social-Democratic leaders. We know all these ringleaders of anti-communism by name and it is not on them that we count in speaking of joint working-class action. Most of the rank and file in the Social-Democratic parties support peace and social progress, although their idea of how to win them is different from ours, from the communist idea. It is in the struggle against reaction and fascism that Communists and Social-Democrats should find a common language. It is high time for the representatives of all trends in the working-class movement to brush aside the mountebanks of anti-communism and to sit around one table to work out a mutually acceptable platform of joint working-class action in defence of their interests, in defence of peace.

It is imperative, in the name of further progress, for the Communist and Workers' Parties to reinforce their ranks ideologically and organizationally, to further consolidate them on the basis of Marxism-Leninism, and to strengthen their fraternal international connections.

The Meetings of Representatives of Communist and Workers' Parties in November 1957 revealed complete unity of views among the fraternal parties. The Declaration of the Meeting was unanimously approved by all the Communist and Workers' Parties, and has come to be a charter of international unity for the world communist movement. The Declaration condemned revisionism as the principal danger, and also dogmatism and sectarianism. Practical experience has fully proved the conclusions drawn in the Declaration to be correct. And we take guidance from them at present.

A further consolidation of forces has taken place inside each Communist Party since the November Meetings. The international Communist movement has become still more united. The revisionists failed to turn any of the fraternal parties away from the Marxist-Leninist path.

The contentions of the revisionists have been refuted by reality, by the practical struggle of the working class, by the entire process of social development. The chief revisionist theses—about the changed character of capitalism, the crisis-free development of the capitalist system, the peaceful growing of capitalism into socialism, and so forth—have been refuted.

The international communist movement has condemned the views and policies of the Yugoslav revisionists. . . . They want to conceal the substance of their differences with the Marxist-Leninists. And the substance is that the Yugoslav revisionists deny the need of international class solidarity, that they depart from working-class views. They are trying to make all and sundry believe that there are two blocs in the world—two military camps. But then everybody knows that the socialist camp, which comprises the socialist countries of Europe and Asia, is not a military camp but a community of equal nations fighting for peace and a better life for the working people, fighting for socialism and communism. The other camp is the imperialist camp, which seeks at all costs to maintain its system of oppression and violence, and threatens mankind with war. We did not think up these camps. They emerged in the course of social development.

The Yugoslav leaders claim that they stand outside blocs, and above camps, although in point of fact, they are in the Balkan bloc comprising Yugoslavia, Turkey and Greece. It may be recalled that the latter two countries are members of the aggressive NATO bloc and that Turkey is also a party to the Baghdad Pact. The leaders of the League of Communists of Yugoslavia deeply resent our telling them that they are sitting between two stools. They insist that they are sitting on their own, Yugoslav stool. But for some reason that Yugoslav stool is vigorously propped up by U.S. monopolies. And it is for this reason that this "keep-out-of-blocs" stand, this neutrality which the leaders of the League of Communists of Yugoslavia advertise so much, smacks quite a bit of the U.S. monopolies, which keep giving handouts to "Yugoslav socialism." In the history of the class struggle there has never been an instance of the bourgeoisie materially or morally supporting its class enemy, helping him to build socialism.

If Yugoslavia is behind in her development, if she does not march but zigzags along the socialist road, the responsibility for this falls entirely on the revisionist, anti-Marxist line of the leadership of the League of Communists of Yugoslavia, which has its own special idea about the role of the Party in the building of socialism. The Yugoslav revisionist minimize the Party's role and, in effect, reject the Leninist principle of the Party being the guiding force in the struggle for socialism.

We have the friendliest feelings for the fraternal peoples of Yugoslavia and for the Yugoslav Communists, the heroes of the underground and partisan struggle. On a number of foreign policy issues, we hold common views. We shall continue to develop trade with Yugoslavia on a mutually beneficial basis. We shall strive for co-operation with Yugoslavia on all issues on which our attitudes will coincide in the struggle against imperialism and for peace.

How will matters stand in the Party sphere? That will depend on the League of Communists of Yugoslavia. Its leaders have isolated themselves from the international communists movement of their own accord. It is therefore up to the League of Communists of Yugoslavia to make a turn towards a rapprochement with the Communist Parties on the basis of Marxism-Leninism, something which would also be in the interests of the Yugoslav people.

It is said that the "dependence" of the Communist and Workers' Parties on Moscow is borne out by statements to the effect that the C.P.S.U. stands at the head of the international communist movement. Reference is made in this respect to the well-known thesis in the Declaration of the Moscow Meeting which says that "the camp of socialist countries is headed by the Soviet Union."

We convey our sincere thanks to the fraternal parties for their recognition of the historic role of the Soviet Union and the C.P.S.U.

It must be emphasized, however, that there always has been, as there is now, complete equality and independence for all the Communist and Workers' Parties and the socialist countries in the communist movement and in the socialist camp. As a matter of fact, the Communist Party of the Soviet Union does not control any of the other parties, nor does the Soviet Union control any other country. There are no "superior" and "subordinate" parties in the communist movement. All the Communist and Workers' Parties are equal and independent. All of them bear responsibility for the destiny of the communist movement, for its failure and its successes. And each Communist and Workers' Party is responsible to the working-class and communist movement. In the struggle for working-class interests, for socialism, the Communist Parties apply the universal tenets of Marxism-Leninism to the specific historical and national conditions in their countries. Only a Marxist-Leninist Party, which is connected with the working class, with the people of its country, is able to know the specific conditions of struggle; it alone can work out a political line conforming to these conditions and taking account of the traditions of the working-class movement in its country.

* * *

We have always held the view, and still do so, that none must retire to their national "domains" and withdraw into their own shells. . . .*Success in the national cause of the working class is inconceivable without the international solidarity of all its contingents.*

We are united by the great theory of Marxism-Leninism and by the struggle to put it into practice. We shall always preserve the purity of the Marxist-Leninist ideology, shall fight against opportunists, against revisionists of all shades, and shall always be loyal to the working class. It is in this that we see our international duty to the world communist and working- class movement.

Great changes have now taken place in the world. There are countries that make up the world socialist system and countries that form the world imperialist system. But there are also countries that are not socialist but cannot be regarded as belonging to the imperialist system. Having won national independence as a result of a liberation struggle, these countries want to follow a path of their own, bypassing the capitalist stage of development, so that, having done away with colonial oppression, they can start building a society on different principles.

Many of the leaders of these countries say that they want to build socialism. True, they pronounce the word "communism" with difficulty, and it is not always clear what they mean by socialism. But there can be no doubt that they are well disposed to the socialist countries, do not consider them to be their antagonists, do not regard them as opponents of their striving to build a new life without imperialists and colonial oppression. That is the reason why good, friendly relations have formed between the socialist countries and these states and why normal economic ties are developing between them. We are acting in common in the struggle for peace and the security of the peoples, for banning atomic and hydrogen weapons, against the colonialist policy of the imperialists.

Now if we take the countries forming the world socialist system and the countries waging a courageous struggle against imperialism and colonialism, for their freedom and national independence, we shall find that the scales have already turned in favour of these peace-loving countries and not in favour of the imperialist states. These peace-loving countries exceed the imperialist states in territory, population and natural wealth.

*   *   *

We want to compete with the capitalist countries in peaceful fields—the development of the productive forces, of the country's economic potential, and the improvement of the material and cultural standards of the people. We want each system to show its economic and spiritual powers in the process of this competition. To put it in the language of businessmen, which should be more understandable to representatives of the capitalist world, let us display our "goods"—the socialist and the capitalist world each its own. And let each system show how long its working day is, what material and spiritual benefits accrue under it to the working man, what housing he has, what opportunities he has for education, what part he takes in government, in the political life of his country, and who is master of all the material and cultural riches—he who works or he who does not work but has capital.

We think that the social system which gives the people more material riches, which provides the people with unlimited opportunities for spiritual growth, is progressive, that it is the system of the future.

And who will be the judge, who will decide which social system is better and more progressive? Naturally, we will not agree to the ideologists of the capitalist world being the judges. And we do not expect that the bourgeois ideologists will agree to our being the judges. It is safe to say that both will stand their ground. So who will be the judges? It will be the peoples. It is they who decide which system is better. We are sure that the peoples will make the right choice, and that they will do so without starting a war between countries, without hydrogen and atom bombs.

* * *

When strategic plans are built on false premises, they may lead to miscalculations that hold disastrous consequences for peace. If a country imagines at a certain moment that its adversary lacks the weapon to strike at its territory, it may be tempted to use that propitious moment for starting a war. Since certain U.S. statesmen think that today their territory is invulnerable, they may arrive at the conclusion that the moment is propitious for them to start a war and to pay the price of that war with the blood and lives of Britons, Frenchmen, Italians, Germans, Turks, and their other allies, whose territory would, in the event of war, be laid waste with intermediate- and short-range rockets, while the United States would, in the opinion of these most narrow-minded "strategists," be able to safeguard itself from destruction.

The readiness displayed by U.S. leaders to sacrifice their allies, their disregard for the destiny of mankind for the sake of their narrow interests, is a mercantile approach, a policy of merchants of death who for the sake of enrichment are prepared to sell out not only their friends, but even their own fathers.

* * *

I think it is high time for the American strategists to give up the illusion that in the event of a military conflict the territory of the United States would remain invulnerable. For a long time now this has not been true and has been so much wishful thinking on the part of America's generals. In point of fact, the Soviet Union today has the means to deliver a crushing blow to the aggressor at any point on the globe. After all, it is not mere talk when we say that we have organized serial production of intercontinental ballistic missiles. And we say this not to threaten anyone, but to make it quite clear how matters stand.

For this reason we call on the statesmen of the U.S.A. and other Western Powers to appraise correctly the Soviet proposals, which are aimed at strengthening peace.

Take the question of West Berlin. Dulles says that West Berlin must not be surrendered. Surrendered to whom? Is there anything in the Soviet proposals that speaks of surrendering West Berlin?

If West Berlin were not a hotbed of unrest and conflicts in the heart of the German Democratic Republic, there would be no Berlin question, either. But the situation in West Berlin today is such that all sorts of unpleasant things may be expected there. It may be compared with a burning fuse in a powder-magazine or with a time bomb whose clockwork may touch it off at any moment. Why should we preserve such a situation? Would it not be better to-put out the fuse and remove the time bomb? It would be difficult to find another solution that would be in the interests of both German states and at the same time would not be offensive and detrimental to the other powers concerned. The conversion of West Berlin into a free city could now be such a solution. It is a solution that does not affect the established pattern of life in the city and, given proper guarantees, would preclude outside interference in its internal affairs.

We are, therefore, prepared to participate with the United States, Britain and France in devising a status for West Berlin that would guarantee its normal development, its contacts with all countries with which it may wish to maintain them, and access for those countries to the free city. We also agree to the United Nations participating in safeguarding the status of the free city, and are prepared to discuss the form in which this may be done. Such proposals and their fulfilment must, naturally, be elaborated with the participation of the German Democratic Republic, because Berlin is in its territory. In our opinion, the conversion of West Berlin into a free, demilitarized city would enable us to settle other disputes and would help guarantee security in Europe and, consequently, throughout the world.

Perhaps I am repeating myself, but this is a question to which we shall have to return again and again until we get all the interested parties to see the utter gravity of the situation, to consider what the maintenance of such a situation may lead to, and to take the right view of the matter. The Soviet Union will not slacken its efforts to reach the goal it has set itself.

It is well known that we abide firmly by the principle of non-interference in the affairs of other contries or parties. This we have stated again in no uncertain terms at our congress.

But look at the foul and provocative methods which the Yugoslav revisionists are now resorting to in an attempt to injure the unity of the socialist countries. As I mentioned in the report, the Yugoslav revisionists are making up all sorts of fabrications about alleged differences between our Party and the Communist Party of China. In the last few days they have gone still further and, apparently in an effort to bolster up their inventions, have drawn in a "substantial witness" and specialist on questions of the "disagreement between the U.S.S.R. and the Chinese People's Republic," the American Senator Hubert Humphrey. You will remember that this Senator recently visited the Soviet Union, and I had a talk with him. Hoping to make a big stir, Humphrey in his speeches and articles told no end of fairy-tales, such as the story that he had brought a special message from the Soviet Government to President Eisenhower (there was, of course, no such message) and that I had confided two top secrets to him. Indeed, I could find myself no better partner for passing on secrets to than Mr. Humphrey! Senator Humphrey's wild imagination ran riot when he began to make up his inventions about the relations between the Soviet Union and the Chinese People's Republic. In this he even excelled the well-known cock-and-bull story-teller, Baron Munchausen.

And now the Yugoslav revisionists have taken this fabricator as a witness. The very idea that I could have been in any way confidential with a man who himself boasts of his twenty-year record of struggle against communism is laughable. Anybody who has the slightest knowledge of politics, not to speak of a knowledge of Marxism-Leninism, will see that it is unthinkable to have a confidential talk with Mr. Humphrey on the policies of the Communist Parties, on our relations with our best friends, the leaders of the Communist Party of China.

Things must be in a bad way with the Yugoslav revisionists since they pick up all sorts of absurd tales.

KHRUSHCHEV

Report to the Supreme
Soviet *January 14, 1960*

Introduction In September, 1959, Khrushchev visited the United States. He made a strong and generally favorable impression on the American people, and they on him. His talks with President Eisenhower at Camp David reinforced his belief that the United States would risk war only under extreme provocation. This had two important consequences: it encouraged Khrushchev in his belief that he could win major concessions—for example, on Berlin—without having to risk war; and it encouraged him to believe that he could at the same time achieve a *détente* with the West that would enable him to reduce Soviet military spending. Subsequent events were to show that Khrushchev could not achieve a *détente* while attempting to force concessions; moreover, he could not win the concessions he desired without assuming unacceptable risks of war. In January, 1960, however, the irreconcilability of Khrushchev's aims—concessions plus *détente*—had not yet been revealed, and both shaped his January 1960 speech on strategy in the nuclear age.

After noting the substantial decline in international tension since Stalin's day, Khrushchev holds out the promise that further improvements may result from the forthcoming Paris summit conference. He says that the reason the United States allots so much money to its military establishment is to provide profits for the capitalists; but this implies that the reason is *not* to get ready for war. (Earlier, especially in 1954, some top Soviet leaders had argued that the West's defense budgets were so high because it was planning to initiate war.)* Moreover, according to Khrushchev, the West has now begun to fear that its accumulation of arms, by stimulating the arms race, inadvertently increases the danger of war. A turning point in the cold war, then, appears to be at hand.

Khrushchev goes on to propose a far-reaching measure to reduce substantially Soviet conventional armed forces. This proposal would seem to follow logically from his previous remarks about the West, but Khrushchev does not explicitly link the two: evidently he is reluctant to base his proposal on the prediction of the West's good behavior.† Khrushchev justifies the reduction in the military forces on two grounds: the increased fire power made possible by nuclear weapons; and, second, the increased strength of the socialist camp. Recall that when Khrushchev rejected the doctrine of the inevitability of war four years earlier, he did not justify this by reference to nuclear weapons; he said it was the advent of the socialist camp, i.e., the world's progress towards the final end posited by Communist ideology, that made it possible to reject one of its tenets. Those four years had brought substantial advances in the use of nuclear technology by the Soviet Army.

The reduction proposed is far-reaching, not only in money and personnel, but also in its downgrading of entire branches of the Soviet armed forces, particularly the Air Force and the Navy. Measures like this one

---

* Khrushchev at times seems to acknowledge that the United States at one time was far superior to the USSR in military power.

† He does warn the West, however, that if it does *not* live up to his expectations, Soviet military spending will again rise. (Subsequently, at the time of the second Berlin crisis in 1961, Khrushchev did increase spending because of the alleged aggressiveness of the West.)

doubtless led important military chiefs to oppose Khrushchev on his day of reckoning in October, 1964, when he desperately needed their support.

In his effort to show the military and the Soviet people that reduced military spending is warranted, Khrushchev exaggerates Soviet strategic nuclear power. His implicit claim that even the United States could be wiped from the face of the earth by Soviet rockets (i.e., ICBM's) is, in retrospect, patently false. In part, it was meant to reassure the Soviet people and the military (few of whom could have known the facts about the Soviet ICBM program) that the cuts were justified. As mentioned earlier, such claims of missile superiority were also meant to serve Khrushchev's efforts to elicit concessions from the West, particularly in Berlin.

Khrushchev's statement, early in the speech, that the government which first violated the unilateral test ban then in effect "would assume a grave responsibility before the peoples" is ironic: the government Khrushchev here condemns turned out to be the Soviet government, which resumed testing in September, 1961. Reversals like this one led some observers to believe that Khrushchev was only the "first among equals" in the Soviet leadership and not infrequently had to act contrary to his will. My own view is that Khrushchev was himself the author of such reversals, which were brought about by changed circumstances.[*]

This speech is notable not only for its discussion of nuclear strategy, but also because it lays bare a crucial moment in the cold war. In his January 1960 speech, Khrushchev evidently is of the opinion that Communism can afford to bring the cold war to an end, because in the absence of both war and cold war its victory is inevitable. Khrushchev's primitive belief in Communist ideology enables him to speak passionately here of a peaceful competition of the two systems for the favor of the peoples, in which a warless victory will be won because of the truth and efficacy of Communist ideas. The peoples of the world will compare the performance of the two systems and then freely choose Communism. If this

---

[*] See M. Rush, *Political Succession in the USSR* (New York: Columbia University Press.), 1965.

dream of ending the cold war was not realized, probably it was because of no single event—like the crash of the U-2 reconnaissance plane on Soviet territory May 1, 1960—but rather because its fundamental premise was false: the people do not freely choose communism. Moreover, they may try to throw it off. This neither Khrushchev nor his associates was prepared to accept, and short of this it seems questionable that the cold war can end.

Some Questions of the Present International Situation

Comrade Deputies, we have noted more than once that the international situation has definitely improved of late. You all remember, of course, what the international situation was like several years ago—say, in 1952-1953. Comparing the situation in those years with what we have today, we can draw only one conclusion—the clouds of war menace have begun to disperse, though not as fast as we should have liked.

To be sure, it would be wrong to picture the recent course of events as a sort of straight line, starting somewhere at a rather high point of international tension and dropping to ever lower points. If it were possible to gauge the degree of international tension in the same way as, say, temperature is measured—with a mercury column—the thermometer would show us several drops and rises. But the general tendency is that international tensions are beginning to relax and the "cold war" champions are suffering defeat.

The Jubilee Session of the U.S.S.R. Supreme Soviet, held on the 40th anniversary of the Great October Revolution [1957], advanced a proposal for an East-West conference of leaders to ease international tension. We note with pleasure that the efforts of the Soviet Government to bring about such a meeting have yielded positive results.

Not long ago we reached agreement with Dwight Eisenhower, the U.S. President, Charles de Gaulle, the French President, and Harold Macmillan, the British Prime Minister, to hold a Summit conference in Paris on May 16. It is understood that this conference will be followed by a number of further top-level meetings.

It would be imprudent to try to forecast the possible results of the forthcoming conference, since those results will depend not only on us, but also on our partners. It is important to stress, however, that there are to be serious talks with the leaders of the major Western Powers with a view to reaching a mutual understanding on the more pressing international issues and eliminating the causes of international tension. As far as the Soviet Union is concerned, we should like the meeting to be beneficial and fruitful.

We are deeply convinced that, given reasonable consideration for the interests of the parties concerned and general readiness to meet each other half-way, any controversial question, however thorny and complicated, can be settled to mutual advantage and in the interest of peace. And there are any number of issues of this kind awaiting settlement. To begin with, there are the issues of general and complete disarmament, of a peace treaty with Germany—including the question of making West Berlin a free city—of a ban on atomic and hydrogen weapons tests, and of East-West relations. It is first of all these issues that we have proposed placing on the agenda of the coming Summit meeting.

It is only natural that the people everywhere should pin great hopes on the meeting in question for the strengthening of peace and friendly co-operation among the nations. True, isolated voices can be heard, particularly in some small countries, expressing apprehension that the Great Powers, having reached agreement among themselves, may throw the interests of small countries overboard, ignoring the views of the states not represented at the conference. Permit me to state here that these apprehensions are absolutely groundless. As far as the Soviet Government is concerned, it has never had and does not have any intention of reaching agreement behind the backs of other countries on matters directly affecting their interests. We consider that any attempts to derive unilateral benefits of any kind at the expense of other countries would be altogether at variance with the aims of the planned meeting, whose results should benefit universal peace and, consequently, all countries, big and small.

The meetings, and the frank and very useful talks, which took place between President Eisenhower and myself at Camp David, as also those I had with Prime Minister Macmillan of Great Britain during his stay in Moscow early last year, suggest that a spirit of realism, frankness and co-operation will prevail at the coming Summit talks as well. Recent experience is conclusive proof that personal meetings and contacts between the leading statesmen are, in the circumstances, the most effective and promising method of improving relations between states and reaching agreement on outstanding international issues.

* * *

It is hard to believe that there is anyone in the United States who does not realise the disastrous consequences which a new world war would have. Neither millions, nor even billions of dollars can safeguard aggressors against defeat if they should start up a new war.

Those circles in the United States, and indeed in the other NATO countries, who today advocate the continuation of the "cold war", find themselves shackled by contradictions born of the "cold war" policy. On the one hand, these circles have an interest in the arms race because it brings them profits. On the other, they cannot but see that the arms race increases the danger of a war whose flames would devour all their fortunes, including the profits made from the arms race. Hence a number of contradictory phenomena in the policy of the capitalist countries, which alternately show a tendency to international co-operation and to an aggravation of international tensions.

One example of these contradictory tendencies is now furnished, unfortunately, by the stand which the U.S. Government has taken on the issue of discontinuing atomic and hydrogen weapons tests. . .The people of the world received as a good, encouraging omen the decision, taken of its own accord by each of the negotiating states, to refrain from further nuclear tests. For over a year, no test explosions of atomic or hydrogen weapons have been carried out anywhere in the world. This gratifying fact inspired the peoples with the hope that the existing situation could be made final through the earliest possible conclusion of an appropriate international treaty putting an end to nuclear tests once and for all.

But on December 29 last Mr. Eisenhower, the U.S. President, made a statement which implied that the United States would consider itself free to resume nuclear weapons tests after December 31, 1959. And although the President's statement says that the United States will not resume tests without advance notice, it evidently means that the United States may now resume nuclear explosions at any time.

The announcement of this decision by the U.S. Government caused regret and alarm in every single country of the world.

It is easy enough to imagine what the consequences would be if any country were to resume nuclear weapons tests in the present situation. The other nuclear powers would be compelled to adopt the same course. An impetus would be given to the resumption of an absolutely unlimited race in the testing of nuclear weapons by any power and in any conditions. The government that resumed nuclear weapons tests first would assume a grave responsibility before the peoples.

It would be difficult to reconcile a decision by any one of the three powers to resume nuclear weapons tests with the commitments made by it before all the members of the United Nations. . . .

Awareness of the fact that the international situation has changed and that a radical shift has occurred in the relation of forces between the socialist and the capitalist countries is gaining ground in the Western countries. It appears that the ossified notions of the nature and prospects of East-West relations, notions that took shape over the years, are right now undergoing a definite change in those countries, above all probably in the United States. This is the subject of numerous statements by statesmen and politicians. Special committees, such as those set up by the U.S. Senate, publish voluminous studies on the further course of Western foreign policy.

There are now many politicians in the West who have learned from experience that the old "positions of strength" policy is untenable, but who have not yet come to recognize the needs of a genuine policy of peace and honest co-operation with the Soviet Union and the other socialist countries. It is clear that the contradictory conclusions and inferences of certain Western circles stem from confusion in the face of the outstanding successes and achievements of the Soviet Union and the socialist camp as a whole.

While in the United States, we saw that the more far-sighted of the American statesmen, businessmen and intellectuals, to say nothing of the workers and farmers, want peace and tranquillity, and not a continued arms race and nervous strain. Since the launching of the Soviet sputniks and space rockets, which demonstrated the possibilities of modern technology, the American people have become fully aware of the fact that the United States is now no less vulnerable militarily than any other country. I think no one will suspect me of trying to intimidate anyone by these words. This is simply the actual state of affairs and it is not we alone who see it that way, but also Western statesmen, including those of the United States. No matter to what U.S. audience we spoke of the need of peaceful co-existence and disarmament, our statements on these points always met with understanding and, moreover, brought what I would call a most favourable response and approval from the Americans.

Today popular sentiment in the United States, Britain, France, Italy and other countries is such that even those circles which are still clinging to a "cold war" policy are unable to come out openly against the idea of disarmament and peaceful co-existence. That is why, at this stage, they are adapting themselves to the situation, re-grouping their forces, manoeuvering, and trying to camouflage themselves. But their positions have been underminded, and their strength is dwindling in the face of the peoples' irresistible urge for peace. Our task is to strike at the "cold war" supporters unrelentingly, hitting them harder and harder, so as to isolate them, and to pillory them in the eyes of world opinion. Our most effective weapon in this noble cause is the peace policy of the Soviet Government and its indefatigable effort towards ending the "cold war" for good.

Recent years have been rich in international events which led to the consolidation of the international position of the Soviet Union and the other socialist countries. We have every reason to say that never throughout the glorious history of the Soviet state has the defence of our country been so reliably safeguarded against any eventualities or encroachments from outside as it is now. Never before has the Soviet Union's influence on international affairs, and its prestige as a bulwark of peace, been as great as it is today.

For General and Complete Disarmament

Comrade Deputies, you know that at its Twentieth and Twenty-First Congresses our Party arrived at the conclusion that in the present situation there is no longer any fatal inevitability of war and that it is possible and necessary to banish war from the life of human society for all time. General and complete disarmament is a clear path leading to the deliverance of mankind from the calamities of war.

On behalf of the Soviet Government, I submitted a programme for general and complete disarmament to the United Nations on September 18, 1959.

Our proposals are simple and clear to anyone. They are supported by all who strive to make the Second World War the last world war in human history, to prevent a third world war from ever breaking out. To prevent another war, we must destroy the means of warfare and put the states in conditions where none of them will be able to start hositlies against another state. This is precisely what the Soviet Government is proposing. Our proposals provide for the disbandment of all armed forces and the destruction of all types of weapons.

The Soviet Union is prepared itself and proposes to the other countries that they abolish war ministries and general staffs and do away with military service. To put it in a nutshell, the idea of our proposals is to reduce practically to zero the level of the armed forces and armaments of states, leaving them only strictly limited contingents agreed for each country, and equipped with small arms, for the maintenance of internal order and the protection of the personal safety of citizens.

We are satisfied with the fact that at the General Assembly all the U.N. member states adopted a resolution approving the idea of general and complete disarmament. The Ten-Nation Committee which is shortly to begin discussing disarmament questions has been instructed to consider our proposals.

It should also be noted that our partners at the coming negotiations, on whom the results of the examination of the Soviet disarmament proposals will chiefly depend, lent an attentive ear to the Soviet proposals, although they added reservations to their positive statements, specifically with regard to establishing control. We are somewhat surprised at those reservations because our proposals provide for all that is needed to ensure reliable international control over the realisation of general and complete disarmament.

* * *

There are those in the West who allege that disarmament is fraught with grave consequences for the economy of the capitalist countries. They argue that if the production of bombs, guns, submarines and other means of destruction were to be stopped, that would lead to ruin and to the loss of employment and means of subsistence by hundreds of thousands of people. But this sort of talk is fit only for people who can see no other way of developing the economy than by subordinating it to the interests of war preparations.

The least we can say about assertions of this kind is that they are utterly unsubstantiated. I had occasion to talk with many representatives of American business who take a far less gloomy view of the matter and are confident that U.S. industry is well able to cope with the task of converting the entire economy to the output of goods intended for peaceful uses.

Indeed, there is good reason to expect that the conversion of production capacities to the manufacture of peace-time goods would make it possible to sharply reduce the taxes levied on the population, to increase the capacity of the home market and at the same time to spend more on education, health and social maintenance. And would it not increase to a tremendous extent the opportunities for a foreign trade free from the artificial restrictions prompted by considerations that have nothing to do with economic advantage? How many countries in the world need peace-time goods and not weapons!

There can be no doubt that, given disarmament, the opportunities of selling peace-time products in the foreign market would increase immensely and world trade would have excellent prospects of expansion.

It is not one particular state or group of states that would benefit from disarmament, for disarmament would pave the way to a lasting peace and to economic progress in all countries and for all peoples.

The Soviet Union has proved not only by words, but also by deeds, that it is seeking a solution to the disarmament problem. Immediately after the Second World War, a large-scale demobilisation of the armed forces was carried out in our country. In later years the Soviet Union dismantled all its military bases on foreign soil.

The Soviet Union went further still. Striving to put an end to the arms race and set about taking practical disarmament steps as soon as possible, our country effected a further reduction of its armed forces. It is well known that in the last four years the Soviet Union has unilaterally reduced the strength of its armed forces by a total of another 2,140,000. Soviet troops have been withdrawn from the Rumanian People's Republic and the strength of our troops stationed under existing agreements in the German Democratic Republic, the Polish People's Republic and the Hungarian People's Republic has been reduced considerably.

I should like to report to the Deputies to the Supreme Soviet on the changes that have occurred in the numerical strength of our armed forces over the past 30-odd years.

After the Civil War the Soviet Government demobilised the bulk of the armed forces and reorganised them. As a result, by 1927 we had 586,000 men serving in the Red Army and Navy. This was also determined to a degree by the international situation at that time.

The Japanese imperialist aggression in the Far East and the advent of fascism to power in Germany were the reason why we increased our armed forces, which by 1937 were 1,433,000 strong.

Then, with the outbreak of the Second World War, which exposed the Soviet Union to the immediate threat of attack by Hitler Germany, our armed forces were increased again, so that by 1941 they were 4,107,000 strong.

Hitler Germany's treacherous attack on the Soviet Union and the bloody four-year war that followed compelled us to increase the strength of our armed forces to 11,365,000 by May 1945.

As a result of the demobilisation carried out immediately after the war, by 1948 the strength of the Armed Forces of the U.S.S.R. was down to 2,874,000. The Soviet Union undertook a substantial reduction of its armed forces in the hope that the Western Powers, too, would be guided by the idea of preserving peace and friendship and would strengthen the relations established between the countries of the anti-Hitler coalition. But our hopes were not realised. As a result of the formation of the aggressive NATO bloc in the West and in view of the atom-bomb blackmail at a time when we had no such bomb yet, the Soviet Union had, with a view to strengthening its defence against the eventuality of provocation, to increase the strength of its troops, which in 1955 reached 5,763,000.

Subsequently, between 1955 and 1958, as I have already reported, we reduced our armed forces by 2,140,000, so that their present strength is 3,623,000.

These, then, are the data on the state of the Armed Forces of the Soviet Union over the past decades.

A New Proposal for Reducing the
Armed Forces of the Soviet Union

Comrade Deputies, today the Soviet Government is submitting to the Supreme Soviet a proposal for a further substantial reduction of the Armed Forces of the U.S.S.R. As in the past, we consider it possible to effect this reduction unilaterally, and irrespective of the progress of disarmament discussions by the Ten-Nation Committee or other international agencies.

The Council of Ministers of the U.S.S.R. is submitting for your consideration and approval a proposal for reducing our armed forces by another 1,200,000. If this proposal is approved by the Supreme Soviet, our Army and Navy will be 2,423,000 strong. In other words, the strength of our armed forces will be below the level indicated in the proposals which the United States, Britain and France put forward during the discussion of the disarmament problem in 1956. Those proposals fixed the level of the armed forces of the U.S.S.R. and the United States at 2,500,000 each. We accepted that proposal and on more than one occasion advanced it ourselves—on the understanding, of course, that this would be only a first step in the reduction of armed forces. In particular, we mentioned this figure in the Soviet proposals submitted to the U. S. General Assembly in the autumn of 1956. More than three years have passed since, but no agreement has yet been reached on the matter. Now we propose reducing the armed forces to a still lower level and we do so of our own accord, without procrastination, without wasting time and effort and without the nervous strain occasioned by interminable disarmament disputes with our partners.

* * *

The security of his country, the safeguarding of the achievements of the Revolution and the successful building of communism in our country are the prime concern of every Soviet citizen, and all the more so of a Deputy to the Supreme Soviet—an elected representative of the people. That is why the very first question prompted by the proposals we have submitted is whether the defence potential of our country will still be adequate when the measure we are suggesting has been carried out. Why is it that, at a time when our ill-wishers have not yet discarded the very phrase "policy from positions of strength", we, instead of countering strength with strength, are, in fact, willing to reduce our Army and Navy and, consequently, expenditure on armaments? What is the reason? Are we not being somewhat careless with regard to the security of our country?

We have made a detailed and comprehensive study of the matter and consulted the military, the General Staff, and we reply without hesitation:

Our defence will be quite adequate and we have taken everything into account realistically.

What is the evidence backing this realistic appraisal and warranting so momentous a decision? What is the evidence on the strength of which the Deputies can adopt this decision with firm conviction that it will not prejudice the defensive capacity of our country?

Our confidence in the soundness of the suggested measures is based on the fact that the Soviet Union is going through a period of unprecedented upsurge in the entire national economy. It is based on the unbreakable moral and political unity of Soviet society. Soviet scientists, engineers and workers have made it possible to equip our armed forces with weapons that were unknown to man—atomic, hydrogen, rocket and other modern weapons. It is our economic progress, and the achievements of our scientific and technical genius, that make it possible to reduce the armed forces. We are also taking into account the growth and consolidation of the mighty socialist camp, which is a reliable stronghold of peace.

* * *

Allow me, Comrade Deputies, to express on your behalf, and on behalf of the Soviet Government and the Central Committee of the Communist Party of the Soviet Union, the most sincere gratitude to all scientists, engineers, technicians and workers... to whose knowledge and effort we owe great achievements in developing atomic and hydrogen weapons, rockets and all the other means that have made it possible to raise the defence potential of our country to so high a level, which in turn enables us now to undertake a further reduction of the armed forces.

The Soviet Union has stockpiled the necessary amount of atomic and hydrogen weapons...

Our country has powerful rocketry. The present level of military technique being what it is, the Air Force and the Navy have lost their former importance. These arms are being replaced and not reduced. Military aircraft is almost entirely being replaced by rockets. We have now drastically reduced, and apparently will reduce still further, or even discontinue, the production of bombers and other obsolete craft. In the Navy, the submarine fleet is acquiring great importance, whereas surface ships can no longer play the role they played in the past.

Our armed forces have to a considerable degree been switched to rocket and nuclear weapons. We are perfecting, and will go on perfecting, these weapons—until they are banned.

The Central Committee of the Communist Party and the Soviet Government can inform you, Comrade Deputies, that the weapons we have now are formidable ones, but what is in the hatching, so to speak, is still more perfect, still more formidable. The weapon that is being developed and is, as they say, in the portfolio of our scientists and designers is an incredible weapon.

* * *

In our time, a country's defensive capacity is not determined by the number of men under arms, of men in uniform. Apart from the general political and economic factors, of which I have already spoken, a country's defence potential depends in decisive measure on the fire-power and the means of delivery that country commands.

The proposed reduction will in no way reduce the fire-power of our armed forces, and this is the important thing. In fact, the reason why states maintain armies is to possess an adequate fire-power, such as will be able to stand up to a probable enemy and restrain him from attack, or repulse him effectively should he try to attack.

The Soviet Army today possesses such armaments and such fire-power as no army has ever had. I want to re-emphasise that we already have such an amount of nuclear weapons—atomic and hydrogen weapons and an appropriate number of rockets to deliver them to the territory of a potential aggressor—that if some madman were to provoke an attack on our country or on other socialist countries, we could literally wipe the country or countries attacking us off the face of the earth.

It is perfectly clear to all sober-minded people that atomic and hydrogen weapons are particularly dangerous to the countries that are densely populated. Of course, all countries will suffer in one way or another in the event of a new world war. We, too, shall suffer much, shall sustain great losses, but we shall survive. Our territory is immense and our population is less concentrated in large industrial centres than is the case in many other countries. The West will suffer incomparably more. If the aggressors start up a new war, it will be not only their last war, but also the end of capitalism, for the peoples will see clearly that capitalism is a source of wars, and will no longer tolerate that system, which brings suffering and calamities to mankind.

Considering all this, the Soviet people can be confident and calm—the Soviet Army's present armament makes our country completely impregnable.

Of course, impregnability is a rather relative term. After all, we must not forget that our enemies—for some states avow themselves to be our enemies, making no secret of their military and political aims—will not mark time. If they do not yet have as many rockets as we have, and if their rockets are less perfect, they have a chance to overcome their temporary lag, to improve their rocketry, and will perhaps draw level with us sooner or later.

The United States, for instance, has set out to overtake the Soviet Union in rocket production within five years. It will certainly do its utmost to help its rocketry out of its present state and raise it to a higher level. But it would be naive to imagine that we will meanwhile sit back and relax. Indeed, the Americans themselves are saying: Why, are the Russians going to play dice and wait for us?

Naturally, we will do everything to use the time we have gained in the development of rocket weapons and to keep our lead in this field until an international agreement on disarmament is reached.

But a question suggests itself here. Since the possibility must not be ruled out that some capitalist countries will draw level with us in modern armaments, cannot they commit treachery and attack us first in order to exploit the factor of a surprise attack by so formidable a weapon as atomic rockets and thereby secure advantages that may help them win? No. Modern means of warfare give no such advantage to either side. . .

Let us suppose, that some state or group of states were to succeed in preparing and carrying out a surprise attack on a power possessing nuclear and rocket arms. Would the aggressor—even allowing for a moment that he succeeded in striking a surprise blow—be able to put out of action at once all the stocks of nuclear weapons, all the rocket installations on the territory of the power attacked? Of course not. The state subjected to a surprise attack—provided it is a big state, of course—would in any case be able to rebuff the aggressor effectively.

We are aware that our country is surrounded by foreign military bases. We therefore distribute our rocket installations in such a way as to have a double and even treble reserve. Ours is a vast territory and we are in a position to disperse our rocket installations and to camouflage them well. We are developing such a system that if some means of retaliation are knocked out, we shall always be able to resort to the duplicating means and hit the targets from reserve positions.

That should be quite enough to have a sobering effect on anyone with a normal mentality, on people who are prepared to answer for their actions to the peoples and who hold the destinies of the peoples dear. There is no vouching for madmen, of course. Madmen have always existed and will probably not become extinct in the future, either. The only thing is not to forget that whereas in the past the advent of such madmen to power resulted in bloody wars, it would in our day be a calamity defying comparison. The peoples should see to it that the governments, parliaments and other offices on which the safe-guarding of peace depends should not be infiltrated by people who set themselves insane, criminal aims. The peoples must show great vigilance to prevent madmen from using rocket and nuclear weapons against mankind, until a solution is found to the problem of general and complete disarmament and, consequently, of the destruction of all means of warfare.

The Lessons of the Past Must Not be Forgotten

Western leaders have not yet renounced the policy "from positions of strength" and "on the brink of war" . . . .

There was some sort of logic in that policy when the Western Powers had economic superiority and the monopoly of a powerful weapon like the atom bomb, although, even then, that was no reason for pursuing a policy "from positions of strength."

Today, however, when the Soviet Union has atomic and hydrogen weapons, when our country has demonstrated to the world its superiority in rocket engineering, when the economy of the Soviet Union and the other socialist countries is flourishing, when the solid unity of the socialist camp is a reality and when all peoples are striving to join efforts to ensure peace, the policy "from positions of strength" is becoming utterly pointless.

* * *

We must state most unequivocally that if rabid fascists, such as are now being allowed to assume authority and command, build up the Bundeswehr and command the NATO armed forces, were to gain the upper hand in West Germany, and if those vermin tried to crawl out of their confines, far from being allowed to crawl as far as Moscow or Stalingrad, as they did during the Hitler invasion, they would be crushed on their own soil.

The policy of the Government of the Federal Republic of Germany shows most dangerous trends. Unless checked by the forces of peace, these trends may have most deplorable consequences and may lead to a third world war.

We cannot help wondering why the war preparations of the Federal Republic of Germany are meeting with support on the part of France, Britain and other countries that suffered from Hitler's onslaught. How can those countries encourage West Germany to rearm, help her with their own hands to build up her armed forces and equip them with modern weapons?

Some politicians of West German's NATO allies say frankly and plainly, though they do so behind the scenes and not in public: Please believe us and try to understand that if the Federal Republic of Germany stays out of NATO, if it has no army and spends nothing on armaments, it will have great economic advantages over the other Western countries and will become a still more formidable competitor in trade. The West German economy *is* strong and it is ahead of those of the other NATO countries, except the United States. It follows that, to such Western politicians, economic progress in West Germany on peaceful lines is a very dangerous thing, while the entry of the Federal Republic of Germany into NATO and its participation in the arms race is almost a blessing. They are not averse to handicapping their West German rival with the burden of arms and large armed forces so as to weaken West Germany economically and create more favourable conditions for competing with her in the world market.

The proponents of this most peculiar concept seem to forget that the arms they are giving to the German revanchists will not be used as the givers see fit. For the Government of the Federal Republic of Germany, while accepting the weapons, has its own aims in view. It wants, with the aid of the army and a powerful economy, to win a dominant position in Western Europe and give orders to its NATO allies. In point of fact, it is not so far away from this goal. West Germany already holds many key positions in NATO. . . .

These facts, comrades, go to show again how pressing is the problem of concluding a peace treaty with both German states, whose solution has long been urged by the Soviet Government. Such a treaty would write *finis* to the Second World War for good, assure the peaceful and democratic development of the whole of Germany and make her neighbours confident that West Germany will not revert to the road of aggression. The Soviet Government holds a peaceful settlement with Germany to be an international problem whose solution brooks no delay, a problem of the utmost importance.

We will do all in our power to have this problem settled at last. It is our earnest desire to find a solution to the German problem in common with our allies in the struggle against Hitler Germany. We proceed on the understanding that the question of West Berlin will also be settled thereby through agreement. But if all our efforts towards concluding a peace treaty with the two German states are still not crowned with success, the Soviet Union, together with the other countries that are willing to do so, will sign a peace treaty with the German Democratic Republic, with all the attendant consequences.

Peaceful Objective of the Soviet Proposals

Comrade Deputies, some of the Soviet citizens, as well as our friends, the peace supporters in other countries, may perhaps wonder whether the new big reduction of the Soviet Armed Forces will not stimulate activity on the part of the military alignments opposing us. The United States will have larger armed forces than the Soviet Union. If the Federal Republic of Germany has nine divisions today, it is going to have as many as 12 divisions before long. The NATO military command has about 50 divisions at its disposal in Europe alone. Besides, the European countries in the North Atlantic alliance have over 30 divisions under their national control.

That being so, will not the reduction of the Soviet Army expose our country, and indeed the cause of peace, to danger? Will it not tempt the aggressive forces, the enemies of communism, to begin a war against the Soviet Union and the other socialist countries and thereby plunge mankind into a new carnage? Will it not undermine or lead to the loss of the Soviet "deterrent," to use the current Western term?

We have considered that and can report to the Supreme Soviet that the defence potential of our country will not diminish in the least. In present-day conditions, wars would not be waged the way they were before. They would have little in common with the wars of the past. In the old days the nations tried to keep their armies close to the frontiers so as to raise a living wall, as it were, of soldiers and guns at the right moment. If any country wanted to invade another, it had to attack the troops stationed thus on the border. That was how wars used to begin. At first fighting broke out on the frontiers of the belligerents and that is where the troops were massed.

If a war were to start now, hostilities would take a different course since the nations would have means of delivering their arms to points thousands of kilometres away. It is first of all deep in the belligerents' territory that a war would start. Furthermore, there would be not a single capital, no large industrial or administrative centre, and no strategic area left unattacked in the very first minutes, let alone days, of the war. In other words, the war would start in a different manner, if at all, and would proceed in a different manner.

A reduction of the numerical strength of our armed forces will not prevent us from maintaining the country's defensive power at the proper level. We shall still have all the means required for the defence of our country, and our enemy will know it very well. In case he does not, we are warning him and telling him outright: By reducing the numerical strength of our armed forces, we shall not be diminishing their fire-power. On the contrary, their fire-power will increase many times over in terms of quality.

If our Western partners decline to follow our example, they will disappoint not only progressive people, but all nations as well. If the Western Powers persist, they will thereby reveal their aggressiveness and their desire to continue the arms race and preparations for a new war. By their policy of arms race, they will be exposing themselves still more in the eyes of the peoples.

Economically, this policy will overload the budgets of the capitalist states and lead to an increasing tax burden.

It goes without saying that we shall have to spend a certain amount on defence, pending agreement on general and complete disarmament. But this expenditure will be cut down as the armed forces will have been reduced. Besides, this money will be used more effectively. Obviously, such a situation will benefit our country as it will help us to increase our economic power and to provide additional opportunities of promoting the standard of living, increasing our material wealth, building more homes and reducing the working day. It follows that the large armies in the countries of the military alignment opposing us are our involuntary allies who will make it easier for us to achieve our main objective, that is, to surpass the most developed capitalist countries in all fields—science, output of machinery and implements of labour, production of consumer goods, and meeting the requirements of the people.

I should like to comment on some speculations which are now rife abroad concerning our disarmament proposals and which our ill-wishers will in all probability indulge in still more following the new, and so very impressive, reduction of the Soviet Armed Forces.

It is often alleged in the West that the Soviet Union wants disarmament because it is having difficulties in fulfilling its Seven-Year Economic Development Plan. They go so far as to assert that the Soviet Union put forward its disarmament proposals for the sole purpose of releasing funds to fulfil the Seven-Year Plan. Of course, that is nothing but an invention of the Soviet Union's ill-wishers. If there are those in the West who imagine that the state of the Soviet Union's economy does not permit of keeping an army strong enough to assure our country's defence, so much the worse for those who think so.

Our economy, as I have already reported, is making good progress and has reached an unprecedented level of prosperity. But we have a still brighter future in store, because we have fulfilled the programme for the first year of the Seven-Year Plan and, moreover, produced a large amount of goods over and above it. Consequently, far from having any difficulties, we have favourable conditions for a substantial overfulfilment of the Seven-Year Plan. The allegations about difficulties in fulfilling the Seven-Year Plan will therefore not hold water.

* * *

The proposal for the reduction of the Soviet Armed Forces, which the Government is submitting to the Supreme Soviet, will save us approximately 16,000 million to 17,000 million rubles a year. [The dollar value of the saving would be in the range of two to five billion dollars.] It will be a very tangible saving for our people and country. It will help us very considerably in fulfilling and overfulfilling our economic plans.

It is not from economic or budgetary weakness but from strength and power that we are undertaking a reduction of the armed forces. In doing so, we are guided by the peaceful aspirations of our people. And it should be clear to anyone that if there arose a situation calling for more spending on the maintenance of the armed forces, our budget and our economy would permit of more than another ten million rubles being set aside for the promotion of our country's security. If our country were threatened with immediate attack, we could not only keep our armed forces at their present strength, but could also increase them considerably. Our budget, our economy, would be able to bear the strain, and we could still provide sufficient investments to fulfil the Seven-Year Plan.

* * *

The reduction of our armed forces, that is, the reduction of expenditures on armaments, will provide even better opportunities for promoting our economy and, consequently, increasing assistance to the so-called underdeveloped countries.

Now as before, we declare that if agreement is reached on general and complete disarmament, which will release enormous means, it will be possible as a result to render greater assistance to all economically underdeveloped countries.

Peaceful coexistence of all countries irrespective of their internal order, of their social systems, is the fundamental question today, the question of questions in international relations. . . .

As it is, however, there exists two camps in the world today, each with a different social system. The countries in these camps shape their policies along entirely different lines. In these circumstances, the problem of peaceful coexistence, that is, of safeguarding the world against the disaster of a military conflict between these two essentially antagonistic systems, between the groups of countries in which the two systems reign supreme, is of paramount importance. It is necessary to see to it that the inevitable struggle between them resolves solely into a struggle between ideologies and into peaceful emulation, or competition, to use a term that the capitalists find easier to understand. Each side will demonstrate its advantages to the best of its ability, but war as a means of settling this dispute must be ruled out. This, then, is coexistence as we Communists see it. We are upholding such coexistence with might and main, and will continue to do so. We consider that it is indispensable and inevitable in the present conditions, unless, of course, one heads deliberately for the lunacy of nuclear-rocket war.

Some Western politicians are now trying to mislead and intimidate unenlightened people who as yet know little about communist theory and to whom our communist philosophy is not clear. They seek to talk them into believing that since the Communists proclaim their faith in the victory of communist ideology and the ultimate triumph of socialism and communism throughout the world, it follows that the Communists harbour aggressive designs, that they want to conquer the world, to rule all peoples, and so on. Need we prove that these allegations are nothing but brazen lies and slander?

The enemies of communism misrepresent our aims because they are afraid of the influence which the peace policy of the socialist countries exerts on the peoples. We have never said, of course, that our aim is to conquer the world or a part of it. What does "conquer" mean? It means forcibly to impose one's terms, one's political system, one's ideology, on the other side. But then that is not coexistence, it is interference in the internal affairs of other countries, it is war. It is something we are most emphatically opposed to.

We consider that it is impossible forcibly to impose on other peoples something they object to, something they do not want. The Communists are firmly convinced that no ideology, including communist ideology, can be implanted forcibly, by war, by bayonets.

But there is yet another side to the matter, which the ideologists of imperialism are also trying hard to conceal. No state frontiers can stop the spread of communist ideology, of Marxism-Leninism. . . .

No bayonets, no prisons or force, can stem the ideas of communism, for the simple reason that Marxism-Leninism is an expression of the vital interests of the working people, that it is the truth. Communist society is a society based on complete justice, freedom, equality, and genuine respect for man. Whatever guards one may post, however much one may try to fool people, they will in the end see and understand what is true and what isn't, what is good and what is bad. That is why we are confident that the cause of communism will triumph in the end. Communism will win, but not in the sense that the socialist countries will conquer the other countries. No, the people of each country will themselves weigh all the facts and when they have appreciated the essence of Marxism-Leninism, they will of their own free will choose the more progressive social system.

* * *

While today capitalist propaganda still succeeds in scaring some little-informed people with communism, we can say with confidence that it is a strictly temporary phenomenon. When these people have seen what is what, they will be ashamed of their present error, and not every grandfather will make bold to confess to his grandchildren that there was a time when he was against communism.

* * *

For decades and even centuries, the imperalists and colonialists plundered the countries of Asia, Africa and Latin America which they now have so "generous" an intention of helping. They extracted untold wealth from the bowels of those countries but deliberately kept those who extracted it for them in poverty and ignorance, and exploited them mercilessly. That is why dozens of countries in Asia, Africa and Latin America are poor today and rank as economically underdeveloped. It is not at all because the soil in those countries is poorer than elsewhere or the populations less capable and industrious, but because foreign exploiters profited by their labour and resources, and waxed rich at their expense.

The time has come when the robbed are beginning to realise who robbed them and who is to blame for their plight. And they are already raising their voice in reminder. That is why the colonialists are beginning to sense that the hour of reckoning will come soon, and are trying to extricate themselves somehow from this situation.

The existence and progress of the Soviet Union and the other socialist countries are no doubt playing a tremendous part in the growth of the self-consciousness of the colonial or former colonial and semi-colonial countries. Their progress is there for all to see. Once these countries—China and some others, for instance—were themselves exploited and economically backward. But today they have changed beyond recognition. They have made immense progress in economy and culture, and in the building of a new society. The socialist states thereby graphically demonstrate the advantages of socialism as a more just and progressive   social system. . . .

The moribund capitalist society is being succeeded by a new, just society which provides equal conditions for all and offers all benefits to every working man. The road of this new society is strewn with the magnificent flowers of freedom, equality, abundance and peace, and its victorious advance is irresistible. Such is the law of historical progress. . . .

KHRUSHCHEV

Report on the World Meeting of Communist Parties
January 6, 1961

Introduction Khrushchev's troubles with President Eisenhower when the U-2 crashed in the USSR were followed by new troubles with Mao Tse-tung. In June, 1960, Khrushchev suddenly withdrew Soviet technicians from Communist China. Mao was not intimidated by this act of escalation, and the polemics grew much sharper. There was a confrontation of the two sides when the world Meeting of Communist Parties took place in Moscow in November, 1960. Their differences were not resolved in the Meeting's Declaration, a compromise document in which each side could find authority for its own views when polemics were later resumed. Early in January Khrushchev reported on the Meeting to Soviet ideologists, and took the occasion to set down the Soviet interpretation of the Declaration. Publication of this speech, just as the Kennedy Administration took office, produced a strong impression on the new President. According to Arthur Schlesinger, Jr. (at that time a presidential aide), Kennedy "took it as an authoritative exposition of Soviet intentions" and was "alarmed" by it.* Fearing that Khrushchev's doctrine on

---

* *A Thousand Days* (New York: Houghton Mifflin, 1965) pp. 302-3.

"national liberation wars" presaged a strategy of subversion and guerrilla warfare in the underdeveloped areas of the world, Kennedy began to develop a defensive strategy of "counter-insurgency." Its chief application, with fateful consequences, was to be in Vietnam.

In this Report, Khrushchev repeats and develops his previously stated views on war. A world nuclear war would be a disaster for Communism, and a local war—the USSR refused to speak of "limited war," as the West does—would tend to become a world war. Therefore, both kinds of war must be deterred. Significantly, Khrushchev feels obliged to deny that in the absence of "military cataclysms" proletarian revolution would not occur. Communist propaganda repeatedly had called attention to the connection between war and Communist revolution, partly with the object of warning the West not to resort to war; but propaganda aside, Stalin seems really to have believed that only when war had prepared the necessary conditions could Communists seize power, and this view may have continued to find advocates after Stalin's death. (Note that while Mao believes *violence* to be necessary for a Communist revolution, he has not said that *war between states* is.)

Khrushchev does not point to proletarian revolutions in history that were unconnected with war. (Actually, with the exception of Cuba, all Communist regimes have been established in the aftermath of world war.) Instead, he asserts that the general crisis of capitalism has "become much deeper" than it was after World War II. One aim of this surprising statement is to show that even without war a revolutionary situation is developing.

Khrushchev also takes issue with another Stalinist thesis on war—that it is more likely to occur between capitalist countries than between the two camps. He argues the opposite view, and makes the avoidance of war a central problem of Soviet foreign policy. This has important policy implications. First, the USSR must have the military means to *deter* the West; this was a requirement that Khrushchev discussed often and at length. Second, the USSR must avoid provocative action against the West; Khrushchev states this second requirement discretely:

In rebuffing the aggressive actions of imperialism, our Party and Government always display firmness and self-control. In upholding the interests of the socialist camp, we invariably strive to direct developments in such a way as not to allow imperialist provocateurs to launch a new world war.

But this posed a problem: so long as the USSR was careful "not to allow imperialist provocateurs to launch a new world war," it could not take the "resolute measures" necessary to compel the West to make major concessions. Khrushchev had failed to resolve this dilemma in the Berlin crisis of 1959; in the second Berlin crisis, which he initiated five months after this speech (June 1961), he was no more successful.

Comrades, the Meeting of Representatives of Eighty-One Marxist-Leninist Parties, held in Moscow in November 1960, will go down in the history of the world communist and working-class movement as one of its most vivid chapters. The Meeting made a profound analysis of the contemporary international situation and worked out a line common for our movement on the major issues. As a result of the Meeting, which proceeded in an atmosphere of fraternal unity, the millions-strong family of Communists of all countries has drawn still closer together on the basis of Marxism-Leninism, and multiplied its strength in the heroic struggle for the triumph of peace and socialism. . . .We have every reason to state firmly that the unity of the world Communist movement, which the imperialist reactionaries fear so terribly, is now stronger than ever. This is a great success for our common cause.

Our Epoch is the Epoch of the Triumph of Marxism-Leninism

Now that a world socialist system exists and there is a marked upsurge of anti-imperialist national-liberation revolutions, we have had to determine the further course and outlook of world development. And this is impossible without a profound understanding of the essence, content and nature of the decisive tasks of the present epoch.

The question of the character of the epoch is not an abstract and purely theoretical question. Inseparably linked with it are the general strategy and tactics of world communism, and of every Communist Party.

* * *

What, then, are the requirements which a Marxist-Leninist characterization of our epoch should meet? It should give a clear idea of what class holds the key place in this epoch, and what are the basic content, trend and tasks of social development. Secondly, it should cover the entire revolutionary process from the emergence of socialism to the complete victory of communism. Thirdly, it should show the forces aligned with the working class, which holds the key place in our epoch, and the movements that are part of the general torrent against imperialism.

At a time when the socialist revolution has triumphed in many countries, when socialism has become a powerful world system, when the colonial system of imperialism is on the point of final collapse, and imperialism in a state of decline and crisis, the definition of our epoch should reflect these decisive developments.

The Statement of the Meeting defines the epoch in these terms:

"Our time, whose main content is the transition from capitalism to socialism initiated by the Great October Socialist Revolution, is a time of struggle between the two opposing social systems, a time of socialist revolutions and national-liberation revolutions, a time of the breakdown of imperialism, of the abolition of the colonial system, a time of transition of more peoples to the socialist path, of the triumph of socialism and communism on a world-wide scale."

The main distinguishing feature of our time is that the world socialist system is becoming the decisive factor in the development of human society. This is also directly expressed in the sphere of international relations. In the present conditions premises have been created for socialism to determine more and more the character, methods and trends of international relations. This does not mean that imperialism is an "insignificant factor" which can be thrown off the scales. Not at all. Imperialism is still very strong. It controls a powerful militaristic machine.

Imperialism has built up a gigantic peacetime war machine and a ramified system of blocs, and has subordinated economy to the arms drive. The U.S. imperialists are bent on bringing the whole world under their sway, and are threatening mankind with nuclear-missile war. Modern imperialism is increasingly tainted by decay and parasitism. Marxist-Leninists do not, and must not entertain any illusions with regard to imperialism in their evaluation of the prospects of international development.

The facts indicating that the imperialists are pursuing a policy of outrageous provocations and aggressions are countless. That is no novelty. The novelty is that all the intrigues of the imperialists are not only being conclusively exposed, but also firmly repelled, and their attempts to start local wars are being frustrated.

The present balance of world forces enables the socialist camp and the other forces of peace for the first time in history to set themselves the entirely realistic task of forcing the imperialists, under pain of the downfall of their system, to refrain from starting a world war.

In connection with the possibility of preventing a world war, I should like to deal with the prospects of the further development of the general crisis of capitalism. It is common knowledge that both the first and the second world wars greatly influenced the onset and aggravation of the general crisis of capitalism. Does it follow that world war is an indispensable condition for further intensification of the general crisis of capitalism? Such an inference would be absolutely wrong, because it distorts the Marxist-Leninist theory of socialist revolution and inverts the true causes of revolution. Proletarian revolution is not caused solely by military cataclysms; first and foremost, it is a result of the development of the class struggle and the internal contradictions of capitalism.

At present the capitalist world is not split into two imperialist camps as it was prior to the two world wars. But it is far from united, and is rent by bitter internal conflicts. Even behind the so-called "Atlantic solidarity" there is the unprepossessing picture of internal strife and conflict, and increasing resistance to United States leadership and *diktat*. The revival of German militarism and revanchism in the heart of Europe is restoring the complex entanglement of Anglo-German, Franco-German and other imperialist contradictions. One has only to compare the present state of capitalism with what it was after the end of the Second World War to see clearly that its general crisis has become much deeper.

Having made a profound analysis of the international situation as a whole, the Meeting reached a conclusion of great theoretical and political significance, namely, that *"a new stage has begun in the development of the general crisis of capitalism"*. The feature of this stage is that it originated not in connection with a world war, but in an environment of competition and struggle between the two systems, the increasing change in the balance of forces in favour of socialism, and the intense aggravation of all the contradictions of imperialism, an environment where the successful struggle of the peace forces for the practice and consolidation of peaceful coexistence has prevented the imperialist from wrecking world peace by their aggressive actions, an environment of rising struggle by the masses for democracy, national liberation and socialism. All this speaks of the further development and deepening of the general crisis of capitalism.

Our comrades-in-arms of the Communist Parties in the capitalist countries bear this in mind when charting their further tactical course of struggle for the working-class cause. And we can confidently say that the near future will be marked by new successes for the combined forces of world socialism, the working class and the national-liberation movement.

Full-Scale Building of Communism in the U.S.S.R.
and the Prospects of the World Socialist System

The changes wrought by socialism in all spheres of life in the People's Democracies are so profound that now we can say with legitimate pride that not only in the Soviet Union but also in all the other countries of the socialist camp the socio-economic possibilities of restoring capitalism no longer exist. The world socialist system has entered upon a new stage in its development.

In all probability we will not pursue a policy of developing iron and steel to the full. The likelihood is that we will divert some of the funds into agriculture and light industry. Communism cannot be built by offering nothing but machines, iron, steel and non-ferrous metals. People should have a chance to eat and dress well, to have good housing and to enjoy other material and cultural amenities.

This is not a revision of our general line, it is rather a rational utilisation of our material possibilities. When we were surrounded by enemies and our industry was weaker than that of the capitalist countries, we economised on everything—even on schools, as Lenin said. Things are different now. We have a powerful industry, and our armed forces are equipped with the most up-to-date weapons. Why deny ourselves the things we can have without prejudicing the further development of our socialist state?

The first stage of the full-scale building of communism, encompassed by the Seven-Year Plan, is at the [same time the] decisive stage in the fulfilment of the basic economic task of the U.S.S.R. In 1950, the industrial output of the Soviet Union amounted to less than 30 per cent of U.S. output. Today, it is approximately 60 per cent. Economists estimate that in 1965 the Soviet Union will surpass the United States in physical output, and by about 1970 in output per head of population.

The peoples of the other socialist countries, too, are working with devotion to solve the basic economic task of socialism. The time is not far off when socialism will advance to first place in world production, and capitalism will suffer defeat in the sphere of material production, this decisive sphere of human endeavour. To be sure, after the Soviet Union fulfils and overfulfils its Seven-Year Plan, and thanks to the rapid rates of economic development in the People's Democracies, the countries of the world socialist system will be producing more than half of the world industrial output.

The victory of the Soviet Union in the economic competition with the United States, and the victory of the socialist system as a whole over the capitalist system, will be a major turning point in history, one that will have a still more powerful revolutionising influence on the working-class movement of the world. When this happens even the most inveterate sceptics will see that socialism alone provides everything needed for man's happiness, and will choose in favour of socialism.

The most important thing today is to win time in the economic competition with capitalism. The faster our economic development, the stronger we will be economically and politically and the greater will be the influence of the socialist camp on the trend and rate of historical development, on the future of the world.

The countries of the world socialist system are drawing closer to each other; their co-operation in all fields is growing. This is a natural development. There are no insoluble contradictions between the socialist countries. Nor can there be. The more developed and economically stronger countries are rendering disinterested fraternal aid to the economically less developed. . . .

The world socialist system is at present an aggregate of the national economies of sovereign, independent countries. The steady strengthening of bonds between the national economies of the socialist countries is a law of the world socialist system as a whole. There is good reason to say that the further development of the socialist countries will follow the line of consolidating the world system of socialist economy. As the Statement points out, the Marxist-Leninist parties at the helm in these countries are unanimous in their striving actively to further this process.

They are working jointly for a correct solution of the problems of specialization and co-ordination of production and the international division of labour. By so doing, they are helping to utilize the advantages of socialism more fully. . . .

The consolidation of the common economic basis of the world socialist system and the creation of the material basis for the more or less simultaneous transition of all the peoples of the socialist system to communism will proceed more rapidly, the more fully the internal resources of each of the socialist countries are utilized and the better the advantages of the socialist international division of labour are employed, with the different levels of economic development being evened out. By gradually eliminating the disparity in levels of economic development, that arose in the course of history, we are showing the peoples of the world the communist way of ending the economic and cultural backwardness to which imperialism doomed them. The effectiveness of this way was first demonstrated by some of the formerly backward peoples of Central Asia and the Caucasus, who, with the generous aid rendered by the more developed socialist nations, the Russian nation first and foremost, rapidly overcame their backwardness and caught up with the industrially developed regions of the country. This process is now taking place throughout the socialist system.

The Communist and Workers' Parties have defined, in the spirit of Marxism-Leninism and proletarian internationalism, the right principles governing the relations among the socialist countries and nations. It stands to reason that some shortcomings and snags are bound to crop up in such a new and momentous undertaking. But the socialist community is characterised not by incidental shortcomings, but by the essentially internationalist nature of socialism, by the internationalist policy of the fraternal parties and countries, and the epoch-making successes achieved through this policy. As to the shortcomings, we must remove them, guided by the principles of Marxism-Leninism, international solidarity and fraternal friendship, seeing our aim in consolidating the socialist camp.

*   *   *

Prevention of a New War is the Question of Questions

Comrades, the Meeting centred its attention on the issues of war and peace. All of us at the Meeting saw clearly that prevention of a world-wide nuclear war was the most burning and vital problem facing mankind.

Lenin pointed out that since the First World War the issue of war and peace had become the basic question of the policy of all countries—a matter of life and death for tens of millions. Lenin's words sound even more forcefully today, when weapons of mass annihilation threaten unprecedented destruction and death to hundreds of millions of people. There is no task more pressing today than to avert such a catastrophe.

The Meeting charted ways and means of making still more effective use of the new possibilities of averting world war afforded by the emergence of the socialist camp and its increased might, by the new balance of forces in the world. The peoples trust that the Communists will use all the might of the socialist system and the enhanced strength of the international working class to rid mankind of the horrors of war. . . .

. . . Our Party, always vigilantly on guard against the danger emanating from imperialism, is educating the Soviet people accordingly and doing everything to prevent the enemy from ever taking us by surprise. We alert the peoples to the danger of war in order to heighten their vigilance and rouse them to action, to rally them to the struggle against world war.

The attitude of the Communist Party of the Soviet Union to questions of war and peace is known to all. It has been stated time and again in the resolutions of its congresses and in other Party documents.

Wars arose with the division of society into classes. This means that the ground for all wars will not be completely eliminated until society is no longer divided into hostile, antagonistic classes. The victory of the working class throughout the world and the triumph of socialism will destroy all the social and national causes of war and mankind will be able to rid itself of this dreadful scourge.

In the present conditions we must distinguish between the following kinds of war: world war, local war, and war of liberation or popular uprising. This is necessary in order to work out the proper tactics in regard to each.

Let us begin with the problem of *world wars*. . . . The Communists are the most resolute opponents of the world wars, as they are of wars between states in general. Only the imperialists need these wars in order to seize foreign territories and to enslave and plunder the peoples. Prior to the emergence of the world socialist camp, the working class was unable to exert any decisive influence on the decision of whether there should or should not be a world war. In those circumstances the finest representatives of the working class advanced the slogan of turning imperialist war into civil war, that is, of the working class and all working people using the situation created by the war to win power. A situation of that kind obtained during the First World War, and was used classically by the Bolshevik Party, by Lenin.

In our time the conditions are different. The world socialist camp with its powerful economy and armed forces is exerting an ever-growing influence on the questions of war and peace. To be sure, acute contradictions and antagonisms between the imperialist countries and the urge to profit at the expense of others, the weaker countries, still exist. However, the imperialists are compelled to keep in mind the Soviet Union and the entire socialist camp, and are afraid to start a war between themselves. They try to minimise their differences. They have formed military blocs and have drawn many capitalist countries into them. Although these blocs are torn by internal conflicts, their members are united, as they themselves say, by their hatred of Communism and, naturally, by their common imperialist nature and aspirations.

In the present circumstances it is not war between the capitalist, imperialist countries that is most likely to occur, although this possiblility should not be ruled out entirely. The imperialists are preparing war chiefly against the socialist countries, and above all against the Soviet Union, the most powerful of the socialist countries. They would like to sap our might and thereby restore the one-time dominance of monopoly capital.

The task is to raise insurmountable obstacles to the unleashing of war by the imperialists. Our possibilities for blocking the warmongers are growing, and we can consequently prevent a world war. It stands to reason that we cannot as yet completely exclude the possibility of war, since imperialist countries continue to exist, but it is now much more difficult for the imperialists to start a war than was the case previously, before the powerful socialist camp came into existence. The imperialists can start a war, but they have to think of the consequences.

I have said before that the maniac Hitler, if he had had an inkling of how his sanguinary gamble would end and of his having to commit suicide, would have thought twice before starting the war against the Soviet Union. But at that time there were only two socialist countries—the Soviet Union and the Mongolian People's Republic. Yet we smashed the aggressors, and in doing so made use also of the contradictions existing between the imperialist states.

Today the situation is entirely different. At present the imperialist camp is confronted by the socialist countries, which are a mighty force. It would be wrong to underestimate the strength of the socialist camp, its influence on world developments and, consequently, on the question of war or peace. Now that there is a mighty socialist camp with powerful armed forces, the peoples can undoubtedly prevent war and thus ensure peaceful coexistence, provided they rally all their forces for active struggle against the bellicose imperialists.

Now about *local wars.* There is much talk in the imperialist camp today about local wars, and the imperialists are making small-calibre atomic weapons for use in such wars. They have even concocted a special theory on local wars. Is this mere chance? Not at all. Some of the imperialist groups fear that a world war might end in the complete destruction of capitalism, and are laying their stakes on local wars.

There have been local wars in the past and they may break out again. But the chances of the imperialists' starting wars of even a local nature are dwindling. A small-scale imperialist war, no matter which of the imperialists starts it, may develop into a world thermo-nuclear, missile war. We must, therefore, fight against world wars and against local wars.

The aggression of Britain, France and Israel against Egypt is an example of a local war started by the imperialists. They wanted to strangle Egypt and thereby intimidate the other Arab countries fighting for their independence, and also to scare the rest of the peoples of Asia and Africa. When we were in London, British statesmen, Mr. Eden included, spoke to us quite frankly about their desire to settle accounts with Egypt. We told them plainly: "If you start a war, you will lose it. We shall not be neutral." When that war broke out, the United Nations formally condemned it, but this did not disturb the aggressors; they went ahead with their dirty business and thought they would soon reach their goal. The Soviet Union, and the socialist camp as a whole, came to the defence of Egypt. The stern warning which the Soviet Government issued to Eden and Guy Mollet stopped the war. Local war, the gamble in Egypt, failed ignominiously.

That was in 1956 when the balance of forces between the socialist and imperialist countries was not what it is now. We were not as powerful then as we are today. Moreover, the rulers of Britain, France and Israel expected to profit by the difficulties that had arisen in Hungary and Poland. Spokesmen of the imperialist countries whispered to us, "You have your difficulties in Hungary and we have ours in Egypt, so don't meddle in our affairs." Be we told the whisperers where to get off. We refused to shut our eyes to their knavish acts. We intervened and frustrated their aggression.

There you have an example of how a local war started by the imperialists was thwarted through the intervention of the Soviet Union and the entire socialist camp.

I have already said that local wars may re-occur. It is our task, therefore, always to be on the alert, to summon to action the forces of the socialist camp, the people of all countries, all peace-loving forces, in order to prevent wars of aggression. If the people of all countries are united and roused, and if they fight indefatigably and combine their forces both in each country and on an international scale, wars can be prevented.

Now about *national-liberation wars.* Recent examples of wars of this kind are the armed struggle waged by the people of Viet Nam and the present war of the Algerian people, which is now in its seventh year.

These wars, which began as uprisings of colonial peoples against their oppressors, developed into guerilla wars.

There will be liberation wars as long as imperialism exists, as long as colonialism exists. Wars of this kind are revolutionary wars. Such wars are not only admissible, but inevitable, for the colonialists do not freely bestow independence on the peoples. The peoples win freedom and independence only through struggle, including armed struggle.

Why was it that the U.S. imperialists, though eager to help the French colonialists in every way, did not venture directly to intervene in the war in Viet Nam? They did not do so because they knew that if they gave France armed assistance, Viet Nam would receive the same kind of assistance from China, the Soviet Union and the other socialist countries, and that the fighting could then develop into a world war. The outcome of the war is known—North Viet Nam won.

A similar war is being waged today in Algeria. What kind of a war is it? It is an uprising of the Arab people of Algeria against the French colonialists. It has assumed the form of a guerilla war. The U.S. and British imperialists are helping their French allies with arms. Moreover, they have allowed France, a member of NATO, to transfer troops from Europe to fight the Algerian people. The people of Algeria, too, get help from neighbouring and other countries who appreciate their love of freedom. But this is a liberation war, a war of independence waged by the people. It is a sacred war. We recognise such wars; we have helped and shall continue to help peoples fighting for their freedom.

Or take Cuba. A war was fought there too. But it began as an uprising against a tyrannical regime backed by U.S. imperialism. Batista was a puppet of the United States and the United States helped him actively. However, the U.S.A. did not directly intervene with its armed forces in the Cuban war. Led by Fidel Castro, the people of Cuba won.

Can such wars recur? Yes, they can. Are uprisings of this kind likely? Yes, they are. But they are wars in the nature of popular uprisings. Can conditions in other countries reach the point where the cup of popular patience overflows and the people take up arms? Yes, they can. What is the Marxist attitude to such uprisings? It is most favourable. These uprisings cannot be identified with wars between countries, with local wars, because the insurgent people fight for the right of self- determination, for their social and independent national development; these uprisings are directed against corrupt reactionary regimes, against the colonialists. The Communists support just wars of this kind whole-heartedly and without reservations, and march in the van of the peoples fighting for liberation.

Comrades, mankind has arrived at the stage in history when it is able to solve problems that were too much for previous generations to solve. This applies also to the most burning problem of all, that of preventing world war.

The working class, which today rules in a vast section of the world and in time will rule throughout the world, cannot let the forces doomed to destruction drag hundreds of millions into the grave with them. For a world war in the present conditions would be waged with missiles and nuclear weapons, that is, it would be the most destructive war in history.

Among the H-bombs already tested there are bombs several times more powerful than all the explosives used in the Second World War and, indeed, ever since mankind existed. . . . The well-known American physicist, Linus Pauling, says that the areas likely to suffer powerful nuclear blows are inhabited by about a thousand million people and that 500 to 750 million people are likely to perish within sixty days of a nuclear blow. Nor would nuclear war spare the people in the countries not directly subjected to bombing; in particular, many millions would die of subsequent radiation.

We know that if the imperialist maniacs were to begin a world war, the peoples would wipe out capitalism. But we are resolutely opposed to war, chiefly because we are thinking of the destiny of mankind, its present and its future. We know that the first to suffer in the event of war would be the working people and their vanguard—the working class.

There exists in the world today not just one country of workers and peasants, but a whole system of socialist countries. It is our duty to safeguard peace and ensure the peaceful development of this grand creation of the international working class, and to protect the peoples of all countries from a new war of annihilation. The victory of socialism on a world scale, inevitable by virtue of the laws of history, is now near. Wars between countries are not needed for this victory.

A sober consideration of the inescapable consequences of a nuclear war is indispensable if we are to pursue, with due consistency, a policy of averting war and mobilising the masses for this purpose. Because the very realization of what a nuclear war implies strengthens the resolve of the masses to fight against war. It is necessary, therefore, to warn the masses about the deadly consequences of a new world war and so arouse their righteous anger against those who are plotting this crime. The possibility of averting war is not a gift from above. Peace cannot be got by begging for it. It can be secured only by active purposeful struggle. That is why we have been waging this struggle, and will continue to do so.

In rebuffing the aggressive actions of imperialism, our Party and Government always display firmness and self-control. In upholding the interests of the socialist camp, we invariably strive to direct developments in such a way as not to allow imperialists provocateurs to launch a new world war.

We aim to expose the aggressive nature of all the politico-military alignments of the imperialists, such as NATO, SEATO, and CENTO, and to work for their isolation and eventual dissolution. We have repeatedly declared that we are ready to follow suit and dissolve the Warsaw Treaty Organization. All the nations of the world will gain from the dissolution of the military alignments.

This would be a real and redoubtable contribution to peace and the improvement of the international climate, and a big achievement for the policy of peaceful coexistence. All their efforts notwithstanding the imperialists have in recent times failed to draw a single new state into their military blocs. It is significant that all the newly-independent states have declared their intention to pursue a policy of non-participation in military blocs.

Of special importance for peace in Europe, and not only in Europe, is the struggle against the revived West Germany. The Soviet Union is waging this struggle together with the German Democratic Republic, Poland, Czechoslovakia and other socialist countries in various ways, the most important being the struggle for a peace treaty. The initiative of the socialist states in advancing a programme for the peaceful settlement of the

German question, and for the solution, on this basis, of the question of West Berlin, has done much to unmask the aggressive elements in the U.S.A., the Federal Republic and other NATO countries as opponents of a *detente*. The international position of the German Democratic Republic—the outpost of socialism in Western Europe—has been strengthened.

The positions of the U.S.A., Britain and France have proved to be especially vulnerable in West Berlin. These powers still cling to the old pattern, but they cannot fail to realise that sooner or later the occupation regime in that city will end.

It is necessary to keep on bringing the aggressive-minded imperialists to their senses, and to compel them to reckon with the real situation. And should they balk, we shall take resolute measures. We shall then sign a peace treaty with the German Democratic Republic, since we are firmly resolved to conclude a peace treaty with Germany at long last, to end the occupation regime in West Berlin, and thereby remove the thorn from the heart of Europe.

There are two trends in evidence in the capitalist camp towards the socialist countries—one bellicose and aggressive, and the other moderately sober. . . .

Fear for the future of capitalism dominates the ruling classes of the imperialist camp. The more reactionary groups show growing nervousness and a tendency towards reckless acts and aggression, whereby they hope to mend their fences. At the same time, there are also groups among the ruling circles of these countries who realise the dangers that a new war holds for capitalism. Hence the two trends: one aimed at war, the other at accepting in some form the idea of peaceful coexistence.

The socialist countries take both of these trends into account in their policy. They work for negotiations and agreements with the capitalist countries on the basis of constructive proposals, and promote personal contacts between statesmen of the socialist and capitalist countries. We should continue to use every opportunity of exposing the cold war warriors, the protagonists of the arms drive, and of showing the masses that the socialist countries are sincere in their efforts to safeguard world peace.

Abolition of Colonialism and the Further Development of the Newly-Free Countries

Comrades, the peoples that have gained national independence have become another mighty force in the struggle for peace and social progress.

The national-liberation movement is striking ever more telling blows at imperialism, helping to strengthen peace and accelerate the social progress of mankind. At present, Asia, Africa and Latin America are the most important centres of the revolutionary struggle against imperialism. Some forty countries have won national independence since the war. Nearly 1,500 million people have broken free from colonial slavery.

The Meeting noted with good reason that the breakdown of the system of colonial slavery under the impact of the national-liberation movement is second in historical significance only to the rise of the socialist world system.

A splendid new chapter is opening in the history of mankind. It is easily imagined what great things these peoples will do after they completely oust the imperialists from their countries and feel themselves masters of their own fate. This multiplies enormously the progressive forces of mankind.

Take Asia, for example, that ancient cradle of human civilisation. What incalculable strength the peoples of that continent possess! What a great role the Arab peoples with their heroic traditions and all the peoples of the Middle East, those liberated or in the process of liberation from political and economic dependence upon imperialism, could play in resolving the issues now confronting mankind!

The awakening of the peoples of Africa is one of the outstanding events of our epoch. Dozens of countries in North and Central Africa have already won independence. The south of the continent is beginning to seethe. The fascist dungeons in the Union of South Africa will undoubtedly crumble to dust, and Rhodesia, Uganda and other parts of Africa will become free.

The forces of the national-liberation movement are multiplying largely because one more front of active struggle against U.S. imperialism, Latin America, has come into being in recent years. Only a short time ago that vast continent was identified by a single concept—America. And that concept accorded largely with the facts, for Latin America was bound hand and foot by Yankee imperialism. Today, the Latin American peoples are showing by their struggle that the American continent is not a preserve of the U.S.A. Latin America is reminiscent of an active volcano. The eruption of the liberation struggle has wiped out dictatorial regimes in a number of Latin American countries. The thunder of the glorious Cuban revolution has reverberated throughout the world. The Cuban revolution is not only repulsing the onslaught of the imperialists; it is spreading and taking deeper root, and constitutes a new and higher stage of the national-liberation struggle, one in which the people themselves come to power and become the masters of their wealth. Solidarity with revolutionary Cuba is the duty not only of the Latin American peoples, but also of the socialist countries, the entire international communist movement and the proletariat all over the world.

Lenin [sought to rouse] the working masses to revolutionary activity and organization, irrespective of the level they had attained, in using communist theory in the specific conditions of their countries, and in merging with the proletarians of other countries for the common struggle.

This task had not yet been effected anywhere when Lenin first set it, and there was no book to tell how it should be carried out in practice. The Communist Parties in countries now fighting for national independence and in the newly-independent countries are in an incomparably more favourable position, for there is now a vast store of experience in applying Marxist-Leninist theory to the conditions existing in countries and areas which capitalism had doomed to age-long backwardness.

This experience gained by the world communist movement is a rich treasure-house for all Communists. Obviously, only the Party operating in the country concerned can make proper use of this experience and work out the right policy.

Bourgeois and revisionist politicians claim that the national-liberation movement develops independently of the struggle for socialism waged by the working class, independently of the support of the socialist countries, and that the colonialists themselves bestow freedom on the peoples of the former colonies. The purpose of these fabrications is to isolate the newly-independent states from the socialist camp and to try and prove that they should assume the role of a "third force" in the international arena instead of opposing imperialism. Needless to say, this is sheer humbug.

It is a historical fact that prior to the victory of the Great October Socialist Revolution, the peoples failed in their attempts to break the chains of colonialism. History proves that until socialism triumphed in at least a part of the world there could be no question of destroying colonialism.

The imperialist powers, above all the United States, are doing their utmost to hitch to their system the countries that have cast off the colonial yoke and thereby strengthen the positions of world capitalism, to infuse fresh blood into it, as bourgeois ideologist put it, and to rejuvenate and consolidate it. If we look at the facts in the face, we have to admit that the imperialists have powerful economic levers with which to exert pressure on the newly-free countries. They still manage to enmesh some of the politically independent countries in the web of economic dependence. Now that it is no longer possible to establish outright colonial regimes, the imperialists resort to disguised forms and means of enslaving and plundering the newly-free countries. At the same time, the colonial powers back the internal reactionaries in all these countries; they try to impose on them puppet dictatorial regimes and to involve them in aggressive blocs. Although there are sharp contradictions between the imperialist countries, they often take joint action against the national-liberation movement.

But if we consider all the factors shaping the destinies of the peoples that have shaken off colonial rule, we shall see that in the final analysis the trends of social progress opposing imperialism will prevail.

However, these matters are resolved in bitter struggle within each country. The Statement of the Meeting contains important propositions on the basic issues concerning the development of the national-liberation movement. It defines the tasks of the Communist Parties and their attitude to the various classes and social groups. The Statement expresses the identity of views held by the Marxist-Leninist parties, and calls for the maximum utilisation of the revolutionary possibilities of various classes and social strata and for the drawing of all allies, even if inconsistent, shaky and unstable, into the struggle against imperialism.

The Communists are revolutionaries and it would be a bad thing if they failed to see the new opportunities, to find new ways and means of reaching the set goal with the greatest certainty. Special note should be taken of the idea set forth in the Statement about the formation of national democratic states. The Statement describes the main characteristics of these states and their tasks. It should be stressed that in view of the great variety of conditions in those countries where the peoples, having achieved independence, are now making their own history, a variety of forms for solving the tasks of social progress is bound to emerge.

Correct application of Marxist-Leninist theory in the newly-free countries consists precisely in taking note of the peculiarities of the economic, political and cultural life of the peoples and in seeking forms for uniting all the sound forces of the nations, ensuring the leading role of the working class in the national front, in the struggle for the final eradication of the roots of imperialism and remnanats of feudalism, and for paving the way for the ultimate advance to socialism.

Today, when the imperialist reactionaries are striving to foist the policy of anti-communism on the young independent states, it is most important to give a truthful explanation of the communist veiws and aspirations. The Communists support the general democratic measures of the national governments. At the same time, they explain to the masses that these measures are not socialist at all.

Nobody appreciates and understands the aspirations of the peoples now smashing the fetters of colonialism better than the working people of the socialist countries and the Communists of the whole world. Our world outlook and interests of all the working people, for which we are fighting, impel us to do our best to ensure that the peoples follow the right road to progress, to the flowering of their material and spiritual forces. By our policy we must strengthen the peoples' confidence in the socialist countries.

The aid extended by the U.S.S.R. and the other socialist states to the newly-independent countries has but one aim—to help strengthen the position of these countries in the struggle against imperialism, further the development of their national economy and improve the life of their people. Noting that the working class of the developed countries is deeply interested in the advance "towards independence" of the colonial countries "as rapidly as possible", Engels wrote: "One thing alone is certain: the victorious proletariat can force no blessings of any kind upon any foreign nation without undermining its own victory by so doing."

The international duty of the victorious working class consists in helping the peoples of the economically underdeveloped countries to smash the chains of colonial slavery, and in rendering them all-round aid in their struggle against imperialism, for the right to self-determination and independent development. However, it does not follow that socialist aid exerts no influence on the prospective development of the newly-free countries.

* * *

The Soviet Union submitted to the Fifteenth U.N. General Assembly a Declaration on the Granting of Independence to the Colonial Countries and Peoples.

After an acute political struggle which raged round this proposal both within and without the U.N., the General Assembly adopted the Declaration. The basic point made in the Soviet Declaration—the need for abolishing colonialism in all its forms and manifestations rapidly and for all time—was in the main reflected in the resolution adopted by the United Nations. This was a big victory for the progressive forces and all the socialist countries, which are firmly and consistently championing the freedom and independent national development of the peoples.

It should be stressed that when the matter was debated in the General Assembly the colonialists were isolated by the socialist and neutralist countries—the countries that are working for the abolition of the colonial system. Even some of the members of the aggressive blocs, such as Norway and Denmark, voted for the abolition of colonialism. The colonialists comprised a wretched group of nine countries that abstained during the voting. This is highly indicative. It shows the world what countries favour abolishing the colonial system, and what the so-called "free countries" stand for. Is it not revealing that the group of countries which abstained included the United States, Britain, France, Spain, Portugal and Belgium?

Though doomed, colonialism still has considerable power of resistance and does untold harm to many peoples. All the moribund and reactionary elements are rallied round it. Colonialism is the direct or indirect cause of the many conflicts that threaten humanity with another war. Colonialism, which has caused bloodshed on so many occasions, is to this day a source of the war danger. It manifests itself again and again in outbursts of malicious fury, as eloquently illustrated by the bloodshed in Algeria, the Congo and Laos; it still holds tens of millions of people in its tenacious clutches. And not all the peoples that have won national independence enjoy its fruits, because their economies are still dominated by foreign monopolies.

The peoples of the socialist countries, the Communists and progressives all over the world, see their duty in abolishing the last remnants of the colonial system of imperialism, in safeguarding from the intrigues of the colonial powers the peoples now liberating themselves, and in helping them to realise their ideals of liberation.

Some Ideological Questions of the Communist Movement

...The road to socialism lies through proletarian revolution and the dictatorship of the proletariat. As regards the forms of the transition to socialism, these, as pointed out by the Twentieth Congress of the C.P.S.U., will become more and more varied. The transition to socialism will not everywhere and in all cases be necessarily associated with armed uprising and civil war. Marxism-Leninism holds that the forms of transition to socialism may be peaceful and non-peaceful. It is in the interests of the working classes, of the masses, that the revolution be carried out in a peaceful way. But if the ruling classes respond to the revolution with violence and refuse to submit to the will of the people, the proletariat is obliged to break their resistance and go the length of a resolute civil war.

We are convinced that increasingly favourable conditions for socialist revolutions will arise with the growth of the might of the world socialist system and the better organisation of the working class in the capitalist countries. The transition to socialism in countries with developed parliamentary traditions may be effected by utilizing parliament, and in other countries by utilizing institutions conforming to their national traditions. It is not a question of using the bourgeois parliament as such, but of employing the parliamentary form, making it serve the people and filling it with a new content. It is thus not a matter of electoral combinations or simple skirmishes at the ballot box. Communists leave that sort of thing to the reformists. Such combinations are alien to them. For Communists the absolute condition for winning a stable majority in parliament is to unify and consolidate the revolutionary forces of the working class and of all the working people, and to launch mass revolutionary actions. To win a majority in parliament and transform it into an organ of people's power, given a powerful revolutionary movement in the country, means to smash the military-bureaucratic machine of the bourgeoisie and to set up a new, proletarian people's state with a parliamentary form.

It is quite obvious that in the countries where capitalism is still strong and commands a huge military and police apparatus, the transition to socialism will be inevitably attended by sharp class struggle. Political leadership by the working class, headed by the communist vanguard, is the decisive condition no matter what the forms of transition to socialism are.

* * *

It stands to reason that the working class in each country, and its communist vanguard, must decide what forms and methods of struggle are to be employed in the concrete historical situation.

It should be stressed in this connection that in the present conditions the following thesis, formulated in the Statement of the Meeting of Representatives of the Communist and Workers' Parties, acquires particular importance:

"The Communist Parties, which guide themselves by the Marxist-Leninist doctrine, have always been against the export of revolution. At the same time they fight resolutely against imperialist export of counter-revolution. They consider it their internationalist duty to call on the peoples of all countries to unite, to rally all their internal forces, to act vigorously and, relying on the might of the world socialist system, to prevent or firmly repel imperialist interference in the affairs of any people who have risen in revolution."

For The Further Consolidation Of The Communist Movement On The Principles Of Marxism-Leninism

. . . The very essence of Leninism implies that no Marxist-Leninist party can permit either in its own ranks, or in the international communist movement, any actions liable to undermine unity and solidarity.

* * *

It should be noted that at the Meeting the delegation of the C.P.S.U. expressed its point of view concerning the formula that the Soviet Union stands at the head of the socialist camp and the C.P.S.U. at the head of the communist movement. Our delegation declared that we regarded this formula above all as a high appreciation of what our Party, founded by

Lenin, has done, and expressed its heartfelt gratitude to all the fraternal parties. Our Party, reared by Lenin, has always seen its prime duty in fulfilling its internationalist obligations to the working class of the world. The delegation assured the Meeting that the C.P.S.U. would continue to hold high the banner of proletarian internationalism and would spare no effort in carrying out its internationalist duties.

Yet the C.P.S.U. delegation suggested that the formula should not be included in the Statement or any other document of the communist movement.

As for the principles of relations between the fraternal parties, the C.P.S.U. expressed its views very definitely on this matter at its Twenty-First Congress. We declared to the whole world from the rostrum of the Congress that in the communist movement, and in the socialist camp, there has always been, and is, complete equality and solidarity of all the Communist and Workers' Parties and socialist countries. The Communist Party of the Soviet Union does not in fact govern other parties. There are no "superior" and "subordinate" parties in the communist movement. All the Communist Parties are equal and independent, all bear responsibility for the state of the communist movement, for its victories and setbacks. Every Communist and Workers' Party is responsible to the working class, to the working people of its country, to the entire international working-class and communist movement.

The role of the Soviet Union does not lie in its leading the other socialist countries, but in its being the most powerful country of the world socialist system, in having accumulated extensive positive experience in the building of socialism, and in being the first to embark on the full-scale building of communism. It is stressed in the Statement that the Communist Party of the Soviet Union has been, and remains, the universally recognised vanguard of the world communist movement, being its most experienced and steeled contingent.

At the present time, when there is a large group of socialist countreis each facing its own specific tasks, when there are eighty-seven Communist and Workers' Parties, each with its own tasks, it is impossible to lead all the socialist countries and Communist Parties from any single centre. It is both impossible and unnecessary. Seasoned Marxist-Leninist cadres capable of leading their parties and their countries have grown up in the Communist Parties.

Furthermore, it is well known that the C.P.S.U. does not in fact issue directives to other parties. Being called "the head" spells no advantages to our Party or the other parties. Quite the reverse. It only creates difficulties.

As evident from the Statement, the fraternal parties agreed with the arguments brought forward by our delegation. The question may arise: Will our international solidarity be weakened by the fact that this proposition is not written down in the Statement? No, it will not. At present there are no rules regulating relations between parties, but we have a common Marxist-Leninist ideology, and loyalty to this ideology is the main condition of our solidarity and unity. It is essential that we guide ourselves consistently by the directions of Marx, Engles and Lenin, that we perserveringly put into effect the principles of Marxism-Leninism. The international solidarity of the communist movement will then constantly increase.

Our Party, being an internationalist party, closely follows the struggle of its class brothers in all countries of the world. We are well aware of the difficulties which the Communists have to overcome in the struggles under capitalism.

From the rostrum of the Meeting the delegation of the C.P.S.U. expressed our Party's boundless solidarity with the fighters for communism in the capitalist countries, and especially with our comrades languishing in the prisons of Spain, Portugal, Greece, West Germany, the U.A.R., Iraq, Iran, the U.S.A. and Paraguay, and with all the other prisoners of the capitalists. We are confident that our words of greeting will encourage the selfless fighters for the people's happiness.

* * *

Representatives of the Communist and Workers' Parties exchanged opinions on questions concerning the current international situation, and discussed the pressing problems of the communist and working-class movement, or, as comrades put it figuratively at the Meeting, "we synchronised our watches". Indeed, the socialist countries and the Communist Parties need to synchronise watches. Whenever someone's watch is fast or slow, it is adjusted, so as to show the right time. The communist movement, too, needs to synchronise its watch, so that our mighty army marches in step and advances with confident stride towards communism. Putting it figuratively, Marxism-Leninism and the jointly prepared documents of the international communist meetings are our timepiece.

Now that all the Communist and Workers' Parties have adopted unanimous decisions at the Meeting, each Party will strictly and undeviatingly abide by these decisions in everything it does.

The unity of every Communist Party, the unity of all the Communist Parties, is what makes up the integral world communist movement which is to achieve our common goal, the victory of communism throughout the world. The main thing required of all the Communist and Workers' Parties today is perseveringly to strengthen with the greatest of energy the unity and cohesion of their ranks. . . . In this connection I want to emphasise our continuous effort to strengthen bonds of fraternal friendship with the Communist Party of China, with the great Chinese people. In its relations with the Communist Party of China our Party always proceeds from the premise that the friendship of our two great peoples, the unity of our two Parties, the biggest parties in the international communist movement, are of exceptional importance in the struggle for the triumph of our common cause. Our Party has always exerted, and will continue to exert, every effort to strengthen this great friendship. We have a common goal with People's China, with the Chinese Communists, as with the Communists of all countries—to safeguard peace and to build communism; common interests—the happiness and well-being of the working people; and a firm common basis of principle—Marxism-Leninism.

The Communist Party of the Soviet Union and the Soviet people will do their utmost further to strengthen the unity of our Parties and our peoples, so as not only to disappoint our enemies but to jolt them even more strongly with our unity, to attain the realisation of our great goal, the triumph of communism.

Comrades, we live in a magnificent time! Communism has become the invincible force of our epoch. The further successes of communism depend to a tremendous extent on our will, our unity, our foresight and determination. By their struggle, by their work, the Communists, the working class will achieve the great aims of communism on earth.

Men of the future, the Communists of the coming generations will envy us, they will keep going back in their thoughts to our times, when the lines of the Party anthem ring out with special force:

> *We'll change forthwith the old conditions,*
> *Let those who labour hold the reins.*

The Communist Party of the Soviet Union has been, is, and will always be loyal to the doctrine of Marxism-Leninism, to proletarian internationalism and friendship among the peoples. It will always fight for world peace, for the victory of communism, as the great Lenin taught us!

KHRUSHCHEV

Report to the XXII Party
Congress   *October 17, 1961*

Introduction Tension between the two camps remained high in the year following the U-2 incident of May 1960. The debacle of the United States-sponsored invasion of Cuba at the Bay of Pigs (April 1961) persuaded Khrushchev that the young and inexperienced John F. Kennedy could be maneuvered into making large concessions on Berlin. He initiated a new Berlin crisis in June, again with a six-month deadline. President Kennedy reacted sharply, dispatching additional United States military forces to central Europe and asking Congress for more money for defense. Khrushchev in turn responded by announcing a new increase in Soviet military spending, by erecting the wall in East Berlin to prevent East Germans from escaping (August, 1961), and by renewed nuclear testing, thereby violating a three-year moratorium.

This sequence—Khrushchev's demands, Kennedy's rejoinder, and Khrushchev's response—resulted in a rapid escalation of tension that Khrushchev was unwilling to sustain. Moreover, United States officials made it clear about this time that their previous uncertainty about the size of Soviet ICBM forces had been resolved; they were again confident that the United States was superior in strategic nuclear forces. Convinced of the danger he faced in trying to extract concessions on Berlin, and satisfied that the exodus of East Germans had been stemmed by the Berlin Wall, Khrushchev, in the Report to the Congress, withdraws the deadline for acceptance of his proposal—although not the proposal itself.

In discussing the capitalist camp, Khrushchev revises the portrait of imperialism that he presented in January, 1960, when he denied that the United States aimed at war. He now argues that men have gained ascendancy in the capitalist states who are not content with profits from the arms race but seek additional profits from war. "Adventurous actions may well be expected" that could lead to a terrible war. The Report reflects Khrushchev's realization that his earlier assessment had been overly optimistic. He now recognizes the need to *choose:* he could seek major concessions from the West *or* aim at *detente* and a reduced arms race, but he could not hope to achieve both. From subsequent developments it would appear that at this juncture he opted for a policy of seeking concessions.

Khrushchev evinces concern that nationalism may weaken Soviet hegemony in the bloc, particularly in the face of the growing challenge from Communist China. He warns Yugoslavia that its policy of "development in isolation from the world socialist community" may result in the overthrow of socialism, a warning that is doubtless intended for other states as well. Khrushchev professes confidence in the "permanence" of what has been achieved, and in further progress "within the framework" of the socialist camp. He warns, however, that particular countries might be severed from the socialist system as the result of discord and nationalism stimulated from the outside. To avert such dangers Khrushchev calls on the socialist countries to rally round the Soviet Union, and to strengthen their armed forces and security organs. In 1968, faced with Dubchek's Czechoslovakia, Khrushchev presumably would have been tempted to act as his successors did, and as he himself had acted in 1956 in Hungary.

The Present World Situation
and the International Position
of the Soviet Union

Comrades, the chief content of the period following the Twentieth Congress of the C.P.S.U. is the competition between the two world social systems—the socialist and capitalist systems. . . .

The fact that it has been possible to prevent war and that Soviet people and the peoples of other countries have been able to enjoy the benefits of peaceful life must be regarded as [a] chief result of the activities of our Party and its Central Committee in increasing the might of the Soviet state and in implementing a Leninist foreign policy, as a result of the work of the fraternal parties in the socialist states and of greater activity by the peace forces in all countries.

During recent years, as we know, the imperialists have made a number of attempts to start a new war and test the strength of the socialist system. During the past five years the U.S.A. and its closest allies have repeatedly resorted to brutal force, have rattled the sabre. But on each occasion the Soviet Union and the other socialist countries have checked the aggressor in good time. Of particular, fundamental importance were the actions of the socialist countries in defence of the peoples struggling for their liberty and independence. The masses are getting to realise more and more that the Soviet Union and all the socialist countries are a reliable support in the struggle the peoples are waging for their liberty and independence, for progress and peace.

* * *

The Further Growth of the Might of the Socialist System and Its Conversion into the Decisive Factor in World Development. Strengthening of the International Brotherhood of the Socialist Countries

In the period under review an important stage in the development of the world socialist system has been completed. Its specific features are these:

The Soviet Union has launched the full-scale construction of communism; the majority of the People's Democracies have abolished multiformity in their economies and are now completing the building of socialism; fraternal co-operation and mutual aid between the socialist countries have been developed in every way. Not only in the Soviet Union, but in all socialist countries, social and economic possibilities for the restoration of capitalism have now been eliminated. The growing might of the new world system guarantees the permanence of the political and socio-economic gains of the socialist countries. The complete victory of socialism within the framework of the community of genuinely free peoples is certain.

* * *

The appearance of a large group of sovereign socialist states in the world posed the problem of organising their mutual relations and co-operation on a basis that was new in principle. By their joint efforts, the fraternal parties have found and are improving new forms of inter-state relations—economic, political and cultural co-operation based on the principles of equality, mutual benefit and comradely mutual aid. The growing fraternal rapprochement between the socialist countries, together with their political and economic consolidation, constitute one of the decisive factors of the strength and durability of the world socialist system. We joined forces voluntarily in order to march forward to a common goal together. The union was not imposed on us by anyone. We need it as much as we need air.

In the first stage of the development of the world socialist system, relations between the countries were effected mostly by way of bilateral foreign trade and scientific and technical exchanges, the dominant forms being aid and credits granted by some countries to others.

In recent years the experience of the fraternal parties has brought into being a new form—direct co-operation in production. Take, for instance, the co-ordination of the basic indexes of development in certain branches of the economy for the 1956-60 period, agreed upon by the member countries of the Council for Mutual Economic Aid. This was an important step forward. Since 1959 state plans for economic development have been co-ordinated. It has become the practice to arrange periodical consultations and exchanges of opinion between the leaders of parties and governments on important economic and political problems. The collective organs of the socialist states—the Warsaw Treaty Organisation and the Council for Mutual Economic Aid—have grown stronger.

We have every ground for speaking of a durable socialist community of free peoples existing in the world today.

The profound qualitative changes that have taken place in the socialist countries and in relations between them are evidence of the growing maturity of the world socialist system which has now entered a new stage of development. The chief thing now is, by consistently developing the economy of each socialist country and all of them collectively, to achieve preponderance of the socialist world's absolute volume of production over that of the capitalist world. This will be a great historic victory for socialism. The achievements of our country, which is the first to have entered the path of full-scale communist construction, facilitate and accelerate the advance of the other countries of the world socialist system towards communism.

* * *

Comrades, Lenin's statement to the effect that socialism exercises its influence on world development mainly by its economic achievements is today more valid than ever. The all-round, growing effect which the building of socialism and communism is having on the peoples of the non-socialist countries is a revolutionising factor that accelerates the progress of all mankind.

Socialism is firmly maintaining priority in rates of economic development and is ahead of the capitalist countries in the development of a number of highly important branches of world science and technology. The imperialist countries have lost their former monopoly in supplying the world non-socialist market with means of production, and also in granting credits, loans and technical services. The peoples of Asia and Africa who have liberated themselves from the foreign colonial yoke are looking more and more frequently to the socialist countries, and borrowing from them experience in the organisation of certain spheres of economic and social life. In the world socialist system they seek protection and support in their struggle against colonialist encroachments on their liberty and independence.

* * *

In the same way as a mighty tree with deep roots does not fear any storm, so the new, socialist world does not fear any adversities or upheavals. The counter-revolutionary insurrection in Hungary, organised by internal reaction with the support of the imperialist forces, and the intrigues of enemies in Poland and the German Democratic Republic showed that in the period of socialist construction the class struggle may, from time to time, grow stronger and take on sharp forms. In the future, too, the remnants of internal reaction may, with imperialist backing, attempt to sever one country or another from the socialist system and to restore the old bourgeois regime. The reactionary forces speculate on the difficulties that are inevitable in an undertaking as new as the revolutionary transformation of society, and continue planting their agents in the socialist countries.

* * *

The intrigues of the imperialists must always be kept in mind. Our gigantic successes in building the new way of life must not lead to complacency and relaxation of vigilance. The greater the achievements of socialism and the higher the living standards in each socialist country, the more solidly the people will muster around the Communist and Workers' parties. That is one aspect of the matter, and a very encouraging one. There is, however, something else that must be borne in mind. As the unity of the peoples of all socialist countries grows the hopes the imperialists have of restoring the capitalist regime, of the socialist countries degenerating, are gradually fading away. World reaction, therefore, is more and more turning to the idea of striking a blow at the socialist countries from outside in order to win capitalist world dominion through war or, at least, to check the development of the socialist countries.

The most rabid imperialists, who act in accordance with the principle "after us the deluge", openly voice their desire to set out on a new war venture. . . . Blinded by class hatred, our enemies are prepared to plunge all mankind into the holocaust of war. The possibilities the imperialists have of implementing their aggressive plans are, however, becoming fewer. They behave like a feeble and covetous old man whose strength is exhausted, whose physical capacity is low, but whose desires persist.

The imperialists, of course, may set out on dangerous adventures, but they have no chance of success. They are prepared to try other ways as well. To weaken the socialist community the imperialists try to set the peoples of the fraternal countries at loggerheads or to sow discord among them, to revive the remnants of national strife and artificially stir up nationalist sentiment.

A great historical responsibility rests with the Marxist-Leninist parties, with the peoples of the socialist countries—to strengthen tirelessly the international brotherhood of the socialist countries and friendship between nations.

As long as the imperialist aggressors exist we must be on the alert, we must keep our powder dry and improve the defences of the socialist countries, their armed forces and their state security organs. If the imperialists, contrary to all common sense, venture to attack the socialist countries and hurl mankind into the abyss of a world war of annihilation, that mad act will be their last, it will be the end of the capitalist system.

*Aggravation of the Contradictions in the Capitalist
Countries. Growth of the Revolutionary Struggle and
Upsurge of the National-Liberation Movement*

Comrades, the Twentieth Congress of the Party analysed the situation in the capitalist countries and drew the conclusion that they were moving steadily towards new economic and social upheavals. This conclusion has been borne out. In the years that have elapsed there has been further aggravation of contradictions both within the capitalist countries and between them, colonial empires have been disintegrating and the struggle of the working class and the national-liberation movement of the peoples have assumed huge proportions.

The general trend—the further decay of capitalism—has continued to operate inexorably. Although there has been some growth in production, the economy of the capitalist countries has become still more unstable and reminds one of a man sick with fever, so often does its short-lived recoveries give way to depressions and crises. The U.S.A., the chief capitalist country, has experienced two critical recessions in five years, and there have been four such recessions in the post-war period as a whole. The crisis of 1957-58 involved countries whose share in capitalist industrial output amounts to almost two-thirds of the whole. . . .

In recent years there have been some significant changes in the alignment of forces in the capitalist world.

First, the United States of America has lost its absolute supremacy in world capitalist production and commerce. Its share in capitalist world industrial output dropped from 56.6 per cent in 1948 to 47 per cent in 1960, its exports from 23.4 per cent to 18.1 per cent and its gold reserves from 74.5 per cent to 43.9 per cent. The result is that the United States today occupies approximately the same position among the capitalist countries as it did before the Second World War.

West Germany has drawn level with Britain in industrial output, and as far as exports are concerned takes second place after the U.S.A. In post-war years U.S. monopolies have invested huge sums of money in the economy of West Germany and Japan. For a number of years these two countries were actually relieved of the burden of their own war expenditure because the U.S.A. provided them with armaments at the expense of the American taxpayers. West Germany and Japan have made huge investments in the key branches of the economy to renew their constant capital and reorganise production on modern lines. As a result they are already serious rivals to Britain, France and even the United States in the world market.

The contradictions that existed between the imperialist powers before the war have reappeared and new ones have emerged. The struggle between British and West German imperialism for supremacy in Western Europe is growing fiercer. French imperialism, in its struggle against British imperialism, is seeking support in yesterday's enemy, the West German monopolies. But this unnatural alliance, like a marriage of convenience, is more and more frequently operating against France herself. There are profound contradictions dividing the U.S.A. and Britain and other imperialist states. They are manifested in NATO and other aggressive blocs. . . .

In their talks the leaders of the Western Powers do not conceal that their policy is one of arming West Germany. Their argument is something like this—if West Germany does not rearm and does not spend money on armaments, she may become a still more powerful and dangerous rival. In short, there are some very acute contradictions in the imperialist camp.

In their fear of the future the imperialists are trying to unite their forces and to strengthen their military, political, commercial, customs and other alliances. The reactionaries count on aggression against the socialist countries as a way out. In the pre-war period they placed great hopes on Hitler Germany. Today the role of the chief aggressive force belongs to the United States of America which has become the centre of world reaction. The U.S. imperialists are acting in alliance with the West-German militarists and revenge-seekers and are threatening the peace and security of the peoples. In our times, however, it has become dangerous for the imperialists to seek a way out of their contradictions in war.

The position of imperialism in Asia, Africa and Latin America, where the colonialists until recently oppressed hundreds of millions of people, is getting shakier. The revolutionary struggle of the peoples of those continents is rapidly gaining momentum. In the course of the past six years twenty-eight states have won political independence. The sixties of our century will go down in history as years of the complete disintegration of the colonial system of imperialism.

It must not be forgotten, however, that although the colonial system has collapsed, its remnants have not been eliminated. Many millions of people in Asia and Africa are still suffering under colonial slavery and are struggling for their liberation. For seven years the blood of Algerian patriots has been flowing in the fight for freedom. The French monopolies do not want to end the war in Algeria although that "dirty war" against a peaceful people is costing thousands of lives and is a heavy burden on the French and Algerian peoples. Portugal, a small state with an area no more than two-thirds of our Vologda Region, holds in bondage colonies with an area nearly twenty-five times its own size. The Dutch colonialists stubbornly refuse to return to the Indonesian people their ancient land of West Irian. The U.S.A. is maintaining its grip on the Chinese island of Taiwan and the Japanese island of Okinawa. Against the will of the Cuban people the U.S.A. retains its hold on the military base of Guantanamo which is on Cuban soil.

The forces of imperialism are opposing any effort on the part of the peoples to achieve liberty and independence, democracy and progress. On the pretext of various commitments, the imperialists strive to smother the national-liberation movement, and by entering into deals with internal reactionary forces intervene brazenly in the home affairs of young states. That was the method they used in Iran, Pakistan and the Congo and are now using in Laos and Kuwait.

Throughout this period the Soviet Union, in fulfilment of its internationalist duty, has been helping the peoples who struggled against imperialism and colonialism. There are those who do not approve of this position. But we cannot help that. Such are our convictions....

Today the colonialists, sensing that their rule is coming to an end, are putting on a good face in a losing game. They assert that they are leaving the colonies of their own accord. Who will believe them? Anyone can see that they are taking this step because they know that anyway they will be driven out in disgrace. The more prudent of the colonialists are getting out, so to say, five minutes before they are given "a kick in the pants", to put it in popular language.

The colonial powers impose unequal treaties on the newly-free countries, locate military bases on their territories and try to involve them in military blocs, one of the new forms of enslavement. Almost a half of the states that have emerged as a result of the disintegration of the colonial system are shackled by unequal, onerous treaties. In the centre of this refurbished but no less disgraceful colonialism stands the United States of America. Its closest allies and at the same time its rivals are British colonialism and West German imperialism, the latter unceremoniously pushing the British and French monopolies out of Africa and the Middle East.

The countries that have gained their freedom from colonial oppression have entered a new phase of development. The struggle for political independence united all the national forces that suffered under the colonialists and shared common interests. Now that the time has come to tear up the roots of imperialism and introduce agrarian and other urgent social reforms, the differences in class interests are coming more and more into the open. Broad sections of the working people and also that considerable section of the national bourgeoisie interested in the accomplishment of the basic tasks of the anti-imperialist, anti-feudal revolution, want to go farther in strengthening independence and effecting social and economic reforms. Within the ruling circles of those countries, however, there are forces that are afraid to go farther in their collaboration with the democratic, progressive strata of the nation. They would like to appropriate the fruits of the people's struggle and hamper the further development of the national revolution. These forces compromise with imperialism outside the country and feudalism within, and resort to dictatorial methods.

* * *

The sad fate of Pakistan, whose people we wish nothing but good, should set the public thinking in some other countries where influential forces are wrecking national unity and are persecuting progressive leaders, especially the Communists, who have shown themselves to be the stoutest defenders of national independence.

To adopt the path of anti-communism means splitting the forces of the nation and weakening them in face of the imperialists, of the colonialists.

And contrariwise—the sounder the unity of the democratic national forces and the more radically urgent social and economic reforms are carried out, the stronger is the young state. . . .

Revisionist ideas pervade both the theory and practice of the leadership of the League of Communists of Yugoslavia. The line they have adopted—that of development in isolation from the world socialist community—is harmful and perilous. It plays into the hands of imperialist reaction, foments nationalist tendencies and may in the end lead to the loss of socialist gains in the country, which has broken away from the friendly and united family of builders of a new world.

* * *

Attempts are made to blame us Communists for any action by the masses against their oppressors. Whenever the working people of a capitalist or colonial country rise to fight, the imperialists claim that it is the "handiwork of the Communists", or "the hand of Moscow". To be sure, we are glad to have the imperialists attributing to Communists all the good actions of the peoples. By so doing the imperialists unwittingly help the masses gain a better understanding of Communist ideas. These ideas are spreading throughout the world. But, of course, this is not happening because the Soviet Union and the other socialist countries impose them on the peoples. You cannot bring in ideas on bayonets, as people used to say in the past, or in rockets, as it would now be more proper to say.

Certainly, warring classes have always sought the support of kindred forces from outside. For a long time the bourgeois class had an advantage in this respect. The world bourgeoisie, acting in concert, stamped out revolutionary centres everywhere and by every means, including armed intervention. It goes without saying that even at that time the international proletariat was not indifferent to the struggle of its class brothers; but more often than not, it could express its solidarity with them only through moral support. The situation has changed since then. The people of a country who rise in struggle will not find themselves engaged in single combat with world imperialism. They will enjoy the support of powerful international forces possessing everything necessary for effective moral and material support. . . .

The imperialists claim at every turn that the Communists export revolution. The imperialist gentlemen need this slander in order to camouflage, in some way or another, their claims to the right to export counter-revolution.

It is a strange logic these gentlemen have. They are apparently still under the spell of the times when they were able to strangle the liberation movement of peoples. But those times have gone, never to return. The Communists are against the export of revolution, and this is well known in the West. But we do not recognise anybody's right to export counter-revolution, to perform the functions of an international gendarme. This, too, should be well known.

Imperialist attempts to interfere in the affairs of insurgent peoples would constitute acts of aggression endangering world peace. We must state outright that in the event of imperialist export of counter-revolution the Communists will call on the peoples of all countries to rally, to mobilise their forces and, supported by the might of the world socialist system, repel firmly the enemies of freedom and peace. In other words, as ye sow, so shall ye reap.

*Peaceful Coexistence Is the General Line in Soviet
Foreign Policy. The Peoples Are the Decisive Force
in the Struggle for Peace*

Comrades, important changes have come about in the alignment of world forces during the period under review. The world socialist system has become a reliable shield against imperialist military ventures not only for the peoples of the countries that are friendly to it, but for the whole of mankind. And the fact that the socialist community of nations has a preponderance of strength is most fortunate for all mankind. The peace forces, furthermore, have grown all over the world.

A few years ago there were two opposing camps in world affairs—the socialist and imperialist camps. Today an active role in international affairs is also being played by those countries of Asia, Africa and Latin America that have freed, or are freeing, themselves from foreign oppression. Those countries are often called neutralist though they may be considered neutral only in the sense that they do not belong to any of the existing military-political alliances. Most of them, however, are by no means neutral when the cardinal problem of our day, that of war and peace, is at issue. As a rule, those countries advocate peace and oppose war. The countries which have won their liberty from colonialism are becoming a serious factor for peace, for the struggle against colonialism and imperialism, and the basic issues of world politics can no longer be settled without due regard for their interests.

In the capitalist countries, too, the masses are taking more and more vigorous action against war. The working class and all working people are fighting against the arms race and the disastrous policy of the warmongers.

Thus the aggressive policy of the imperialist powers is now being opposed by greater forces. *The struggle which the countries of socialism and all the forces of peace are carrying on against preparations for fresh aggression and war is the main content of world politics today.*

In these past years, the forces of war and aggression have jeopardised world peace more than once. In 1956 the imperialists organised, simultaneously with the counter-revolutionary rising in Hungary, an attack on Egypt. In the second half of 1957 the imperialists prepared an invasion of Syria that threatened a big military conflagration. In the summer of 1958, in view of the revolution in Iraq, they launched an intervention in the Lebanon and Jordan and at the same time created a tense situation in the area of Taiwan, an island which belongs to the People's Republic of China. In April-May 1960 the U.S. imperialists sent their military aircraft into Soviet air space, and torpedoed the Paris summit meeting. Last spring they organised an armed invasion of Cuba by mercenary bands and tried to bring Laos under their sway, to involve her in the aggressive SEATO military bloc. But all those imperialist sorties failed.

It would be a gross error, however, to imagine that the failure of aggressive schemes has brought the imperialists to their senses. The facts show just the opposite. The imperialists continue their attempts to aggravate the international situation and to lead the world to the brink of war. In recent months they have deliberately created a dangerous situation in the centre of Europe by threatening to take up arms in reply to our proposal to do away with the remnants of the Second World War, conclude a German peace treaty and normalise the situation in West Berlin.

In view of the aggravation of the international situation, we were compelled to take proper steps to safeguard our country against the encroachments of aggressors and save mankind from the threat of a new world war. The Soviet Government was compelled to suspend the reduction of the armed forces planned for 1961, increase defence expenditure, postpone the transfer of servicemen to the reserve and resume tests of new and more powerful weapons. We were compelled to adopt these measures; they were unanimously supported by our people and correctly understood by the peoples of other countries, who know that the Soviet Union will never be the first to adopt a policy leading to war. . . .

Certain pacifist-minded people in the West are simple-minded enough to believe that if the Soviet Union made more concessions to the Western Powers, there would be no aggravation of international tension. They forget that the policy of the imperialist powers, including their foreign policy, is determined by the class interests of monopoly capital, in which aggression and war are inherent. When, under the pressure of the masses, the partisans of a more or less moderate policy gain the upper hand, there occurs an international detente and the clouds of war are dispelled to some extent. But the international situation deteriorates when the pressure of the masses slackens and the scales tip in favour of those groupings of the bourgeoisie that capitalise on the arms race and see war as an additional source of profit.

Hence, the peaceful coexistence of countries with different social systems can be maintained and safeguarded only through the unrelenting struggle of all peoples against the aggressive aspirations of the imperialists. The greater the might of the socialist camp and the more vigorously the struggle for peace is waged within the capitalist countries, the more difficult it is for the imperialists to carry out their plans of aggression.

Peace and peaceful coexistence are not quite the same thing. Peaceful coexistence does not merely imply absence of war; it is not a temporary, unstable armistice between two wars but the coexistence of two opposed social systems, based on mutual renunciation of war as a means of settling disputes between states.

Historical experience shows that an aggressor cannot be placated by concessions. Concessions to the imperialists on matters of vital importance do not constitute a policy of peaceful coexistence but mean surrender to the forces of aggression. That we will never accede to. It is high time the imperialists understood that it is no longer they who are the arbiters of mankind's fate and that socialism will exist, develop and gain strength whether they like it or not. But for the time being the imperialist gentry do not seem to have understood this. Adventurous actions may well be expected of them, actions that would spell disaster for hundreds of millions of people. That is why we must curb the aggressors and not aid and abet them. . . *It must be realised that it depends above all on the peoples themselves, on their resolve and vigorous action, whether there is to be peace on earth or whether mankind is to be hurled into the catastrophe of a new world war.* It is necessary to heighten the vigilance of the peoples with regard to the intrigues of imperialist warmongers. Vigorous anti-war action by the peoples must not be put off till the war starts; such action must be launched immediately and not when nuclear and thermonuclear bombs begin to fall.

* * *

Seek the Settlement of International Problems
by Peaceful Means. Expose the Intrigues and Manoeuvres
of the Warmongers. Improve Relations Between Countries

...We have always resolutely opposed the arms race, for in the past, competition in this field not only imposed a heavy burden on the peoples but inevitably led to world wars. We are opposed to the arms race still more firmly now that a tremendous technical revolution has taken place in the art of war and the use of modern weapons would inevitably lead to hundreds of millions of people losing their lives.

The stockpiling of these weapons, which is taking place in an atmosphere of cold war and war hysteria, is fraught with disastrous consequences. It only needs an addlebrained officer on duty at a "button" somewhere in the West to lose his nerve for events to occur that will bring down great misfortune on the peoples of the whole world.

* * *

To mislead people, the imperialists are hypocritically raising a racket over the fact that we were compelled to carry out experimental blasts of nuclear weapons. But the racket did not prevent the peoples from seeing that we had taken this step only because the Western Powers, after bringing the solution of the disarmament problem and negotiations on nuclear weapons tests to a dead end, had set the flywheel of their war machine turning at top speed in order to achieve superiority in strength over the socialist countries. We forestalled them and thus retained the superior position of the socialist camp, which is defending peace.

We were forced to take these measures. It was known that the United States had for a long time been preparing to resume tests, and as for France, she had carried them out repeatedly. In the present conditions, the necessity for the peoples' struggle to get rid of the arms race is all the more obvious. The disarmament problem affects the vital interests of every nation and of mankind as a whole. When it has been solved there will be no more need for nuclear weapons and hence for their manufacture and testing.

The elimination of the remnants of the Second World War is of tremendous importance for the maintenance and strengthening of peace. It is intolerable that sixteen years after the defeat of the Hitler invaders a peaceful settlement with Germany has still not been effected. The Western Powers, headed by the U.S.A., are alone to blame for this unpardonable delay. In flagrant disregard of the interests of the peoples, they set out to revive German militarism as soon as the war was over.

The absence of a peace treaty has already played into the hands of the Bonn revenge-seekers. With help from the U.S. imperialists, they have re-established their armed forces with an eye to further aggression. It is the West German militarists' cherished dream to profit by the unstable situation in Europe to set their former enemies—the powers of the anti-Hitler coalition—upon each other. They dream of absorbing the German Democratic Republic, enslaving other neighbouring countries and taking revenge for the defeat they sustained in the Second World War.

* * *

Recently, while attending the U.N. General Assembly, Comrade Gromyko, the Soviet Foreign Minister, had conversations with the Secretary of State and the President of the United States. He also had talks with the Foreign Secretary and the Prime Minister of Britain. We gained the impression from those conversations that the Western Powers are showing some understanding of the situation and are inclined to seek a solution to the German problem and the West Berlin issue on a mutually acceptable basis.

Some Western politicians offer us would-be good advice by declaring that the signing of a peace treaty would endanger the Soviet Union and the other socialist countries. What are we to make of that? Since when have wars been considered to endanger one side only? . . .

* * *

We consider that at present the forces of socialism, and all the forces championing peace, are superior to the forces of imperialist aggression. But even granting that the U.S. President was right in saying a short time ago that our forces were equal, it would be obviously unwise to threaten war. One who admits that there is equality should draw the proper conclusions. It is dangerous in our time to pursue a position of strength policy.

* * *

Certain spokesmen of the Western Powers say that our proposals for the conclusion of a German peace treaty this year constitute an ultimatum. But they are wrong, for it was as far back as 1958 that the Soviet Union proposed concluding a peace treaty and settling the issue of West Berlin on that basis by transforming it into a free city. A long time has passed since then. We did not rush the settlement of the issue, hoping to reach mutual understanding with the Western Powers. It is fair to ask, therefore, why this talk about an ultimatum? In proposing the conclusion of a German peace treaty, the Soviet Union presented no ultimatum, but was prompted by the need to have this pressing issue settled at last.

The Soviet Government insists, now as before, on the earliest possible solution of the German problem; it is against that problem being shelved indefinitely. If the Western Powers show readiness to settle the German problem, the issue of a time limit for the signing of a German peace treaty will no longer be so important; in that case, we shall not insist that a peace treaty absolutely must be signed before December 31, 1961. The important thing is to settle the matter—to eliminate the remnants of the Second World War by signing a German peace treaty. That is the fundamental issue, the crux of the matter.

The solution of these problems will pave the way to further steps in the sphere of peaceful co-operation, both multilateral and bilateral, between states. What else has to be done for the further strengthening of peace, in addition to the conclusion of a German peace treaty?

The problem of effecting *considerable improvement in the United Nations machinery* has long been awaiting solution. That machinery has grown rusty in the cold war years and has been operating fitfully. The time has come to clean it, to remove the crust that has formed on it, to put fresh power into it, with due regard to the changes that have occurred in the international situation in recent years. It is high time to restore the legitimate rights of the People's Republic of China in the U.N. The time has come for a decision on the question of the German people's representation in the United Nations. As matters stand now, the most reasonable solution would be to conclude a peace treaty with both German states, whose existence is a reality, and to admit them into the U.N. It is time to grant genuinely equal rights in all U.N. agencies to the three groups of states that have come into being in the world—socialist, neutralist and imperialist. It is time to call a halt to attempts to use the U.N. in the interests of the military alignment of the Western Powers.

The problem of the full abolition of colonial tyranny in all its forms and manifestations must be solved in accordance with the vital interests of the peoples. They must be helped to reach, as speedily as possible, the level of the economically and culturally developed countries. We see the way to achieve that goal first of all in making the colonial powers restore to their victims at least part of their loot. The Soviet Union and other socialist countries are already rendering the peoples disinterested, friendly support and assistance in the economic and cultural fields. We shall continue to help them.

The solution of pressing regional political problems could play a fairly important part in achieving a healthier international atmosphere. We attach great importance to the problem of establishing atom-free zones, first of all in Europe and the Far East. A non-aggression pact between the countries in the Warsaw Treaty Organisation and those in the North Atlantic military bloc could go a long way towards promoting security. An agreement could also be reached on the establishment of a zone dividing the armed forces of military alignments, and a start could be made to reduce the armed forces stationed on foreign soil. And if the countries in military blocs were to come to the reasonable conclusion that all military alliances must be disbanded and armed forces withdrawn to within their national boundaries, it would be the best, the most radical, solution of the problem.

In short, given mutual desire, many useful steps could be taken that would help the nations reduce the war danger and then remove it altogether.

We see a way to a better international situation in *more extensive business relations with all countries.*

Our relations with the socialist countries have been, and will continue to be, relations of lasting fraternal friendship and co-operation. We shall expand and improve mutually beneficial economic and cultural ties with them on the basis of agreed long-term plans. Such co-operation will enable us all to proceed even faster along the road of socialism and communism.

Our people derive deep satisfaction from our expanding co-operation with the great Asian powers of India and Indonesia. We rejoice in their successes and realise their difficulties, and we readily expand business co-operation which helps them promote their economy and culture. Successfully developing on similar lines are our relations with Burma, Cambodia, Ceylon, the United Arab Republic, Iraq, Guinea, Ghana, Mali, Morocco, Tunisia, Somali and other Asian and African countries that have freed themselves from foreign tyranny. We will develop business relations with the Syrian Arab Republic.

After long and painful trials a government which declared itself to be successor to the Patrice Lumumba Government was set up in the Congo. The Soviet Government is prepared to help the Congolese people solve the difficult problems facing them in the struggle to overcome the consequences of colonial oppression.

Our relations with Latin American countries have likewise made progress in the period under review, despite the barriers artificially raised by internal reaction and the U.S. imperialists. The heroic people of Cuba, who have broken down those barriers, are establishing co-operation on an equal footing with other countries. And even though the U.S. imperialists stop at nothing—not even at overthrowing lawful governments—to prevent Latin American countries from pursuing an independent policy, events will nevertheless take their own course.

We shall continue assisting newly-independent nations to get on to their feet, grow strong and take a fitting place in international affairs. Those nations are making a valuable contribution to the great cause of peace and progress. In this the Soviet Union and the other socialist countries will always be their true and reliable friends.

We attach great importance to relations with the major capitalist countries, first and foremost the United States. U.S. foreign policy in recent years has invariably concentrated on aggravating the international situation. This is deplored by all peace-loving peoples. As for the Soviet Union, it has always held that the only way to prevent a world war of extermination is to normalise relations between states irrespective of their social systems. That being so, there is a need for joint efforts to achieve this. No one expects the ruling circles of the United States to fall in love with socialism, nor must they expect us to fall in love with capitalism. The important thing is for them to renounce the idea of settling disputes through war and to base international relations on the principle of peaceful economic competition. If realistic thinking gains the upper hand in U.S. policy, a serious obstacle to a normal world situation will be removed. Such thinking will benefit not only the peoples of our two countries but those of other countries and world peace.

We propose to expand and strengthen normal, businesslike economic and cultural relations with Britain, France, Italy, West Germany and other West European countries. Noticeable progress has been achieved in this respect in recent years, and it is up to the other side to improve the situation.

The Soviet Union pays special attention to the promotion of relations with its neighbours. Differences in social and political systems are no hindrance to the development of friendly, mutually advantageous relations between the U.S.S.R. and such countries as Afghanistan or Finland. Our relations with Austria and Sweden are progressing fairly well. We have sought, and will continue to seek, better relations with Norway and Denmark. Relations with our Turkish neighbour have been improving lately. We should like them to go on improving.

The Soviet Union would also like to live in peace and friendship with such of its neighbours as Iran, Pakistan and Japan. Unfortunately, the ruling circles of those countries have so far been unable or unwilling, to disentangle themselves from the military blocs imposed on them by the Western Powers, nor have they been using the opportunities for business co-operation with our country. Their governments' present policies imperil their peoples. Outstanding in this respect is the Shah of Iran, who has gone to the point of agreeing to turn almost half the country into a zone of death in the interests of the aggressive CENTO bloc.

The Soviet Union has exerted considerable effort to improve its relations with Japan. But the government of that country, which is bound to the United States by an unequal military treaty, still refuses to eliminate the remnants of the Second World War. The absence of a Soviet-Japanese peace treaty seriously handicaps wider co-operation between our two countries. The Japanese people are becoming increasingly aware of the great loss Japan is incurring as a result. We hope that sooner or later common sense will win and that our relations with Japan will make proper progress to the benefit of both countries.

The role of *economic ties* as an important element of peaceful co-existence is growing. In the period under survey, Soviet foreign trade has almost doubled in volume. We have stable commercial relations with more than eighty countries. But a great deal more could be achieved in this field if the Western Powers stopped their obstructionist practices and frequent arbitrary actions, which damage business co-operation with the socialist countries. Incidentally, these outmoded practices do more harm to them than to us. Whoever resorts to discrimination, trade barriers and even blockades inevitably exposes himself as a proponent of war preparations and an enemy of peaceful co-existence.

Our country's *cultural relations* have expanded considerably in recent years and we now maintain such relations with more than a hundred countries. Over 700,000 Soviet people go abroad every year, and as many foreigners visit our country. We are willing to continue these mutually beneficial international contacts on a large scale. They can and must play a role in promoting co-operation and understanding among people.

Contacts with the leaders of other countries have become an important factor in Soviet foreign policy. It will be recalled that, despite pressure of business, Lenin, who guided the foreign policy of the Soviet state, received and had talks with American, British, French, Finnish, Afghan, and other foreign leaders. It was his intention to attend the 1922 Genoa Conference. The Central Committee of the Party has regarded it as its duty to follow this Lenin tradition. In pursuing an active foreign policy, members of the Presidium of the C.C. C.P.S.U. have often visited countries of the socialist community. They have paid sixty-five visits to twenty-seven non-socialist countries. I have had to travel far and wide myself. It cannot be helped—such is my duty, such is the need.

We have received many distinguished foreign guests including the heads of state or government of European, Asian, African and Latin American countries. Party and government leaders of the socialist countries have been frequent and welcome visitors to our country. We are prepared to continue meetings with heads of state or government, individually or collectively.

Comrades, events have shown that the foreign policy of our Party, elaborated by the Twentieth Congress, is correct. We have achieved major victories by pursuing that policy. While our strength has increased very appreciably, we shall persevere in our Leninist policy in an effort to bring about the triumph of the idea of peaceful coexistence. *There is now a prospect of achieving peaceful coexistence for the entire period necessary for the solution of the social and political problems now dividing the world.* Developments indicate that it may actually be feasible to banish world war from the life of society even before the complete triumph of socialism on earth, with capitalism surviving in part of the world.

Lenin taught us to be firm, unyielding and uncompromising whenever a fundamental question, a question of principle, is involved. In the most trying conditions, at a time when the only socialist state had to resist the attacks of the whole capitalist world, when the enemy was storming us at the front, in the rear and from the flanks, Lenin spoke with the imperialists in firm, resolute terms, while following a flexible course and always retaining the initiative.

What are the tasks which the present international situation sets before Soviet foreign policy? We must continue:

adhering steadily to the principle of the peaceful coexistence of states with different social systems as a general line of the Soviet Union's foreign policy;

strengthening the unity of the socialist countries through fraternal co-operation and mutual assistance, and contributing to the might of the world socialist system;

promoting contacts and co-operating with all who champion world peace. Together with all those who want peace we must oppose all those who want war;

strengthening proletarian solidarity with the working class and all working people of the world, and rendering the fullest moral and material support to the peoples fighting to free themselves from imperialist and colonial oppression or to consolidate their independence;

vigorously extending business ties, economic co-operation and trade with all countries that are willing to maintain such relations with the Soviet Union;

pursuing an active and flexible foreign policy. We must seek the settlement of pressing world problems through negotiations, expose the intrigues and maneuvers of the warmongers, and establish business co-operation with all countries on a reciprocal basis.

Experience has proved that the principle of the peaceful coexistence of countries with different social systems, a principle advanced by the great Lenin, is the way to preserve peace and avert a world war of extermination. We have been doing, and will do, all in our power for peaceful coexistence and peaceful economic competition to triumph throughout the world.

KHRUSHCHEV

Report to the Supreme Soviet
December 12, 1962

Introduction   After the XXII Congress, Khrushchev looked about for some means of rapidly acquiring a strengthened nuclear capability against the United States to replace the fictitious one that had been exposed. By late Spring 1962, his project for covertly introducing strategic missiles and bombers into Cuba was under way. Khrushchev's aim, as he truly says, was not to acquire the forces with which to initiate war against the United States. Nevertheless, his aims were far-reaching. By making United States strategic forces vulnerable to attack from nearby Cuba as well as from the USSR, Khrushchev hoped to prevent the United States from using its strategic superiority to deter Soviet offensive moves. The Soviet Union would thereby acquire a greater capacity for political maneuver, in Berlin and elsewhere.

The result of Khrushchev's attempt to introduce strategic weapons covertly into Cuba was the historic confrontation in October, 1962, which ended in Khrushchev's precipitous agreement to withdraw the strategic weapons he had introduced into Cuba. The failure of this enterprise, as well as its adventurous character, brought criticism down upon Khrushchev, not only from leaders of Communist states like Fidel Castro and Mao, but also from dissident figures in the USSR itself. Khrushchev was able to maintain his personal rule, however, and in his speech to the Supreme Soviet, which is largely devoted to the Cuban missile crisis and its implications, he undertook to defend his actions.

Contrary to his view in January, 1960, Khrushchev here presents the danger of an all-out nuclear-rocket war as a serious possibility. Activities of the imperialists could "spark" such a war, and during the Cuban missile crisis the world actually was on the "brink" of the world thermonuclear war that "the most rabid imperialists" were gambling on.

Khrushchev had good reason to argue that the world had been at the brink in October, 1962, because, were that the case, his hasty retreat was justified. It is questionable, however, that Khrushchev would have introduced the missiles at a time of great strategic weakness had he not been confident that he could control the risk of war, as he in fact succeeded in doing. He hints at this himself when he says that war would have resulted "if one side or the other had not shown restraint, had not done everything necessary to avert the outbreak of war."

Khrushchev's contention that the USSR achieved its objectives in Cuba in the settlement cannot be accepted at face value. The threat of a United States invasion of Cuba, which Khrushchev eliminated by his withdrawal of Soviet strategic forces, was itself the result of bringing those forces into Cuba. For a Communist, moreover, as some of Khrushchev's critics pointed out, President Kennedy's declaration that the United States would not attack Cuba had little value, and in any case had been made previously.

Khrushchev's extreme "restraint," after having initiated the crisis, led the Chinese Communist leaders to carry their challenge of the USSR further by fresh criticism of Soviet policies. Khrushchev replies in the part of his speech entitled "Against Dogmatism," without mentioning that his antagonist is Communist China, (China is, of course, the "someone" who taught the Albanian leaders to use foul language against the USSR and who goaded them on.) Peking had said of the United States that it is only a paper tiger; Khrushchev replies that it is necessary to show respect for its atomic teeth. Peking had criticized the USSR for making concessions to end the Cuban crisis; Khrushchev replies that Peking, for its own reasons, tolerates colonialists in Hong Kong. (Later in the speech he suggests that Communist China retreated and made concessions to India in order to bring their border war of October, 1962 to an end.) Peking had accused Moscow of retreating in the Cuban confrontation; Khrushchev says such charges evince a desire to provoke a world war (from which the critics mean to stand aside) as the only means whereby the world-wide victory of socialism can be achieved. But such a war is not necessary and would in fact drive people away from the Communist movement. The USSR has too much it treasures to risk war unnecessarily. In treating the brief Sino-Indian border war (which coincided with the Cuban missile crisis), Khrushchev approves of Communist China's withdrawal from territory it conquered in its punitive attack against India, but implies that it would have done better not to have invaded India in the first place.

At this juncture in world affairs, when the Sino-Soviet schism was rapidly widening because of the challenge of Mao's leftist strategy (*dogmatism*), Khrushchev tries to improve relations with rightist Communists like Tito (*revisionism*). Recognizing that the multiplicity of states that are building socialism requires the flexible application of Marxist-Leninist ideology, Khrushchev asserts that differences of interpretation on particular questions should not lead to splits in the Communist movement. But his attempt to keep both Mao's China and Tito's Yugoslavia in the camp eventually met with failure.

Comrade Deputies, extremely important events have taken place in the international arena during the seven months since the last session of the Supreme Soviet of the U.S.S.R. A number of these events constituted a serious threat to peace. The Soviet Government regards it as its duty to analyse the present international situation and to set out the steps in foreign policy it has recently taken.

The foreign policy of a state and its diplomatic activity demand of the ruling political parties and statesmen of the socialist countries a penetrating scientific approach in analysing international affairs and high political skill in order to find solutions [that] take into consideration the real state of affairs, soberly assess the balance of forces and produce results that strengthen the positions of socialism and accord with the interests of all peaceable peoples.

* * *

The principal result of Soviet foreign policy, and the foreign policy of the governments of the other socialist countries, the result of the struggle of all peace forces during this period is that the attack on Cuba, prepared by the aggressive imperialist circles of the United States of America, has been prevented. The direct threat of a thermonuclear world war, which arose in connection with the crisis in the Caribbean, has been averted.

Our Purpose Is Peace, Creation and Communism

Comrade Deputies, the Soviet people, who have passed through the grim school of several wars, and particularly the Second World War which swept like fire over a considerable part of our territory, know well what armed struggle between states means. Naturally, they can understand the better what thermonuclear war may be like.

And when Soviet people are asked, as in the words of the song, *Do Russian people stand for war?*, our answer is clear—we say an emphatic "No!" to war. The same answer is given by the peoples of the other socialist countries. But we are not alone on this planet, and we cannot disregard the fact that the aggressive forces of imperialism support the cold war and further intensify the arms race, that they have ringed the Soviet Union with military bases and are boasting of their military plans for an attack on the Soviet Union and the other socialist countries.

The Soviet people have worked hard to develop the most up-to-date and powerful means of defence—atomic and hydrogen bombs and rocket weapons, including inter-continental ballistic and global missiles. We have developed these weapons. They are the best in the world, and we have enough of them to reply to a blow by our enemies with a lightning, smashing blow which would obliterate the bases spearheaded against us, wherever they are, and the industries forging the weapons for the armed forces of the aggressor.

The NATO militarists like to prate about an "equilibrium of fear", about a "balance of forces of retaliation", and even about a "balance of terror", as a factor capable of guaranteeing peace on earth. But is it sensible to pin one's hopes on peace built on such a foundation? A closer look will show that the world now lives, figuratively speaking, on a mined powder magazine crammed with thermonuclear weapons.

The only choice mankind has in our time is peaceful coexistence or devastating war. But no people in any country needs a military catastrophe. A new war, if permitted to start, would kill people by the million, regardless of nationality and property status. Consequently, there is only one choice: peaceful coexistence. This means renunciation of war among states as a way of settling international disputes. This means their solution through negotiation.

* * *

Counterposed to the line of peaceful coexistence and the solution of international problems by peaceful means, followed by the Soviet Union and the other socialist countries, is the line of the aggressive imperialist circles aimed at maintaining the cold war and increasing international tension. It is their fault that crises flare up, one after another, aggravating the international situation and pushing mankind to the abyss of a world war.

The imperialists are trying to find a way out of their difficulties by assaulting the living standard of the workers of their countries and intensifying the plunder of the economically underdeveloped countries. After the collapse of the colonial empires, the plan of the imperialist monopolies is to preserve intact, and even to intensify, the economic enslavement of the young national states and to keep in chains the peoples which are still in colonial bondage. Thus, we have, on the one hand, a growth of the national liberation movement, which is supported by all progressive mankind, and on the other, an intensification of the attempts of the imperialist powers to crush this movement at all costs.

The most aggressive and adventurist circles of imperialism are trying to resolve their difficulties by a further intensification of the arms race and the preparation of a war of aggression against the socialist countries and the young sovereign states of Asia, Africa and Latin America.

It is becoming increasingly obvious that the centres of aggression created by the imperialists may spark off an all-out nuclear-rocket war.

The aggressive imperialist forces are tying knots of international tension which are fraught with dangerous consequences for mankind. So far the most acute point of this tension was the crisis in the Caribbean.

Solution Of The Crisis In The Caribbean Was a Major Victory For The Policy Of Peace

Comrade Deputies, everyone remembers the tense days of October when mankind was anxiously following the news coming from the Caribbean. In those days the world was on the brink of a thermonuclear catastrophe.

What created this crisis? How did it develop? What lessons must be learned from it? These questions call for a thorough analysis which will help the peace forces better to understand the resulting situation and to define their tasks in the struggle for the further maintenance and consolidation of peace.

But before passing over to this analysis, I should like to recall how the Cuban revolution developed and how the relations between the Soviet Union and Cuba [developed].

* * *

Flouting the generally accepted standards of international relations, the reactionary forces in the United States have been doing everything from the first day of the victory of the Cuban revolution to overthrow Cuba's revolutionary Government and to restore their domination there. They broke off diplomatic relations with Cuba, have conducted and are conducting subversive activities and established an economic blockade of Cuba. Threatening to apply sanctions, the United States began to press its allies not only to stop trading with Cuba, but even not to make ships available to carry food to Cuba from the socialist countries which came to the assistance of their brothers. This is an anti-human policy—a scheme to starve a whole nation.

But even this seemed insufficient to them. They arrogated the functions of a policeman and decided to take the path of military suppression of the Cuban revolution. In other words, they wanted to usurp the right to export counter-revolution.

United States policy *vis-a-vis* Cuba is a most unbridled, reactionary policy. To declare that Cuba threatens America, or any other country, and on this plea to usurp a special right to act against Cuba is simply monstrous.

Seeking to justify its aggressive actions, American reaction claims that the crisis in the Caribbean was created by Cuba herself, adding that blame also rests with the Soviet Union which shipped rockets and IL-28 bombers there.

But is this so? It is true that we brought weapons there at the request of the Cuban Government. But what were our motives in doing that?

Exclusively humanitarian motives—Cuba needed weapons as a means of deterring the aggressors, and not as a means of attack. For Cuba was under a real threat of invasion. Piratical attacks were repeatedly being made on her coast; Havana was shelled, and airborne groups were dropped to carry out sabotage.

A large-scale military invasion of Cuba by counter-revolutionary mercenaries was launched in April last year. This invasion was prepared and carried out with the full support of the United States.

Further events have shown that the failure of the invasion did not discourage the United States imperialists in their desire to strangle Cuba. They began preparing another attack. In the autumn of this year a very alarming situation was created. There was every indication that the United States was preparing to attack the Cuban Republic, using its own armed forces.

Revolutionary Cuba was compelled to take all measures to strengthen her defence. The Soviet Union helped her build up a strong army standing guard over the achievements of the Cuban people. In view of the mounting threat from the United States, the Government of Cuba, in the summer of this year, requested the Soviet Government to render further assistance. Agreement was reached on a number of new measures, including the stationing of several dozen Soviet I.R.B.M.s in Cuba. These weapons were to be in the hands of Soviet military men.

What were the aims behind this decision? Naturally neither we nor our Cuban friends had in mind that this small number of medium range I.R.B.M.s sent to Cuba would be used for an attack on the United States or any other country. . . .

Some people contend that the rockets were supplied by us for an attack on the United States. This, of course, is not a clever deduction. Why should we station rockets in Cuba for this purpose, when we were and are able to strike from our own territory, possessing as we do the necessary number of inter-continental missles of the required range and power.

We do not at all need military bases on foreign territories. It is known that we have dismantled all our bases abroad. All people who have any understanding of military matters know that in the age of inter-continental and global rockets, Cuba—that small far-away island which is only 50 kilometres wide in some places—is of no strategic importance for the defence of the Soviet Union. We stationed rockets in Cuba only for the defence of the Cuban Republic, and not for an attack on the United States. A small country like Cuba cannot, naturally, build up forces such as could launch an offensive against so big a country as the United States.

Only people who are not "all there" can claim that the Soviet Union chose Cuba as a springboard for an invasion of the American continent—of the United States or countries of Latin America. If we wanted to start a war against the United States, we would not have agreed to dismantle the rockets installed in Cuba, which were ready for launching, for battle. We would have used them. But we did not do that, because we did not pursue such aims.

How Events Developed Around Cuba

Developments in the Caribbean confirmed that there was a threat of such aggression. In the last ten days of October, a large-scale build-up of U.S. naval and air forces, paratroopers and marines began in the south of the United States, at the approaches to Cuba. The U.S. Government sent reinforcements to its naval base at Guantanamo, lying on Cuban territory. Big military manoeuvres were announced in the Caribbean. In the course of those "manoeuvres", a landing was to be made on the island of Vieques. On October 22, Kennedy's Administration announced a quarantine of Cuba. The word "quarantine", by the way, was merely a fig leaf in this case. Actually it was a blockade, piracy on the high seas.

Events developed rapidly. The American Command alerted all its armed forces, including its troops in Europe, and also the Sixth Fleet in the Mediterranean and the Seventh Fleet based in the Taiwan area. Several airborne, infantry and armoured divisions, numbering about 100,000 men, were set aside just for an attack on Cuba. Moreover, 183 warships with 85,000 naval personnel were moved to the shores of Cuba. The landing on Cuba was to be covered by a few thousand military planes. Close to 20 per cent of all the planes of the U.S. Strategic Air Command were kept in the air round the clock, carrying atom and hydrogen bombs. Reservists were called up.

The troops of America's NATO allies in Europe were also put on the alert. A joint command was set up by the United States and Latin American countries, and some of these countries sent warships to take part in the blockade of Cuba. As a result of these aggressive steps on the part of the U.S. Government there arose a threat of thermonuclear war.

In face of these intensive military preparations, we, for our part, had to take appropriate measures. The Soviet Government instructed the U.S.S.R. Minister of Defence to alert all the Armed Forces of the Soviet Union, and above all the Soviet inter-continental and strategic rocket forces, the rocket anti-aircraft defences and the fighter command, the strategic air command, and the Navy. Our submarine fleet, including atomic submarines, took up assigned positions. A state of top military readiness was announced in the ground forces, and the discharge of servicemen of senior age groups from the strategic rocket forces, the anti-aircraft defence forces and the submarine fleet was halted. The armed forces of the Warsaw Treaty countries were also fully alerted.

In these conditions, if one side or the other had not shown restraint, had not done everything necessary to avert the outbreak of war, an explosion would have followed with irreparable consequences.

Now, when the tension caused by the events in the Caribbean has been reduced, when we have reached the last stage of settling the conflict, I should like to report to the Deputies of the Supreme Soviet what the Soviet Government did to extinguish the approaching flames of war.

On October 23, immediately after the United States had proclaimed the blockade of Cuba, the Soviet Government, besides taking defensive measures, issued a statement resolutely warning that the United States Government was assuming a grave responsibility for the fate of the peace and was recklessly playing with fire. We frankly told the United States President that we would not tolerate piratical actions by United States ships on the high seas and that we would take appropriate measures with this object in view.

At the same time the Soviet Government urged all peoples to bar the road to the aggressors. Simultaneously, it took certain steps in the United Nations. The peaceful initiative of the Soviet Government in settling the Cuban crisis met with the full support from the socialist countries and the peoples of most other United Nation member states. The United Nations Secretary-General, U Thant, made great efforts to settle the conflict.

However, the Government of the United States continued to worsen the situation. Militarist forces in the United States were pushing developments towards an attack on Cuba. On the morning of October 27 we received information from the Cuban comrades and from other sources which bluntly said that the invasion would be carried out within the next two or three days. We assessed the messages received as a signal of the utmost alarm. And this was a well-founded alarm.

Immediate action was needed to prevent an invasion of Cuba and to preserve peace. A message suggesting a mutually acceptable solution was sent to the United States President. At that moment it was not yet too late to extinguish the fuse of war which had already begun to smoulder. In sending this message we took into consideration the fact that the President's own messages had expressed anxiety and a desire to find a way out of the existing situation. We declared that if the United States undertook not to invade Cuba and would also restrain other states allied with it from aggression against Cuba, the Soviet Union would be willing to remove from Cuba the weapons which the United States described as "offensive".

The United States President replied by declaring that if the Soviet Government agreed to remove these weapons from Cuba, the American Government would lift the quarantine, i.e., the blockade, and would give an assurance that Cuba would not be invaded, either by the United States itself or other countries of the Western Hemisphere. The President declared quite definitely, and this is known to the whole world, that the United States would not attack Cuba and would also restrain its allies from such actions.

We shipped our weapons to Cuba precisely for the purpose of preventing aggression against her. That was why the Soviet Government reaffirmed its agreement to remove the ballistic rockets from Cuba.

Thus, briefly speaking, a mutually acceptable solution was achieved, which meant a victory for reason, a success for the cause of peace. The Cuban question entered the stage of peaceful talks and, as regards the United States, was, so to speak, transferred from the generals to the diplomats.

Talks began in New York on October 29 between representatives of the U.S.S.R., the United States and Cuba, with the participation of U Thant. Comrade Mikoyan, First Deputy Chairman of the U.S.S.R. Council of Ministers, flew to Havana for an exchange of views with the Government of Cuba.

Meanwhile, the two sides set about discharging their commitments. The Soviet Union removed from Cuba all the rockets which the United States described as offensive weapons. The Soviet crews servicing the rocket installations also left. The United States was afforded an opportunity of convincing itself that all the ballistic rockets which were in Cuba had indeed been removed, and this has been confirmed in statements by United States officials.

At the same time, seeking to expedite a settlement of the crisis in the Caribbean, we agreed to withdraw the Soviet IL-28 planes from Cuba within a month, although they are obsolete as bombers. By December 7 these planes had already been removed from Cuba. They had been shipped to Cuba only to be used as a kind of flying coastal defence artillery, to operate under the cover of anti-aircraft facilities.

For its part, the United States Government on November 21 lifted the naval blockade of Cuba and withdrew its warships from that region. The United States Command withdrew from the Florida region the ground and air forces concentrated there for an attack on Cuba and demobilised the reservists who had been called up. The additional troops sent to Guantanamo during the crisis were also removed from that base. At the same time, the President reaffirmed the United States' assurance that there would be no invasion of Cuba.

Taking this into consideration, we also cancelled the military measures we had been obliged to take in connection with the worsening of the Cuban crisis. The Republic of Cuba, in its turn, began demobilising the men called up for the defence of their country, and they are returning to peaceful work and to their families.

* * *

Some Lessons and Conclusions

From this there follow some obvious results of the normalisation now beginning in the Cuban situation.

1. It has been possible to avert the invasion which was imminently threatening the Republic of Cuba and, therefore, to avert an armed conflict, to overcome a crisis which was fraught with the danger of universal thermonuclear war.

2. The United States publicly, before the entire world, pledged itself not to attack the Republic of Cuba, and to restrain its allies from so doing.

3. The most rabid imperialists who were gambling on starting a world thermonuclear war over Cuba have not been able to do so. The Soviet Union and the forces of peace and socialism have proved that they are in a position to impose peace on the advocates of war.

Which side triumphed? Who won? In this connection it can be said that it was reason, the cause of peace and the security of peoples, that won. The sides displayed a sober approach and took into account that unless such steps were taken as could help to overcome the dangerous development of events, a third world war might break out. As a result of mutual concessions and compromise, an understanding was reached which made it possible to remove dangerous tension, to normalise the situation.

Both sides made concessions. We withdrew the ballistic rockets and agreed to withdraw the IL-28 planes. This gives satisfaction to the Americans. But both Cuba and the Soviet Union received satisfaction, too. An American invasion of Cuba has been averted, the naval blockade has been lifted; the situation in the Caribbean area is returning to normal; People's Cuba exists and is growing stronger and developing under the leadership of its revolutionary government and its dauntless leader, Fidel Castro.

Some people allege that the United States compelled us to yield on certain points. But if this yardstick is applied, these people should say that the United States, too, was compelled to yield. Settlement of outstanding issues between states, without war, by peaceful means—this is precisely the policy of peaceful coexistence in action. Had we agreed to put our relations on such a basis, had the United States' relations with Cuba been built on the basis of the United Nations Charter, it would not have been necessary to take our rockets to Cuba and to install them there.

We are satisfied with this outcome of the Caribbean events; unquestionably all the other peoples favouring peaceful coexistence are also satisfied. This has made it possible for them to live and work in conditions of peace.

Now let us imagine for a minute what could have happened had we copied diehard politicians and refused to make mutual concessions. It would have been like the two goats in the folk tale who met on a footbridge over a chasm and, having locked horns, refused to make way for each other. As is known, both crashed into the chasm. But is this a wise course for human beings?

Among the ruling circles of the United States there are some politicians who are rightly called "wild". The "wild men" insisted and continue to insist on starting war as soon as possible against the Soviet Union and the countries of the socialist camp. Is it not clear that if we had taken an uncompromising position, we would only have helped the camp of the "wild men" to take advantage of the situation in order to strike a blow at Cuba and touch off a world war?

In justice it should be noted that among the leading circles of the United States there are also some people who take a saner view of the situation and, considering the present balance of forces in the international arena, realise that, if the United States touched off a war, it would not win it, and would fail to achieve its purpose.

* * *

The Cuban Government has rightly posed the question that any settlement of the Caribbean crisis must be of a long-term nature and include guarantees for the Cuban Republic which would safeguard her from aggression and ensure the Cuban people the possibility to build their new life in a peaceful environment. . . . Who is to blame for the fact that the relations between Cuba and the United States have still not been normalised? The answer is clear: it is none but the ruling circles of the United States, who do not want to negotiate with their neighbour. However, we are still hopeful that reason will prevail. Sooner or later the United States will have to agree to a normalisation of relations with Cuba.

* * *

It should be clear to all that our country will never leave revolutionary Cuba in her hour of need. The Soviet Union will honour its promise to help revolutionary Cuba. Revolutionary Cuba will not remain defenceless.

In our times, the imperialists cannot disregard the growing might of the Soviet Union and of the other socialist countries. We have the necessary number of powerful intercontinental rockets, which will enable us to strike back if war is started against us.

The militarists who boast that they have nuclear submarines against the Soviet Union, with Polaris missiles and other "surprises", as they put it, would do well to remember that we are not exactly rustics either.

* * *

Why do I recall such unpleasant things as inter-continental missiles and atomic submarines? Because we are compelled to do this by the irresponsible statements of certain leaders of the United States and its allies.

When the Cuban events were at their height and there was imminent danger in the air, many people in the West said it was necessary to seek a reasonable solution of disputes in order to prevent war. But now, when the shock has passed, so to speak, some of them are beginning to say that disputes should be settled by concessions by one side only. This is an unwise and dangerous policy.

We are not surprised that the main tune in the discordant chorus of the advocates of a "tough line" is called by Adenauer and his like.

Still, I should like to tell the cold war Chancellor that there was no cause for him to rejoice at the "toughness" of the West, which allegedly forced us to withdraw rockets from Cuba. I can assure you, Herr Chancellor, that when we decided to install some forty rockets in Cuba, we did not touch that "share" of them which are reserved for you, should you start an aggression in Europe. . . .

Indeed, consider for a moment that a knot of tension has been created in Europe, say over the question of a peace treaty with Germany. I imagine that the American militarists and critics like Adenauer, who prompt them from behind, will claim that "firmness" pays off for the West, and that an even tougher position should therefore be taken.

One can say to these people: Do you imagine that we shall undertake—under your pressure—to withdraw rockets from the Soviet Union, or be frightened by the threat of bombing? I shall tell you frankly, gentlemen: If you build your policy on such calculations, you will make a gross miscalculation.

Such methods will not enable you to remove pressing international problems from the agenda, including the question of a German peace settlement. They must be solved. But you apparently want to bury these questions, and us with them. If anybody thinks that there is a shovel big enough to bury us with our rocket weapons, we can say that the Soviet Union and other socialist countries, have a shovel just as big, perhaps bigger.

To take this road—the road of settling disputes from positions of strength—might provoke a really devastating world war. And the Western statesmen should bear it in mind.

Against Dogmatism, For Creative Application
Of The Marxist-Leninist Teaching

Comrade Deputies, it should be said that during the peaceful adjustment of the conflict in the Caribbean shrill voices of discontent were also heard from another side, from people who even call themselves Marxist-Leninists, although their actions have nothing in common with Marxism-Leninism. Whom I mean are the Albanian leaders. Their criticism of the Soviet Union in effect echoed the criticism coming from the most reactionary, bellicose Western circles.

* * *

The Albanian leaders are like . . . unreasoning boys. Someone has taught them foul language, and they go about and use it against the Communist Party of the Soviet Union. Yet it is their mother! For using this foul language they get the promised three kopeks. If they use stronger and more inventive language they get another five kopeks, and praise.

What do they want, these people who call themselves Marxists-Leninists? Why are they pressing for the same thing, in fact, as Adenauer, that is, pushing us to conflicts, to an aggravation of the international situation? It is a true saying: If you go to the left, you'll finally come to the right. Objectively, during the Cuban crisis they acted like people provoking a conflict. They wanted to bring about a collision between the Soviet Union and the United States. But what does that mean? It means provoking a world thermonuclear war.

I wonder how they would behave in such a war? I do not think that they would want to take part in it. Obviously, they would prefer to sit it out. But the question arises: What do they want? Can it be that they want the blood of the peoples of the Soviet Union, Cuba and other socialist countries to flow?

* * *

The critics of a peaceful settlement of the conflict say: Don't you see that one cannot trust the word of the United States, that history knows many instances when treaties were violated? Yes, history has such instances, but if one proceeds from this alone, one would have to acknowledge that people now have no other prospect except mutual extermination. To assert this means, wittingly, or unwittingly, to take the road of militarism, to regard war as the only method of settling disputes.

Are international disputes really bound to be settled through war and not through negotiations? No, reaching a settlement of disputes between states through war is madness, which can hold only suffering and disaster for the peoples. It has nothing in common with the teaching of Marx and Lenin. It is tantamount to denying international treaties and agreements, denying the principle of peaceful coexistence. Reasonable standards of international relations exist, and we must not undermine, but strengthen them. Vituperation will not settle disputed issues.

* * *

It is, of course, true that the nature of imperialism has not changed. But imperialism today is no longer what it used to be when it held undivided sway over the world. If it is now a "paper tiger", those who say this know that this "paper tiger" has atomic teeth. It can use them and it must not be treated lightly. It is possible in relations with imperialist countries to make reciprocal compromises, while, on the other hand, one must have all the means to smash the aggressors, should they unleash war.

Some people confined themselves to cursing when difficult conditions were created for Cuba. . . .

Of course, this was a critical time and the Government of the United States understood the possible development of events. It understood that if its armed forces set off a war in Cuba, and both Cubans and Soviet men in Cuba would be burnt in this conflagration, no force would restrain the Soviet Union from striking a crushing retaliatory blow. That is why the United States Government displayed reason at the crucial moment of the crisis. . . .

No one blames the People's Republic of China for leaving fragments of colonialism intact. It would be wrong to prod China into actions which she considers untimely. If the Government of the People's Republic of China tolerates Macao and Hong Kong it must clearly have good reasons for it. It would, therefore, be ridiculous to charge that this is a concession to the British and Portuguese colonialists, that this is appeasement.

* * *

But the hour will come when our Chinese friends will find this position intolerable and will tell the colonialists in a loud voice, "Get out!" And we shall welcome that step. But it is for our Chinese friends themselves to decide when this is to be done. We are not hurrying them. On the contrary, we say: "Settle this matter in your country's interests and the interests of the whole socialist camp."

Some dogmatists have slipped to Trotskyist positions and are prodding the Soviet Union and the other socialist countries on to the course of unleashing world war. They would like to impose the same kind of provocative policy that Trotsky followed in his time. Clearly, the Albanian leaders and those who are goading them on have lost faith in the possibility of the victory of socialism without war between states; possibly they never appreciated the possibility, believing that only through war, by destroying millions of human beings, is it possible to achieve communism. But that folly cannot make the peoples of other countries follow the Communist Parties! It can, on the other hand, repel millions upon millions of people from the communist movement. . . .

We have travelled a long road in forty-five years. Now we are advancing with even greater strides. What we used to cover in five years we are now covering in a month. Do we have anything to treasure? Of course, we have; we have prospects; we have confidence in the ultimate victory of our ideas. We seek these victories not on the road of war, but on the road of peaceful creation and peaceful competition with capitalism. We reject not only world thermonuclear war, but all wars between states in general, with the exception of a just war of liberation and a defensive war waged by people who are the victims of aggression.

Naturally, if a war is imposed on us from whatever quarter, we shall stand up for ourselves and for our allies, and shall use all the means we have at our disposal. We shall, however, do everything in our power to avoid a military clash, in order to exclude wars altogether from the life of society.

* * *

To preserve peace, to preserve the great gains of socialism, we are ready to agree, and do agree, to reasonable political compromise, firmly abiding by the principles of the Marxist-Leninist teaching. We follow the injunctions of Lenin, who time and time again stressed the possibility and need for compromise in politics.

Let Us Search Persistently For Peaceful Settlement Of Outstanding Issues

Comrade Deputies, in examining the present international situation, one cannot overlook the regrettable events which have occurred in the area of the Indian-Chinese border. It is well known that it wasn't a week or a month ago that the border conflict began there. It began as long ago as 1959. Recently this conflict has worsened and developed into armed clashes, in the course of which thousands of men have fallen on both sides.

* * *

Suddenly a bloody border conflict flared up between the People's Republic of China and India, in which both the Chinese people and the Indian people have suffered heavy casualties. This has grieved us deeply.

War can be started by an accidental rifle shot. One accidental shot, two in reply, then another three in reply to these two. This is how war sometimes begins, but to end a war is not so easy even for experienced statesmen.

On the question of border disputes we maintain Leninist views. The forty-five-year experience of the Soviet Union suggests that there are no border disputes which, given a mutual desire, cannot be settled without resort to arms. It is from these positions that Soviet people evaluate the developments on the Chinese-Indian border.

* * *

But in the world there also exist forces, the international imperialist circles, which rejoice in the aggravation of the Indian-Chinese conflict. They attach far-reaching provocative plans to it. They hasten to offer arms, so that Indians and Chinese may kill each other. The imperialist powers are ready to loosen their purse-strings and to display "generosity", give armaments "free", as a "gift". To the imperialists this conflict is a real godsend.

* * *

Therefore, we regard as reasonable the step taken by the Government of the People's Republic of China in announcing that it had unilaterally ceased fire and started to withdraw its troops on December 1. We are most happy about that and welcome such actions on the part of the Chinese comrades.

Some might say: "How is it that you claim this is a reasonable step, if it was taken after so many lives have been lost, after so much blood has been shed? Would it not have been better if both sides had refrained from resorting to arms?" Yes, of course, that would have been better. We have said this more than once, and we repeat it again. But if it was not possible to prevent such a course of events, it is better to display courage now and to end the clash. Is not this wisdom worthy of statesmen?

Of course, there might be some people who would say: "Look, the People's Republic of China is withdrawing its troops essentially to the line on which this conflict broke out. Wouldn't it have been better not to have advanced from the positions which those troops occupied at the time?" Such reasoning is understandable. It shows that people are displaying concern, and regret what has happened.

But, comrades, some people try to put a different construction on the decision taken by the Government of the People's Republic of China. They ask: "Isn't this a retreat?" They also ask the question: "Isn't this a concession on the part of the Chinese comrades?" Of course, such questions are asked and apparently will be sprung by those who love to cavil, in order to hurt the feelings of this or that side, to kindle enmity between India and China and to profit from that.

* * *

There are some persons who are already saying that apparently China desisted from hostilities because India had begun to receive support from the American and British imperialists, who are supplying her with armaments. "Therefore," such people say, "the People's Republic of China realised that if the armed conflict continued to develop it might grow into a major war which would result in still greater casualties."

Yes, clearly, our Chinese friends considered the situation and this also testifies to their wisdom and their understanding of the fact that when a war breaks out between friendly neighbouring peoples, the imperialists always try to profit from that. . . .

Undoubtedly, the measures taken by the Government of the People's Republic of China will be duly acclaimed by peace-loving peoples. Indeed, why wage war? Did China ever have the aim of invading India? No, we reject such contentions as slanderous. And, of course, we also absolutely rule out the idea that India wanted to start a war with China. That is why we sincerely welcome the steps taken by the Government of People's China and in no way consider that it has made some sort of retreat. No, the

Government of the People's Republic of China has displayed reason, a correct understanding of the situation and has made efforts to stop the military clash and to normalise the situation.

* * *

Live In Peace And Friendship With Our Neighbours

We Communists must take account of how the process of history is developing, how the struggle for socialism is developing in practice in various countries. Already, many countries of Europe and Asia have embarked on the socialist road. Naturally, each Communist Party in these countries tries to apply creatively the principles of Marxism-Leninism to the concrete historical, geographical and other conditions of its own country, and on this basis it exercises its guidance of the people in building socialism and communism. It is clear that our understanding cannot completely coincide on all questions that confront this or that Communist or Workers' Party in the struggle for the building of a new society. A different interpretation of concrete questions of socialist construction, a different approach to this or that question, cannot be ruled out. This is so in practice and, apparently, this is how it will be when other peoples embark on the socialist road.

Therefore, it would be wrong to work out some set pattern and to keep to it in the relations with other socialist countries. It would be a mistake to brand as renegades all who do not conform with this pattern. What then? Are we to press for the complete expulsion of a Communist Party from the ranks of our movement? Is it possible to ignore the fact that the people of such a country are building socialism? Or perhaps we must turn a blind eye to the very existence of such a people and struggle against it? To act in that way would be tantamount to adopting the bestial laws of the capitalist world and to apply them to the relations between Communist Parties and socialist countries. . . .

We are fighting for a better future for mankind, for communism under which the genuine brotherhood of all the peoples of the world will come into being. We are deeply convinced that in the future, with the complete victory of communism, as Lenin taught, the state frontiers that now divide peoples will be no more. National isolation will completely disappear, and the peoples will form a single family as brothers.

In advancing to this cherished goal we must do everything possible to overcome differences if they appear among Communists of different countries. Our duty is to help a party that has committed errors or has deviated from the standards of the international revolutionary workers' movement, from Marxism-Leninism, to help it to realise its mistakes and to mend them, so that it may occupy a worthy place in the family of all the fraternal parties. . . .

Some people contend that Yugoslavia is not a socialist country. Then, it is permissible to ask: What sort of a country is it? In answering that question, one must proceed from the Marxist-Leninist teaching, from an objective analysis of the country's social development, the nature of its social and political system. Subjectivism is impermissible here! One must not think that some Buddha-like individual can, ignoring facts, utter truths and determine which country is socialist and which is not. In this connection, knowledge of Marxist-Leninist theory, a profound analysis of reality is required.

As is well known, there have been no landowners or capitalists in Yugoslavia for a long time now, and no private capital, no private enterprises or landed estates, no private banks. We see also that the Yugoslav Communists and their leaders are channelling their efforts into the development of their economy, the consolidation of the gains of socialism. Therefore, if one is to base oneself on objective laws, on the teaching of Marxism-Leninism, it is impossible to deny that Yugoslavia is a socialist country. . . .

The Albanian leaders are again attempting to boost the cult of Stalin's person. They want the restoration of the abnormal atmosphere that existed in the communist movement during the days of the cult of the individual.

Our Party has subjected Stalin's errors and abuses to sharp and vigorous criticism, although it does not deny his services to the Party and to the communist movement. We have done this not only for the sake of historical truth, but also so as to establish all the necessary guarantees against the recurrence of anything similar in the future, against the recurrence of phenomena that are alien to Leninism, the danger of which Lenin himself pointed out in his time.

We have done so not only in the interests of our Party and our people, but also in the interest of the entire world communist movement, for the sake of the struggle for the world-wide victory of socialism. . . .

The anti-Leninist ideology of the personality cult lies at the base of the whole of the present erroneous line of the Albanian leaders. They are doing everything in their power to preserve in Albania a situation in which, uncontrolled and unpunished, they are able to violate all the standards of Party and government life so as to satisfy their own interests. Hoxha and Shehu know that they would not have remained in power if they had slackened their regime of repression and persecution. The people would not tolerate them in the leadership, because their hands are smeared with the blood of the best sons of the Albanian Party of Labour.

* * *

One of the negative effects of the Stalin personality cult on the international communist movement was the spread of Left-sectarian, dogmatic views, which gravely harmed the great cause of the struggle for socialism and which weakened the influence of Marxism-Leninism on the broad masses of the people. As Lenin had warned, underestimation of the struggle against Left-wing opportunism resulted in neglect of that disorder, which has long since ceased to be an infantile one. . . .

Soviet Communists, to whom there is nothing higher than the unity of the ranks of the world communist movement, will wage a resolute struggle both against Right-wing opportunism and against the Left-wing opportunism which today is no less dangerous than revisionism.

* * *

BREZHNEV

Report to the XXIII Party Congress *March 29, 1966*

Introduction After Khrushchev's defeat in the Cuban crisis, he seemed to commit himself to a policy of détente, and was reconciled to the prospect of being unable to elicit large concessions from the West, at least in the short term. In mid-1963, a limited test-ban treaty was negotiated, a "hot line" linking White House and Kremlin was set up for rapid communication during emergencies, and jamming of the West's broadcasts to the Soviet Union ceased. Khrushchev's belated effort to fit the objectives of Soviet foreign policy to the means available might have enabled him to consolidate his personal position, had it not been for the egregious failures of his agricultural policies and a slow-down in the rate of Soviet industrial growth. Even so, his personal position was sufficiently strong that his lieutenants had to resort to a conspiracy in order to remove him. In October, 1964, Khrushchev was suddenly ousted and a collective leadership headed by his heir apparent, Leonid Brezhnev, seized power. Within a few months the new leadership had to face the problem of shaping a policy on Vietnam, where the United States had escalated the level of violence in order to prevent the collapse of the Saigon regime.

Through its commitments to provide Hanoi with weapons for air defense and the Viet Cong with arms and supplies, Moscow was able to regain a measure of influence on Hanoi's policies while limiting the risk of a confrontation with the United States. The increasing United States involvement in Vietnam tended to deflect American military power and diplomacy away from the European theater. The USSR acquired new room for maneuver and the focus of its foreign policy, which under Khrushchev had been on the United States, now shifted to Europe.

Brezhnev delivers his Report not as a personal ruler, but as spokesman for a collective leadership. In style Brezhnev suffers by comparison with Khrushchev: he is turgid, flat, wordy and schematic, where Khrushchev's style was generally lively and expressive of his character and temperament. Brezhnev intones the ideological formulae—the increasing contradictions of capitalism and the growing successes of the working class—with the bureaucrat's respect for ritualistic orthodoxy. What political character lay beneath the bureaucratic exterior and what credo underlay the verbal formulae was still to be revealed.

The increased importance of "the national liberation movement" for Soviet foreign policy is revealed by the fact that an entire section of Brezhnev's Report is devoted to it. Even so, the new leadership early met with serious reverses in two underdeveloped countries, when local upheavals negated the steady progress of past years. In Indonesia, where the USSR had invested the equivalent of many hundreds of millions of dollars in economic and military assistance, Sukarno was overthrown by a military coup and the Communist Party was severely damaged and driven underground. In Ghana, the USSR was deprived of its chief ally in Africa when Nkrumah was overthrown after a decade in power. Neither setback could properly be charged to failings of the post-Khrushchev leadership, which in any case showed no signs of modifying its policies as a result of the setbacks.

Difficulties in the Communist world—particularly with Communist China and Rumania—were handled cautiously and without Khrushchev's close personal involvement. The new leadership was all for conferences, delegations (200 from 60 fraternal parties!), meetings, and palaver as a way of keeping communications open while relying on "the objective identity of the basic interests of all revolutionary contingents" to reconcile "subjective" differences. The method had something to be said for it if it helped Moscow to make correct decisions as necessary. But this was something the collective leadership in Moscow found hard to do.

In discussing relations with the West, Brezhnev takes a firmer stand, reflecting increased hostility arising from the Vietnam war. He says, the thesis that "it is possible to curb the aggressor and avert another war remains valid. But. . . ."—and the "but" is perhaps intended to convey fresh doubts. Basically, however, the Soviet position in Europe seemed secure. Moscow had acquired room for maneuver, but seemed to lack the interest or capacity to exploit it with major initiatives.

Insofar as concerns the international situation in the period that has elapsed since the 22nd Party Congress, there has been a steady growth in the international influence of the Soviet Union and the entire world system of socialism, the countries and peoples fighting for independence and progress against the yoke of colonialism have scored fresh victories, the struggle of the working class in the capitalist countries has become more active and there has been a further development of the international communist and labour movement.

On the other hand, there has been a continued exacerbation and deepening of the general crisis of capitalism. Imperialism, primarily imperialist circles in the USA, has on a number of occasions resorted to insolent provocative acts, going so far as war adventures. This has resulted in an exacerbation of the international situation.

The increased aggressiveness of imperialism by no means signifies that there has been a change in the alignment of world forces in its favour. On the contrary, this aggressiveness is a reflection of the growing difficulties and contradictions confronting the world capitalist system in our day. The events of the past few years have again shown that no matter what methods and means imperialism resorts to, it is not in a position to check the course of historical development. Contemporary revolutionary forces are continuing their offensive. The peoples' fight against imperialism is increasing.

The [Central Committee of the Communist Party of the Soviet Union] has taken into consideration all the complications of the world situation in elaborating the course of the Party and the state in foreign policy; it has been guided by the vital interests of the peoples of the Soviet Union and by the desire to ensure peaceful conditions for the building of communism and socialism in the countries of the world socialist community and to prevent the unleashing of a new world war. In elaborating and implementing foreign policy the Central Committee proceeded from its internationalist revolutionary duty both to the fraternal socialist countries and to the working people of all countries.

The results of past years show that the political line of the CPSU is correct and enjoys the full support of the entire Soviet people. Our chief task is to work for the implementation of this line. Loyalty to the cause of communism, proletarian internationalism and socialist solidarity has been and will always be the law of life and struggle of the great Party of Lenin.

The International Status Of The USSR.
The Activities Of The CPSU
In The Sphere Of Foreign Policy

The World Socialist System, The Efforts Of
CPSU To Strengthen Its Unity And Might

The world socialist system is making steady progress. The basic laws of socialist construction are common to all countries, they are well known and have been tested in practice. Nevertheless, as the socialist countries develop, they are constantly coming up against new problems engendered by the realities of life in all its complexity and variety. It stands to reason that there are no ready-made solutions to these problems, nor can there be any. The development of the world socialist system, therefore requires a constant creative approach, on the tried and tested basis of Marxism-Leninism, to the problems that arise, it requires the pooling of experience and opinions.

Business-like contacts and political consultations between the leaders of the fraternal parties of socialist countries have developed into a system. During the year and a half that have elapsed since the October (1964)

Plenum of the CC, members of the Presidium and Secretaries of the CC, and many members of the CC CPSU have, on a number of occasions, met leaders of the Communist and Workers' Parties of almost all the socialist countries for negotiations and detailed talks. Our friendly meetings, sincere talks, our pooling of opinion and experience, always take place in a spirit of comradeship, profound mutual respect and common loyalty to the great ideals and aims of socialism.

Such meetings make it possible to summarise and use, in good time and more fully, all that is worthwhile in the practical activities of each country and of the entire socialist system, to elaborate more successfully the policy of communist and socialist construction in [all our] countries and the most correct line in international affairs. Everything, all our experience, tells us that this is a practice that is very necessary and useful and we should like to see it developed in every way. . . .

The Council for Mutual Economic Assistance is acquiring increasing importance in expanding the economies of the participant countries. Economists are now busy working on problems of greater specialisation and co-operation in production and more rational dovetailing of economic plans. Like many fraternal parties, we are of the opinion that only in this way can the national economies of the socialist countries keep pace with the tempestuous scientific and technical revolution of our days and thus ensure conditions for further achievements in the economic competition with capitalism.

The economy of the socialist countries is developing more rapidly than that of the countries of the bourgeois world. Suffice it to say that in the period 1961-65, the industrial output of the world socialist system increased by 43 per cent and that of the capitalist system by 34 per cent. As you see, the difference is substantial and, apart from that, industrial growth figures in capitalist countries are not an indicator of higher living standards as they are in the socialist countries, but are primarily evidence of the growing profits of the monopolies and the progressive militarisation of capitalist economy.

In the sphere of military co-operation, there has been a further consolidation of our relations with the socialist countries in the face of growing aggressive acts on the part of the imperialist forces headed by the USA, a strengthening and improvement of the mechanism of the Warsaw Pact. The Warsaw Pact is the reliable protector of the gains of the peoples of the socialist countries. The armies of the Warsaw Pact countries are equipped with the most up-to-date weapons. In field exercises, in the air and at sea, co-operation between the armed forces of the allied states is being developed, the power of modern weapons tested and the fraternity of the armed forces of the Warsaw Pact countries strengthened. If the need arises the closely knit family of signatories to the Pact will rise solidly in defence of the socialist system, and the free life of our peoples, and deliver a crushing blow at any aggressor.

As far as the CPSU is concerned we shall continue to do all we can to extend and consolidate military co-operation of the fraternal socialist countries.

Comrades, co-operation and solidarity are the main sources of the strength of the socialist system. The development and deepening of this co-operation is in accordance with the vital interests of each individual country and of the socialist system as a whole, it promotes the cohesion of our ranks in the struggle against imperialism.

Such cohesion is particularly necessary in the present situation when the US imperialists are escalating their aggression against the Vietnamese people, have launched an unprovoked attack on the Democratic Republic of Vietnam, a socialist country. The CPSU is working consistently for united action by all socialist countries in assisting fighting Vietnam. Permit me, comrades, to speak at greater length about the events in Vietnam and our support of the fraternal Vietnamese people somewhat later.

The CPSU and the Soviet people fully support the fraternal Korean people who are fighting against US imperialism to unify Korea on a democratic basis. Our Party, all the Soviet people, are confident that the Korean people will be victorious and that Korea will be united and free.

The heroic people of Cuba, the first American country to carry out a socialist revolution, are fighting and building socialism under difficult circumstances. Cuba is not alone: she is a member of the mighty community of socialist states. Our people are wholeheartedly with the Cuban people in their efforts to build a new society. The Soviet Union has been giving all-round support to fraternal Cuba, and will continue unswervingly to do so.

While speaking of the consolidation of the world socialist system, comrades, we must at the same time note that our relations with the Parties of two socialist countries, with the Communist Party of China and the Albanian Party of Labour unfortunately remain unsatisfactory.

Our Party and the Soviet people sincerely desire friendship with People's China and its Communist Party. We are prepared to do everything possible to improve relations with People's Albania and the Albanian Party of Labour.

You know that in November 1964 there was a meeting in Moscow between the CPSU and a delegation of the CC CPC. Somewhat later our delegation had a talk with the leadership of the CPC in Peking. It was proposed to the Chinese comrades that a new meeting be held at the highest level in Moscow or Peking. We still believe that such a meeting would be valuable, and are prepared at any moment to examine existing differences with the leadership of the CPC in order to find a way of overcoming them on the principles of Marxism-Leninism.

We are convinced that our parties and our peoples will ultimately overcome all difficulties and will march side by side in the fight for our common, great revolutionary cause.

Exacerbation of the Contradictions of
The Capitalist System. Development of the
Class Struggle of the Proletariat

Comrades, in its foreign policy the CC CPSU has paid regard to the processes taking place in the capitalist world. The capitalist system as a whole is gripped by a general crisis. Its inherent contradictions are growing more acute. In their efforts to surmount these contradictions and hold their ground in the struggle against socialism, the bosses of the bourgeois world pinned strong hopes on state regulation of the economy, scientific and technical progress and on greater military production. However, this has not, nor could it have cured capitalism of its basic ailments. Although economic growth in the main capitalist countries has been more rapid since the war than between the two world wars, it is obvious that capitalist economy has remained unstable. Periods of relative rises in production are succeeded by recessions. Such rises and drops have occurred in many capitalist countries, particularly in the United States.

When to this is added the mounting inflation, the tremendous growth of the national debt and the indebtedness of the population, it becomes clear that the hidden destructive forces inherent in the capitalist economy are still operating and that it will not escape new upheavals.

The law of the uneven economic and political development of capitalist countries is operating implacably; the contradictions between the capitalist states are growing more acute. For a number of years economic growth in the West-European countries and Japan was more rapid than in the United States, but in the last few years the tables have turned. Economic growth in the USA has been accelerated, while in Western Europe and Japan rates of growth have sharply fallen.

The US monopolies have taken advantage of this and mounted a fresh offensive in the world markets. American capital is again being invested heavily in the industries of Italy, the Federal Republic of Germany, Britain and other countries. However, unlike the early postwar years, the US monopolies are having to deal now with stronger competitors, who are hitting back at the dollar more and more frequently.

The competitive struggle in Western Europe, including the Common Market and other state-monopoly associations, has also become sharper. A process of disintegration has set in [in] the imperialist blocs, as a consequence of the contradictions among the member countries. The United States in no longer able to direct the latters' policy as sweepingly as before. It is long since any serious politician, let alone the people has given credence to the myth about a "threat of Soviet aggression", which once helped forge these blocs. American aggression, on the other hand, is a patent fact. The allies of the United States are becoming increasingly conscious of the dangers involved in blind conformance with Washington policies. Thus, a new area of contradiction and rivalry is appearing within the capitalist world. . . .

Since NATO was founded more than a thousand million dollars have been spent in building up and improving its war machine. . . .

The facts play havoc with the lying tales of "people's capitalism" and the "welfare state" spread by bourgeois ideologists. What sort of general welfare is it if, say, the 1965 net profits of the US monopolies aggregated 45,000 million dollars, or 4 times as much as annual average during the Second World War, while 32 million Americans, as the US Government itself admits, live in poverty? . . .

Headed by the Communist Parties, who are their vanguard, the proletariat of the capitalist countries are waging an active struggle against war, against the colonial policy of the imperialists, and in support of peoples that have become victims of imperialist aggression. The resounding political successes scored lately by the working class and all the "Left" forces of France speak plainly of their increasing influence on the country's social life, and of the growing political maturity of the masses. The working class of Italy stands in the van of a broad progressive front and is frustrating reactionary attempts at encroaching on the democratic gains of the people. During the period under review there has been a great upsurge in the United States, in the fight against racial discrimination, in the campaign for the civil rights of the 20 million American Negroes. Large sections of the American nation are protesting more and more vigorously against the US aggression in Vietnam.

Other social strata opposing monopoly oppression—the bulk of the peasants and the intelligentsia—are rallying more closely round the working class. A broad anti-monopoly front is being formed. This process promotes closer unity of the people and stimulates their struggle for the ultimate goal—for the revolutionary transformation of society, for socialism.

Times are becoming increasingly difficult for capitalism. Its doom is becoming more and more obvious. But the capitalists will never give up control of their own free will. It is only through tenacious class battles that the working class and the rest of the working people will achieve victory.

The CPSU Works for the Unity of the
World Communist Movement

Half a century ago, when our Party led by Vladimir Lenin marshalled the people to assault capitalism, there were 400,000 Communists in the world. Today, 88 Communist Parties in all continents have a membership of nearly 50 million. . . .

* * *

Since 1960 the number of Communists in the world has increased by 14 million. . . . More and more, the Communists are winning the sympathies of the people. In a number of European and Latin American countries, the Communist Parties have grown into a major political force. A quarter of all electors vote for Communists in these countries.

The Communists are the most active fighters for the unity of the working-class movement. Lately, distinct headway has been made in the struggle for such unity, although it still encounters considerable difficulties. These are due above all to the right-wing leaders of the social-democratic parties. But it is not these leaders who represent the true interests of the working-class movement. The working class is becoming increasingly conscious of the dangers implicit in the policy of the right-wing social-democratic leaders, who are bent on safeguarding capitalism and maintaining the split in the working-class movement. The masses are becoming increasingly convinced from their own experience that nothing but concerted efforts will yield tangible results in the struggle against monopoly capital. The working class wants unity and we are deeply convinced that this will be achieved.

The collapse of imperialism's colonial system and the emergence of a large group of young independent states on the world scene confronts the *Communist movement in Asia, Africa, and Latin America* with new tasks. Born in the flames of national liberation revolutions, it is gaining strength in the struggle for their consummation, for the consolidation of freedom and independence, and for social progress.

The Communists tread a thorny path in the countries of the capitalist world, falsely styled "free". Every step made by the communist movement there involves grim struggle against an experienced, treacherous and ruthless foe. . . . For many years now, the Communist Parties of Spain, Portugal, Greece, West Germany, Venezuela, Peru, the South African Republic and a number of other countries have had to operate underground. The Communist Party of the United States is fighting gallantly in most difficult conditions, withstanding the assault of a giant coercive police machine, and hounded continuously by anti-communist ideologists in the pay of the bourgeoisie.

Unable to defeat the Communists in politico-ideological combat, bourgeois reaction resorts to terrorism against the Communist Parties and to physical violence against loyal sons of the proletariat and all the working people.

The whole of our Party and all our nation condemn the anti-communist terror in Indonesia. The reactionary forces in that country have, without trial, brutally exterminated tens of thousands of people whose only "guilt" was their being members of the Communist Party. The persecution and banning of the Communist Party prejudices the unity of the revolutionary forces of Indonesia, undermines the anti-imperialist front and greatly damages the interests of the friendly Indonesian people. We demand that the criminal butchery of Communists, those heroic fighters for Indonesia's national independence and the interests of the working people, be stopped at once.

In. . .recent years, executioners have depleted the Communist ranks of many outstanding leaders. Many gallant fighters for the happiness of their peoples, for socialism have been tortured and done to death by the police. These men are immortal. They will live on in the memory of generations.

No tortures, no terror by the reaction can break the Communists. We are proud that our movement produces wonderful heroes, that it produces models of ideological devotion, civic and personal courage.

Comrades, the successes of the Communist movement are incontestable. But Communists take a sober view of the situation. Vladimir Lenin taught us to take into account not only victories but also setbacks, in order to draw from them the correct conclusions.

Giving leadership to the class struggle is a great and complicated art; today, it is probably more intricate than ever before. The conditions in which the fraternal parties are waging the struggle vary from country to country. New social strata, whole nations, are joining the revolutionary struggle. They have different traditions, different economic conditions and different experience in struggle. All this affects the activities of the respective Communist Parties.

The experience of the revolutionary movement during the last few years has again demonstrated that success is achieved by Parties that adhere to the tried and true Leninist principles of strategy and tactics, and take account of the existing situation. Experience shows that deviations from the Marxist-Leninist line either to right or "left" become doubly dangerous when they are combined with nationalism, great-power chauvinism and hegemonic ambition. Communists cannot help drawing the proper conclusions from this.

Comrades, you know that the world communist movement has run into serious difficulties over the last few years. The attitude of the CPSU on this score is well known to the Congress delegates. We regret deeply that the differences from which none but our common adversaries benefit have not been overcome to this day. This, we believe, goes against the interest of every fraternal party and the common interest of the entire world communist movement. . . .

Greater unity calls for the observance of the collectively defined rules governing relations between Parties, those of complete equality and independence, non-interference in each other's internal affairs, mutual support, and international solidarity. The Communist Parties possess vast experience in revolutionary work and none can find the right conclusions for the problems that arise before them better than they themselves. The CPSU is opposed to any and all hegemonic trends in the communist movement. The CPSU stands for truly internationalist relations between all the Parties on the basis of equality.

* * *

The conferences and meetings held lately by representatives of Communist Parties have served to strengthen the unity of the world communist movement. Our Party attaches great importance to such contacts. In the last 18 months alone, we have had meetings with more than 200 delegations from 60 fraternal parties. Further multilateral and bilateral meetings, the continuous exchange of experience, and comradely discussions of current problems—this is a correct and useful practice in the relations between fraternal parties and, at the same time, a good way of promoting the solidarity of the communist movement.

The Central Committee of the CPSU fully shares and supports the fraternal parties' view that international conferences of Communist Parties are an important and tested form of securing the international unity of Communists, and holding collective discussions of new problems. We stand for a new conference when the conditions for it are ripe.

* * *

The facts confirm that the overwhelming majority of the Communist Parties are strongly in favour of the international unity of the revolutionary vanguard of the international working class. The objective identity of the basic interests of all the revolutionary contingents is the foundation on which the unity of Communists rests and flourishes. Today, at this Congress, the CPSU again repeats the appeal to all Communists: Close the ranks tighter for the struggle against the common enemy—imperialism!

* * *

Development of the National Liberation Movement. Our Party's Support of the National Liberation Struggle

...In the past few years the cause of national liberation has made considerable progress. The world has witnessed the emergence of another 17 independent states, including the Algerian People's Democratic Republic, Kenya, Uganda, Tanzania and Zambia. Almost the whole of Asia and Africa have now shaken off the yoke of colonial slavery. This is a great gain in the people's liberation struggle against imperialism.

But there are still countries in the world today where the imperialists are seeking by force of arms to preserve the shameful colonial system. In Angola and Mozambique, in "Portuguese" Guinea and in South Arabia patriots are heroically fighting the foreign enslavers and invaders. In South Africa and in Southern Rhodesia the resistance of the people to the racist regimes is mounting. Our Party and the entire Soviet people actively support this struggle; we are giving effective all-round assistance to peoples fighting against foreign invaders for freedom and independence and shall continue to do so. We are firmly convinced that the day is not far distant when the last remnants of colonialism will be destroyed and the peoples will raise the banner of national freedom in the liberated territories. That is the sentence passed by history, and it is irrevocable.

The peoples of the countries that have won state independence are working to abolish the grim aftermaths of colonial rule. These countries have vast natural resources. Nevertheless, on a population basis, output is only one-fortieth to one-twentieth that of the economically developed countries. But the peoples who have achieved independence are fully determined to overcome their age-old backwardness.

The new life in the liberated countries is burgeoning in fierce combat with imperialism, in a sharp struggle between the forces of progress and the forces of internal reaction. Some social strata, supported by imperialism, are trying to direct the development of the liberated countries along the capitalist road. Others, expressing the interests of the bulk of the people, are working to promote development along the road of social progress and genuine national independence.

Experience shows that, the struggle for social progress and national independence is more successful, where there is greater unity of all patriotic, progressive and democratic forces. Communists, being as they are, selfless fighters against imperialism for the interests of the people, are active in this struggle. Unquestionably, where this is forgotten and where

Communists are even persecuted, the cause of strengthening national independence and freedom is harmed. . . .

The capitalist monopolies still have considerable control over the economy and resources of many of the developing countries in Asia, Africa and Latin America and are continuing ruthlessly to pillage them. The USA, Britain and other Western powers are draining nearly 6,000 million dollars a year out of these countries as profits on capital investments.

Wherever they can, the imperialists try to utilise the internal contradictions in the newly-free countries. They provoke clashes between various social, national and tribal groups and strive to set various politicians against each other; they try to move to power those belonging to the most reactionary and corrupt elements who enrich themselves through ties and collaboration with foreign capital. In some countries they succeed in setting up anti-popular regimes, whose representatives are not averse to being the direct accomplices of imperialism in the international arena as well.

The imperialists ignore the national sovereignty of the newly-free countries. They cynically lay claim to the right of intervening, by force of arms, in the internal affairs of other peoples. An example of this is the recent resolution of the House of Representatives of the US Congress on armed interference in the internal affairs of Latin American countries, a resolution which has evoked indignation throughout the world. Essentially this is an attempt to legalise aggressive imperialist action like the recent US armed intervention in the Dominican Republic.

All this is a manifestation of the policy of neo-colonialism, the struggle against which the whole of progressive mankind regards as one of its cardinal tasks. There is no doubt whatever that the people who have risen to fight for independence will carry this struggle on until final victory is achieved and will oppose all attempts to re-enslave them.

The CC CPSU informs the Congress with satisfaction that in the past few years our relations with the overwhelming majority of the independent countries of Asia and Africa have developed successfully. There has been a considerable extension of trade, economic and cultural co-operation between the USSR and these countries. Nearly 600 industrial, agricultural and other projects are being built in Asian and African countries with the aid of our design organisations and with the participation of Soviet building specialists. Soviet geological surveying teams are working in many of these countries, in jungles and sun-scorched deserts, helping the young countries to explore their mineral resources and make it serve their national economy.

More than 100 educational and medical institutions as well as research centres have been built or are under construction in these countries with Soviet assistance. The number of students from Asian, African and Latin

American countries studying at Soviet institutions of higher learning and technical schools has almost doubled in the past five years. The number of Soviet teachers, doctors and other specialists in the cultural field now working in 28 Asian and African countries has increased fourfold. In these countries Soviet people are working selflessly, conscientiously, without sparing themselves. They are contributing greatly towards strengthening friendship between our countries. The proletarian internationalism of the Soviet people is manifested in all this.

Our Party and Government are also rendering all possible support to the newly-free countries in the international arena as well. The USSR actively opposes imperialist interference in the internal affairs of the young national states. It opposes the attempts of the neo-colonialists to provoke conflicts between the independent countries with the object of exhausting their strength in internecine struggle. On many vital international issues we are successfully cooperating with the independent countries of Asia, Africa and Latin America. We shall continue to promote this co-operation in the interests of progress and peace.

Comrades, an important development of the past few years has been the emergence of a number of newly-free countries on the road of progressive social development. Experience has thereby confirmed the conclusion drawn by the 1960 Moscow Meeting of Communist and Workers' Parties, and recorded in its Statement: the masses "are beginning to see that the best way to abolish age-old backwardness and improve their living standard is that of non-capitalist development. Only in this way can the peoples free themselves from exploitation, poverty and hunger".

Major social reforms have been carried out in such countries as the United Arab Republic, Algeria, Mali, Guinea, the Congo (Brazzaville) and Burma. Foreign monopolies are being driven out. Feudal estates are being confiscated and capitalist enterprises nationalised. The state sector in the economy is being enlarged, industrialisation implemented and broad social legislation adopted in the interests of the people. It goes without saying that the form and scale of these processes differ in the different countries. The revolutionary creative work of the peoples who have proclaimed socialism as their objective is introducing features of its own into the forms of the movement towards social progress.

We have established close, friendly relations with the young countries steering a course towards socialism. Naturally, the further these countries move towards the objective they have chosen the more versatile, profound and stable our relations with them will become. The relations between the CPSU and the revolutionary democratic parties of these countries are likewise developing.

The achievements scored by the newly-free countries that have taken the road of social progress is evoking the special hatred of the imperialists, who are spinning a web of conspiracies against them. Recent developments show that the reactionary forces have become more active, particularly in the African continent. Imperialist plots have been exposed and thwarted in a number of African countries. In face of the intrigues and plots of the imperialists and the conspiracies of the agents bribed by them, the liberated peoples are doing the only correct thing, they are resolutely repelling the enemies of freedom and progress and displaying increasing vigilance. The Communist Party and the entire Soviet people indignantly condemn the criminal policy of plots and subversion against independent countries.

Special mention must be made of the courageous liberation struggle of the peoples of Latin America.

Only recently the USA regarded Latin America as a reliable bastion. Today in every country in that continent the people are waging a struggle against US imperialism and its accomplices—the local military, feudal lords and bourgeoisie, who are linked up with foreign monopolies. This struggle is headed by the working class and the Communist Parties.

An important factor of our day is the consolidation of the unity of the Asian, African and Latin American peoples in the struggle against imperialism. The Afro-Asian solidarity movement, the movement for the unity of the Arab peoples and for the unity of the peoples of Africa, and the solidarity movement of the peoples of the three continents are in line with the vital interests of these peoples and we actively and ardently support them.

The successes of the national liberation movement are inseparably bound up with the successes of world socialism and the international working class. The firm and unbreakable alliance of these great revolutionary forces is the guarantee of the final triumph of the cause of national and social liberation.

Struggle of the Soviet Union Against the
Aggressive Policy of Imperialism, for Peace
and World Security

The years that have elapsed since the 22nd Congress of the CPSU have witnessed a tense struggle between two opposing trends in the international arena: the peace-loving and the aggressive. . . The imperialists have brazenly interfered in the affairs of other countries and peoples, even going so far as to engage in armed intervention. As a result, there has been an exacerbation of world tension. The threat of war from the aggressive acts of the imperialists, particularly the US imperialists, has increased.

Under these conditions, the Party and the Soviet state have pursued a policy of resolutely rebuffing the forces of aggression, countering any further deterioration of the situation in the world and combatting the threat of a world war. . . .

We have always sided with peoples subjected to imperialist aggression and have rendered them political, economic and, when necessary, military aid; we have exposed the perfidious designs of the aggressors. The Soviet Union's vigorous efforts jointly with other peoples which cherish the cause of freedom and peace have time and again compelled the imperialists to retreat.

In speaking of mounting world tension and of the threat of a world war, special mention must be made of US imperialist aggression against Vietnam. In flagrant violation of the Geneva Agreements, the USA has piratically attacked the Democratic Republic of Vietnam and is waging a barbarous war against the people of South Vietnam. This imperialist power, which styles itself a champion of freedom and civilisation, is using almost all the known means of destruction and annihilation against a peace-loving country situated thousands of miles away from America, a country that has never harmed US interests. More than 200,000 US troops, US aircraft carriers, huge bombers, poison gases and napalm are being used against the heroic patriots of Vietnam. Irresponsible statements threatening to escalate military operations still further are being made in Washington. Recently the US State Department officially declared that there is a "programme" of destroying vegetation and crops in Vietnam with chemicals in order to deprive the Vietnamese of food sources. Such is the real face of US imperialism. Through its aggression in Vietnam the US has covered itself with shame which it will never live down.

But no matter what outrages the aggressors commit they can never break the will of the Vietnamese people who have risen in a sacred struggle for the freedom of their country, for their life and honour, for the right to order their own destiny. Their heroic, just struggle will go down in history as a splendid example of unyielding courage, staunchness and determination to achieve victory.

A powerful movement in support of Vietnam is mounting throughout the world. Moral and political isolation of the US aggressors is being intensified. The Vietnamese people enjoy the assistance of the Soviet Union and other socialist countries and the sympathy and support of the broad masses of all countries. Indignation against the war in Vietnam is growing among the American people as well. All this is promoting the best internationalist traditions of the world working class.

The Soviet Union and the peace-loving peoples of the whole world demand that the USA stop its aggression against Vietnam and withdraw all interventionist troops from that country. Continuation of this aggression, which the American military are seeking to extend to other Southeast Asian countries, is fraught with the most dangerous consequences to world peace.

We categorically declare that if the aggressors escalate the shameful war against the Vietnamese people they will have to contend with mounting support for Vietnam from the Soviet Union and other socialist friends and brothers. The Vietnamese people will be the masters of their country and nobody will ever extinguish the torch of socialism, which has been raised on high by the Democratic Republic of Vietnam.

As a consequence of US aggression in Vietnam and other aggressive acts of American imperialism our relations with the United States of America have deteriorated. The US ruling circles are to blame for this.

The USSR is prepared to live in peace with all countries, but it will not reconcile itself to imperialist piracy with regard to other peoples. We have repeatedly declared that we are prepared to develop our relations with the USA, and our stand in this has not changed. But for these relations to develop the USA must drop its policy of aggression. Good fruit of peaceful co-operation cannot be grown on the poisonous soil of aggression and violence. Our Party and our Government categorically reject the absurd standpoint that the great powers can develop their relations at the expense of the interests of other countries and peoples. All countries, big and small, have the same right to respect of their sovereignty, independence and territorial integrity. And nobody has the liberty to violate this right.

Comrades, the Soviet Union is vitally interested in ensuring European security. Today West-German imperialism is the USA's chief ally in Europe in aggravating world tension. West Germany is increasingly becoming a seat of the war danger where revenge-seeking passions are running high. West Germany already has a large army in which officers of the nazi Wehrmacht form the backbone. Many leading posts in the Government are occupied by former nazis and even war criminals. The policy pursued by the Federal Republic of Germany is being increasingly determined by the same monopolies that brought Hitler to power.

The Rhineland politicians fancy that once they get the atomic bomb frontier posts will topple and they will be able to achieve their cherished desire of recarving the map of Europe and taking revenge for defeat in the Second World War.

One of the most ominous factors endangering peace is the bilateral military alliance that is taking shape between the ruling circles of the USA and the FRG. This factor remains an object of our unflagging attention.

US and West-German imperialism are a peculiar sort of partners. Each wants to make use of the other for his own designs. Both seek to aggravate tension in Europe—each in accordance with his own considerations. The West-German militarists entertain the hope—an unrealisable hope, of course—that this will enable them to carry out their revenge-seeking plans. The USA, for its part, wants some pretext to enable it, more than 20 years after the war, to continue keeping its troops and war bases in Europe and thereby have the means of directly influencing the economy and policy of the West-European countries.

The Washington rulers count on West Germany continuing faithfully to serve the interests of the US imperialists in Europe, and if necessary, on pushing the West Germans into the inferno of war first. In the meantime, Bonn is hoping to involve the USA and its other NATO partners more deeply in its revenge-seeking plans and thereby secure a revision of the results of the Second World War in its favour. It is not difficult to see that all these designs are spearheaded against the Soviet Union and other socialist countries, against peace and security in Europe and the whole world.

The threat stemming from the aspirations of the West-German revenge-seekers is well appreciated by the peoples of Europe. In the course of half a century many European countries have twice been the victims of German aggression. Like us, the peoples of eight socialist countries know only too well the predatory ways of the German militarists. The burden of German occupation has been experienced by most of the West-European peoples. Today, therefore, the struggle against the threat of another war is the vital affair of all European peoples. Even in West Germany itself more and more people are protesting against the bellicose policy of the Bonn rulers.

* * *

The balance of forces in Europe today is not at all what it was like on the eve of the Second World War. Nobody will succeed in changing the present frontiers of the European countries. Even by climbing on the shoulders of their US ally, the West-German imperialists will not become taller. They will only hurt themselves more when they fall. The aggressors are now opposed by such a mighty, invincible force that if they unleash war it will bring them nothing but destruction.

* * *

We will never agree to, nor reconcile ourselves to the West-German militarists obtaining nuclear weapons. If, in spite of everything this does happen, the necessary measures will be taken. The responsibility will devolve wholly on the ruling circles of the FRG and on those who encourage them. Nobody has the right to forget that after the defeat of the nazi aggressors, the participants in the anti-Hitler coalition—the Soviet Union, the USA, Britain and France—solemnly pledged themselves under the Potsdam Agreement to do everything necessary to prevent Germany from ever again threatening her neighbours, and to preserve peace throughout the world. The Soviet Union will always honour this commitment.

We highly value the fact that our friend and ally, the German Democratic Republic, the first socialist state of the German working people, is vigilantly defending peace in the heart of Europe. It has implemented in practice the peace-loving and democratic principles of the Potsdam Agreement and is consistently pursuing a policy of peace and advocating the strengthening of security in Europe.

As a whole, comrades, the positions of the socialist community in Europe are now firm and reliable. This is an important factor helping to consolidate socialism throughout the world and ensuring the security of all peoples.

As a counterbalance to the bellicose and the revenge-seeking policy of US and West-German imperialism in Europe the Soviet Union is consistently advocating the strengthening of European security and peaceful, mutually advantageous co-operation among all European states.

We profoundly believe that the conclusion drawn by the international communist movement that it is possible to curb the aggressor and avert another world war remains valid. But to make this possibility real the broad masses must participate in the struggle; there must be vigorous, ever-mounting action on the part of all the peace forces; the peace movement, trade unions, women's associations, youth leagues and other mass democratic organizations must redouble their activity.

The socialist countries play a special role in the defence of peace. We are well aware of this, and for that reason the CPSU shows tireless concern for strengthening our country's defensive might and consolidating our military alliance with other socialist countries. The CPSU sees its duty in keeping the Soviet people in a state of unceasing vigilance with regard to the intrigues of the enemies of peace and does everything to prevent the aggressors, if they try to violate peace, from ever taking us by surprise and to make certain that retaliation overtakes them inexorably and promptly.

Comrades, while exposing the aggressive policy of imperialism we are consistently and unswervingly pursuing a policy of peaceful coexistence of states with different social systems. This means that while regarding the coexistence of states with different social systems as a form of the class struggle between socialism and capitalism the Soviet Union consistently advocates normal, peaceful relations with capitalist countries and a settlement of controversial interstate issues by negotiation, not by war. The Soviet Union firmly stands for non-interference in the internal affairs of other countries, for respect of their sovereign rights and the inviolability of their territories.

It goes without saying that there can be no peaceful coexistence where matters concern the internal processes of the class and national liberation struggle in the capitalist countries or in the colonies. Peaceful coexistence is not applicable to the relations between oppressors and the oppressed, between colonialists and the victims of colonial oppression.

As regards state relations of the USSR with capitalist countries we want these relations to be not only peaceful, but also to include the broadest mutually advantageous contacts in the economic, scientific and cultural fields.

At this Congress we can note with satisfaction that our peace-loving policy has had notable success in the period under review. The Soviet Union has good relations with most countries.

The USSR has always attached great importance to relations with neighbouring countries and we are pleased to note that our good-neighbourly policy has yielded beneficial results. Our relations with Finland and Afghanistan are characterised by trust, friendship and co-operation. Normal relations are taking shape with the Scandinavian countries, although it cannot be said, of course, that there are no obstacles to their further development. The Soviet people welcome the certain turn for the better that has taken place in recent years in the Soviet Union's relations with Turkey and Iran.

The CC CPSU and the Soviet Government have always paid great attention to improving relations with such major Asian countries as India and Pakistan, which can virtually be considered our neighbours as well.

The Tashkent meeting of the leaders of India and Pakistan with the participation of the Soviet Prime Minister in conformity with the Soviet Government's proposal was an event of world-wide significance. The very fact that this meeting was held, the results achieved by it and the positive assessment of these results by world opinion speak eloquently of the great trust that the peoples have for the peace-loving foreign policy of the Soviet Union.

The Soviet Union supports Cambodia, a country friendly to us, in her just struggle to preserve and strengthen her independence, neutrality and territorial integrity.

There has been a considerable improvement in our relations with France. This is a positive development stemming from a community of interests in a number of key international issues, and from long-standing traditions of friendship between our peoples. Further development of Soviet-French relations may serve as an important element in strengthening European security.

In recent years our relations, particularly in the economic field, with such a major European country as Italy have begun to improve. We are prepared to develop these relations.

An activisation of Soviet-British relations would undoubtedly be useful. The future will show how far British foreign policy makes this activisation possible.

We can note that lately there has been a certain advance in our relations with Japan with whom we are developing mutually advantageous economic ties. But we cannot help taking into account the fact that there are US troops and war bases on Japanese territory in the immediate proximity of Soviet frontiers. Recently Japan and the South Korean Government, a puppet of Washington, have signed a militarist treaty which we emphatically condemn. All this, of course, hampers the development of our relations with Japan.

The dismantling of foreign military bases on alien territory and the withdrawal of foreign troops from such territory have been and remain a major international issue. The imperialist powers, primarily the United States of America, have established numerous military bases scattered throughout the world and have stationed contingents of their armed forces on the territories of other countries. These bases and armed forces are being used to further interests alien to peace; they are being used as a means of bringing pressure to bear on peace-loving countries, and frequently for open armed interference in their internal affairs. The Soviet Union considers that it is high time to end this situation which threatens the peace and security of countries, high time to dismantle military bases on foreign territory and withdraw foreign armed forces from this territory. We shall continue to pursue a policy aimed at achieving this purpose in the interests of strengthening world peace and security.

In furtherance of the vital interests not only of the Soviet people but also of the broadest masses in all countries the Soviet Union is waging a consistent struggle to slow down and stop the arms race started by imperialists, to reach agreement on practical steps towards general and complete disarmament. Soviet policy on these issues enjoys the understanding and support of many countries.

In the period under review the USSR had continued to take an active part in the work of the United Nations. The admittance of many newly-free countries to UN membership has substantially changed the situation in that organisation, and the change has not been in favour of the imperialists. In the UN the Soviet Union undeviatingly strives to facilitate the unity of countries opposing aggression and thereby enhance the role played by the UN in the struggle for universal peace and the independence of the peoples. On the initiative of the Soviet Union the UN General Assembly at its latest session adopted important resolutions against interference in the internal affairs of countries and against the proliferation of nuclear weapons. We shall continue to regard the UN as an arena of active political struggle against aggression, for peace and the security of all peoples.

The Communist Party of the Soviet Union considers that at this stage in the struggle for an improvement of the international situation, and for the consolidation of peace and the development of peaceful co-operation among nations it would be most important to achieve the following:

To put an end to US aggression in Vietnam, withdraw all US and other foreign troops from South Vietnam and enable the Vietnamese people to decide their internal affairs by themselves; accept the position set forth by the Government of the Democratic Republic of Vietnam and the National Liberation Front of South Vietnam as a basis for the settlement of the Vietnam problem.

To ensure strict adherence to the principle of non-interference in the internal affairs of states.

To conclude an international treaty on the non-proliferation of nuclear weapons; completely remove the question of the nuclear armament of the [Federal Republic of Germany] or of giving it access to nuclear weapons in any form; implement the aspiration of the peoples for setting up nuclear-free zones in various parts of the world; secure a solemn obligation on the part of the nuclear powers to refrain from using nuclear weapons first; reach an agreement on the banning of underground nuclear tests—implementation of these steps aimed against the threat of a nuclear war would open the road for a further advance towards the complete banning and destruction of nuclear weapons.

To initiate talks on European security; discuss the proposals of socialist and other European countries for a relaxation of military tension and a reduction of armaments in Europe and the development of peaceful, mutually advantageous relations between all European countries; convene an appropriate international conference for this purpose; continue to look for ways to a peaceful settlement of the German problem—one of the cardinal problems of European security—so that on the basis of recognition of the now existing borders of the European countries, including those of the two German states, the survivals of the Second World War in Europe can be completely eliminated.

Such are our proposals. Many of them have been put forward earlier. Naturally, we do not regard them as all-embracing and are prepared to give our closest attention to all other proposals aimed at improving the international situation and strengthening peace.

Comrades, we have every reason to declare that our country's international position is stable. The peace-loving foreign policy of the Communist Party and the Soviet Government reliably serves the interests of communist construction and the cause of preserving and strengthening world peace and security. The CPSU will continue to pursue this tested course.

The quicker our country moves forward in building [a] new society the more successfully will our international tasks be resolved. By the will of history the Land of Soviets was the first in the world to raise the banner of communist construction. The Soviet people led by their Leninist Communist Party will continue with honour to hold aloft this great, invincible banner.

BREZHNEV

Report to the Karlovy Vary Conference
April 24, 1967

Introduction Brezhnev's speech, which is largely devoted to European security, was delivered when the Soviet Union's prospects were at a high point in the post-Khrushchev period. "The great cultural revolution" had been working its destructive effects in Communist China for almost a year, increasing its diplomatic isolation and weakening its challenge to the USSR. The United States had fallen deeper into the mire of Vietnam. While the USSR was having its own difficulties in East Europe—particularly with Rumania—they still seemed manageable, or at least tolerable. The NATO countries, no longer believing the USSR to be aggressive, had begun to turn their attention away from the problem of security against the Soviet threat in Europe. As a result, NATO's cohesiveness had continued to decline.

Soon after Brezhnev gave this speech the outlook for the USSR began to darken. Israel's sudden defeat of Arab military forces in June, 1967 was a setback for the USSR, which had supplied the Arab armies. Still further ahead, in 1968, lay the crisis of Soviet relations with

Czechoslovakia. In April 1967, however, when the Conference met, the international situation looked quite good.

Brezhnev lists the gains for the USSR from the U.S. involvement in Vietnam: one-half million U.S. soldiers "tied up" in Southeast Asia; a decline in U.S. prestige; hatred for the United States in Asia; dissent from U.S. Vietnam policy by some NATO allies. Capitalism in West Europe, having been revived with American support, is trying to establish itself as "a force independent of the United States." While the *intention* is to strengthen capitalism in Europe—which has not yet overcome its fundamental weakness—the *effect* has been to accentuate the division within world capital and to open new opportunities for the workers' movement. This struggle, waged in Europe, has favorable consequences in Vietnam and elsewhere.

Any discussion of European security from Moscow's viewpoint inevitably focuses on the danger posed by West Germany. After repeating the standard arguments, Brezhnev touches on some sensitive themes. He says politicians in West Germany consider partnership with the United States necessary for their revanchist plans; he does not here assert, however, that the United States intends to support those plans. At the same time, the notion (frequently expressed in the West) that the USSR actually welcomes the U.S. presence in Europe—because this binds West Germany to the more moderate European policies of the United States—gets no support from Brezhnev. On the contrary, he says West German revanchist hopes are fed by the presence of United States forces in Europe. It seems not unreasonable to suppose that Moscow will fear West Germany only so long as there remains a danger that U.S. military force might be brought to bear in support of West Germany's particular national objectives. Moscow may be confident that once U.S. troops were removed from Europe, it could readily cope with any threat from West Germany.

Fifty years after the Revolution, Brezhnev continues to express a certain defensiveness about Moscow's failure to support the world Communist movement more vigorously, and to take greater risks on its behalf. He answers this charge (one that is central in Peking's attacks on the Soviet leadership) with the assertion that international tension is bad for the Communist movement; *détente,* on the other hand, has enabled West European Communist parties to increase their influence. This answer would hardly have satisfied Lenin! Nevertheless, the Soviet leaders remained good Bolsheviks in their willingness to incur the consequences of heightened tension when necessary, as they were to show in August, 1968, with the invasion of Czechoslovakia.

The Situation in the World and
The Struggle for European Security

... At their 1957 and 1960 conferences, Communists drew important conclusions about the basic tendencies of modern world development. The intervening period has confirmed the correctness of these conclusions.

We are not over-simplifying in the least our evaluation of the international situation. We state with conviction that during the years since the Moscow conferences detachments of the revolutionary movement have taken up new positions and continue their advance, though perhaps not as rapidly as we would like. The world socialist revolution is a complex process in the progress of which a stubborn struggle is developing, and difficulties arise at certain stages.

Important and positive processes are taking place in the socialist system. The majority of socialist countries is experiencing deep transformations in the forms and methods of managing the national economy, striving to make more effective use of the internal possibilities of socialism and to master more fully the natural laws of the development of a socialist economy. The communist parties of the socialist countries devote increasing attention to improving socialist democracy, to further developing the political activity of the masses, and to drawing them into the administration of all aspects of social life; intensive and interesting research is proceeding everywhere in this field. The economic, political, and defense cooperation of the socialist states continues to improve and becomes increasingly regular and thorough. In many respects this cooperation is now being raised to a new and higher level.

Of course, evaluating the situation in the world socialist system, we cannot ignore in its recent development the well-known position of the leadership of China and the violation of the cooperation of the CCP and the CPR with other fraternal parties and socialist countries. Discussion of this problem is not included on the agenda of our conference, but the problem exists nonetheless and has a negative influence on the communist and the entire liberation movement.

The national liberation movement continues to broaden and deepen. In the sixties, the Algerian revolution was victorious, the positions of the democratic forces in the UAR were strengthened, Syria took the path of social progress, and the foundations of progressive socio-economic development were laid in a number of countries of the so-called third world.

On this path, conflicts cannot be avoided, as evidenced, in particular, by the events in Ghana and Indonesia. Naturally, after former colonies and semicolonies have achieved national independence, indigenous reactionary elements, relying on support of foreign imperialists, attempt to push these states on to the path of capitalist development and cooperation with the forces of international reaction. But the forces of progress, and primarily communists, are called upon to act with even greater persistence and flexibility.

The wave of the revolutionary movement against U.S. imperialism and local reaction is ever growing in the Latin American countries. Important changes are taking place in the workers movement in the developed capitalist countries. Because of the active work of the communist and workers parties, and the actions of the internal natural laws of capitalism, antimonopolist feelings are increasing in the broad strata of the working people of these countries; a clear move to the left by the popular masses is observed.

This creates fresh opportunities in the struggle for the unity of the working class and all progressive forces and in the struggle for socialism. Of course, the comrades from West Europe present at this conference know all these processes and problems much better and we shall therefore limit ourselves to a general statement on the shifts that have been noted.

The leaders of imperialism are aware of the weakening of their positions; they see the strength of the revolutionary detachments opposing imperialism. In recent years, Western leaders have exerted vast efforts to improve their class tactics and strategy in this new situation, both on the national and the international plane, and to find new ways and means to combat world socialism and the revolutionary and liberation movement.

Imperialism counts more and more on the disunity of socialist states and on a split in the liberation movements.

At this time, the most malignant expression of the predatory nature of imperialism, and of its main force, American imperialism, is the U.S. aggression in Vietnam. The U.S. imperialists wage a shameful and hopeless war there. They will never conquer a a people who have fought unsparingly for their freedom and independence for over 20 years. The patriots of Vietnam, relying on varied aid from the socialist countries and support from the progressive forces of the world, successfully resist the interventionists. In so doing, they also strike telling blows at the positions of U.S. imperialism. This is not only because about one-half million U.S. soldiers, a large navy, and a large proportion of the U.S. Air Force are tied up in the southeast Asia region. It is also a fact that the aggression in Vietnam has resulted in a most profound undermining of U.S. prestige and political positions throughout the world.

The aggression in Vietnam has aroused millions upon millions of people against the United States. It builds up hatred for the U.S. interventionists in the minds of Asian people. This is a factor with which the U.S. leaders will have to deal for many years. The U.S. dirty war in Vietnam has also intensified the contradictions in the camp of the U.S. allies; many of them want nothing to do with it.

It is well known that the socialist countries, including the Soviet Union, actively help fighting Vietnam with political, economic, and military support. It could not be otherwise, for imperialist aggression is taking place against a socialist country, the DRV. I can assure you, comrades, that we Soviet communists will continue to fulfill our international duty with regard to struggling Vietnam and render it the necessary help.

The war in Vietnam today constitutes the most serious threat to general peace. On all continents vast masses of people of different classes, belief, and convictions demand that the United States stop its bombings of the DRV and cease aggression in Vietnam. This concerns not least of all Europe itself, where the demonstrations against U.S. aggression are becoming increasingly inflamed. I think we all agree that the struggle in this sector at the same time contributes to the cause of European security.

Finally, the events in Vietnam remind us again of how vital is the task of strengthening the unity of the world communist movement. It is clear that if it were possible to support Vietnam in agreement with and jointly with China, the task of ending U.S. aggression would be considerably eased. Allow me to repeat here what we have already stated at the SED congress a few days ago: the CPSU Central Committee and the Soviet Government are prepared to implement unity of action with China in the planning and practical implementation of assistance to struggling Vietnam. We are prepared for such unity of action on the widest possible scale.

Those, comrades, are some of the international factors which must be taken into account when discussing the question of European security.

In evaluating the present European situation, we proceed first of all from the changes which have taken place here since World War II. One of the most important sociopolitical factors of the postwar period is that precisely in Europe—that is, in that part of the world where capitalism was born and where it turned into a social system which for centuries determined the course of all world development—capitalism's positions have been weakened to a great degree.

This is manifest in the collapse of capitalism and the victory of socialist revolutions in eight states of East and Central Europe. This is also manifest in the fact that the bourgeoisie has been able to retain its domination over the remaining part of Europe to a considerable degree only by relying on the military, political, and economic help of the United States.

West European capitalism, relying on American support and taking advantage of the opportunities presented by the association of the forces of the monopolies and the authority of the state, as well as on the achievements of the scientific-technical revolution, and by extensively resorting to maneuvers in the field of social relations and political life, was later able to get out of the difficult crisis in which it found itself immediately following World War II. Of course, this does not at all signify the restoration of the previous political might of European capital. Its fundamental weakness remains.

The new correlation of sociopolitical forces on the continent has found its reflection in the foreign policy of the main capitalist powers of Europe. The chief detachments of European capitalism, whose interests are frequently in sharp contradiction, are striving by every means to avoid methods and forms of struggle with one another which might threaten the foundations of capitalism with new shocks.

Having restored their economic potential, certain capitalist countries in Europe are now striving to pursue a more and more independent policy. No small part in this is played by the intensifying contradictions between the interests of the European and American magnates. In place of pro-American policy concepts, new concepts which aim at transforming capitalist Europe into a force independent of the United States and capable of playing an independent role in the world arena are increasingly blazing a path for themselves.

To us communists, it is quite clear that such plans are called upon to strengthen European capitalism and its international positions. But something else is obvious, too; these plans simultaneously shake the united front of world capital, which opens up new opportunities for the European and world workers movement for the development of the struggle for peace and security in Europe and throughout the world.

Comrades, the draft statement which our conference is discussing stresses that the problem of Europe is not merely a regional problem and is not an isolated internal affair of the European peoples alone. On what is this conclusion based? We cannot forget that it was precisely in Europe that the conflagration of world war twice started, and that even today there exists on this continent one of the most serious hotbeds of international tension. If a new war started in Europe it could become thermonuclear and envelop the whole world. European security is an important condition for preventing a nuclear clash.

But this is not all. Even today the struggle for peace in Europe pins down the aggressive forces of the imperialists to a certain extent and prevents them from taking part in suppressing the liberation movement in other parts of the world. It is a fact, comrades, that despite stubborn efforts the United States has not managed to attract its NATO European allies into the Vietnam adventure, as occurred during the Korean War. This is a result of the struggle of the communist parties, of the working class of the whole world, and of all peace-loving forces.

To tie down the forces of imperialism in Europe and thwart their aggressive plans is not to simply narrow the circle of action of imperialism's aggressive policy, although this is important in itself, but is also to deal it a defeat which would have effects everywhere. This would also be a real help to the liberation struggle of the peoples on all other continents.

I believe, comrades, that I express the general opinion when I say that in displaying concern for the interests of European security we also fulfill our international duty to the peoples of the whole world!

American and West German Imperialism, The Main Threat to European Peace

It might be asked: Why do we sharply pose the question of military danger in Europe today? Is the threat so serious? Yes, comrades, there are grounds for this. We do not want to exaggerate the danger of war, but neither do we wish to underestimate it.

Where and in what do we see the threat to European security today?

We answer: The threat to peace in Europe is borne by the aggressive forces of American and West German imperialism. What is the increasingly close partnership of these forces built upon? For American imperialism, collusion with the ruling circles of the Federal German Republic is the chief means, convenient for the United States and in essence not very expensive, of preserving its military-strategic positions in Europe. And this gives the United States significant levers for pressuring the policy and economics of the West European countries. As far as West German politicians are concerned, in their calculations partnership with the United States opens up for them real opportunities for implementing revanchist plans.

The aggressive policy of German imperialism has brought vast calamities to many European countries. This is well known not only by the peoples of the Soviet Union but also by the peoples of Poland, Yugoslavia, Czechoslovakia, France, Britain, Belgium, Holland, Norway, Denmark, and other European states.

The Soviet people have not forgotten and never will forget that 20 million Soviet citizens gave their lives in the name of the victory over fascism. We had to develop vast efforts to heal the wounds of war, to restore thousands of destroyed towns and villages.

The Soviet people, engaged in peaceful creative labor today, will not let their achievements and the achievements of other fraternal socialist countries be threatened again. We recall the lessons of the war today not because we seek atonement for the past, but because we are concerned about the future. The vital interests of all peoples of Europe demand that aggression by German imperialism—on its own or in alliance with anybody else—be excluded forever.

The foundations of Europe's postwar structure were defined by the Potsdam agreement. Its main demand is for eradication of militarism and nazism so that Germany shall never again threaten its neighbors and world peace. This demand has force now and in the future.

The Potsdam principles have been fully implemented in the GDR. But they are ignored in the Federal German Republic, where German militarism is alive and where German nazism, too, is being galvanized. The fact that the bacillus of nazism was not destroyed in West Germany, as demanded by the Potsdam agreement, is news to no one. But now, when the neo-Nazis have come openly into the political arena, the matter looks more serious.

The danger grows especially in connection with the fact that Federal German ruling circles have made revanchist demands the keystone of their official state policy. It is not some irresponsible bawlers and extremists from the soldiers unions or refugee organizations but the Government of West Germany which makes absurd claims about the right to speak on behalf of the whole German people, which refuses to recognize existing borders in Europe, which makes claims on West Berlin, and which seeks loopholes for the nuclear armament of the Federal German Republic.

If one adds to all this the fact that the Bonn authorities keep the Communist Party under prohibition and suppress other progressive forces, then a whole raft of political and ideological means of preparing revenge can be seen to be at hand. The present Federal Government speaks willingly about its love of peace. But it is characteristic that through this it seeks all sorts of elastic formulas in order to avoid giving up revenge-seeking aims. Thus, how can one believe in the sincerity of the peace-loving statements of the Federal German ruling circles? Is it not clear that in this way the new government only wants to delude European public opinion in order to escape its isolation and thus insure firmer positions for achieving its plans?

The Soviet Union does not at all believe that all European peoples should shun West Germany; the path to international cooperation with equal rights, to participation in European affairs, is open to it as to all other states. We know that there are in the German Federal Republic considerable forces which oppose the aggressive and reactionary policy of West German imperialism. The miners of the Ruhr, Stuttgart steelworkers, and Mannheim chemical workers have shown in the class clashes that a movement against militarism and fascism is growing in West Germany itself. The mass peace marches and meetings of protest against the war in Vietnam show that peace is as dear to the West German working people as to all peoples.

For our part, we have stated more than once and state again: The Soviet Union is not against improving relations with the Federal Republic and is ready to do everything necessary to this end. If the present Federal Government displays sobriety in its approach to the existing situation in Europe, if it does not encroach upon the interests of other states and people, and demonstrates by deeds its desire to strengthen peace on our continent, then we shall be among those who support such a course.

But for us, as for all to whom peace and security of the peoples are dear, there has not been and cannot be any compromise at the expense of the peace and security of the peoples. The longer the German Federal Republic leaders hang on to revanchist doctrines, the stronger will be the rebuff by the Soviet Union and all the European peoples.

Facts show that the military threat which today stems from German imperialism is an indisputable reality. In the past 10 years the German Federal Republic has created one of the largest armies in West Europe, numbering almost half a million troops, and a sufficient quantity of command cadres to enable numerous armed forces to be mobilized in a short period, as was done on the eve of World War II.

The West German imperialists, of course, do not have the power to achieve their revanchist aims. The Soviet Union and other socialist countries have sufficient military might to strike a crushing blow at an aggressor who would dare start a war. But the revanchists could plunge the European countries, and eventually the whole world, into the horrors of another war, and this danger must be clearly recognized.

The military presence of the United States in Europe encourages West German militarism and increases the threat to peace in Europe. Hundreds of thousands of U.S. troops on European soil, U.S. military basis, U.S. aircraft carriers and atomic submarines patrolling the seas around the continent, U.S. bombers flying in European skies with their nuclear loads—all this creates a constant threat to the security of the peoples of Europe.

* * *

We do not hide the fact that the buildup of military efforts by the NATO countries forces the Soviet Union and the other socialist countries to raise their level of military preparedness and to devote considerable sums to defense needs.

* * *

In the past few years, plans for the so-called "modernization" of NATO have been urgently proposed, artificial arguments have been raked up to save this "holy alliance" of U.S. and European reaction at any price. This even went as far as to assert that NATO is capable of playing a positive role in developing contacts between West and East. It is difficult to conceive a more absurd argument! . . .

Experience shows that the process of expanding political, trade-economic, and cultural relations between the European socialist and capitalist countries proceeds faster when our Western partners put their national interests first and act directly contrary to the recommendations of the NATO Council, ignoring the discriminatory measures it has introduced in relations with the socialist countries.

* * *

The Way to Security in Europe

In the present international situation, there are real possibilities for implementing these measures. We are convinced that a Europe can and must be created in which security for each state and each people would at the same time be security for all. Our conviction in this rests not only on an understanding of the deepest desires of the European people, but also on a realistic evaluation of the forces opposing the policy of military adventures and preparations for aggression.

The community of socialist states is a very important factor in postwar Europe. The strength of their foreign policy rests on the fact that its basic aims coincide with the vital interests of the broad popular masses of all the countries of our continent.

* * *

A very important prerequisite for security in Europe is recognition of the existence of two German states with different social systems. The shortsighted policy of "nonrecognition" of the GDR, which in effect serves only the interests of the West German revanchists, conflicts irreconcilably with European reality and serves as a serious source of international tension. The GDR has been living and flourishing for almost two decades, and the Soviet Union and the other socialist countries of Europe consider the strengthening of the GDR's international position as an important aim of their policy.

In the age of the atom and rockets, new problems have arisen connected with insuring European security. The people of Europe can well imagine what the appearance of nuclear weapons would mean in the hands of a state advocating the revision of European frontiers. Therefore, the inadmissability of further proliferation of nuclear weapons is not only a general world problem but also one of the key questions of European security.

Negotiations are now in progress to conclude an international treaty on the nonproliferation of nuclear weapons. The Soviet Union and the other socialist countries are striving to successfully conclude this work to have a nonproliferation treaty open for signing by all states of the world.

In weighing the possibilities opened up by the development of events in Europe, we cannot ignore the fact that in two years the governments of the NATO countries will have to decide whether NATO is to be extended or not. In our opinion, it is quite correct that communists and all progressive forces should try to use this circumstance to develop still more widely the struggle against the preservation of this aggressive bloc.

* * *

For several countries, including those of northern Europe, neutrality could be an alternative to participation in military-political groupings of powers. The CPSU thinks that much depends on the initiative of the neutral states and on their good services in the cause of strengthening European peace. The Soviet Union would be ready to welcome initiatives serving this end.

Overcoming the division of the world and Europe into military blocs or alliances is part of the general struggle of the peoples to limit and completely end the arms race, to check militarism, and to clean the political atmosphere in Europe and throughout the world. From this point of view, there would be considerable significance in partial measures to reduce military tension in Europe, from the establishment of nuclear-free zones in separate regions of the continent to the liquidation of foreign military bases.

There is no justification whatever for the constant presence of the U.S. fleet in waters washing the shores of southern Europe. One would like to ask: What are the grounds, 20 years after the end of World War II, for the U.S. Sixth Fleet to cruise the Mediterranean and to use military bases, ports, and supply bases in a number of Mediterranean countries? This poses a serious threat to the independence of all coastal countries. The time has come to demand the complete withdrawal of the U.S. Sixth Fleet from the Mediterranean.

In Europe there are not only the U.S. military bases but also bases of a different kind. They are the subversive espionage and sabotage centers, the broadcasting stations, and various organizations which have been created by the Americans in the German Federal Republic and other West European countries and which engage in slanderous propaganda directed against the socialist countries. The time has come to question the activities of all venomous breeding grounds on European soil which poison relations. The development of bilateral relations between European nations could be an important prerequisite for the strengthening of European security. The present trend toward a detente in Europe is very much the result of the improvement of bilateral relations between East and West European countries. . . . The Soviet Union is ready to exchange opinions on the preparation of bilateral agreements and treaties with the governments of the European countries which, on their part, wish to develop their relations with our country.

There is yet another important and promising trend in the efforts of European peoples and states which has a direct bearing on the solution of tasks of consolidating European peace. This is cooperation in the field of economy, science, and technology, as well as culture, on both a bilateral and an all-European basis.

The foundations for this have already been laid. It is our opinion, however, that this is only the beginning. The developing scientific and technological revolution, the increasing efforts to consolidate national independence and liberation from the dollar diktat, suggest to the European states many ways and projects in a great variety of fields—from the construction of a gas pipeline crossing the continent to the introduction of a unified color television system for all Europe.

The field of the peaceful use of atomic energy also arouses interest in many countries. We are willing to agree with other European countries on cooperation in conducting nuclear research and the use of atomic energy for peaceful purposes. The realization of this proposal will make it possible for states which relinquished their right to the manufacture and acquisition of nuclear weapons to participate in all the advantages offered mankind by the peaceful energy from the split atom.

Another important field for cooperation on an all-European basis is the joint work on such problems as the purification of European rivers and seas, the unification of efforts of countries in the struggle against such diseases as cancer, cardiovascular diseases, and so on. . . .

The Peoples—Decisive Force in the Struggle for European Security

. . . The split in the working class movement in West Europe has not yet been overcome; along with the militant vanguard of the working class, the communists, there are also the Social Democrats who speak on behalf of the working class. It has already been said more than once that unity of action of communists and socialists could secure a drastic change in the entire political situation in West Europe; it could create a serious barrier to the course of the forces of reaction and aggression. It is for this reason that the CPSU highly appreciates the policy of fraternal parties which is directed toward overcoming the split of the working class. . . .

Nor can one fail to mention in this connection the Social Democratic Party of Germany, whose leaders have for many years refused to adopt an independent policy in questions of foreign policy and have followed in the wake of the CDU, the party of the German monopolies. Representatives of the German Social Democratic Party are now members of the government. They have acquired great possibilities for influencing the foreign political course of West Germany to benefit the cause of peace and the security of nations. Unfortunately, so far they do not appear to have undertaken anything serious in this direction.

* * *

All our parties are united by the common Marxist-Leninist ideology, by common ultimate aims. We know that the fraternal parties work under different conditions and therefore take different tactical steps, the result of the specific conditions of their work. But all this does not prevent our parties from cooperating closely, from drawing up agreed positions, from striving for unity of action in the struggle for the common end. And we are convinced that the solidarity of communists will continue to grow. In this respect, our conference is the best reply to those bourgeois politicians who maintain that communism has split along national lines.

It is our party's profound conviction that the necessary conditions for achieving, within a short period of time, the consolidation of our ranks by means of concerted joint efforts do exist. We maintain this view firmly and are doing everything to implement this idea, hand in hand with the other fraternal parties.

If this task is tackled with the energy and adherence to principles characteristic of Marxist-Leninists, differences can be overcome. Naturally, this will demand effort and good will of all parties, without exception. The duty of communists does not permit anyone to stand aside waiting for the time when unity will come by itself. He who does not understand this, who fails to do everything he can to strengthen our solidarity, takes upon himself a heavy responsibility in the face of history, in the face of the international working class. . . .

The problem of European security is not simply a foreign policy problem, but also a very important social problem. In putting forward this thesis, our party relies on practical experience accumulated in Europe in the postwar decades.

What does this experience teach? It teaches in particular that the "cold war" and the confrontation of military blocs, the atmosphere of military threats, seriously hamper the activity of revolutionary, democratic forces. In conditions of international tension in bourgeois countries the reactionary elements become active, the military raise their heads, antidemocratic tendencies and anticommunism are strengthened.

And conversely, the past few years have shown quite clearly that in conditions of slackened international tension the pointer of the political barometer moves left. Certain changes in relations between communists and social democrats in certain countries, a noticeable falling-off in anticommunist hysteria, and the increase in the influence of West European communist parties is most directly correlated with the reduction in tension which has taken place in Europe.

There has been continuous confirmation of one of the fundamental propositions of communist strategy: that the struggle for peace does not contradict the struggle for socialism. If it is true that the struggle for peace helps the struggle for socialism, then it is no less true that the struggle against imperialism and reaction and for democracy and social progress is an important condition for stabilizing peace and international security. Militarism and reaction are twins, and an improvement of the situation in Europe is inseparable from the determined struggle against fascist or semifascist regimes which still exist in several capitalist countries of Europe.

From this platform we once again declare our solidarity with the heroic struggle of the communists and democrats of Spain and Portugal. In our opinion, a vital task for the European workers movement is a struggle against the persecution of democratic and peace-loving forces in the German Federal Republic, primarily for a lifting of the ban on the German Communist Party.

* * *

BREZHNEV

Speech to the International Conference of Communist and Workers' Parties June 7, 1969

Introduction Steady deterioration in relations with Communist China led to intensified Soviet efforts to convene a Conference of Communist Parties. Opposition to such a meeting increased after the Soviet Army invaded Czechoslovakia in order to reverse that country's radical course of liberalization. With the passage of time, however, Czechoslovak resistance to the USSR waned and the Soviet leaders finally succeeded in getting most of the world's Communist Parties to attend. Brezhnev's speech to the Conference is in three parts: the first deals with the international situation, particularly the world of imperialism against which the Communist world is called upon to unite; the second deals with the Communist world, chiefly Soviet grievances against Mao's China: the third (little of which is printed here) deals with internal politics.

In assessing the "contradictions" between capitalist states, Brezhnev finds that they have lost something of their former intensity as imperialism has become preoccupied with the struggle against its chief enemy, the world socialist movement. On the other hand, within capitalist societies Brezhnev sees signs of a shift in favor of the revolutionary forces; the rising generation, in particular, "is in revolutionary ferment." In Asia and Africa, it is the peasantry which is a mighty revolutionary force. Brezhnev calls upon Communists to rally these allies of the working class to the struggle against imperialism.

In discussing the dangers to Communist unity, Brezhnev speaks of both the rightist danger of opportunism, exemplified by Czechoslovakia (although it is not named), and the "leftist" danger of adventurism, exemplified by Communist China. He acknowledges his concern at Peking's inroads in the world Communist movement. Peking's foreign policy is aimed more against the Soviet Union than against imperialism, and the Chinese press even speaks of preparing for war against the USSR. Brezhnev may have Peking in mind when he speaks of the developing need for a system of "collective security in Asia."

Presumably, this new analysis of the international situation had important implications for Soviet foreign policy, but this speech does not spell them out. Would the internal weakening of the West, and particularly of the United States, encourage the USSR to try to settle particular issues of the cold war on favorable terms, while concentrating its energies to deal with the challenge from Peking? Or would Moscow choose to apply new pressures at points where the West is vulnerable in order to demonstrate to the Communist world that it has not lost its revolutionary fervor? Perhaps Moscow had not yet settled upon a definite strategy, but was maintaining a flexible posture to deal with the kinds of unpleasant surprises (like the emergence of a radical reformist government in Czechoslovakia) and unexpected targets of opportunity (like the Castro revolution in Cuba) that had been so abundant in the 1960's.

Dear Comrades,

The principal item on the agenda of our [Conference] is the question of the tasks of the struggle against imperialism at the present stage and of unity of action of Communist and Workers' Parties and of all anti-imperialist forces. . . .

We are convinced, comrades, that our [Conference], at which most of the Communist Parties in the world are represented, will play a major role in stimulating the actions of the fighters against imperialism. It will contribute towards uniting the entire world front of the forces championing peace, democracy, national independence and socialism.

At the same time, we are confident that the work of this Conference and the joint struggle for the aims which it will chart will help to surmount the difficulties that have emerged in the communist movement and strengthen its unity on the principled foundation of Marxism-Leninism.

* * *

I. The Present International Situation and the Tasks of the Anti-Imperialist Struggle

Comrades, a little under nine years have passed since representatives of the Communist Parties of all continents last gathered in order to jointly map out the further course of their revolutionary struggle. This has been an extremely important and eventful period. To us Communists it has brought many successes and opened up further possibilities for achieving the great aims of our movement. At the same time, this period has brought serious problems and complications.

* * *

The peoples are making a stern claim on imperialism. Through its fault the vital problems that face mankind in acute form remain unresolved though they could be successfully settled already today. . . .

The growth of socialism's might, the abolition of colonial regimes and the pressure from the working class movement increasingly influence the inner processes and policies of imperialism. Many important features of modern imperialism may be explained by the fact that it is compelled to adapt itself to new conditions, to the conditions of struggle between the two systems.

First and foremost, we cannot afford to ignore the fact that the imperialism of our day still has a powerful and highly developed production mechanism. We cannot afford to ignore the fact that modern imperialism makes use also of the possibilities placed before it by the increasing fusion of the monopolies with the state apparatus. The programming and forecasting of production, state financing of technological progress and scientific research and steps aimed at achieving a certain restriction of market spontaneity in the interests of the biggest monopolies are becoming more and more widespread. In some countries this is leading to a certain enhancement of the efficacy of social production.

The economic, scientific and technological achievements of the socialist countries and the class struggle are compelling capitalism to make some concessions to the working people in the social sphere. It seeks to camouflage the rising level of exploitation of the working people. Monopoly capitalism thereby tries to avert social and economic upheavals fraught with the greatest danger to the bourgeois system.

To meet the challenge of socialism and strengthen their positions, the imperialists are combining their efforts on an international scale and taking recourse to various forms of economic integration. International monopoly associations are being set up with the support and participation of the bourgeois governments. Imperialist military and political alliances are becoming more active.

It goes without saying that today, despite all this, the ineradicable inter-imperialist contradictions remain a vital law governing capitalist society. These contradictions are made all the more acute by the circumstance that the reciprocal penetration of capital of these countries is intensifying and the interdependence of their national economies is increasing. The growth of contradictions between the imperialist powers finds its expression particularly in the weakening of aggressive military blocs, chiefly NATO.

As as whole, however, under conditions of the deepening general crisis of capitalism, a certain shift of the centre of gravity of imperialism's strategy is taking place in the world arena. The policies of imperialism are being increasingly determined by the class objectives of its general struggle against world socialism, the national-liberation revolution and the working class movement.

There is no doubt at all that imperialism will continue to look for new possibilities for prolonging its existence. We cannot ignore all this in our policy.

However, in speaking of these aspects of modern imperialism without underrating the strength and potentialities of our adversaries, we consider that neither must they be overrated. The deep-rooted, truly ineradicable inner contradictions undermining capitalism, chiefly the contradiction between labour and capital, are becoming more and more acute precisely in our day. Under the onslaught of the forces of socialism and democracy its positions in the world continue to grow weaker. Today, more fully than ever before, it is exposing itself as a system of social and national inequality, oppression and violence.

Massively socialising production and centralising its management, state-monopoly capitalism is deepening to bursting point the basic contradiciton of the bourgeois system, the contradiction between the social nature of production and the private mode of appropriation. The unnatural character of the situation in which production complexes, some of which serve more than one country, remain the private property of a handful of millionaires and billionaires is becoming increasingly evident to the peoples. The need for replacing capitalist by socialist relations of production is becoming ever more pressing.

The further imperialism goes in its attempts to adapt itself to the situation, the deeper become its inner social and economic antagonisms. The development of capitalist economy is marked by periodic recessions. The unevenness and one-sidedness of the development of individual countries is becoming more pronounced. All this cannot fail to engender serious difficulties within these countries and boost the growth of contradictions between them. This is shown by the constant [budgetary] deficit, the extremely acute outbursts of currency and financial crises, and the rising cost of living and inflation which in the 1960's have become a chronic disease in many capitalist countries. This disease is now frequently called a "creeping crisis".

* * *

The trend, intrinsic to imperialism, to abolish democratic freedoms and towards the fascisation of social and political life likewise harbours a tremendous threat to the peoples. Lenin had emphasised that reaction in all spheres is inherent in imperialism. In the 1960s a great deal of new convincing evidence of this has come to the fore.

The influence of the so-called military and industrial complex, i.e., the alliance of the largest monopolies with the military in the state apparatus is growing rapidly in the most developed capitalist states. This sinister alliance is increasingly pressuring the policy of many imperialist countries, making it still more reactionary and aggressive.

Where the exploiters find themselves unable to ensure the "order" required by them within the framework of bourgeois democracy, power is placed in the hands of openly terrorist regimes of the fascist type. There are many examples of this in our day. These regimes enjoy the financial and political support of the ruling circles of imperialist powers and of the largest monopolies.

* * *

One of imperialism's gravest threats to the peoples of the whole world is that of another world war.

Militarism has always been part and parcel of imperialism. But today it has acquired truly unparalleled proportions.... Suffice it to say that during the past five years US military expenditures amounted to nearly 350,000 million dollars or 20 per cent more than the total during the Second World War. Yet today the imperialist governments are drawing up new plans for building up armaments over whole decades in advance. Implementation of these plans will be a further heavy burden on the shoulders of the working people and increase the threat of another world war.

In the 1960s alone the USA and other imperialist states have launched armed attacks on Vietnam, Cuba, Panama, the Dominican Republic, the Arab countries—this list can be continued.

Combined with the stockpiling by the principal imperialist powers of weapons of mass annihilation, the policy of military gambles makes the imperialism of our day a constant menace to world peace, a threat to the lives of many millions of peoples, to the existence of whole nations. For that reason the struggle against imperialism is at the same time a struggle to deliver mankind from the threat of a world thermonuclear war. . . .

We hold that it would be a gross error to underrate the threat of war created by imperialism, above all US imperialism, the main force of world reaction. Millions of people must be made to understand what is being brought to mankind by the imperialist policy of unleashing wars, by the existence of aggressive blocs, by the policy aimed at revising existing state frontiers and by subversive activities against the socialist countries and the progressive regimes in the young national states. Our task is to see to it that the peoples not only appreciate the entire danger of this policy of the imperialists, but also multiply their efforts in the struggle to frustrate the aggressive designs of imperialism.

An extremely important form of the struggle against the threat of imperialism starting another world war is to organise a collective rebuff to the actions of the aggressors whenever they launch military adventures in any part of the world. The most striking example of this is the rebuff which US aggression has received in Vietnam.

* * *

In many ways the situation on the front of the anti-imperialist struggle is now determined by the course of the economic competition between socialism and capitalism. It may be said with gratification that in this sphere the socialist countries have scored many achievements. If we take, for instance, the member countries of the Council for Mutual Economic Assistance, we shall find that during the past ten years their national income has increased 93 per cent, while in the developed capitalist states the national income rose 63 per cent in the same period. Occupying 18 per cent of the world's territory and having only 10 per cent of the world's population, the CMEA countries now account for approximately one-third of the world's industrial product. On this foundation the people's standard of living is rising and increasing possibilities are opening for further successful economic, scientific and cultural development.

Parallel with this, economic co-operation between socialist countries is deepening and improving. In this sphere, as in the economic development of separate countries, the main accent today is on the qualitative aspect, on promoting the efficacy of social production and economic relations. Precisely this task is served by the economic reforms carried out in the European socialist countries. The same aim is pursued by the comprehensive long-term programme of further socialist integration, whose main directions were defined at a special CMEA session held recently in Moscow.

Much has to be done to achieve these purposes. But we are on the right path. . . .

* * *

The struggle of socialist countries against imperialism is not only economic, ideological and political. Imperialism, which has been and remains aggressive by nature, constantly enlarges its military machine and, as the events in Vietnam have shown, is prepared to put it to use. Strength, and not a little strength at that, is needed to defend the socialist gains. That is why, like other fraternal Parties, the CPSU ceaselessly concerns itself with ensuring the steady growth of the socialist states' defence might and with promoting close co-operation among them in the sphere of defence. This year important decisions have been taken to improve direction of the Warsaw Treaty armed forces. Co-ordination between the armed forces of the allied countries is systematically perfected and their combat skill is growing. The armies of the Warsaw Treaty and other socialist countries are being equipped with the most up-to-date armaments.

* *

Active relations between ruling Communist Parties are the nucleus, the cornerstone for promoting many-sided cooperation among socialist states.

In recent years the contacts between the leaderships of our Parties have become more operative, comradely and businesslike. Practically all problems of any essential significance which are of common interest are discussed collectively. Naturally, this helps to work out the most effective solutions, averts possible mistakes and deepens understanding between us.

Comrades, the achievements of world socialism are indisputable. At the same time, it is common knowledge that in the development of the world socialist system there are difficulties as well. Permit me to dwell on this question in somewhat greater detail.

Lenin emphasised that the road to socialism "will never be straight, it will be incredibly involved" (Collected Works, Vol. 27, p. 130). The CPSU, which had to be the first to blaze the road to socialism, knows from its own experience that this is not an easy road. After all, this road involves a fundamental break with many age-old traditions affecting the interests of all classes and social groups, the creation of an absolutely new type of social relations and the bringing up of people with a new psychology, a new world outlook. It involves, especially where relations between states are concerned, the surmounting of deep-rooted national strife and distrust.

Life itself and the practice of socialist transformations have shown that the seizure of political power by the proletariat and the socialisation of the means of production only create the objective prerequisites, the objective possibilities for resolving all these problems. The way these possibilities are realised in practice depends chiefly on the ruling Communist Parties, on their ability to resolve in a Marxist, in a Leninist way the complex problems posed by life. This ability does not come at once. It comes as a result of generalising the practical experience of the people, as a result of thought and an analysis of the traversed road and of possible prospects.

But it is not only a matter of the objective complexity of the very process of building socialism and new relations between socialist countries. Many of the difficulties which these countries encounter in the course of their development are closely linked with imperialism's constant striving to pressure the socialist world, to exert economic, political and ideological pressure on it. The attempts of the imperialists to undermine the positions of socialism from within and inject elements of discord and alienation into the relations between socialist countries do not cease for a single day. Wherever vigilance is blunted, where Communists underestimate the need for a class approach to social phenomena, the intrigues of the imperialists lead to definite results—to the activation of Right-opportunist and even openly anti-socialist elements and to the intensification of nationalistic sentiments.

However, none of the difficulties arising during the building of socialism in one country or another have been able to or can cancel the general principles underlying socialist development. The practice of the socialist countries has reaffirmed the significance of the ideas of Marx and Lenin that the development of socialist society proceeds on the basis of general laws, that in one form or another the dictatorship of the proletariat, i.e., state leadership of the building of socialism by the working class, is inevitable during the entire period of transition from capitalism to socialism.

The whole experience of the political struggle proves again and again that the victory of the trend towards consolidating fraternal relations between socialist states and that the progress of the socialist system itself are indissolubly linked with the strengthening of the leading role of the Communist Parties in the building of socialism and communism. Our Party highly values the determined struggle which the Communists of fraternal countries wage against any attempts to weaken the leading role of the Communist Parties, replace socialist democracy with political liberalism of the bourgeois type and erode the positions of socialism. To be as firm as Lenin in defending and upholding the principles of socialism is the lesson which life teaches us.

We fully subscribe to the provision formulated in the draft of the Main Document that the main direction in cementing the socialist system is steadfastly to implement the principles of socialist internationalism, correctly combine the national and international tasks of socialist countries and promote fraternal mutual assistance and support between them, on the basis of a consistent observance of the equality of all socialist countries, of their sovereignty and independence and of non-interference in their internal affairs.

World socialism absorbs all the wealth and diversity of the revolutionary traditions and experience deriving from the creative activity of the working people of different countries. In this connection we should like to say that our Party constantly studies that experience and utilises everything of value that may be applied in the conditions obtaining in the Soviet Union, everything that really helps to strengthen the socialist system and embodies the general laws of socialist construction that have been tested by international experience.

Nobody can deny that the ruling Communist Parties have accomplished and are engaged in extensive work of historic significance. Naturally, it cannot be said that ways of resolving all problems have been found and that we know all and are able to do all. Life does not stand still. In place of resolved problems others arise, which are linked with the need for a further improvement of socialist social relations. Like other Communist Parties of socialist countries, the CPSU seeks to resolve these problems creatively, in good time and consistently in line with the principles of Marxism-Leninism, taking into account the concrete conditions of its own country and the international situation.

By working for a further strengthening of fraternal relations between sovereign and equal socialist states and mobilising the working people for fresh achievements in the building of socialism and communism, the Communist Parties directing the building of the new society fulfil their duty to their own peoples and their internationalist duty to the working class of the whole world.

Comrades, one of the decisive sectors of the anti-imperialist struggle naturally runs through the capitalist countries themselves. The blows which the revolutionary forces are dealing imperialism in its very citadels are highly important for the whole of world development. The 1960s have introduced many new elements in this front of struggle as well.

A sharpening of the class struggle in the capitalist world is an inexorable fact. Suffice it to say that from 1960 to 1968 a total of over 300 million persons took part in the strike struggle, as compared with 150 million over the preceding 14 years. This fact alone gives the lie to the assertions about a weakening of the working class's fighting spirit.

* * *

Of very great importance is the fact that the strikers have ever more frequently succeeded in imposing their demands on the capitalists. This lends the working people confidence in their strength, and stimulates the further development and extension of the front of struggle. The working class sees for itself that while the bourgeoisie may still be mounting counter-attacks, its strength is far from what it used to be.

Under the changing world balance of forces and the sharpening of the class struggle in the bourgeois countries, capitalism has to resort to new means and methods of struggle which in many ways appear even to clash with the habitual "classic" features of the capitalist system. In an effort to reinforce their social hinterland areas, the capitalists combine methods of suppression with partial satisfaction of the working people's demands—a method which Lenin said was one of "concessions of the unessential while retaining the essential" (Collected Works, Vol. 24, p. 64)—sowing the illusions that the working class can achieve its aspirations through agreements with the employers, without a revolutionary transformation of society, within the framework of the capitalist system.

Quite a few people in many capitalist countries fall captive to these illusions. It is, after all, a fact, for instance, that at election time a sizable section of the workers cast their votes for capitalist candidates and their placemen. But for all the machinations of the capitalists, the social struggle in the 1960s showed signs of shifts in favour of the revolutionary forces whose importance it is hard to exaggerate.

In this situation Communists face new problems and tasks whose successful solution will largely predetermine the further development of the struggle for the working class cause.

* * *

The antagonism between imperialism, which intensifies social oppression and rejects democracy, and the masses of people, who are fighting for their vital rights and striving for freedom and democracy, is growing sharper. In some countries the discontent among the people is so great that sometimes as little as a spark is enough to set off a powerful social explosion. Such explosions are becoming ever more frequent everywhere, including the United States, where the most acute social contradictions, the struggle against the war in Vietnam and the fight for Negro civil rights are tangled in a tight knot. It is a long time since imperialism has been confronted with such violent forms of social protest and with general democratic action of the present scale and pitch. Ever more frequently broad masses of peasants, intellectuals, white-collar workers, students and middle strata of the urban population actively join with the working class in this struggle.

In these conditions, it is inevitable that elements of surprise and spontaneity should arise in the course of the anti-imperialist struggle in the advanced capitalist countries. Experience shows that in such a situation special importance attaches to the problem of relations between the working class and its allies. This is a question both of jointly taking various concrete political actions and of planning long-term co-operation on a mutually acceptable basis.

As the draft Main Document correctly says, the requisites are emerging for uniting all democratic trends in a political alliance capable of decisively limiting the role of the monopolies in the economy of countries, putting an end to big capital rule and carrying out a fundamental transformation which would ensure favorable conditions for the struggle for socialism.

The working class is the leading force of the alliance. It is the only class capable of leading this alliance to victory, and of raising the struggle to a new level, securing the complete abolition of the power of capital and the triumph of socialism. No other class, no other social stratum of society is as organised and strong. The numerical strength of the working class ranks is enormous. Its revolutionary experience is exceptionally rich. Its ideological, cultural and spiritual level has been rising from year to year. The political and moral prestige enjoyed by it in society has grown immeasurably.

While intensifying their work in the midst of the working class, including the rather sizable section of it which is not unionised, the Communist Parties in the capitalist countries devote much attention to their activity in the most diverse mass organisations of which workers are members—co-operatives, sports clubs, and democratic circles of religious bodies taking part in the struggle for peace—in short, wherever there are large numbers of working people.

Work in the midst of the peasant masses of the capitalist states continues to be of great importance. The working peasants remain the chief allies of the working class, despite the fact that there has been a considerable diminution of their numerical strength in the advanced capitalist countries. The concentration of agricultural production in the hands of big entrepreneurs entails ever spreading ruin of the small and middle farmers and an aggravation of social contradictions in the countryside. In many capitalist countries the 1960s were marked by large-scale peasant strikes, with the peasants fighting for their rights more and more frequently demanding unity of action with the working class.

A new light is now shed on many aspects of work with the intelligentsia, especially with that section of it which together with the working class is engaged in industry and is being subjected to growing exploitation. The professions requiring mental work are becoming increasingly massive. The engineering and technical intelligentsia in the capitalist countries is now being drawn not only from the bourgeoisie but also from the middle sections and in part from among the working people as well. To a considerable extent all this is changing the intelligentsia's attitude to the capitalist system and brings its interests closer to those of the working class.

The Communist Parties must take these changes into account. Experience has shown that more extensive work with the intelligentsia makes it more active in the anti-imperialist struggle.

It is natural that the fraternal Parties now devote considerable attention to work among the young people. It is a fact after all that the rising generation in the capitalist countries, including the students, is in revolutionary ferment. Young people are actively coming out in opposition to imperialist wars, to the militarisation of bourgeois society, and to the attempts of the bourgeoisie to curtail the working people's democratic rights.

It is true that frequently youth actions reveal a lack of political experience and connection with the vanguard of the revolutionary struggle. That is why these actions are often spontaneous and assume politically immature forms. An effort to use this is made by extremist elements essentially hostile to communism, and sometimes by direct imperialist agents. There is no doubt, however, that once the young fighters against imperialism have mastered the theory of scientific socialism and have acquired experience of class battles, they will do great things.

* * *

The increasing possibilities of combatting imperialism accordingly increase the role of the Communist Parties and of their work among the masses. On the activity of Communists will largely depend world development in the closing third of the twentieth century. One cannot fail to see that not only the material but also the socio-political conditions are maturing for a revolutionary replacement of capitalism with the new social system, for socialist revolutions.

By closing the fighting ranks of staunch revolutionaries, carrying Marxist-Leninist ideology into the midst of the working class masses and rallying the allies of the working class round it, Communists fulfil their historic mission in the struggle against imperialism, for the triumph of socialism.

Comrades, the fighters for national liberation and social emancipation in the countries of Asia and Africa comprise one of the important and active contingents of the world-wide anti-imperialist front.

The 1960s have brought considerable changes into the alignment of forces in that part of the world. In that period, 44 former colonies won independence. But more than 35 million people remain in colonial slavery. The peoples of the last colonies are waging a heroic, as a rule, armed struggle for their liberation. Soviet Communists fully support this just struggle.

The socialist orientation of a number of young states of Africa and Asia is an important achievement of the revolutionary forces and a heavy defeat for imperialism. These countries have scored their first successes in putting through deep-going social and economic reforms, thereby providing fresh practical confirmation of the Leninist conclusion that in our epoch the peoples who win liberation from colonial oppression can advance along the path of social progress, bypassing capitalism. One of the most important conditions which make such development possible is co-operation between the progressive young states and the socialist countries.

The states which have embarked on non-capitalist development are making a tangible contribution to the anti-imperialist struggle. It is true that these states are still few and that there are many difficulties in their development. Apart from the serious internal problems which remain, it should be borne in mind that it is above all against the progressive states of Africa and Asia that the subversive policy of imperialism on these continents is directed. But whatever the difficulties, they cannot minimise the importance of the cardinal fact that a start has been made in a fundamentally new direction for the development of the newly independent countries. And their example will carry the greater conviction the more headway the revolutionary-democratic countries make in their economic and cultural development, the fuller the advantages of non-capitalist development are revealed.

Communists regard assistance to and support of these young countries as one of the most improtant tasks of their foreign policy. The work the Communist and Workers' Parties of the socialist countries have been doing in this direction is generally known. Considerable possibilities in this respect are also open to the fraternal Parties in the developed capitalist countries.

In a number of countries of the former colonial world, as a result of inadequate organisation or of passive attitudes by the progressive forces, power was seized, after the proclamation of political independence, by reactionary elements closely linked up with imperialism. Some of these countries are ruled by military dictatorships, and a reign of terror has been instituted against all progressive forces. The imperialist states use the territories of many of these countries for their aggressive purposes, notably for military bases. The conditions of struggle for Communists and their allies in these countries are in many respects similar to the conditions of the colonial period.

However, what can be said about a considerable number of the states liberated from colonial dependence is, perhaps, that their further path has not yet been clearly defined. An intense struggle for the future rages in these countries between the progressive forces and internal reaction supported by imperialism. In these countries, the process of internal social division is deepening. The working people are ever more actively demanding far-reaching reforms capable of providing answers to burning fundamental problems. On the other hand, the top crust of the national bourgeoisie, guided by its class interests, resists social progress and the pursuit of any consistent anti-imperialist line. An increasingly acute class struggle is unfolding on this basis.

* * *

Imperialism is actively working to slow down the advance towards independence and social progress, to keep its former colonies within the framework of the capitalist system, and to retain them as objects of exploitation, even if in modified form. With their stake on nationalism and separatism, the imperialist forces are trying to weaken the developing countries from within, to range them against each other and to hamper their contacts with the socialist world.

The central question of the revolutionary process in Asia and Africa today is that of the stand of the peasantry, which there constitutes a majority of the population.

The peasants in that part of the world are a mighty revolutionary force, but in most cases they are an elemental force, with all the ensuing vacillations and ideological and political contradictions. Nor could it have been otherwise for the time being, because the great majority of the peasantry still lives in conditions of monstrous poverty and denial of rights, surviving feudal and sometimes even prefeudal relations.

The experience of the revolutionary movement in various parts of the world has shown that the surest way of effectively involving the peasants in the struggle against imperialism, for true social progress, is to establish a strong alliance between them and the working class. That is also the task in the zone of national liberation.

However, history has shaped the situation in such a way that in most states of Asia and Africa there is still no large-scale industry, and a working class has yet to emerge. But wherever industrial development is underway, the working class movement has won substantial positions. The agricultural proletariat of these countries is also active in the struggle. There is no doubt that ahead lies the broadest development of the working class struggle in the young national states against imperialism and its allies. It is the working class movement that will ultimately play the decisive part in this area of the world too.

* * *

In present-day conditions, the problem of relations between the working class and the peasantry in the former colonial countries is largely of an international nature. It is a question of consolidating the alliance of the whole international working class with the peasantry, with all the working people of the young liberated countries. This includes the strengthening of the revolutionary alliance between the national-liberation movement, the young national states and the countries of the socialist community, and the promotion of the closest ties between the fighters for national liberation and the Communist Parties coming forward as the vanguard of the international working class.

In this context we attach great importance to contacts and ties between the Communist Parties and the revolutionary-democratic Parties in the developing countries. These Parties and organisations are our fellow-fighters in the struggle against imperialism, for social progress. At present, the CPSU has contacts and ties with 18 national-democratic Parties, while Soviet mass organisations have connections with democratic organisations in all countries of that part of the world. We believe everything has to be done so that the relations between the Communist Parties and the revolutionary-democratic Parties continue to grow stronger.

* * *

II. Some Problems of the Communist Movement and Unity Action in the Struggle Against Imperialism

* * *

The successes which the Communist Parties have achieved are incontestable. But our Meeting is right to concentrate its attention on unresolved tasks, on the new possibilities in the anti-imperialist struggle, on the difficulties that arise in its path. Such difficulties do exist, and some of them spring from the state of affairs in our movement itself, which is going through a difficult period of its development. Unity has been seriously disrupted in some of its links. Some fraternal Parties have suffered setbacks and even defeats.

There are various reasons for these difficulties.

One of them is connected with the fact that in present-day conditions, when a tremendous social break-up of the pillars of the old world is taking place under the onslaught of socialism and all the revolutionary forces, there is growing resistance from the bourgeoisie. To safeguard its positions it strives to use all the economic and political possibilities of state-monopoly capitalism. In the capitalist countries, anti-communisim has been elevated to the status of state policy. To erode the communist and the whole revolutionary movement from within is now one of the most important directions of the class strategy of imperialism.

Another reason for the difficulties that have arisen is that fresh millions of people belonging to various social strata are being drawn into vigorous political action. Many of them enter politics with a great store of revolutionary energy, but with rather hazy ideas about how to solve the problems agitating them. Hence the vacillations—the swings from stormy political explosions to political passivity, from reformist illusions to anarchic impatience. All this tends to complicate the activity of the Communist Parties, multiplies the number of their tasks and increases the volume of demand on their practical work. In this situation, Communists must display Marxist-Leninist firmness and loyalty to principle and a creative approach to the problems of social development, if they are to keep control of developments, and tackle their problems in the light not only of short-term requirements but also of the long-term interests of the revolutionary movement. Otherwise, grave errors in policy are inevitable.

We cannot afford to ignore the divergences existing in the communist movement today and pretend they do not exist. These differences have been largely caused by the penetration into the communist movement of revisionist influences both of a Right and of a "Left" nature. And these influences are making themselves felt not only in the sphere of "pure" theory. Revisionism in theory paves the way to opportunist practices, which inflict direct harm on the anti-imperialist struggle. Revisionism is, after all, a departure from proletarian class positions, a substitution for Marxism-Leninism of all sorts of bourgeois and petty-bourgeois concepts, old and modernistic.

We share the stand of the fraternal Parties which in their decisions draw attention to the need for resolutely combatting this danger. The Communist Parties justly believe that the interests of their own cohesion, the interests of the whole anti-imperialist movement insistently demand an intensification of the struggle against revisionism and both Right and "Left" opportunism. A principled stand on this issue has always been a most important condition for strengthening a Party's political positions and has always mobilised and enhanced the activity of Communists in the class struggle.

Right-wing opportunism means a slide-down to liquidationist positions and to conciliation with Social-Democracy in policy and ideology. In socialist countries, Right-wing opportunism goes to the extent of repudiating that the Marxist-Leninist Party should play the leading role, and this can lead to surrender of the positions won by socialism and to capitulation to the anti-socialist forces.

"Left-wing" opportunists, behind a barrage of ultra-revolutionary verbiage, push the masses into adventurist action, and the Party onto the sectarian path, which paralyses its ability to rally the fighters against imperialism.

For all their distinctions, deviations from Marxism-Leninism to the Right or to the "Left" ultimately result in similarly harmful consequences: they weaken the militancy of the Communist Parties and undermine the revolutionary positions of the working class and the unity of the anti-imperialist forces.

A frequent feature of "Left" and Right-wing opportunism is concessions to nationalism, and sometimes even an outright switch to nationalistic positions. Lenin showed up this connection a long time ago. He wrote, "The ideological and political affinity, connection, and even identity between opportunism and social-nationalism are beyond doubt." (Collected Works, Vol. 21, p. 154.)

Of course, the struggle against opportunism and nationalism in one country or another is, above all, a sphere within the competence of the fraternal Party concerned. No Party can advance successfully unless it consistently and resolutely upholds the purity of Marxist-Leninist principles. But it is also true that when this struggle is abandoned in some sector of our movement, it is reflected on the movement as a whole.

The stand taken by the leadership of the Communist Party of China offers a striking example of the harm that can be done to the common cause of the Communists by a departure from Marxism-Leninism and a break with internationalism.

Frankly speaking, just recently we had no intention at all of touching on this question at the Meeting. However, the events of the recent period, particularly the nature of the decisions taken by the Ninth Congress of the CPC, have forced us to deal with it. There has arisen a new situation which is having a grave negative influence on the whole world situation and the conditions of the struggle of the anti-imperialist forces.

Peking's present political platform, as you are well aware, was not shaped either today or yesterday. Almost 10 years ago Mao Tse-tung and his supporters mounted an attack on the principles of scientific communism. In its numerous statements on questions of theory the CPC leadership has step by step revised the principled line of the communist movement. In opposition to this it has laid down a special line of its own on all the fundamental questions of our day.

At the same time, Peking started a political offensive against the communist movement. This offensive steadily gathered momentum, assuming ever sharper and open forms. From polemics with the Communist Parties the CPC leaders went on to splitting, subversive activity, to active attempts to range the revolutionary forces of our day against each other. From a folding up of their ties with the socialist countries to hostile acts against them. From criticism of peaceful coexistence to the staging of armed conflicts, to a policy undermining the cause of peace.

The Ninth Congress of the CPC marked a new stage in the evolution of the ideological and political propositions of Maoism. In the new Constitution of the CPC, Mao Tse-tung's thought has been proclaimed the Marxism-Leninism of the modern epoch. Chinese propaganda openly proclaims the task of "hoisting the banner of Mao Tse-tung's thought over the globe".

It is a big and serious task to make an all-round Marxist-Leninist analysis of the class content of the events in China over the last few years, and of the roots of the present line of the CPC leaders, who have jeopardised the socialist gains of the Chinese people. The CPSU, like the other fraternal Parties, is giving it due attention. But in the light of the tasks facing the Meeting there is a need to dwell here, primarily, on the international aspects of the Chinese leadership's policy. It is doubly important to speak about it, because a section of progressive world opinion still believes that the present Chinese leadership has revolutionary aspirations, believes its assertions that it is fighting imperialism.

It seems to us that the Ninth Congress of the CPC revealed whom the Chinese leadership is really fighting, and for what purpose. The Congress indicated the necessity of a "merciless struggle" principally against so-called "modern revisionism". Yet, as we know, under this category Peking classifies not revisionists, but the overwhelming majority of the socialist countries and Communist Parties.

You will recall that the Chinese leadership accused the Communist Parties of France, India, the United States, Italy, Latin America, and other countries of refusal "to conduct revolution", of being renegades, and of other deadly sins. "Traitors", "social strike-breakers", "social-imperialists"—those are the labels attached to many of the Parties represented here. Everybody here knows what insults were showered on all the participants in the present Meeting by the CPC leadership in its reply to our invitation.

The Peking leaders impute "revisionism" to all Parties that do not share their views and aims. They resort to all possible means against these Parties—from slanderous charges of "connivance with imperialism" to organising subversive splinter groups. Such groups now exist in nearly 30 countries. The Peking leadership is trying to give them the nature of an organised movement.

The damage done by Peking's splitting activities should not be under-estimated. Recent class battles clearly showed what great harm Peking's activity, which prods people on to an adventurist path, is doing to the organised struggle of the working class, of all working people.

The present Peking leadership's fight against the Marxist-Leninist Parties for hegemony in the communist movement is linked closely with its Great-Power aspirations, with its claims to territory of other countries. The idea that China has a messianic role to play is drummed into the heads of the Chinese workers and peasants. A wholesale conditioning of minds in the spirit of chauvinism and malicious anti-Sovietism is under way. Children are taught geography by textbooks and maps that show territory of other countries as belonging to the Chinese state. The Chinese people are being oriented to "starve and prepare for war". Nor is any doubt left about what sort of war is meant. Only two days ago the Peking Kuangming jihpao issued the call "to prepare both for a conventional and a big nuclear war against Soviet revisionism". Of course, noisy statements are a far cry from actual possibilities. The Soviet Union has enough strength to stand up for itself, and the Soviet people have strong nerves—they will not be frightened by shouting. But the direction of official Chinese propaganda speaks for itself.

In the light of all this, the policy to militarise China takes on a specific meaning. We cannot help comparing the feverish military preparations with the fanning of chauvinistic feelings hostile to the socialist countries, with the general approach by the Chinese leaders to the problems of war and peace in the modern epoch.

Possibly, many of the comrades here remember Mao Tse-tung's speech in this hall during the 1957 Meeting. With appalling airiness and cynicism he spoke of the possible destruction of half of mankind in the event of an atomic war. The facts show that Maoism calls not for struggle against war but, on the contrary, for war which it regards as a positive historical phenomenon.

The combination of the Chinese leaders' political adventurism with the sustained atmosphere of war hysteria injects new elements into the international situation, and we have no right to ignore it.

Peking's practical activity on the international scene convinces us increasingly that China's foreign policy has, in effect, departed from proletarian internationalism and shed the socialist class content. That is the only possible explanation for the persistent efforts to identify the Soviet Union and US imperialism. What is more, these days the spearhead of Peking's foreign policy is aimed chiefly against the Soviet Union and the other socialist countries. For a start, the Chinese leaders reduced to a minimum China's economic contacts with most of the socialist states and rejected political co-operation with them, ending up with armed provocations on the Soviet frontier. Provocative calls resound from Peking, exhorting the Soviet people to "accomplish a revolution", to change the social system in our country.

The facts show that the Chinese leadership speaks of struggle against imperialism, while in fact helping the latter, directly or indirectly, by everything it does. It helps the imperialists by seeking to split the united front of the socialist states. It helps them by its incitement and its obstructions to relaxation of international tension at times of acute international crises. It helps them by striving to hamper the emergence of a broad anti-imperialist front, by seeking to split the international mass organisations of youth, women and scientists, the peace movement, the trade union movement, and so on.

Naturally, the imperialists make the most of Peking's present orientation in the field of foreign policy as a trump in their political struggle against world socialism and the liberation movement.

To sum up: the attack on the Soviet Union all down the line, the false propaganda, mud-slinging at the Soviet people, at our socialist state, our Communist Party, fanning hatred against the USSR among the people of China and, last but not least, resort to arms; intimidation and blackmail in relation to other socialist states and the developing countries; flirting with the big capitalist powers, including the Federal Republic of Germany—those are the guidelines of China's present foreign policy.

As you know, comrades, in March the Soviet Government, striving to end the clashes organised by the Chinese side on the Soviet-Chinese border, called on the Government of China to refrain from border actions that might create complications, and resolve differences, wherever these occur, by negotiation in a tranquil atmosphere. We proposed that the Soviet-Chinese consultations on border issues, which were begun in 1964, should be resumed in the immediate future. At the same time, we warned them that any attempt to deal with the Soviet Union in terms of armed power would be firmly repulsed.

Recently, the Chinese Government made public its reply. If one may judge from words, the Chinese side does not reject the idea of negotiations. There are also expressions of consent to avoid conflicts on the border and refrain from opening fire. At present, we are preparing a pertinent reply to this Chinese statement. This reply, like the Soviet Government's statement of March 29, will naturally be in complete accord with our principled stand: to settle differences through negotiation and to favour equitable and mutually beneficial cooperation.

It should be pointed out, however, that the statement of the CPR Government can hardly be described as constructive either in content or spirit. The wordy document is full of historical falsifications, distortions of the facts of modern times and of crude hostile attacks against the Soviet Union. It renews groundless territorial claims on the Soviet Union, which we categorically reject.

The future will show whether the Chinese leaders are really eager to negotiate, whether they desire agreement, and what course events will take. However, we cannot afford to overlook the fact that the provocations by Chinese military personnel on the Soviet border have not stopped. At the same time, an unprecedentedly broad and intensive anti-Soviet campaign is being conducted all over China on the basis of the decisions of the Ninth Congress of the CPC. The idea is being drummed into the heads of the Chinese people that the Soviet Union allegedly wants to attack China.

It is needless to refute these fabrications. Not only Communists, but all decent people on earth know perfectly well that our people are preoccupied with peaceful creative labour, building communist society, and that they have never attacked nor intend to attack anyone.

Our policy with regard to China is consistent and based on principle. The Central Committee of the CPSU and the Soviet Government chart their policy on the long-term perspective. We are conscious of the fact that the basic interests of the Soviet and Chinese peoples coincide. We have always persevered and will continue to persevere in our efforts to keep alive the friendly feelings of the Soviet people for the fraternal Chinese nation, and are certain that the Chinese people, too, have the same feelings towards the Soviet Union and the other socialist countries.

At the same time we do not consider it possible to remain silent about the anti-Leninist, anti-popular essence of the political and ideological principles of the present leaders of China. We shall carry on a resolute struggle against Peking's splitting policy and against its Great-Power foreign-policy line. It stands to reason that we shall do everything to safeguard the interests of the Soviet people, who are building communism, from all encroachments.

We do not identify the declarations and actions of the present Chinese leadership with the aspirations, wishes and true interests of the Communist Party of China and the Chinese people. We are deeply convinced that China's genuine national renascence, and its socialist development, shall be best served not by struggle against the Soviet Union and other socialist countries, against the whole communist movement, but by alliance and fraternal cooperation with them.

Comrades, the situation created by the policy of the Chinese leadership introduces a new element into the problem of anti-imperialist unity. We Communists must take a responsible and clear stand. The policy of subverting the communist ranks, of dividing the anti-imperialist forces, can and must be opposed by our firm will for unity, by our deeds and joint actions promoting unity.

In their fight for unity the Communists have a tested weapon. It has brought victory in glorious battles for the cause of the working class, for socialism. That weapon is proletarian internationalism.

The imperialists are conscious of the power of international proletarian solidarity. That is why they bank on nationalism in fighting the socialist forces, the revolutionary movement. They expect thereby to divide and atomise the communist movement, to set the revolutionary contingents one against the other.

Bourgeois propaganda goes out of its way to malign the principle of proletarian internationalism and to oppose it artificially to the principles of the independence, sovereignty and equality of the national contingents of the working class and communist movement. That is the purpose for which imperialist propagandists have fabricated and put into circulation the notorious theory of "limited sovereignty".

As for us, Soviet Communists, we hold that the present world situation again forcefully bears out the validity and viability of Lenin's concept of proletarian internationalism.

In our time, the time of a global confrontation of two worlds—that of capitalism and socialism—Lenin's principles about the internationalist class approach to national problems remain in full force.

As valid as ever, for example, is Lenin's definition that to be an internationalist is to do "the utmost possible in one country for the development, support and awakening of the revolution in all countries". (Vol. 28, p. 292.)

The proletarian Party derives its strength from its ability to use to the full the internal opportunities for struggle in the interest of its people, for its country's progress, and, at the same time, in the interest of the common internationalist cause of revolution and socialism. On the other hand, attempts to "invigorate" the Party's position by weakening, or even breaking off, its international ties, by rejecting united action with other contingents of the communist movement, lead to loss of ideological independence from the bourgeoisie and inevitably injure the political prestige of the Party concerned.

It goes without saying, comrades, that all this does not refute or belittle the principles of the independence, sovereignty and quality of either the socialist countries or of individual national contingents of the world working class and communist movement. Respect for, and strict observance of, these principles is for Communists an unbreakable law precisely because they are internationalists.

Genuine internationalism also implies support of the existing socialist society by all fraternal Parties. We think highly of the stand of our friends who are irreconcilable to any and all slander of socialism. For Communists that is not only a natural expression of their internationalist sentiments, but at once an approach to internationalism as a real policy serving the common cause of revolution. For example, all of us agree that new opportunities have arisen in the struggle for peace, democracy, national independence and socialism by virtue of the radical change in the international arena in favour of socialism, to the detriment of imperialism. But this also means that any weakening of socialist positions in the world is bound to reflect negatively on the positions of all the Communist Parties.

For our Conference, strengthening the unity of the communist movement is an important task. There are adequate objective preconditions for this. But we cannot confine ourselves to merely declaring once again that the interests of the various national contingents of our movement coincide. Unity means action, not words. It is not automatically attainable, and must be fought for.

When still preparing for this Conference, all of us agreed that in order to strengthen the unity of the communist movement we must search for ways to overcome existing divergences. These are of different kinds. And, naturally, different courses must be employed to overcome them. In some cases doubts and questions may be removed through bilateral meetings and comradely discussion. In other cases they may be ironed out through the practical experience of the joint struggle for common aims in the international arena. But there are also differences that concern fundamental problems and the very essence of the communist movement. And it will probably take a long time and uncompromising struggle to overcome them.

Speaking of the line aimed at surmounting differences, we should like to dwell on three points.

To begin with, a word about the significance of joint action against imperialism for solidifying the communist movement. In the present conditions, with Communists bearing a direct responsibility for the destiny of their peoples, for the future of mankind, we cannot afford to put the matter thus: let's first resolve all the differences in our movement, and then come to terms about joint action. The realities require a different approach: differences over specific issues must not interfere with joint communist actions in our common struggle against imperialism; let us jointly tackle the practical tasks related to united action and then, in the course of our joint struggle, we shall see more clearly which views are in accord with the common interests of the communist movement and which go against these interests and interfere, even injure, the common cause. In other words, that which brings the Communists of all countries together should be put at the head of the list in our practical activity.

Secondly, we should like to emphasise the need for expanding in every way the ties and contacts among fraternal Parties. They are essential both as a mechanism for coordinating our actions on the international scene and as a means of comparing notes on current problems and of settling differences. In the present conditions, bilateral and multilateral meetings are doubly useful. The experience of the Vienna Conference of European Communist Parties, that of the Karlovy Vary Conference, the conferences of the fraternal Latin American Parties and meetings held by Communists of the Arab countries bore out the importance of regional meetings to discuss a specific round of questions and promote international communist co-operation. The practice of co-operation in the new conditions has also brought into being such a collective form as world conferences.

The third important way of overcoming differences and fighting for the unity of our movement is to generalise the theoretical work of the Parties, to advance Marxist-Leninist theory on that basis and to safeguard its principles and fundamental ideas. Lenin stressed the need for *theoretically* assessing the new forms of struggle prompted by practice (Vol. 9, p. 212). The practice of recent years has convincingly demonstrated the benefits for the whole communist movement of creatively elaborating such problems as the convergence in our epoch of the democratic and socialist tasks of the revolutionary struggle, of correctly combining peaceful and non-peaceful forms of revolution, and of the possibility of the non-capitalist development for the former colonial countries.

* * *

As we see it, it would be useful to improve the methods of joint theoretical work by the Communist Parties, to devise concrete measures for improving mutual information, for studying each other's experience and organising regular exchanges of opinion. We declare ourselves in favour of regular international theoretical conferences.

* * *

Imperialism cannot expect to succeed if it openly speaks of its true aims. It is compelled to create a system of ideological myths to disguise its true intentions and lull the vigilance of the peoples. For this purpose it has built up a mammoth propaganda machine equipped with all modern means of ideological indoctrination. Indeed, comrades, every hour, by day and by night, the working people of almost the entire world are to one or another extent subjected to the influence of bourgeois propaganda, of bourgeois ideology. The hired ideologists of the imperialists have created a special pseudo-culture designed to befuddle the masses, to blunt their social consciousness. And combatting its corrupting influence on the working people is an important area of communist work.

Comrades, we have a powerful weapon against bourgeois ideology. That weapon is the ideology of Marxism-Leninism. We know its potency well. We are witness to the fact that our ideas are spreading more and more among the masses. Marxism-Leninism is on the offensive today, and we must develop that offensive to the utmost. It is more important than ever to recall Lenin's warning that any relaxation by Communists in ideological work, any standing aloof from it, redoubles the influence of bourgeois ideology.

* * *

At our Meeting we shall collectively define the main lines and concrete tasks in the struggle against imperialism in present-day conditions. By advancing them on behalf of our Parties, which in some countries are followed by entire nations and by the biggest trade unions and other democratic organisations, we shall take a very important step towards uniting all anti-imperialist forces.

* * *

In this connection we should like to go back to the question of the unity of the working class movement and, in particular, to the problem of the relationship between Communists and Social-Democrats.

There is no reason to say that the consistent communist policy of promoting the unity of the working class movement has been fruitless. The differentiation in the Social-Democratic movement is now more pronounced, and a certain section of it, including a few leading personalities, is departing from anti-communist positions. The ties between trade unions of different orientation in separate countries and on an international scale have been activated.

The leadership of a considerable number of Social-Democratic Parties, especially those prominent in the Socialist International, still consider fighting communism, fighting the socialist countries, their main task.

* * *

Our stand in relation to Social-Democracy could not be clearer. We are combatting and shall continue to combat our ideological and political opponents in its ranks from the principled positions of Marxism-Leninism. At the same time, we agree to co-operation, to joint action, with those genuinely prepared to fight imperialism, for peace, for the interests of the working people. There are vital issues in regard to which the need for unity of action by working class Parties, including those responsible for the policy of their countries, is now particularly timely. Above all, this concerns questions related to averting a world war, building up a system of European security and combatting the threat of fascism.

* * *

III. The CPSU Is Loyal to Its Internationalist Duty

Immediately after the Civil War ended Lenin stressed: "We are exercising our main influence on the international revolution through our economic policy" (*Collected Works,* Vol. 32, p. 437). Our Party holds that this proposition preserves its significance to this day. The defence capability of the Soviet Union and, to no small extent, of the entire socialist community, and the possibility of countering the imperialist policy of aggression and war depend on our economic achievements. Our possibilities of supporting the revolutionary and liberation movement throughout the world likewise depend on these achievements. The force of the example of the new social system, which is becoming the best agitator for socialism both among the working people in the capitalist countries and the peoples who have shaken off the yoke of colonialism, also depends on them.

* * *

In the economic sphere the distance separating us from the United States, the most powerful and richest country in the capitalist world, has also shrunk appreciably. In 1960, our industrial output was 55 per cent of the American, while in 1968 it reached about 70 per cent.

* * *

... The international situation prevents us from using all of the country's resources for economic development, improving the working people's living standard and promoting culture. Large resources have to be appropriated for defence. And I can assure you that we maintain it at the highest level. Our Armed Forces reliably protect the borders of our homeland, and together with the allied armies they stand guard over the gains of the fraternal socialist countries, over the peace and security of nations.

* * *

In foreign affairs the Communist Party of the Soviet Union concentrates on making the socialist world stronger today than yesterday, and stronger tomorrow than today. This is concretely embodied in the efforts made by our state, jointly with other socialist countries, to further co-operation in the political, defence and economic spheres.

The Soviet Union, together with other socialist countries, holds active positions in the wide and seething front of the national-liberation movement, and renders firm political support and moral and material help to the peoples fighting for liberation.

* * *

We are well aware that extremely aggressive circles often influence the shaping of the foreign policy of the big capitalist states. To curb the activity of these circles it is necessary to be firm, to expose their increasing provocations and be constantly ready to administer a determined rebuff to agressive encroachments. This is the foreign policy that the CPSU and the Soviet Union pursue.

In the capitalist camp we distinguish a more moderate wing as well. While remaining our class, ideological enemies its representatives assess the present balance of power quite soberly and are inclined to explore mutually acceptable settlements of outstanding international issues in this sphere. In its foreign policy, our state takes into account such tendencies.

Barring the road to the threat of war and without relaxing our vigilant watch of the intrigues of aggressive and revanchist circles, we shall continue to do everything in our power to stamp out the hotbeds of war on our planet.

The burning problems of the current international situation do not conceal from our view longer-term tasks, namely, the creation of a system of collective security in areas of the globe where the danger of another world war, of armed conflicts, is concentrated. Such a system is the best replacement for the existing military-political groups.

At their conference in Karlovy Vary the Communist and Workers' Parties of Europe, both those in power and Parties in the capitalist countries of the continent, drew up a common programme of measures aimed at safeguarding security in Europe. Member-countries of the Warsaw Treaty have advanced a concrete programme of achieving the security of the European peoples, stability of frontiers and peaceful co-operation of European states. The CPSU and the Soviet Union will do everything to implement this programme.

We are of the opinion that the course of events is also putting on the agenda the task of creating a system of collective security in Asia.

* * *

Today, as before, the Soviet Union is prepared to reach understanding on general and complete disarmament, on measures for limiting and restraining the arms race, above all the race for nuclear and missile weapons. To compel the imperialists to curtail the arms race means to shake the positions of the instigators of another war, to switch colossal resources to constructive purposes and to strengthen world peace.

* * *

Suggested Readings

This list is ordered chronologically according to the period with which each is chiefly concerned. The books have been selected for their breadth of view and their interest to the general reader.[*] Since they deal with a controversial subject (which Soviet foreign policy is), and since some of the authors are themselves controversial figures, the serious reader will also find much in them with which to disagree, as this writer has.

Revolution to Nazi Invasion (1917-1941)

Fischer, Louis. *The Soviets in World Affairs,* 1917-1929 (New York: Vintage, 1961).

Beloff, Max, *The Foreign Policy of Soviet Russia* 1929-1941. 2 vols. (New York: Oxford, 1947-49).

Kennan, George, *Russia and the West under Lenin and Stalin* (Boston: Atlantic, Little, Brown, 1961). Chiefly 1917 to 1941.

Degras, Jane, ed., *Soviet Documents on Foreign Policy.* 3 vols. (New York: Oxford, 1951-1953).

World War II and the first period of Cold War (1941-1953)

Stalin's Correspondence with Roosevelt and Truman, 1941-1945 (New York: Capricorn, 1965).

Stalin's Correspondence with Churchill and Attlee, 1941-1945 (New York: Capricorn, 1965).

Churchill, Winston, *The Second World War,* 6 vols. (London: Cassell, 1948-54).

---

[*] For further reading and specialized research the reader should consult the following annotated bibliography: Hammond, Thomas, ed., *Soviet Foreign Relations and World Communism* (Princeton: Princeton University Press, 1965).

Mosely, Philip, *The Kremlin and World Politics* (New York: Vintage, 1960) Essays, chiefly on the decade 1946-1956.

Kennan, George, *Memoirs,* 1925-1950 (Boston: Atlantic, Little, Brown, 1967).

Borkenau, Franz, *European Communism* (London: Faber, 1953). A history of the international Communist Movement.

Post-Stalin: (1953-   )

Dallin, David, *Soviet Foreign Policy After Stalin* (Philadelphia: Lippincott, 1961).

Crankshaw, Edward, *The New Cold War: Moscow vs. Pekin* (London: Penguin Books, 1963).

Lowenthal, Richard, *World Communism: the Disintegration of a Secular Faith* (New York: Oxford University Press, 1966). Essays.

Brzeziński, Zbigniew, *The Soviet Bloc: Unity and Conflict,* Revised Edition (Cambridge: Harvard University Press, 1967).

General

Lederer, Ivo, ed., *Russian Foreign Policy* (New Haven: Yale University Press, 1962). Essays.

Triska, Jan, and David Finley, *Soviet Foreign Policy* (New York: Macmillan, 1968). A textbook which relies on "new techniques of political analysis."

Ulam, Adam, *Expansion and Coexistence, The History of Soviet Foreign Policy,* 1917-1967 (New York: Praeger, 1968).

Khrushchev, N.S., *Khrushchev Remembers* (Boston: Little, Brown and Co., 1970).

Finally, the reader interested in a more extended discussion of the evidence and argumentation for some of the views presented in the introduction to the Reports of the post-Stalin period should see:

Horelick, Arnold, and Myron Rush, *Strategic Power and Soviet Foreign Policy* (Chicago: University of Chicago Press, 1966).